THE BOOK OF THE WASHBURN VALLEY

THE BOOK OF
THE WASHBURN VALLEY

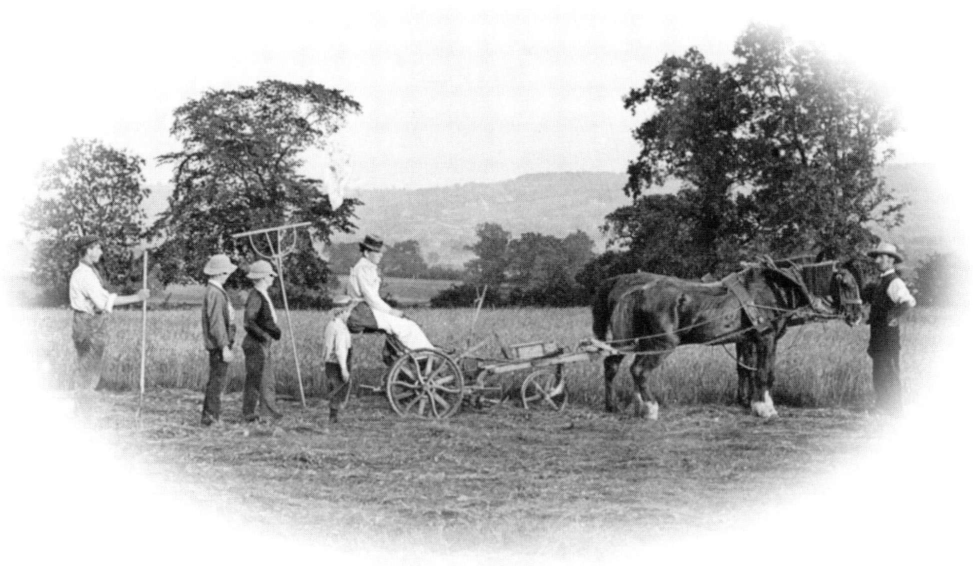

DIANA PARSONS

HALSGROVE

First published in Great Britain in 2014

British Library Cataloguing-in-Publication Data
A CIP record for this title is available from the British Library

ISBN 978 0 85704 240 8

HALSGROVE
Halsgrove House,
Ryelands Business Park,
Bagley Road, Wellington, Somerset TA21 9PZ
Tel: 01823 653777 Fax: 01823 216796
email: sales@halsgrove.com

Part of the Halsgrove group of companies.
Information on all Halsgrove titles is available at: www.halsgrove.com

Printed and bound in the UK by TJ International Ltd

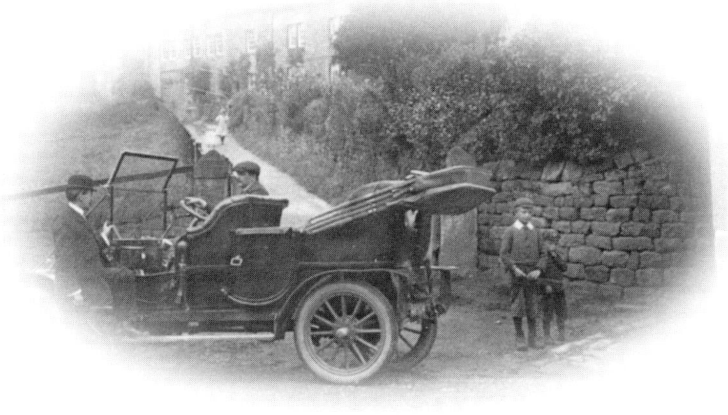

CONTENTS

Preface		7
Introduction		8
Chapter 1	**The Forest of Knaresborough and Haverah Park**	11
Chapter 2	**The Upper Valley**	17
Chapter 3	**The Middle Valley**	43
Chapter 4	**The Lower Valley**	90
Chapter 5	**'The Beautiful Pellucid Waters'**	110
Chapter 6	**Lest We Forget**	116
Principal Printed Sources		125
Acknowledgements		126
Subscribers		127

For Alexandra and William

'... ther is a brooke called Washborne, which beginneth about two myles of Apletrewyke, runneth to Westend Chappell, so to Blubber Houses, thence to Fuyston and Dog Parke to Lindley, to Lethely, and into Wharfe nere Pole.'

Yorkshire Church Notes 1619-1631, Roger Dodsworth, ed. J. W. Clay 1904, Yorkshire Archaeological Society Record Series, Vol. XXXIV, 1904, p.142

Preface

There appears to be no logical reason why the valley of the Washburn is not called Washburndale. It cannot be argued that it is disqualified on the grounds of size for many of Yorkshire's dales are no larger. Moreover the word 'dale' is simply an Old Norse term for 'valley.' However, that it is not generally known as such is perhaps fortunate for, unlike its nearest neighbour Wharfedale, tourism has largely passed it by, and it is rarely busy. For this reason in particular, the valley with its proximity to the large conurbations of Leeds and Bradford has always been valued by the many local people who visit to enjoy its peace and tranquillity.

Many of these visitors pause to wonder about the history of the valley, but little has been written about the area since the late nineteenth century and that is now long out of print. Although this book is an attempt to rectify this situation, it has never been my intention to write either a geological or an archaeological account of the valley. As a historian I am not qualified to do either and must therefore leave those aspects to those who are. Instead it is my hope that this book will provide answers to some of the questions asked and dispel at least some of the myths which abound. Above all, I hope it will provide a lasting tribute to the people of the valley, whose families made its history. Here I must acknowledge the invaluable contribution of David Alred who, in the latter part of the last century, collected almost 2000 images of the area, most of which were generously provided by its residents. Without this archive, the history of the valley would have been lost for ever, and this book could not have been written.

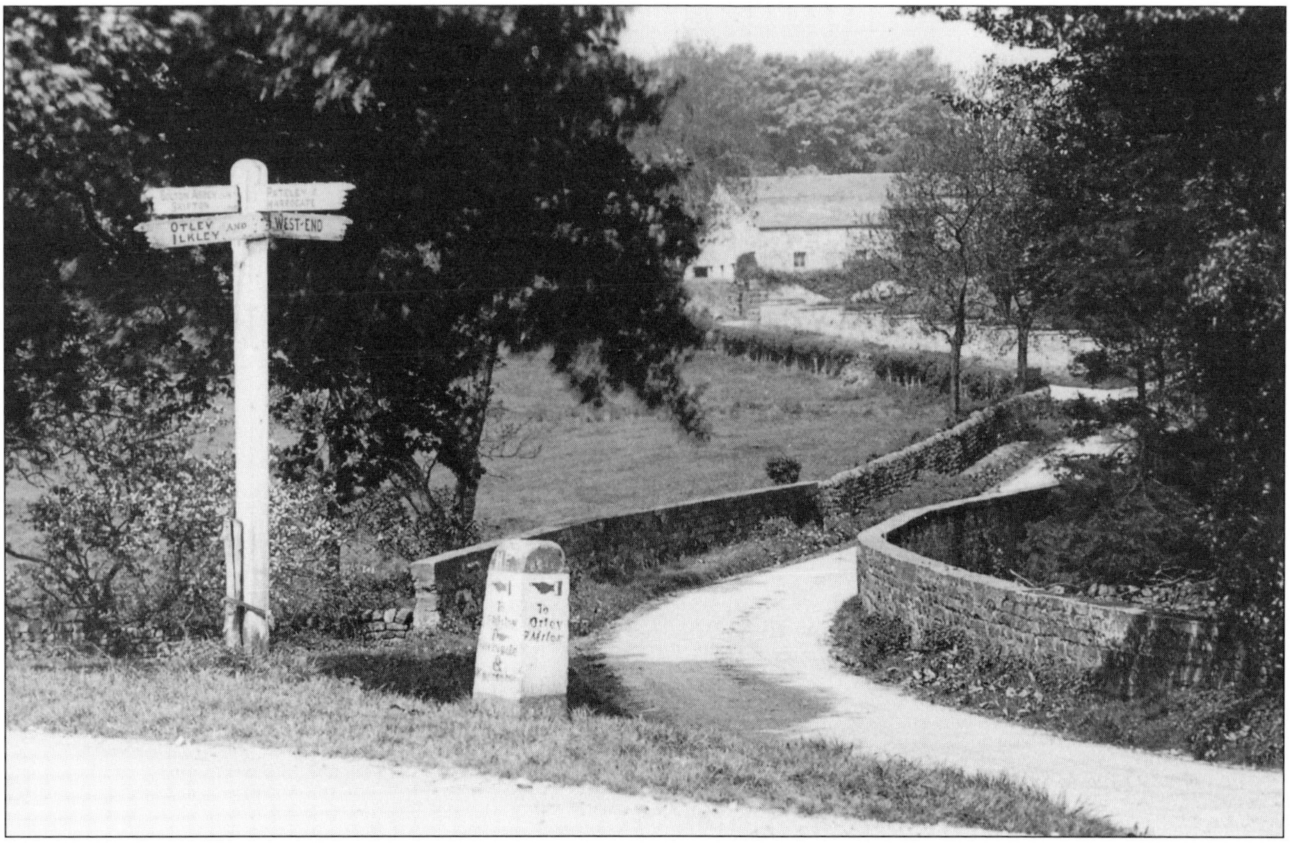

Old road to West End from Blubberhouses.

Introduction

The Washburn Valley straddles the borders of West and North Yorkshire between the towns of Harrogate to the east and Skipton to the west and takes its name from the River Washburn (*uisque* = *water* and *burn* = *small brook*) which rises on the northerly ridge of Pock Stones Moor separating the valley from Nidderdale. Soon joined by the Capelshaw Beck, the river flows in a roughly south easterly direction for approximately 14 miles to its confluence with the River Wharfe at Leathley.

At various times over the centuries the valley has been crossed by Roman infantry, its Royal Forest of Knaresborough has provided a hunting ground for kings, it has been raided by Scots and traversed by Royalist troops, while its river has provided the power for a network of textile mills, and later water for the City of Leeds via the four major reservoirs, Thruscross, Fewston, Swinsty and Lindley Wood.

In more recent times the valley has separated into three more or less distinct areas, the first of which lies north of the A59 Harrogate-Skipton road, and includes the old township of Thruscross. Here the predominant settlement is one of isolated single dwellings in the hamlets of West End, Thruscross Green, Low Green and Bramley Head. These small scattered clusters of population were favoured by ninth century Scandinavian settlers from whom the name Thruscross (*Thori's cros* – Old Norse) may derive, although the

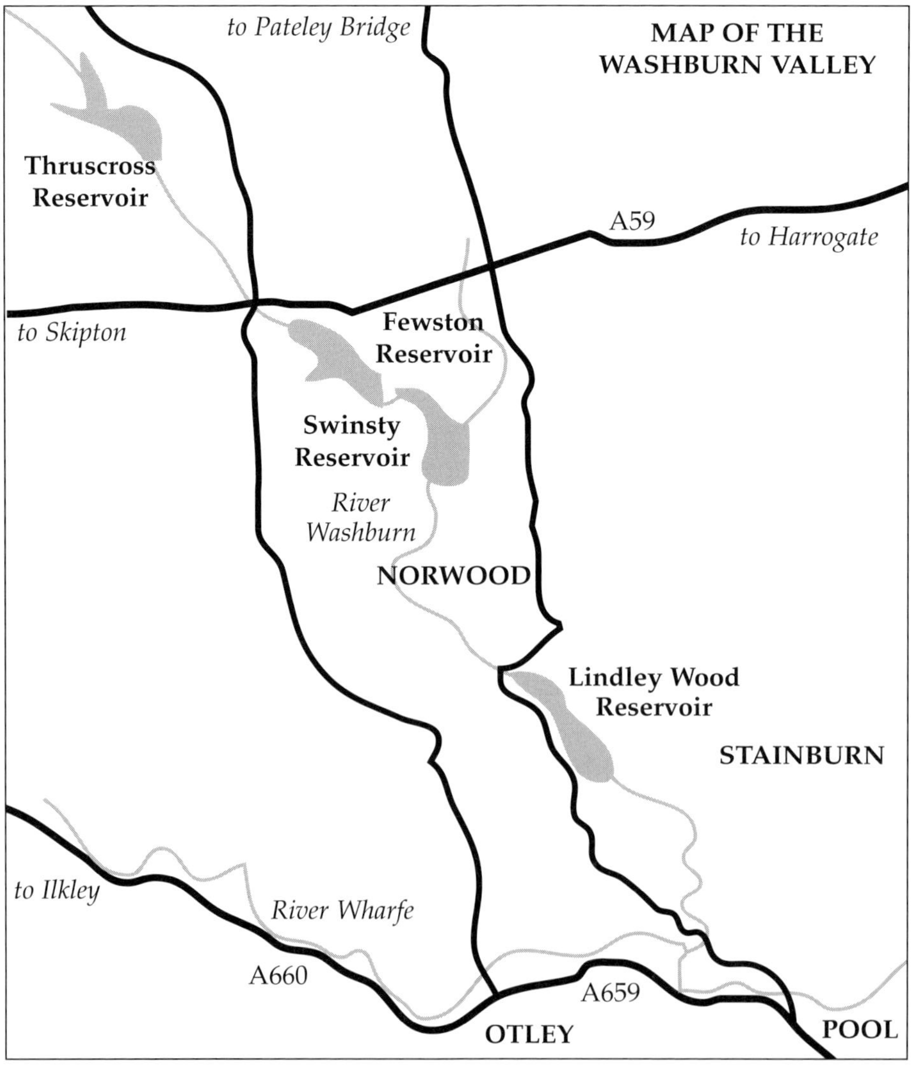

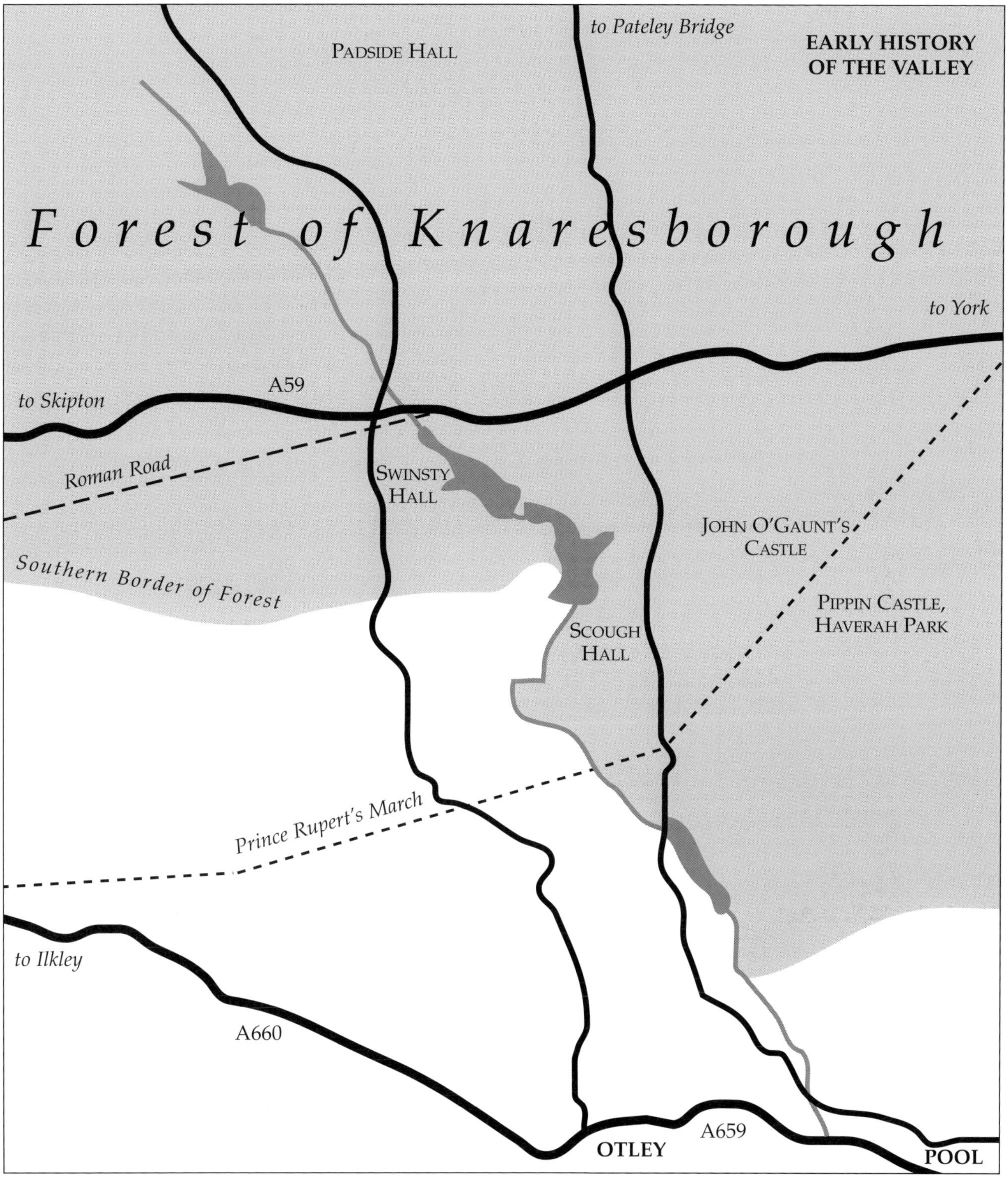

presence of a preaching cross does not necessarily imply the existence of a settlement. In 1086 this part of the valley was described as 'waste without a single plough' but it should not be assumed that this was necessarily the result of the so-called 'harrying of the north' by the King. Instead it may simply have meant that the economically unattractive land had never encouraged settlement, or even that the King's pursuit of game was paramount and therefore incompatible with the creation of villages.

The middle section of the valley lies between the township of Blubberhouses on the A.59 Skipton-Harrogate road, and the hill known as Norwood Edge. It includes Haverah Park with the ruins of the so-called John o' Gaunt's castle, a former hunting lodge, the mysterious Pippin Castle, and the Roman road which crosses Blubberhouses Moor to join the Skipton-Harrogate road on its way to Aldborough. Also included are the townships of Fewston, Timble Great, and Clifton with Norwood. Timble Little, however, as an administrative outlier of the former estate of the Archbishop of York centred on the market town of Otley was never part of the Royal Forest which covered much of the valley.

The third and most southerly section of the valley lies between the old township of Clifton with Norwood and the River Wharfe and is largely outside the Forest boundary. This part of the valley displays a marked difference in the pattern of settlement including the nucleated villages of Farnley and Leathley and the hamlets of Lindley and Stainburn in a fertile pastoral landscape, due in large part to the influence of numerous lay and ecclesiastical landlords.

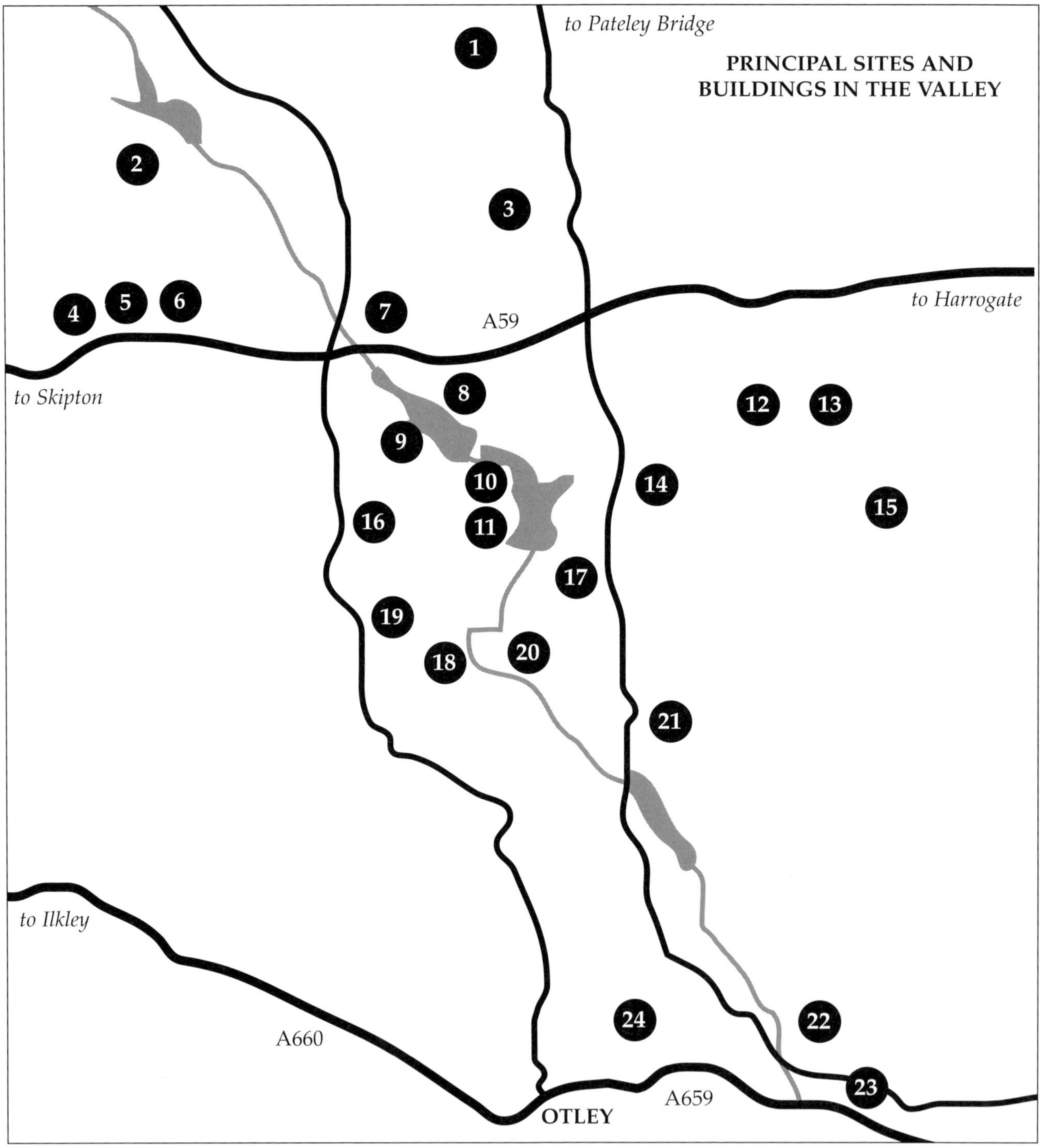

KEY

Blubberhouses Hall	6	Hopper Lane Hotel	7	Norwood Hall	21	Skaife Hall	5
Castley Hall	23	John o'Gaunts Castle	12	Padside Hall	1	Swinsty Hall	11
Cragg Hall	8	Leathley Hall	22	Pippin Castle	15	Thackray	9
East End Manor	13	Low Hall	19	Redshaw Hall	2	Wakefield's Folly	14
Farnley Hall	24	Moorcock Hall	3	Scow Hall	17	Washburn Farm	18
Folly Hall	20	New Hall	10	Shaw Hall	16	West House Mill	4

Chapter 1

The Forest of Knaresborough and Haverah Park

The Old Washburn townships of Timble Great, Fewston, and Clifton with Norwood (now called simply Norwood and not to be confused with Clifton near Otley) lie on the western boundary of the Forest. Twenty miles in length and 8 in width the Forest was the largest in Yorkshire and formed part of the Honour of Knaresborough. Although the first surviving documentary reference to it occurs during the reign of Henry II in 1167, some royal forests were in fact introduced into England by William the Conqueror (1066-1087), and it may therefore have been established much earlier.

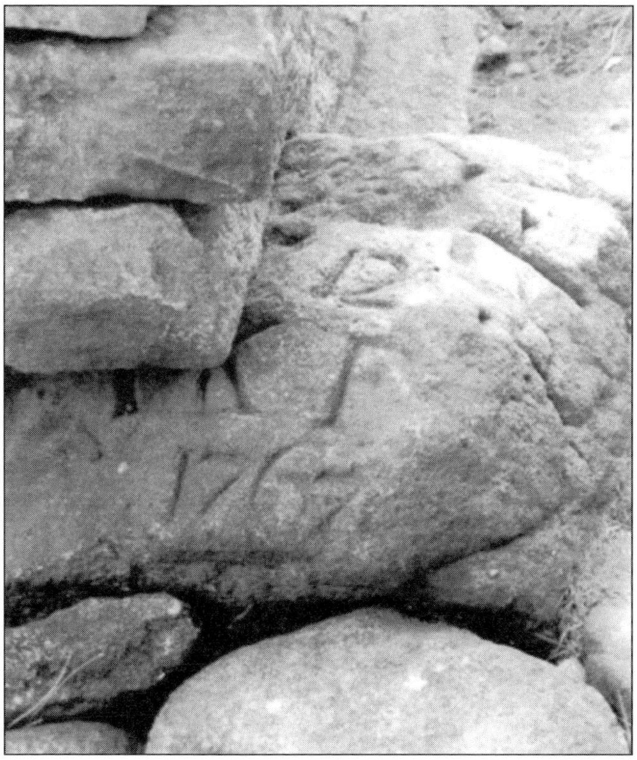

Boundary stone – Forest of Knaresborough.

Historically, the term 'forest' does not necessarily imply a densely wooded area. Rather it was an administrative term for an area of jurisdiction over land where cultivation was often difficult, and where it was necessary for the hunting rights of the King to be protected. The office of Custodian to the Forest was an important one and from 1158 to 1173 it was held by Hugh de Morville, one of the four men involved in the murder of Thomas Becket. Later Custodians included successive Earls of Cornwall and, in 1372, John of Gaunt, Duke of Lancaster, whose son was to become Henry IV.

The residents of the Forest, said to have been 'a most headstrong people', were tenants of the Crown holding their land 'according to the custom of the Forest' for an annual rent of 6d. per Forest acre [1 Forest acre=4 statute acres]. The rules with which they were required to conform were many and varied including the 'lawing' of dogs (ie the removal of claws and three toes of their forefeet to prevent them from hunting), payment to the Crown by executors, on the death of a tenant, of a 'heriot', or fine, of a 'best beast', and punishment by fines and seizure of land in cases of illegal encroachment which often occurred in close proximity to township boundaries, such as at Jack Hill and Bland Hill, Norwood. In addition they required the licensing of all cattle and sheep, any unlicensed stock being impounded following an annual drove. Those who lived outside the Forest boundary, for example the residents of Timble Little, were required to pay an annual sum of nine shillings in order to pasture stock. Pigs were only permitted to graze the Forest in the autumn, any infringement carrying a fine of between two pence and four pence. In 1319 the keeper of Knaresborough Castle was ordered to 'acquit the men and tenants ... in the towns of Timble, Clifton, Foston [Fewston] and Thorscros [Thruscross] of their ... rents for the Michaelmas term last to the amount of £72.3s.7d ...' the tenants being 'ruined to a great extent by the burning of their houses, the abduction of their beasts and the carrying away of their goods by the attacks of the Scotch rebels'.

Wood for the repair of fences and buildings, especially important in the wake of devastation by the Scots raiders between 1314 and 1320, could be cut at any time. At other times fines were also levied for failing to repair property. In 1342-3 the inhabitants of Thruscross were fined a quarter of a mark, or three shillings and four pence, for failing to repair the roof of the corn mill.

HAVERAH PARK

Bordering the western fringe of the Forest were the 2,245 acres known as Haverah Park, a name believed

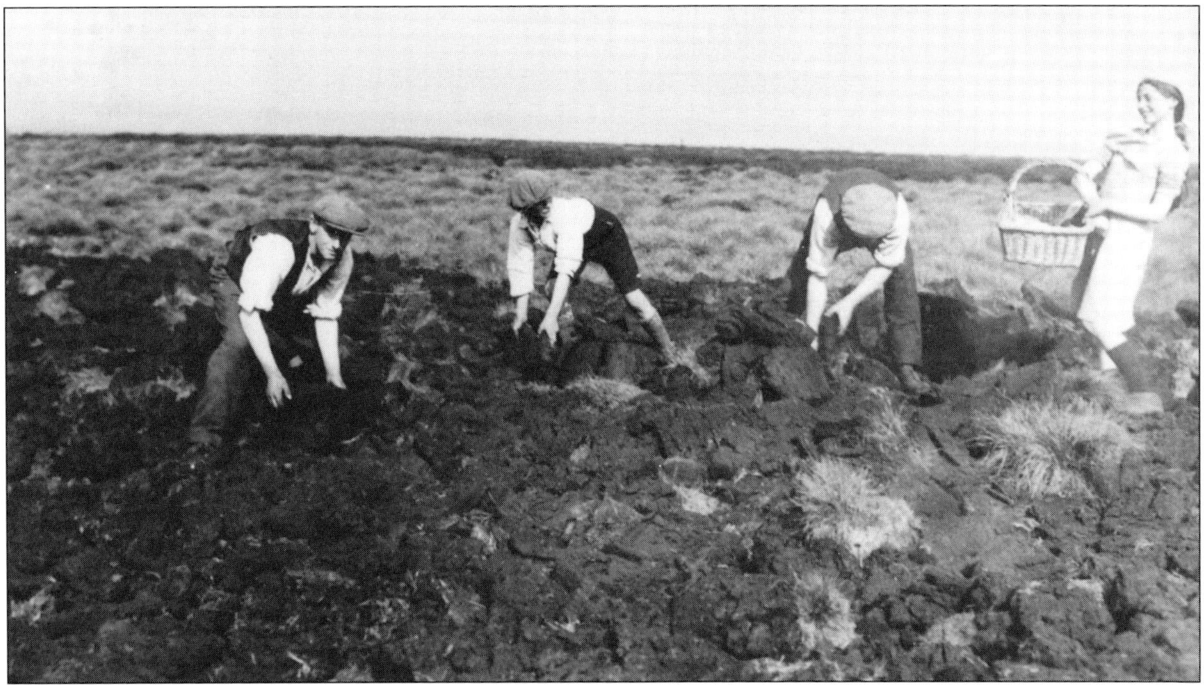

Farms in the north of the valley had rights of turbary on the moor allowing tenants to dig their own peat. Some, if not all farms, never burned anything else. Cutting began in May and many cart loads were taken from the moors by the end of June to be stored in a peat stack at each farm. Members of the Stone family, Charles, and his sons Edward and Robert, have been brought lunch by daughter Annie. In the Second World War peat cutting ceased because of the danger from unexploded devices on land used for military training.

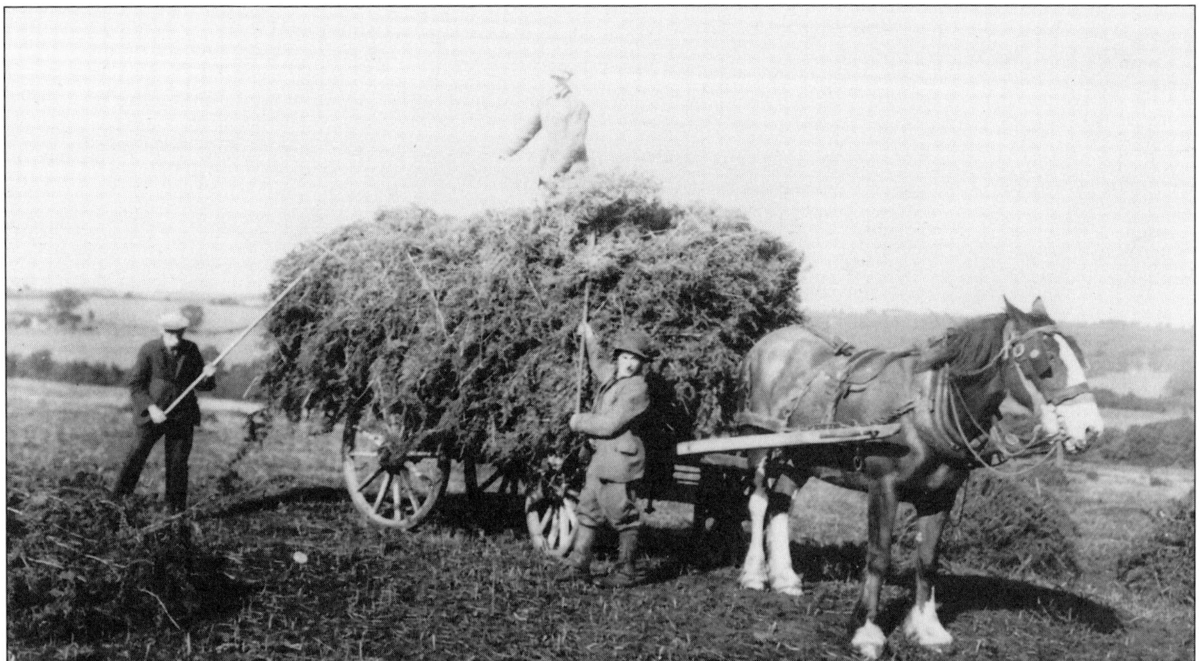

Harvesting bracken at Haverah Park. The bracken would be intended for animal bedding but it was once a source of potash for use in glass and textile manufacture, and under manorial control. In 1660 Thomas Pawson was fined for 'burning Brackans in Farnley Common' in the lower valley.

to be derived from the Old English *haeg* = 'a hunting enclosure', and the Old Norse *vra* 'a nook or corner of land'. First mentioned in 1173 it was granted by Henry II, along with the Honour of Knaresborough, to William de Stuteville. In 1307 two 'parkers' were paid at least eleven pence halfpenny per day to oversee the park where in 1324 and 1330 judicial commissions were issued concerning the poaching of deer from the parks. By 1439, in addition to holding a hundred and sixty deer, it also provided rabbits, hares, wild boar, fowl and fish, all constituting a valuable source of food, as well as a stud farm for the King's horses. In the Forest as well as at Blubberhouses, the forging of iron was an important industry which at Haverah continued to add to the King's coffers until at least 1351.

JOHN O'GAUNT'S CASTLE

Within the park stood the building which later became known as John o' Gaunt's Castle. Probably intended for official visitors, it was first described in royal records during the latter part of the reign of Edward I, and it seems likely that it was mainly used as a hunting lodge or as a residence for a park keeper. Although it is possible that King John may have stayed at the park in 1210 and in 1212, there is no direct evidence of either visit. However, in 1292 Edward I ordered that the lodge should be stocked with wine and stayed there for three days before moving on to Skipton. In 1307 Edward II granted the whole of the Honour to his favourite, Piers Gaveston with 'free chace ... in Haverah'. In 1308 he married Isabella who was granted 'enjoyment of the royal park of ... Haverah' and he may have stayed there between the 13-14 August 1310 when the Privy Seal, court and household were present. He certainly did so in May 1322, and on the 25 and 26 September 1323, perhaps with Isabella. Edward III was also a visitor, and his son, John of Gaunt, Duke of Lancaster, may also have visited in 1372 when the park was granted to him by his father.

In the fourteenth century the building underwent extensive repairs and alterations, perhaps necessary after the previously mentioned Scottish incursions in which Knaresborough had been destroyed by fire. The repairs were carried out under the supervision of 'Master Richard the mason' and one 'Richard of Glatton', and the chapel, a timber-framed building above the gateway, was rebuilt under the direction of Master William of Kendal. Several carpenters were paid two shillings and six pence per week, the masons four pence per day. Two of its chambers, described as the 'Waerhall' and the Queen's Chamber had nineteen windows depicting the arms of the King which were made at York by Master Robert le Verreour at a cost of five pounds ten shillings and sixpence. Further repairs, including those to the battlements, were carried out in 1333 under the then Custodian, John of Newsham, the keeper of the King's horses north of the River Trent. The new stones were cut by several masons working under a Trinitarian friar, Brother William from the House of St Robert at Knaresborough, although the new battlements were actually built by John of Kilburn for which he received the sum of twenty six pounds thirteen shillings and four pence.

Between 1335 and 1337 work on the fort was continued by Edmund of Thedmarsh, then keeper of the King's stud farms. He completed a new moat 26 feet wide and 12 feet deep, and had a pele tower set up on the bank supervised by a master carpenter, John Wynd, on payment of two shillings and sixpence a week. Behind the pele there was a raised platform from which to defend it, and opposite the gate of the fort were doors in a palisade. Seven timber turrets were also constructed along with three perches of brattices or *'ffendours'*, (ie a wooden palisade providing a perimeter fence) adjoining'. The total cost of the work carried out was two hundred and sixty eight pounds.

In the years between 1388 and 1390 the park was the scene of several disturbances one of which was an attempt to murder the master forester, Robert Doufbiggyng who was forced to take refuge in the castle. This attack followed an ambush on Palm Sunday at Fewston church during which some of those assaulted died. The reason for the attacks is unclear, but they perhaps resulted from 'certain malpractices' following a meeting of Foresters. A pardon granted to one of the accused in 1393 recorded his offence as 'destroying the park of Haverah and doing mischief in the parks and chases ... entering the house and destroying the goods and utensils of Robert Doufbiggyng, value forty shillings, abducting the groom of Robert de Rokley, knight, and his greyhound, and detaining them for two days ... and for coming with others on 1 June (1390) ... and slaughtering 16 oxen and cows and destroying household utensils, value £8.'

In 1399 the stewardship of the Forest was transferred to the Duchy of Lancaster. By 1490 it had been leased to Thomas, Earl of Derby and thereafter it passed to the Plumpton family, Sir Robert acquiring the office of Keeper of the Park for an annual rent of £8. In the late sixteenth century a Privy Councillor of Queen Elizabeth surveyed the Forest discovering 'spoiles and waste' and the 'deere pale and lodge' in 'great ruyn and decay' which had allowed the deer to escape. However, by 1608 matters generally had clearly improved for it was reported that the 'soile' in the Forest was 'good and inclosed [and] the tenants generally riche'. Misdemeanours were now apparently dealt with by local magistrates; in 1638 Richard Widdopp of Hartwith in Nidderdale, a yeoman, appeared at the Skipton Quarter Sessions charged with breaking and entering 'the Forest of the Lady Maria, the Queen, called Knaresborough Forest, at Thriscrosse, and hunting with a greyhound, killing and taking away a young male redd deere.'

PIPPIN CASTLE

About a mile to the south of John o' Gaunts Castle is the area known locally as Pippin Castle. It has been suggested, apparently with little foundation, that this was the site of a chapel and burial ground for the inhabitants of the castle. However, the series of three mounds, two oval in shape and a third, rounded and with a depression in the top, perhaps suggest greater antiquity which may only be revealed by archaeological investigation. The site of the nearby 'Siwardergs' mentioned in 1225, which now lies under, or in the vicinity of, Scargill reservoir, may once have been a 'shieling', or summer pasture for grazing, held by someone named Siward.

In 1627 Charles I [1625-1649] demised Haverah for ninety nine years to a consortium of businessmen, but in 1628 it was sold leasehold to the City of London. In 1640/1 a scheme to divide the Forest lands between Charles and the tenants, commoners and freeholders was drawn up but never implemented, perhaps because of the Civil War. After the restoration of the monarchy in 1660 the remainder of the Forest was granted away by Charles II, and Haverah passed into the hands of the Ingilby family of Ripley.

In 1770 an Act of Parliament was obtained for dividing and enclosing the Forest, allotments being granted to Lady Frankland of Blubberhouses, Joshua Hardisty, and Francis Fawkes of Farnley. This Act, later amended, was executed in 1778 when the remainder of the valley was enclosed, the last common fields being those in Timble Great.

PADSIDE HALL

The oldest inhabited domestic house in the Forest of Knaresborough, its name is believed to derive from 'Padda's hillside'. It holds a commanding position at the head of the valley, and for this reason, and also because until 1893 it possessed a watch tower with high windows and a guard room, is believed, perhaps erroneously, to have had a defensive purpose. In 1434 Sir John Pulleyn is said to have died in the house, so at least part of the present house apparently dates from the fifteenth century.

ELSEWHERE IN THE FOREST

In 1086 the Domesday Book recorded that at Fewston in the centre of the valley the King held three ploughlands (approx. 160-180 acres) with four at Besthaim, now lost but probably in the vicinity of Blubberhouses, and another four ploughlands with approximately 3 square miles of woodland at

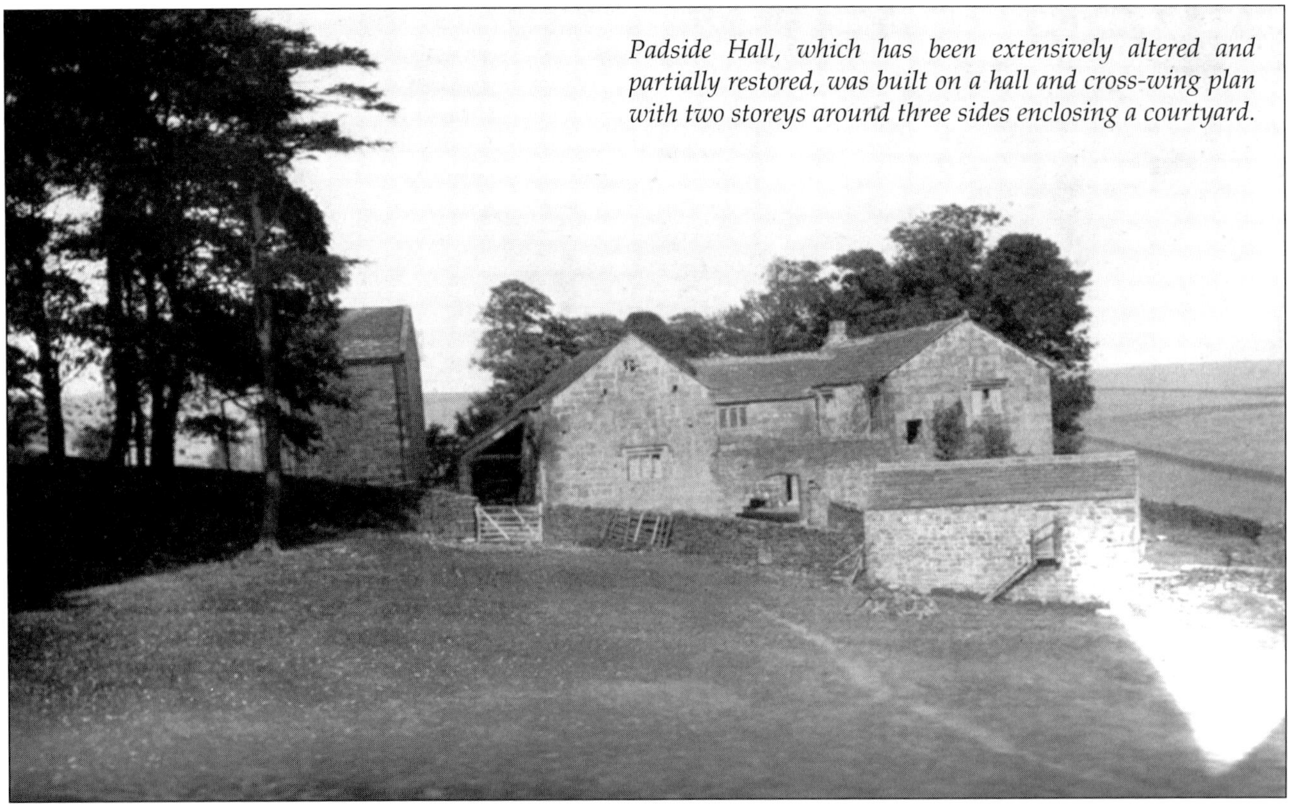

Padside Hall, which has been extensively altered and partially restored, was built on a hall and cross-wing plan with two storeys around three sides enclosing a courtyard.

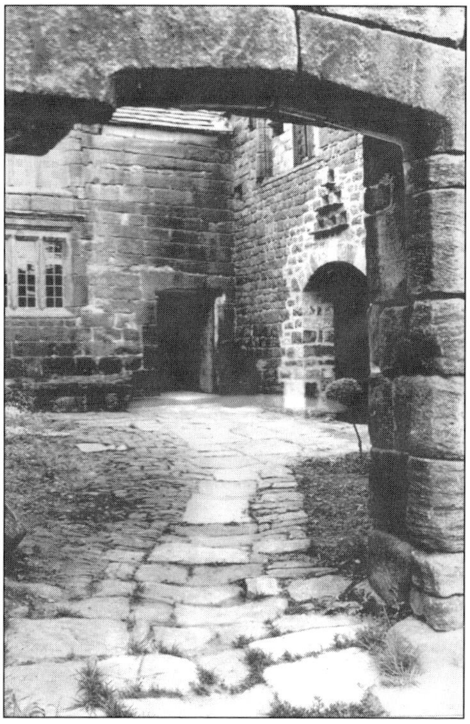

Padside Hall – Courtyard. The tower or stair turret is said to have been on the north-east but was actually on the north-west.

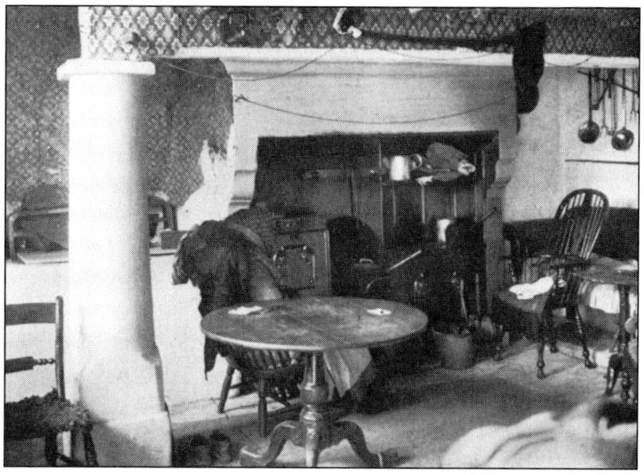

Close observation shows an old lady sitting in the chair. For three hundred years from 1614 the house was the home of the Wigglesworth family, many members of which held the hereditary office of Constable of the Forest up until 1916. Robert Wigglesworth, a substantial farmer, had almost 250 sheep, the largest flock in any Forest inventory. Padside eventually fell into disrepair before a programme of restoration began in the 1970s.

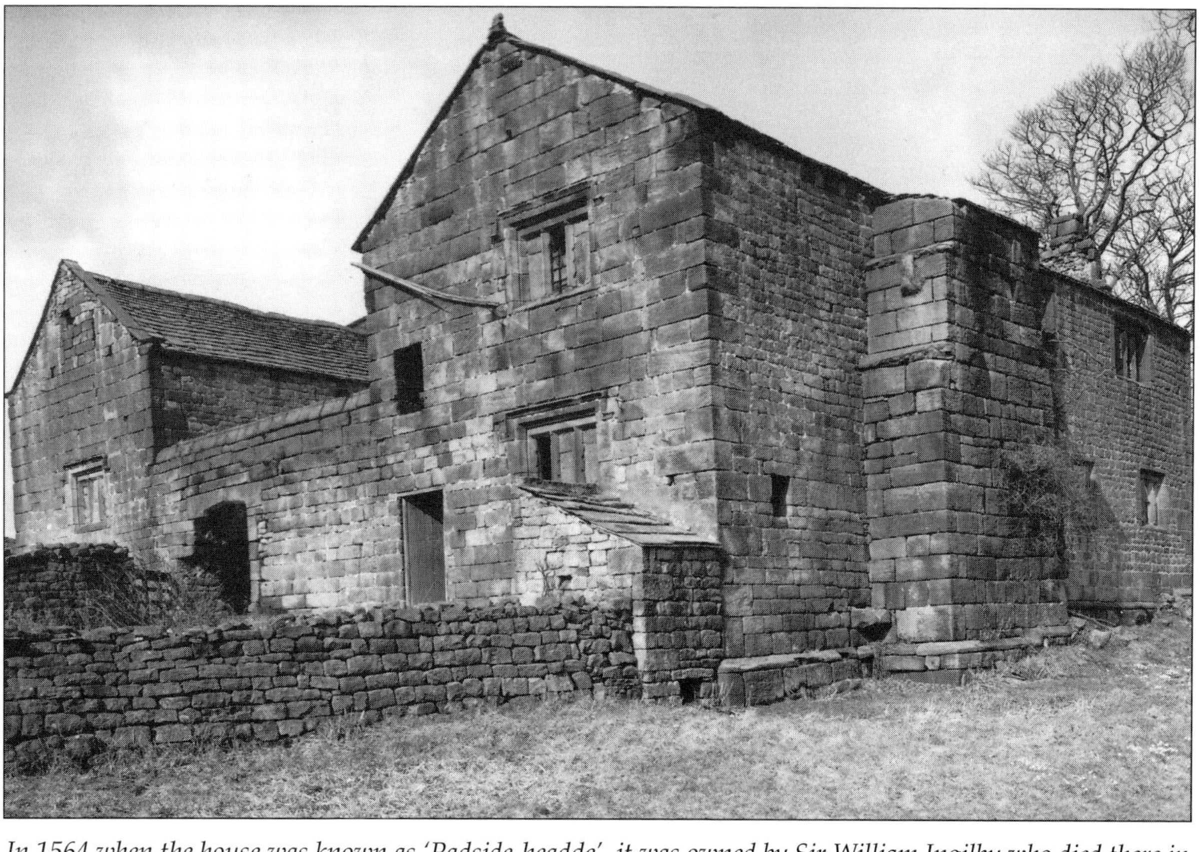

In 1564 when the house was known as 'Padside-headde', it was owned by Sir William Ingilby who died there in 1579. An inventory at that time describes a hall, middle parlour, six chambers, and 'My Lady's parlour' heated from the large chimney. The house later passed to Thomas Bankes of Whixley, and in 1596/7 it was acquired by 'Robert Wygte along with a barn, stable, two garths or parcels of land, and four closes.'

Elsworth which may have been near Jack Hill at Norwood.

At Blubberhouses in 1227 Robert the Forester and his heirs received a forge, the rights of which he later granted to the Augustinian Canons at Bridlington Priory who between 1190-1260 had acquired rights on land at both Timble and Blubberhouses. This grant allowed them to mine and raise iron, to erect forges and to use them as they chose within the bounds of Blubberhouses. Such an acquisition so far from their own house can probably be explained by their need for access to iron. Although such sources existed in the east and north of the county, it is possible that these were already supplying the numerous monastic establishments in that area, thereby forcing the Bridlington canons to look further afield.

In 1267 Henry III ordered his bailiffs to allow the Prior and Convent of Bridlington 'to have and peacefully to hold' the manor of Blubberhouses. This edict seems to have followed a dispute between the Canons of Bridlington and those at nearby Bolton Priory who had grazing rights on the land. The dispute proved to be lengthy and more than twenty years later, following the Archbishop's visitation of 1279-80, an injunction was issued that 'no canon [of Bridlington] was to dwell alone in any manor, or elsewhere, particularly not at Blouberhous, to the injury of his reputation.' The reason for this injunction was not made clear but five months later another visitation to the canons at Bolton gave rise to a suggestion that that house was guilty of laxity. In particular, discipline was poor, the Priory was in debt, and the canons, many of whom were said to be 'troublesome, incompetent or senile', had been plotting against the Prior. As a result of the visitation, carrels, or cupboards for study, were forbidden, money payments were not to be made for clothes and shoes, and any canon going out without good reason was to fast the following day. In addition, there was to be no drinking after Compline except in cases of necessity, and 'at all times drinking and food which tended to pleasure or lasciviousness with any unlawful and disorderly activities, were wholly proscribed.' In 1297 the canons at Bolton hired a bercary, or sheep pasture, at Blubberhouses, thereby extending the scope of their enterprises in the area.

By the early fourteenth century the furnaces in the valley, with the exception of one at Haverah Park which continued at least until 1351, were no longer active. This was probably due to the combination of a shortage of timber resulting from the extensive deforestation of earlier centuries, poor summers, Scottish raiding parties during the early fourteenth century, and outbreaks of plague in the latter part of the century. In 1536 William Wade, Prior of Bridlington, lost his priory's rights at Blubberhouses, then said to be worth ten pounds, and in 1562 the lordship passed from the Crown to Thomas Wood, gentleman, and William Frankland, the latter giving to his brother, Richard and his son, Hugh, 'the Manor of Bluberhouses, and all his lands there and at Fuiston'.

Although there is little hard evidence of significant activity in the valley during the Civil War a letter of 1640 addressed to Ferdinando, the 1st Lord Fairfax by his brother, Charles, did report the presence of 'a body of military in the Forest' which seems to have consisted of a company of men under the command of a Captain Langley. 'They had no good report before they came, yet I hear not of any great enormity since their coming' he reported before adding that the men were 'many weeks behind with their pay' and for that reason he feared 'we shall have ill neighbours in them, and when their ... provisions fail them ... they will cater for themselves.' In 1643 and 1644 it was reported that both Royalist and Parliamentary forces were making occasional raids and 'in the open Forest had taken and wounded a man' and 'before his eyes ravished a woman.' On the 26 June 1644 Prince Rupert's Royalist army left Skipton and was initially billeted at the village of Bolton Abbey. By the 29 June it passed through Denton, home of the Fairfax family, and it is likely that it may then have taken the direct route across the lower part of the Washburn Valley, perhaps via the ford at Dob Park, to the hill now known as Sword Point. The oft repeated suggestion that this hill derives its name from some military involvement cannot however be substantiated and it may in fact be derived from the old placename 'Elsworth' or 'Elsward'. The army may then have continued via Haverah Park and Penny Pot Lane to Harrogate and Knaresborough where it arrived on the 30 June, and at Marston Moor on 2 July. The remnants of the defeated army may also have returned by the same route for on 12 July 1644 it was 'Agreed with Richard Barnvis, for all that piece of ground at Bolton [Abbey] ... to be eaten and soiled by the Prince's horse as they passed through the country – £20.'

Chapter 2

The Upper Valley

The township of Thruscross, the most northerly in the valley, consisted of 6340 acres bounded on the south by the township of Blubberhouses, on the west and north by Rocking Moor and Pock Stones Moor, and on the east by Heyshaw Moor, all of which separate the valley from Nidderdale. Here the land was formerly divided between a number of landlords including the Roundell, Shann and Nicholson families as well as the Duke of Devonshire whose estate still encompasses much of the land for shooting purposes. In 1764 he also owned a smelt mill on the Washburn near Hoodstorth. Between this ridge and the township of Blubberhouses to the south was an area consisting of a number of isolated and scattered dwellings as well as four small centres of population at Bramley Head, West End, Low Green and Thruscross. Here the occupants, usually holding no more than twenty or thirty acres of land by tenure of the Manor of Knaresborough, supplemented their income from farming by the spinning of wool and flax in their own homes, and perhaps also pursuing a trade such as besom making or tanning.

In the present era when it is possible to travel the entire length of the valley in half an hour it is difficult to imagine how insular the smallest communities of the valley were before the arrival of the internal combustion engine. In his diary account of a visit to the township of Thruscross in 1891, John Dickinson gives the impression that the trip was something of an expedition. 'Went to West End ... I was never so high up that way before – very romantic and interesting.' In fact it was only 3 miles from his own home in Timble where he spent almost all his life. Even in the early twentieth century, workmen sent from the estate of the Duke of Devonshire at Bolton Abbey to carry out repairs to property at West End, had to lodge there from Monday to Friday despite living only 4 miles away.

Northerly Section of Upper Valley Pre-Reservoir – Mills and Principal Buildings

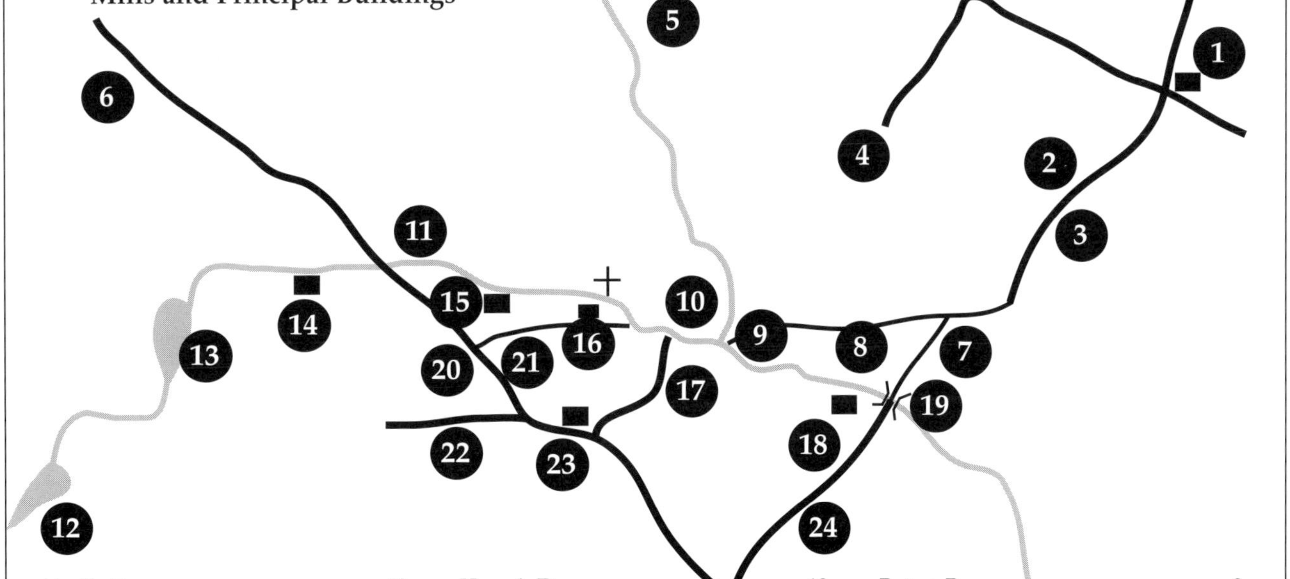

Aked's Dam	12	Harry's Dam	13	Ratten Row	3
Beck Foot Bridge	9	High Mill	14	River Washburn	5
Brake's fold	24	Little Mill	15	School and Corkscrew Lane	23
Bramley head	6	Low Green	10	Scot Lane	8
Capelshaw Beck	11	Maukin Cross	2	Stone House	1
Clogger lane	21	Meeting of the Waters	9	Thruscross	4
Corkscrew Lane	17	Methodist Chapel	20	West End	10
Duke's Lane	22	Mill (Street Lane, Low Mill) Bridge	19	West End (Low) Mill	18
Gate Inn	7	Patrick's Mill	16		

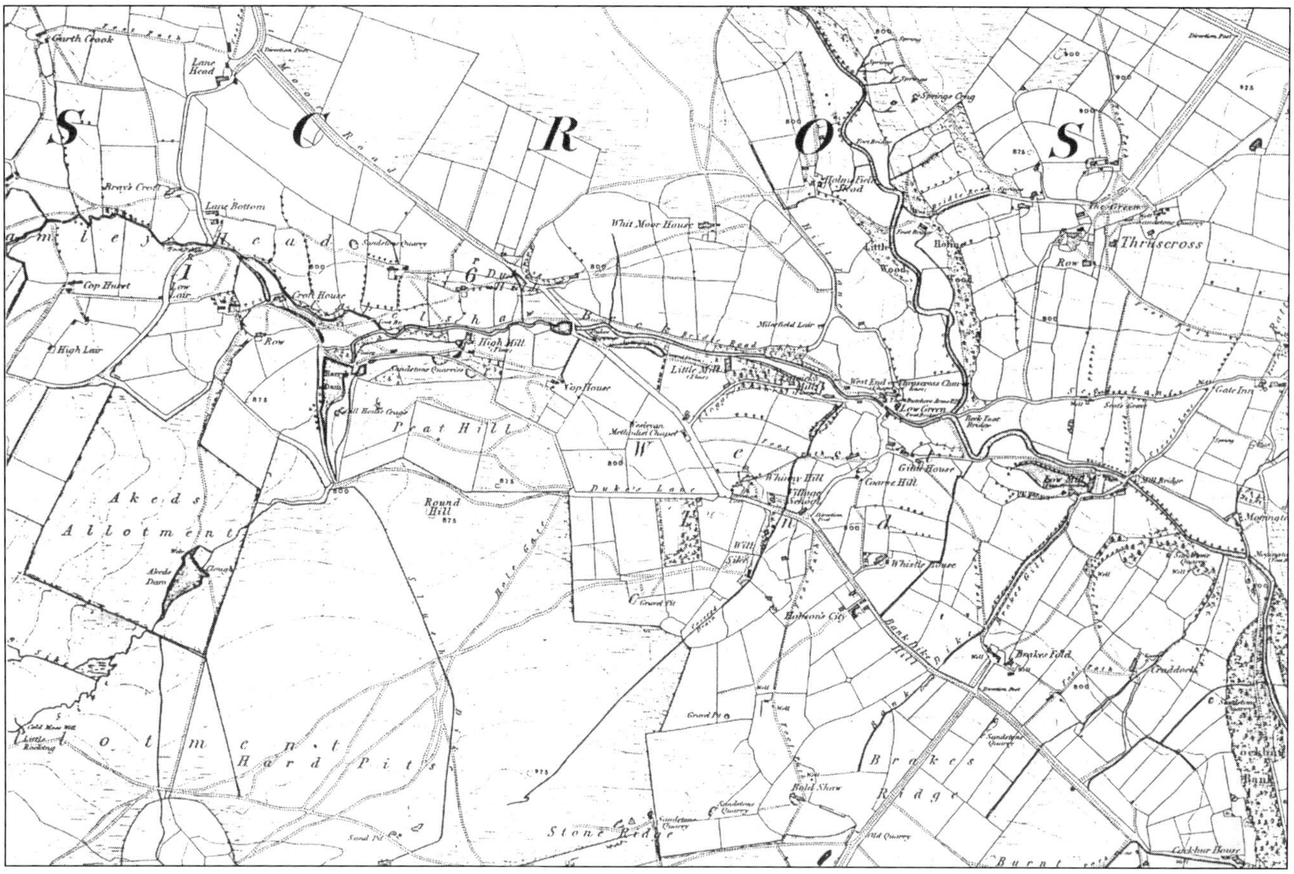

Northerly section of Upper Valley post-reservoir.

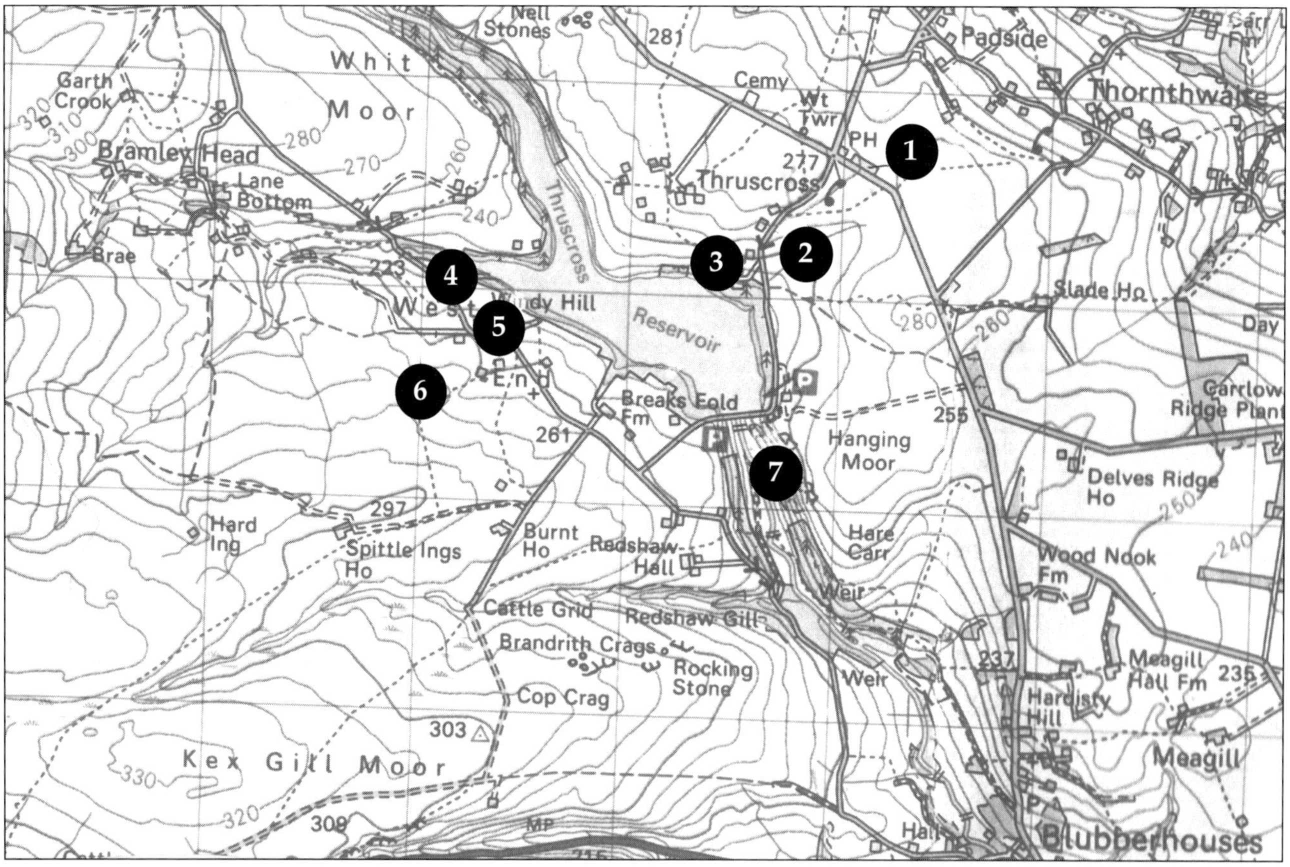

This map shows Blubberhouses. Bramley Head, Breake's Fold, Clogger Lane (4), Thruscross dam (7), Duke's Lane (6), Hardisty Hill, Ratten Row (2), Redshaw Hall, the school (5), Scot Lane (3), The Stone House (1) and Thruscross.

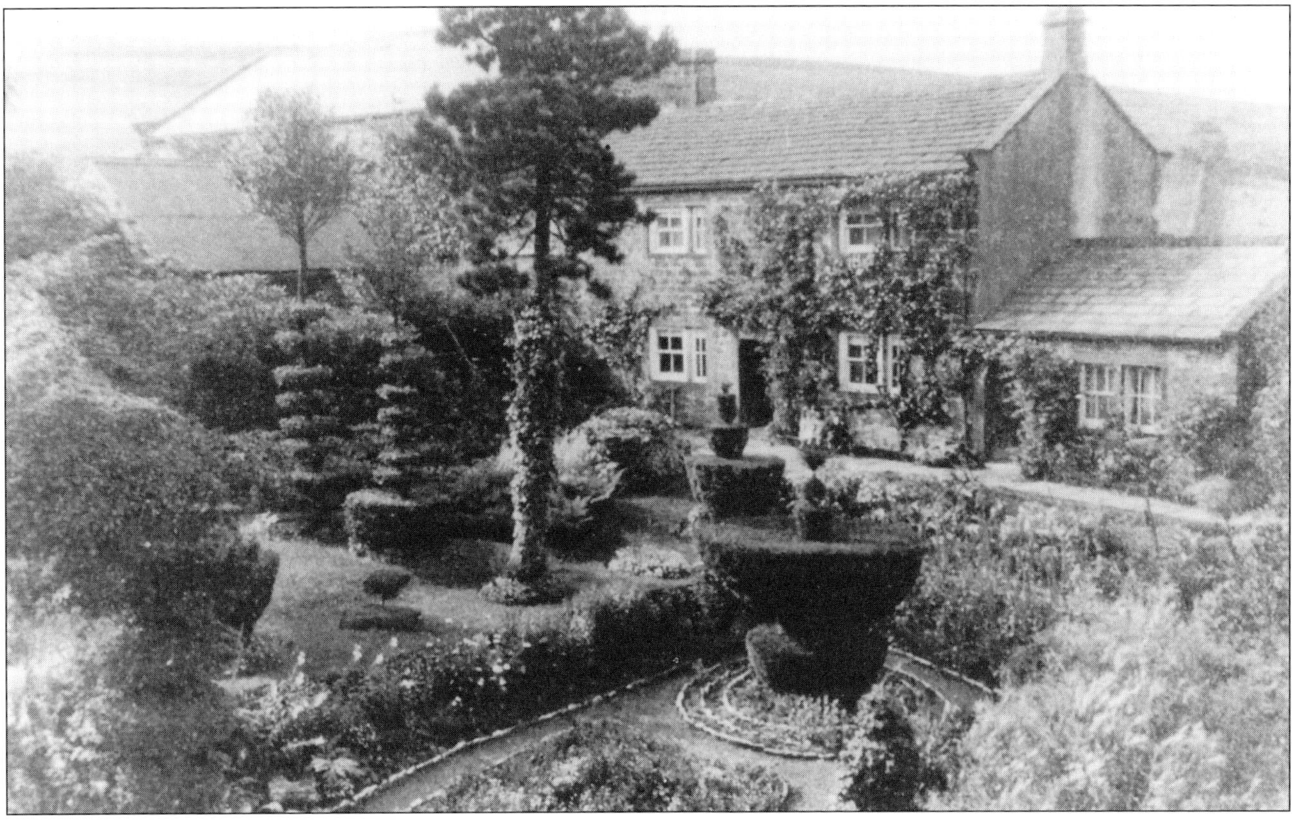

Bray House garden.

BRAMLEY HEAD

The most remote of the township's three communities, Bramley Head consists of only a few farmsteads one of which, Bray House, was built in 1771 when the moor was first enclosed.

In 1841 the house was occupied by the Myers family, Thomas Myers serving as a gamekeeper, initially for Stephen Nicholson of Leeds, and later for the Sheepshanks family, and the Duke of Devonshire, all absentee landlords. Robert, who was born in 1834, was a gamekeeper like his father.

The house was chiefly famed for its garden carved out of the surrounding moorland. Lined with paths of stone and rubble it was equipped with lawn, herbaceous borders, orchard and many varieties of rose and topiary. It later became the home of the Stone family. So famous did the garden become that

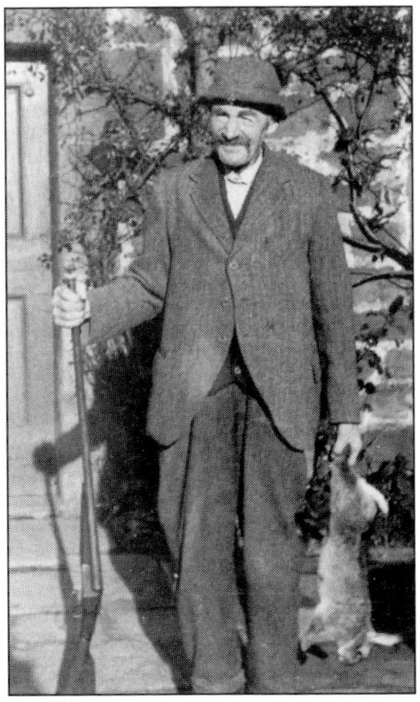

Robert Myers - gamekeeper.

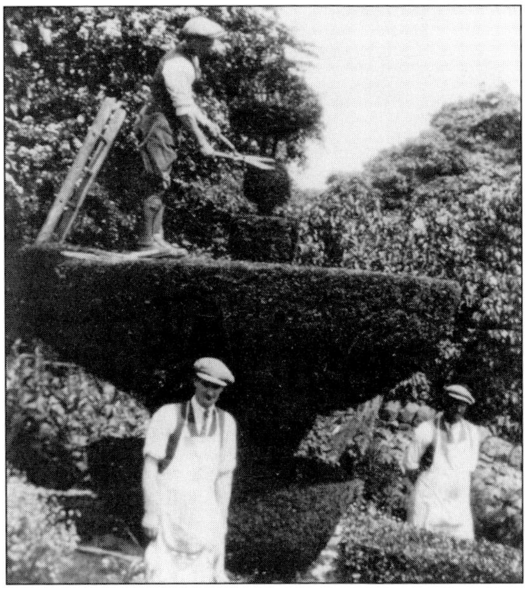

Charles Stone trimming topiary at Bray House.

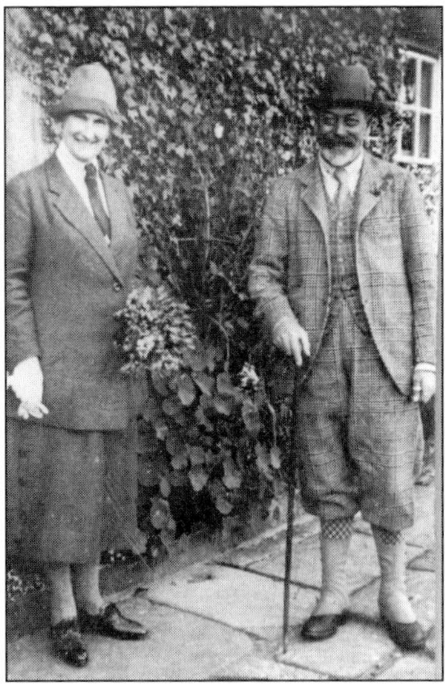

King George V and the Duchess of Devonshire at Spittleings.

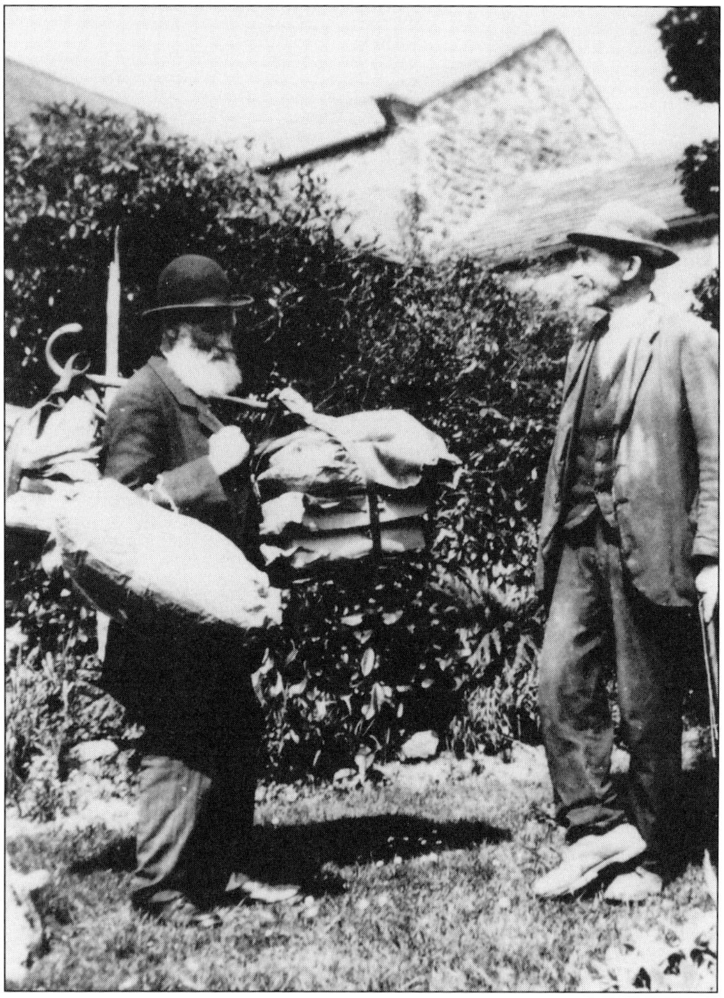

The 'Pinnyman' with Robert Myers.

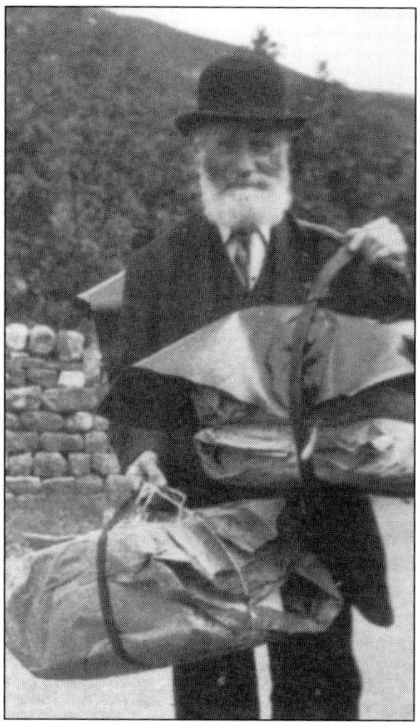

James shortly before his death.

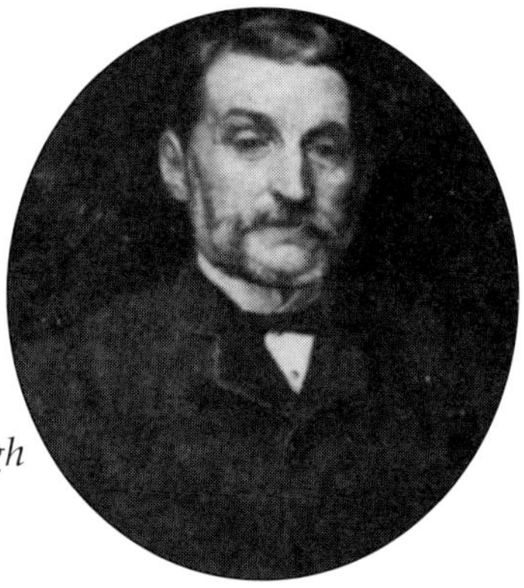

John Denbigh Hannam 1824-1906.

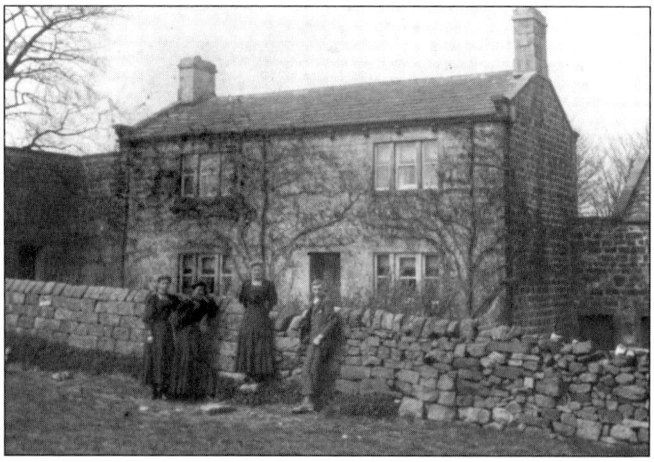

The Browns of Cop Hurst. John Brown and his wife Jane farmed at Cop Hurst for forty years. Born in 1844 John was the son of a lead smelter turned schoolmaster. For many years he served Holy Trinity church, Thruscross, as organist. His wife was the daughter of John Emsley whose father was a former licensee of the Stone House Inn. John and Jane produced ten children of which nine were daughters. The youngest, Lily, became Mrs Hiley, a teacher at nearby Rocking School.

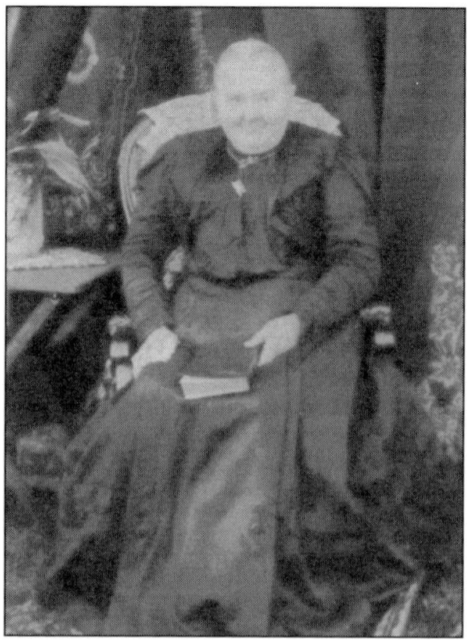

Sarah Jane Brown (née Emsley).

King George V when at Bolton Abbey for the shooting, visited each year to receive a sprig of white heather for his buttonhole.

THE PINNYMAN

A licensed hawker, James Cowley was born in Burnley in 1854, the grandson of a soldier who had served at Waterloo and the son of an itinerant draper who also had a shop in Burnley. As a boy he had travelled the dales with his father, and it amused him that some of his older customers continued to refer to him as 'Young Cowley' long after he had ceased to be young. For over half a century James spent most of the year 'on the road', a very familiar figure greeted eagerly especially by the children who were so excited by his appearance that he was often referred to as the Pied Piper. Always dressed in a tightly buttoned black overcoat and a bowler hat, he carried his wares in two large bundles dangling from a walking stick over his shoulder and could be heard from afar muttering 'where are all these little boys and girls who would like to see in my pack?'

Named after the stiff collars and pinafores among his wares, or as 't'feastman' because he sometimes arrived at the time of the village feast, James was always a welcome visitor. In winter he toiled many miles over snowy moorland roads and tracks to reach his customers at isolated settlements in both neighbouring Nidderdale and the Washburn Valley. A devout Catholic he contrived always to make a base within walking distance of a church where he could hear mass, and claimed he was always able to

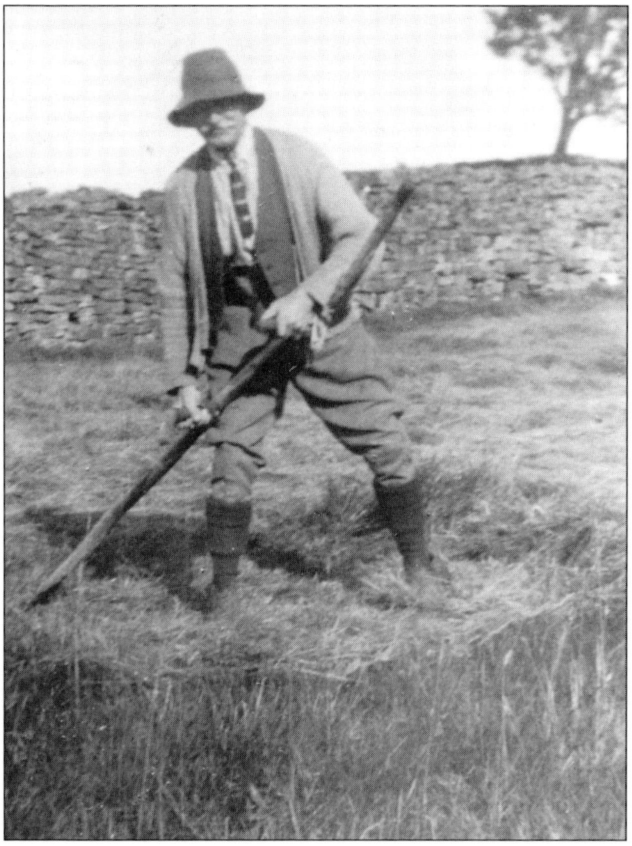

William Nelson Snr scything at Garth Crook 1930s. Members of the Nelson family have lived and worked in the upper valley since pre-Norman times and some were well-known for the making of besoms. William born c.1856 was a farmer and gamekeeper to the Duke of Devonshire. He and his wife, Mary, raised nine children at Garth Crook.

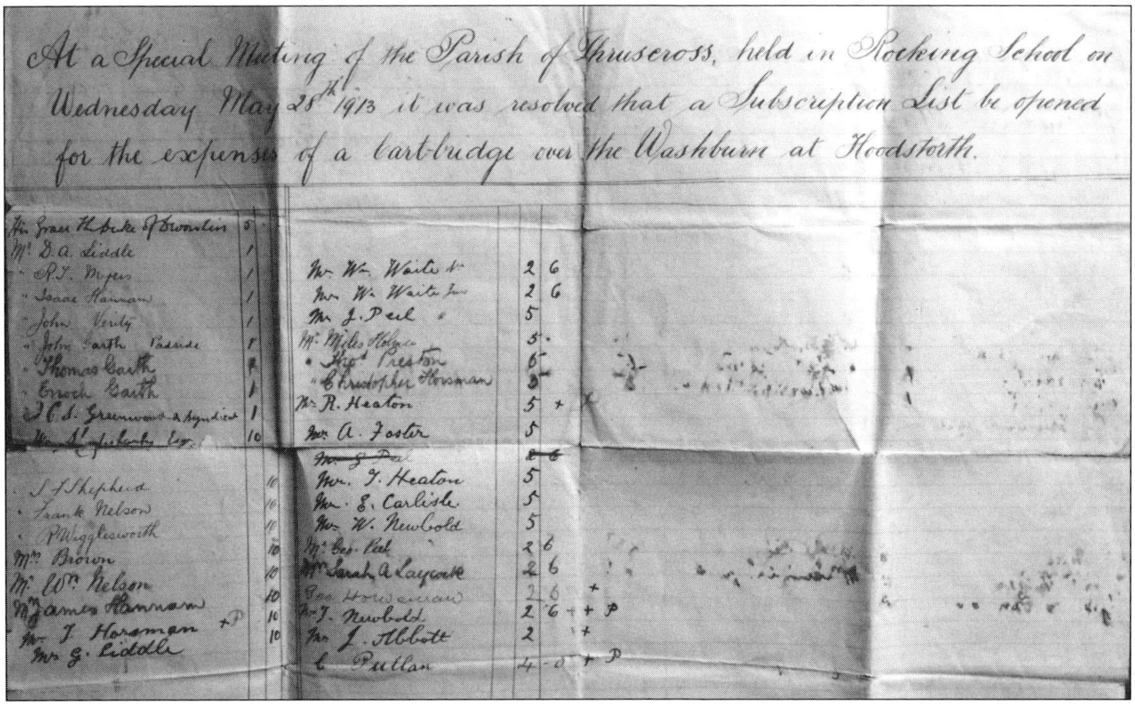

At a Special Meeting of the Parish of Thruscross, held in Rocking School on Wednesday May 28th 1913 it was resolved that a Subscription List be opened for the expenses of a cart bridge over the Washburn at Hoodstorth.

His Grace the Duke of Devonshire	5	Mr Wm Waite Sr	2 6
Mr D. A. Liddle	1	Mr Wm Waite Jun	2 6
" R. T. Myers	1	Mr J. Peel	5
" Isaac Hannam	1	Mr Miles Holgate	5
" John Verity	1	" Richd Preston	5
" John Garth Padside	1	" Christopher Horsman	5
" Thomas Garth	1	Mr R. Heaton	5
" Enoch Garth	1	Mr A. Foster	5
J. C. S. Greenwood & Syndicate	1	~~Mr J. Peel~~	~~5 6~~
[illegible]	10	Mr T. Heaton	5
" J. Shepherd	10	Mr E. Carlisle	5
" Frank Nelson	10	Mr W. Newbold	5
" P. Wigglesworth	10	Mr Geo Peel	2 6
Mrs Brown	10	Mrs Sarah A Laycock	2 6
Mr Wm Nelson	10	Geo Horseman	2 6
Mr James Hannam	10	Mr J. Newbold	2 6
Mr T. Horsman	10	Mr J. Abbott	2
Mrs G. Liddle		C. Pullan	4 0

Subscription list for building Hoodstorth Bridge.

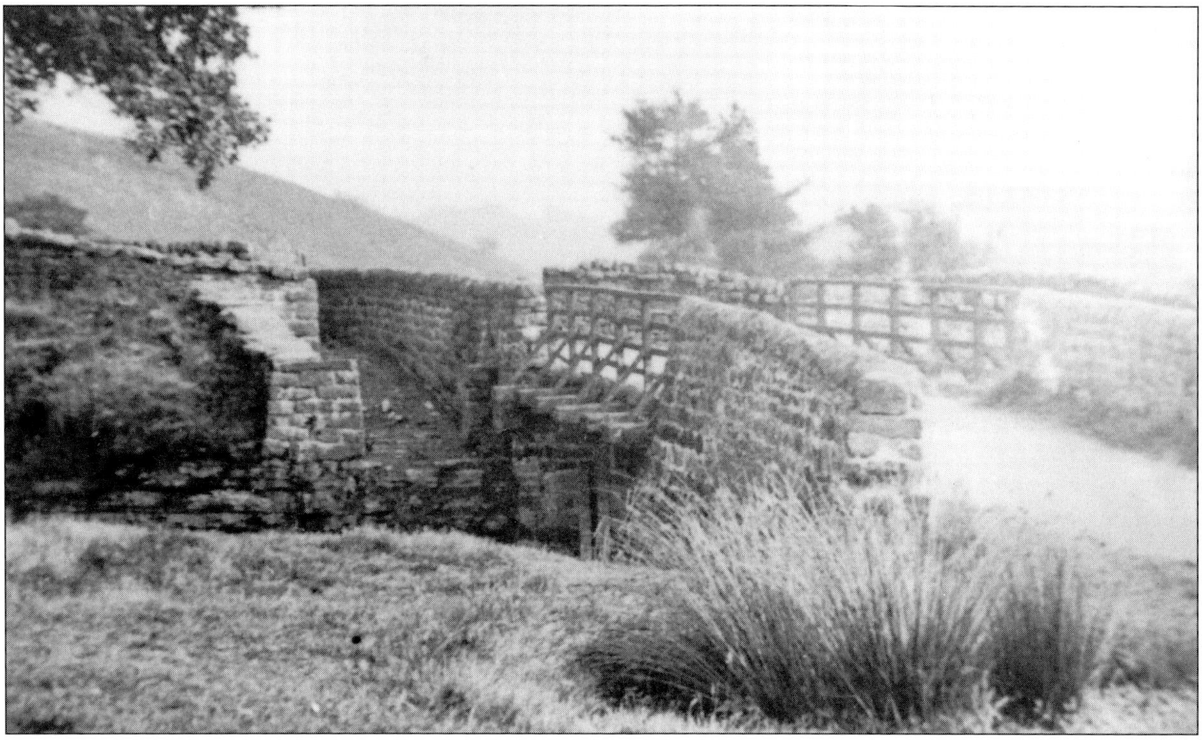

Old Cart Bridge at Hoodstorth, 1913.

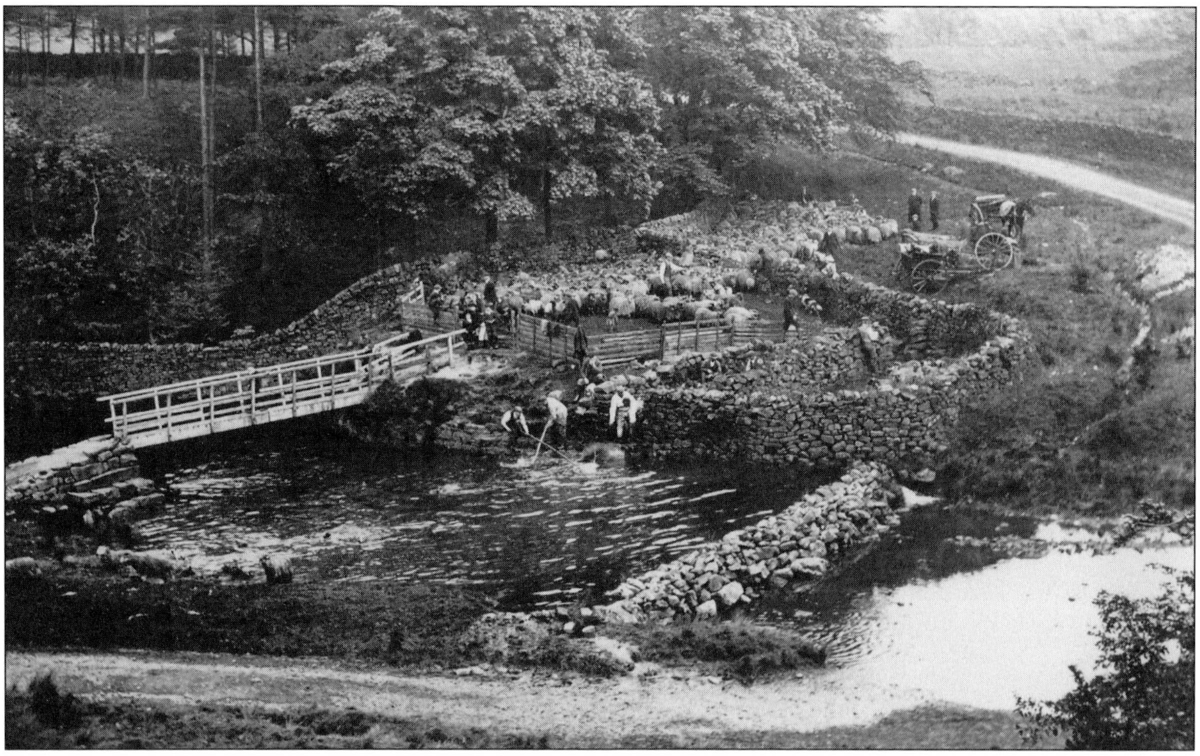

Sheep Dipping at Hoodstorth. Introduced in the mid-nineteenth century, dipping was intended to eradicate infestation and to prepare the wool for shearing. Before the First World War members of the Nelson, Myers, Hannam and Garth families often made this annual event into a special outing with a picnic.

do so. One day, Alfred J. Brown, the Yorkshire writer, met him walking briskly through Nidderdale on his way back to Middlesmoor after both men had been to mass in Pateley Bridge. It was apparently not unusual for James, even in his eighties, to make a round trip of 12 or 13 miles for this purpose. On at least one occasion during the First World War he left Lofthouse in Nidderdale at four in the morning to hear mass 9 miles away at Colsterdale where soldiers in camp underwent preliminary training before going to the front. Arriving at the church to find it deserted, and fearing that he was too late, he managed to find the key and let himself in to pray. Discovered by the priest, he was assured that not only was he in time for mass but was invited to what must have been a very welcome breakfast afterwards. James, the last of the Dales packmen, died at Burnley in 1937 aged eighty-three.

ETHEL PEEL

In 1934 Ethel Garnett, a Bradford girl, married a valley man, Leonard Peel and they became tenants at Lane Head, one of the last farms in the upper valley, with 34 acres for which the rent was £34 per annum. The house was only made habitable after weeks of work. Few of the farms had piped water and Lane Head, with a pump beside the sink, was no exception. There was no electricity and the lavatory was an earth closet in a secluded corner of the garden. In addition, when the couple moved in they found that the boiler had burst, the range was useless and the bedroom floors were rotten.

Before the advent of three cats, the house was full of rats, twenty of which were killed in one week. For a while the house also became home to two hundred chickens in two brooders heated with paraffin lamps. Each morning and evening the new boiler and set pot had to be filled and water also had to be provided daily for an elderly uncle, Joe Hannam, at Lane Bottom Farm, where there was no source of drinking water. All heating of water and cooking was done on the fire. One of Ethel's duties was to take a reading every morning at 9.00 am from the rain gauge which stood in the front pasture at Lane Head. Results were then posted to Leeds once a week. For this she received the sum of ten shillings (50p) a month.

For a former townee like Ethel Peel pig killing, usually in November, was a daunting task. Ethel was forever grateful to Annie Stone who instructed her in the complex arts of scalding, rendering lard, making dripping, brawn and stand pies, and putting meat in brine. The meat was preserved by the men who salted, washed and hung it up to dry ready to keep the family in pork, bacon and ham during the winter months.

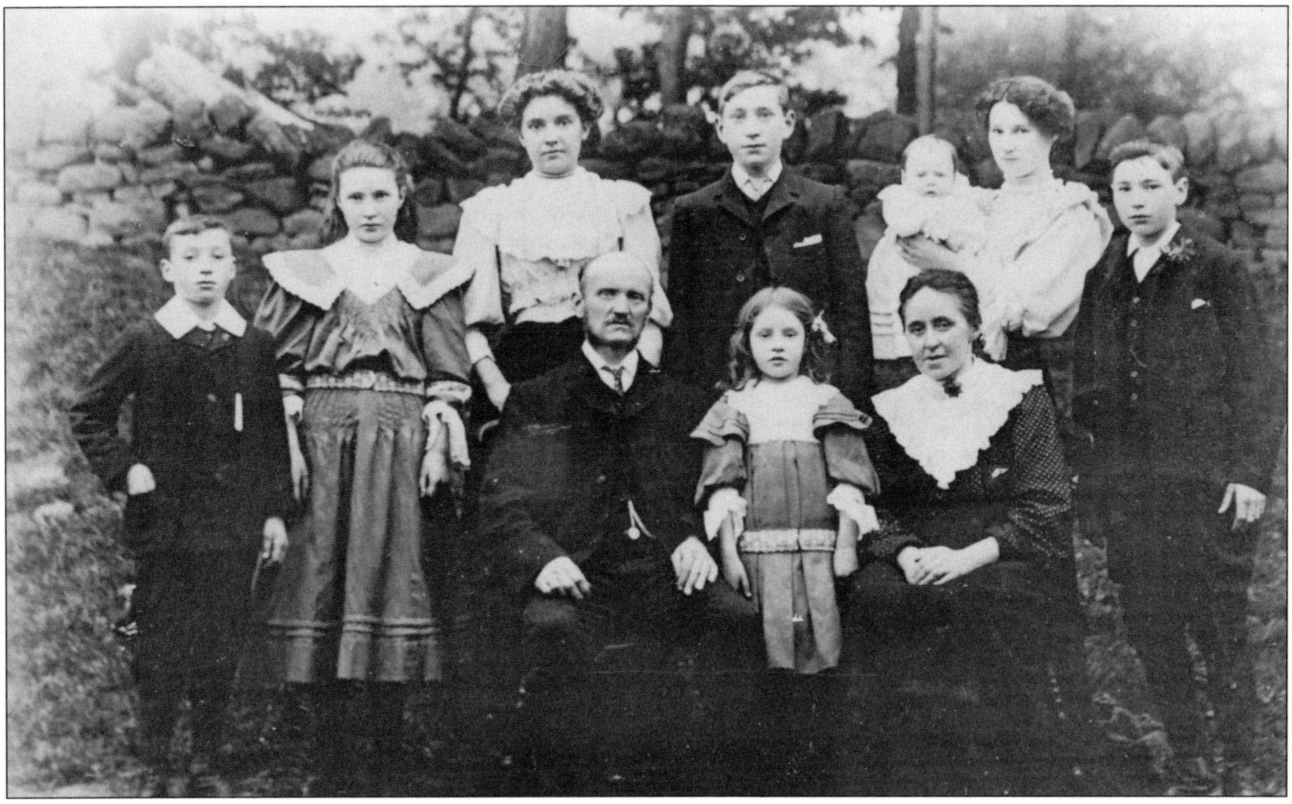

The Abbot Family of Lane Head. Joseph Abbot, farmer, his wife Susannah and their children, Gertrude, Edith, Harry, Thomas, Clarice, Joseph and the baby, Lizzie. In 1901 Gertrude and Edith were employed as hemp rovers probably at Low Mill which spun hemp. Rovers drew out and twisted the fibre used in the manufacture of rope.

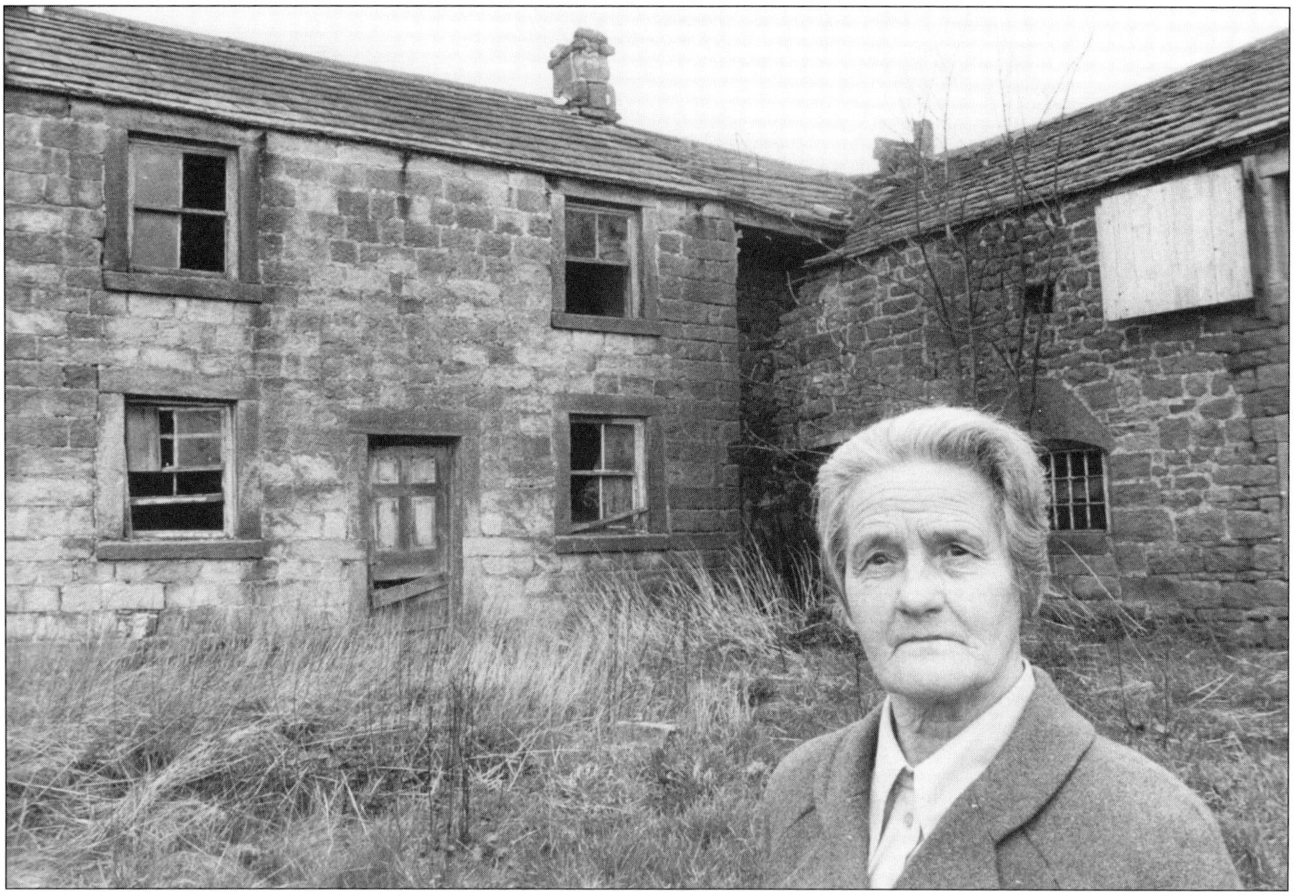

Ethel Peel of Lane Head outside her former home – 'it was a most peculiarly built house'.

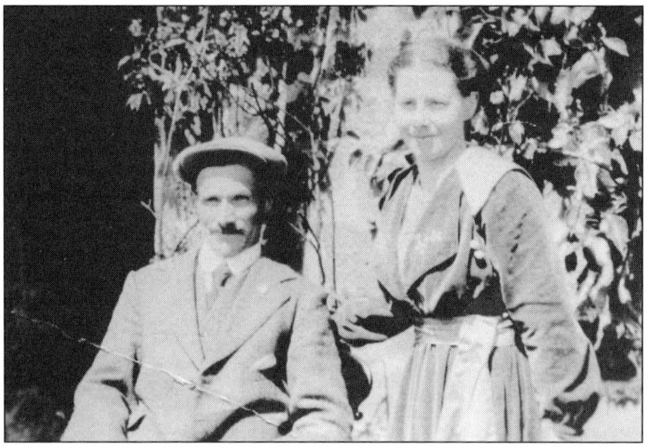

Charles and Annie Stone at Bray Head.

Most farmers kept a couple of cows to provide milk for home use and for making butter. In the 1930s a pound and a half of butter sold at market for one shilling and sixpence of which the carrier received a penny. Eggs sold for less than two shillings a dozen. Although families were usually self sufficient in eggs, milk, cream, butter, meat, vegetables and fruit in season, Mr Wigglesworth's shop in Scot Lane provided basic groceries including yeast and flour for baking bread, cakes and pies. Other vital necessities were supplied by several travelling salesmen including a cobbler, and pedlars like Johnny Myers, Thomas Shepherd and James Cowley.

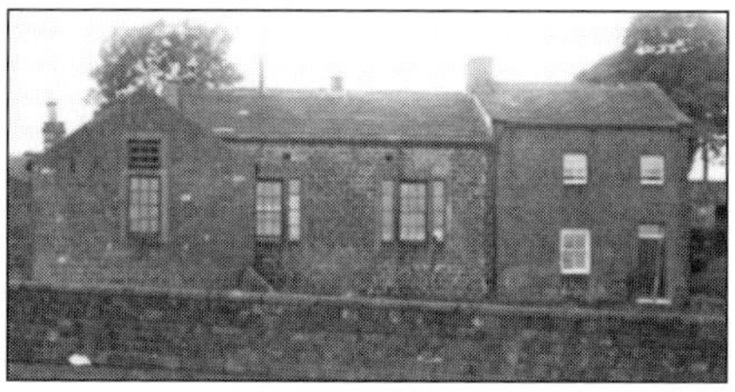

ROCKING SCHOOL

In his will John Breakes of Bramley Head, who died in 1651, left five shillings for 'a small bridge at Bramley Head on the way to West End Chapel'. No doubt it was also used for children attending Rocking School. Prior to the mid-nineteenth century education was only for the sons of the wealthy taught by a private tutor or perhaps a local clergyman. In 1566 Christopher Banks of Thruscross left the sum of eight pounds per annum for seven years so that his son 'shal be brought up in the learninge.' A very basic education would have been provided by a dame school of which there was also one at West End

STEPHEN NICHOLSON

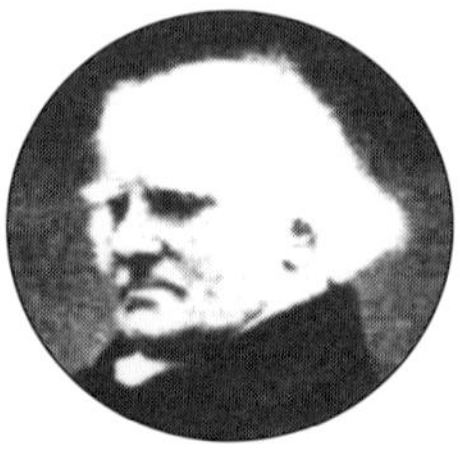

In 1826 Stephen Nicholson, a banker and philanthropist with shooting rights on Rocking Moor, whose home was at the Mansion

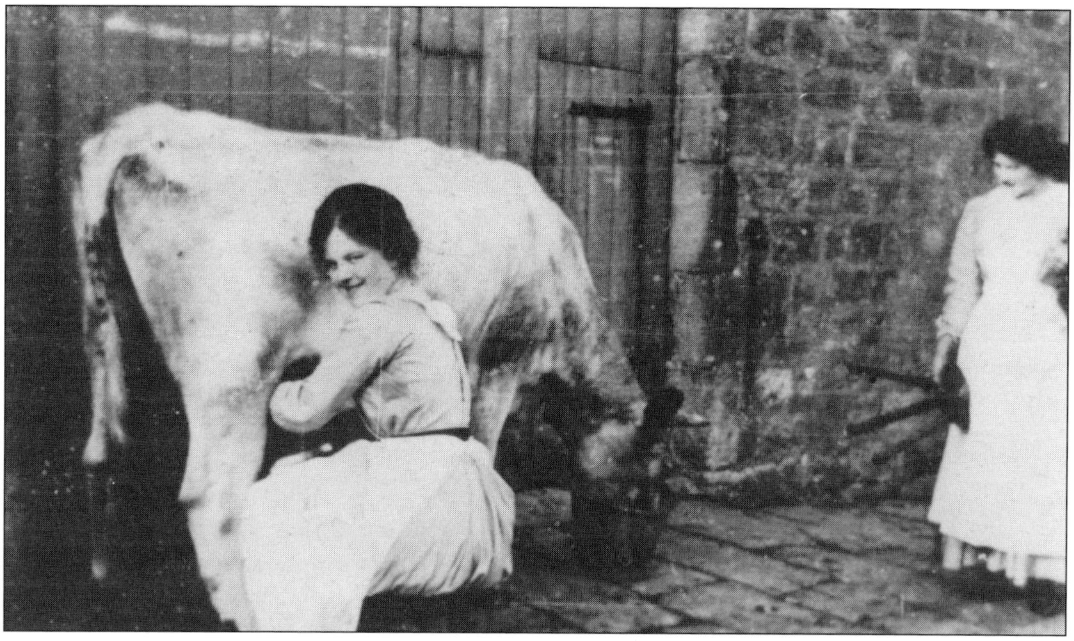

Hand milking – Polly Mudd at Slade House Farm c.1915. Mary Susanna (Polly) was the daughter of William and Frances Mudd. Both she and her older sister, Phyllis, were at one time in service at the home of the Rev. George Hugh Elliott of Holy Trinity church, Thruscross.

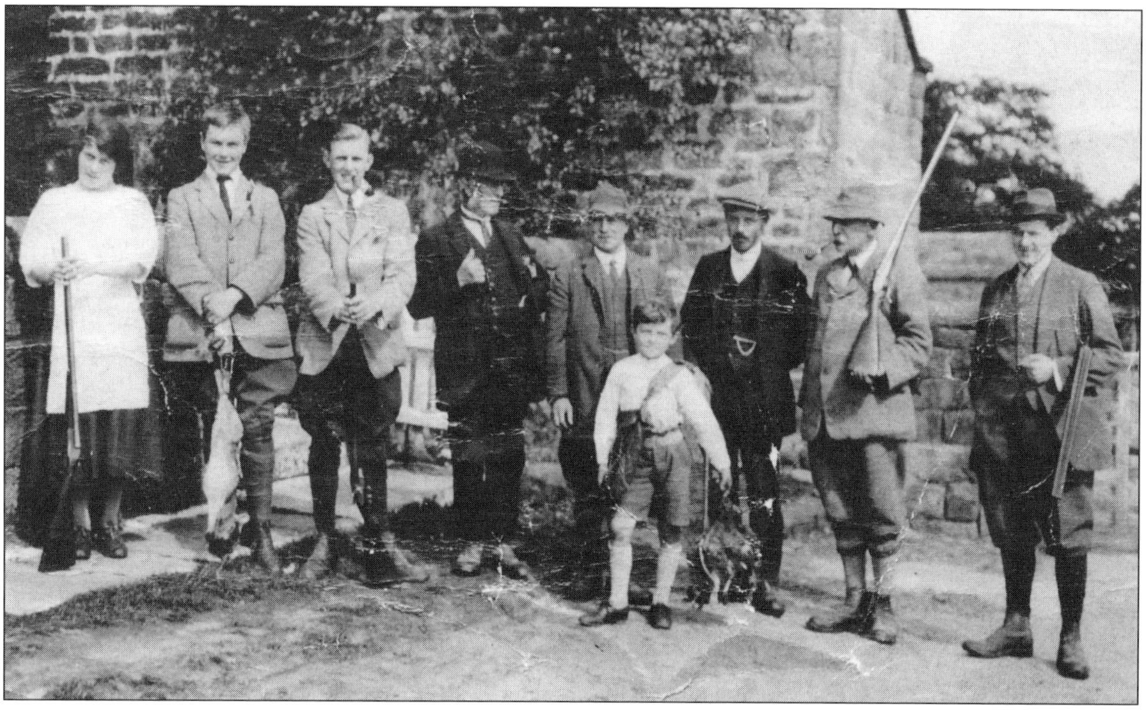

Shooting Party at Slade House 1920s.

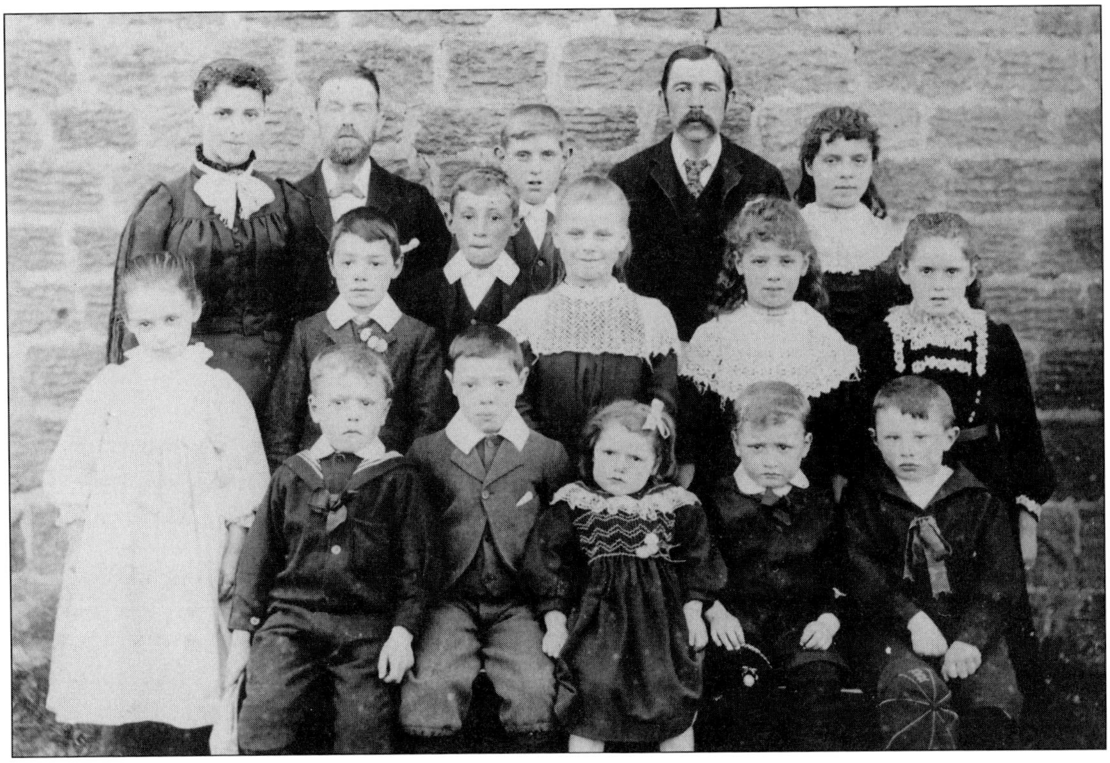

Rocking School pupils and teachers, 1897.

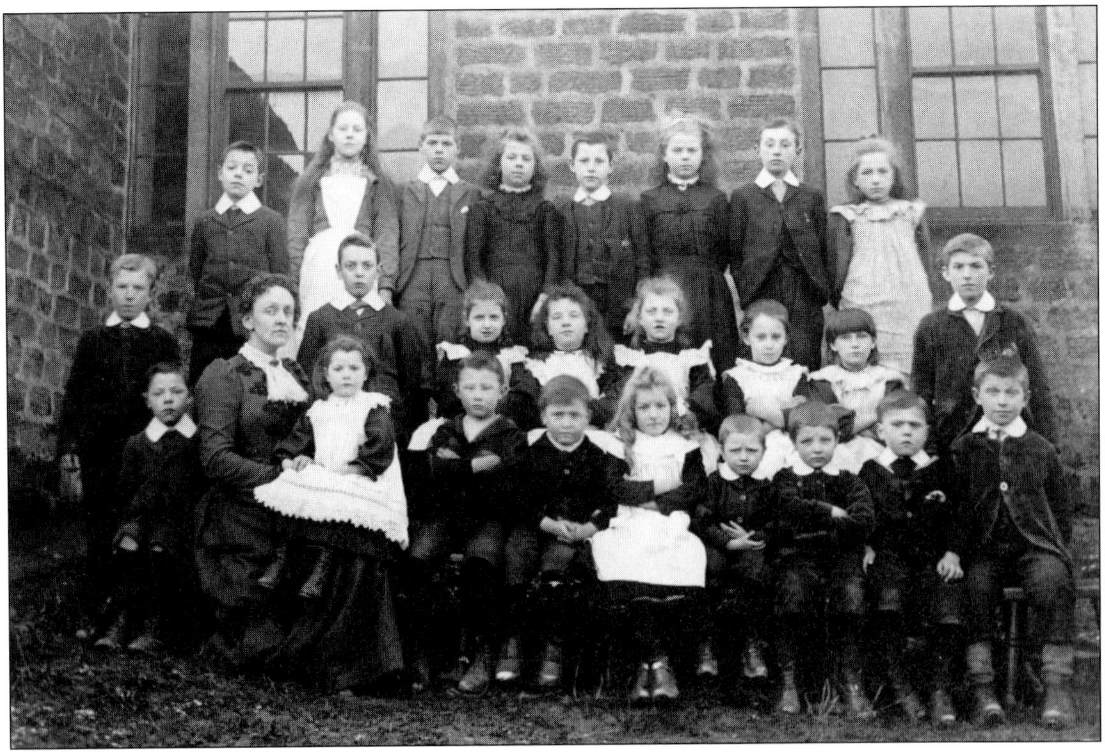

Rocking School pupils c.1900 with Mrs Evelyn Hiley. Mrs Hiley taught at the school for twenty-five years.

in Roundhay Park at Leeds, purchased land for the building of a school on the moor edge.

A suggestion by John Gwyther, then vicar of Fewston, that the building should be conveyed to the Church was declined but the school was however made 'subject to the control and inspection of the vicar.' Instructions were issued that any master appointed should sign an agreement 'that he will keep the interior ... in good repair ... and that he will on receiving a month's notice ... give up possession of the master's house, school and premises and move himself and his family ... without any charge to Mr Nicholson'. The first known teacher was John Rhodes in 1841 who lived on the premises with his wife and three children.

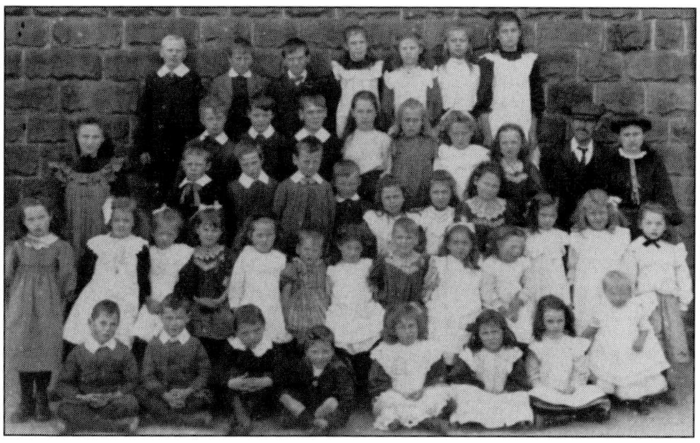

Rocking School pupils 1900-1910 with possibly Thomas and Florence Hyde. Their own eight children may also have been included in the picture.

In 1856 the Nicholson family decided to convey the school to a Trust 'for educational purposes' on condition that should it cease to be a school, it would be restored to the Nicholsons or their representative. John Gwyther was advised to appoint five trustees, and the family indicated their willingness to continue their 'subscription to the ... schoolmaster for one year from the date of the last half yearly payment.' Gwyther also applied for a grant to the National Society for Promoting the Education of the Poor in the Principles of the Established Church, usually shortened to the National Society, but his application was refused on the grounds that no funds were available, presumably because the school had not been conveyed to the Church. However, on the 2 March, 1857, shortly before the death of Stephen Nicholson in 1858, the school was finally conveyed by the family 'to the Minister and Churchwardens of the Chapel or Church of Ease at West End'.

In 1860, needing a grant of £65 to add to the £35 already collected in the parish for alterations to the building, Gwyther approached the Education Department in London for financial assistance, pleading that 'without such a grant ... efforts must stop ... but should you not consent to this, such is the kind interest His Grace the Duke of Devonshire has taken in the matter, I am persuaded he will not let us stand still for a few pounds.' Perhaps His Grace was approached, and perhaps he produced the shortfall. Whatever occurred the mention of his name may have been a shrewd move on Gwyther's part, for

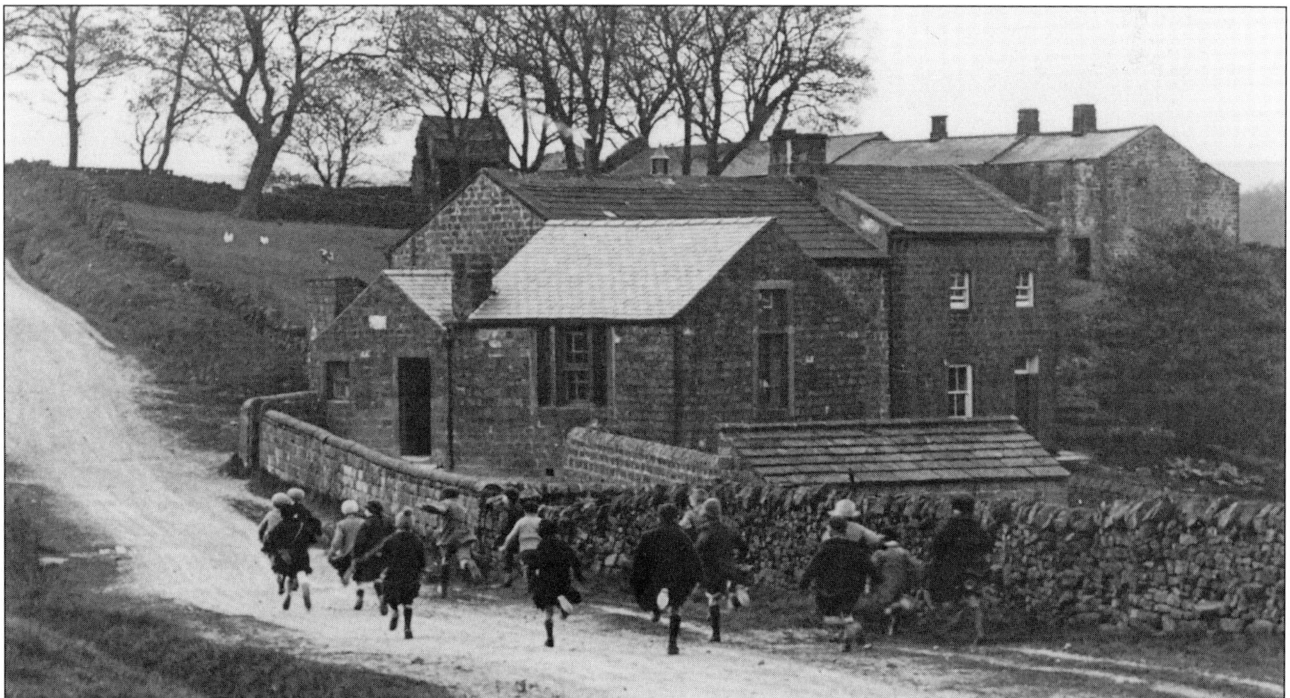

Rocking School, 1930s.

thereafter the school appears to have prospered, the vicar and churchwardens of Fewston administering it for the 'Education of children of the Parish in reading, writing and arithmetic, and the teaching of the Lord's Prayer, Ten Commandments and the Church catechism.'

From 1870 a copy of the Education Act passed in that year had to be displayed in every National School, a timetable drawn up, a portfolio for official papers obtained, new desks provided, and new offices built. A register also had to be kept. In 1876 there were said to be fifty children on the Rocking School roll, twenty six boys and twenty four girls between the ages of six and thirteen, a figure which may however be inaccurate because three years later the master at the school was threatened with the suspension of his certificate for falsifying registration, and the grant to the school was therefore cut by a tenth. The school catchment area included children from Blubberhouses up to the head of the valley. Heavily represented was the Peel family, two brothers having twenty nine children between them.

Over the years teachers also included Mr Fewster and Walter Gledhill, both of whom left to teach in Nidderdale, George Smith, Miss Southwell of Knaresborough, and Mrs Horner. The infants were taught by Mrs Rose Peel and Miss Ida Foster. The last head teacher was Miss Edith Bentley who despite being due to retire in January 1949, stayed on until the school closed for the holiday in July for the benefit of her pupils. The school closed only once – in the 'great snow' of 1933. After its permanent closure in 1949 the children attended school at Fewston.

WEST END WESLEYAN METHODIST CHAPEL

By 1790 the Washburn valley had become part of the Otley Methodist Circuit which included societies in the upper valley. From at least 1823 services were held in the farmhouse of Peter and Ellen Nelson at Clogger Lane end, but in 1829 a Primitive Methodist chapel capable of holding 120 was built at Low Mill. So large was the population at this time that within nine years a gallery had to be added.

In 1837 the Wesleyan Methodists built their chapel near the top of Clogger Lane on land purchased for £18.15s. the previous year from John Hill of Thruscross. The cost of building was £220, but despite much of the work being carried out by volunteers, it opened with a debt of £100. Here too the chapel soon proved to be too small, many people having to listen outside.

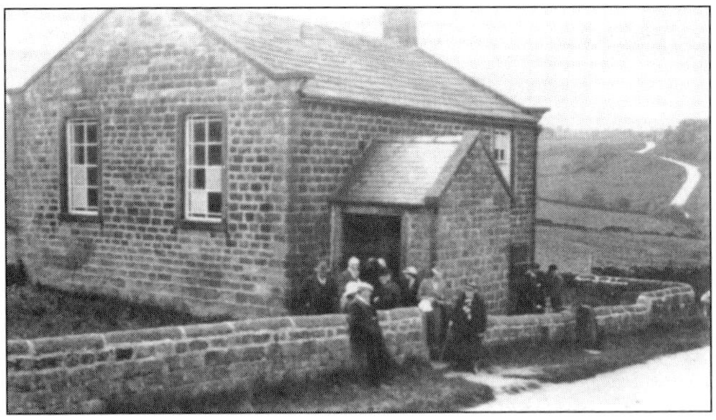

West End Wesleyan Methodist chapel.

There was also a well attended Sunday School and on the first Sunday following the 10 July, Feast Sunday, the chapel became so full that many of those taking part in the service had to remain outside. One pupil, John Verity, who received his first prize in 1871, eventually became the Sunday School superintendent, society steward and trust secretary, as well as the lead singer with 'a truly stentorian approach'. His wife, also a Sunday School scholar, eventually served as the 'poor' steward. In 1874 Charles Gill was presented with a tea service and an inscribed teapot by members of the congregation for his valuable services at the harmonium.

Most if not all of the Methodist chapels were served by itinerant preachers, one of whom, John Metcalfe of Wilsden, first preached at West End in the 1870s when only seventeen. No doubt he was relieved not to be on duty when, in the middle of a sermon on the subject of 'things which cannot be shaken', the gallery, erected in 1838, suddenly collapsed. With great presence of mind the preacher on that occasion, the Rev. Dr George Findlay, a tutor at Headingley Wesleyan College, called for calm before pronouncing the benediction. Unsurprisingly, in their haste to escape 'many people failed to observe the offertory rites'. In 1937 centenary celebrations at the chapel included the reminiscenses of Thomas Marshall, a local preacher for forty-three years, who recalled how in the early days he rode over to the valley from Greenhow above Nidderdale on a donkey which once became stuck on the then narrow Hoodstorth Bridge.

The churches and chapels held many social occasions attended by families, relations and friends who arrived in a flotilla of carts and carriages. Popular events included a tea party with a maypole, sports, whist drives, a 'sit down supper' in Rocking School, a dance every June, and an annual trip to the seaside, initially by train from Darley, later by bus. There were also many parties where, although there was never any conventional alcohol at least for the chapel-goers, the home-made dandelion, rhubarb, cowslip and elderberry wines were perhaps equally effective.

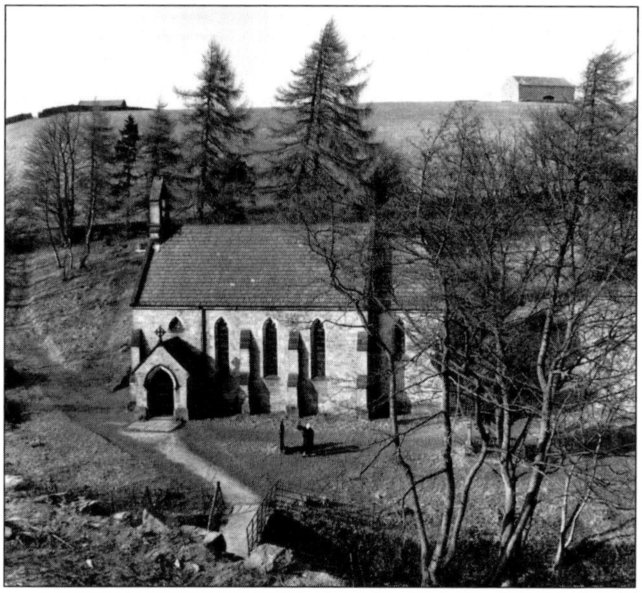

Holy Trinity church, Thruscross.

LOW GREEN

The date of the earliest church in the upper valley is unknown. There was certainly a church there as early as 1669 when the minister of 'West End Chapel of Ease at Thruscross', John Umpleby, was buried in the churchyard. The church is later said to have been dependent on the parish church at Fewston which 'supplied a preaching minister who at Thruscross hath no maintenance but a voluntary contribution'.

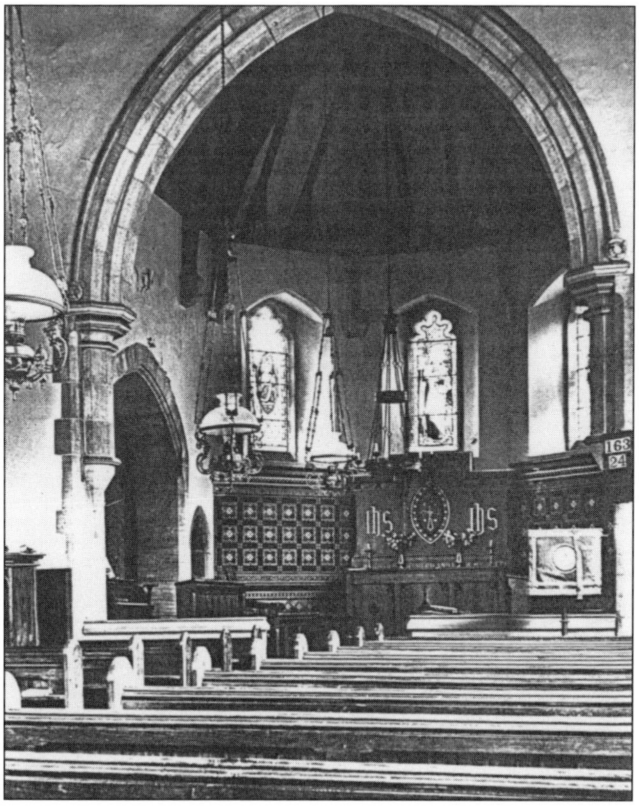

Holy Trinity – interior.

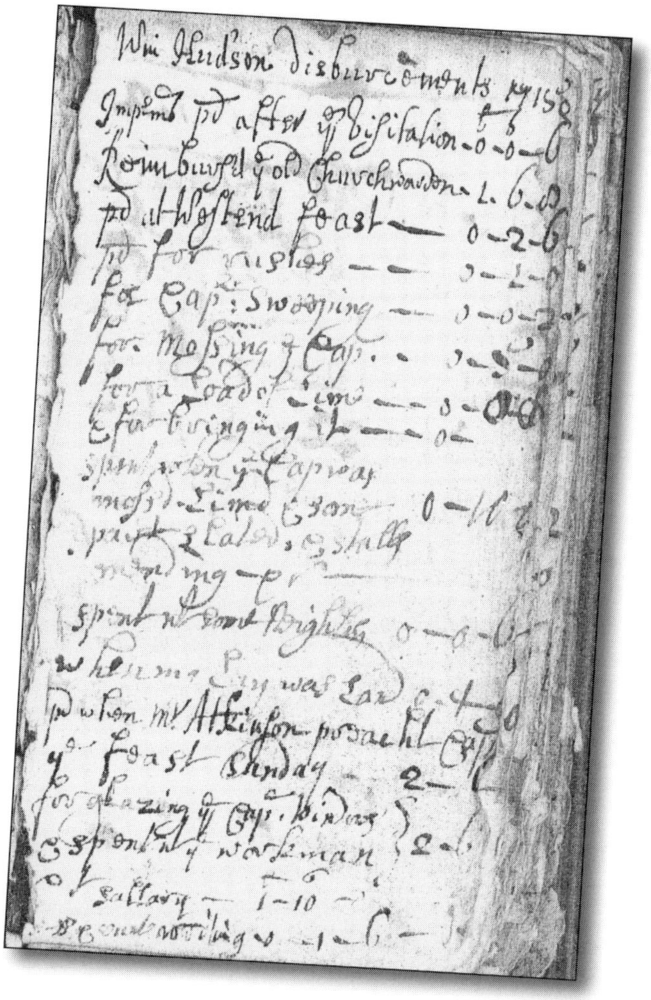

Holy Trinity church – churchwarden's account book 1715.

However, by 1764 the vicar of Fewston, John Whinneray, reported that he served the church every second Sunday in the afternoon, and twice a year held a Communion service for a sum of £5 which was paid by the inhabitants of West End.

By 1831 the church was found to be inadequate for the size of the larger community and in 1841, by which time it was dilapidated, it was rebuilt. In 1875 it was further enlarged with the addition of a chancel and restored, the cost of £1400 being raised by private subscription. Several people gave generously to the fund including the Duke of Devonshire who gave £300 and members of the Hannam family who also contributed towards the provision of an east window illustrating 'the Good Shepherd', but the bulk of the subscriptions consisted of the shillings of many of the parishioners, no doubt encouraged by their vicar, Mr. Ashley of Fewston who then had oversight of the church. 'An earnest and hard-working clergyman' he supplied 'the ministerial duties without payment', was 'much beloved', his 'services well attended, the number of communicants ... increased' and the 'parishioners and schools regularly visited'. Now instead of 'plodding 4 to 6 miles ... o'er moor and fell, o'er crag and torrent ... the inhabitants have them' [his services] 'close at hand'.

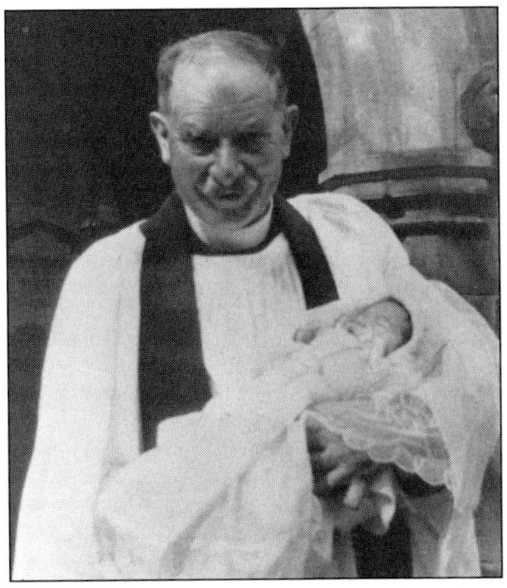

Rev. George Hugh Elliott – baptism of Jean Liddle 1925.

Unfortunately, after further work on the churchyard and bridge, the church found itself overspent to the tune of £350 on lawyers fees and extras, and a further appeal from the pulpit had to be launched. 'Surely such a work must not be suspended, much less cease. But of this there is some danger unless a parsonage be built, and sufficient stipend be raised to make Thruscross a separate parish. To do this and clear off the debt, we should have £2000, a large sum, but the work is urgent and friends sympathize. Can you help us?' The plea was apparently met.

At the Harvest Festival in 1909 the Rev. George Hugh Elliott, Vicar of Thruscross, preached before 'a good congregation' in a church 'prettily decorated' with flowers and fruit sent by Mrs Galloway of Skaife Hall who 'also sent her usual liberal hamper'. On the Monday following, there were sports and a tea in the barn at Redshaw Hall, a custom still maintained in 1941, when the children performed a play entitled 'God's Garden', before a service in the church. Holy Trinity continued until its last service in 1965 after which it was partially demolished and the area flooded. The bodies interred in the surrounding graveyard were transferred to a new plot on higher ground although sadly some of the new graves were not marked.

The water authority – then Leeds Corporation – decided it was unsafe for the church to remain standing in the reservoir. The water level was therefore lowered to allow for demolition in 1966.

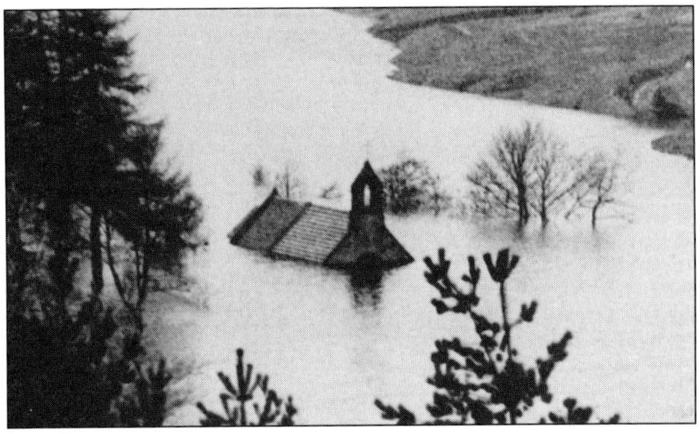

Holy Trinity flooded.

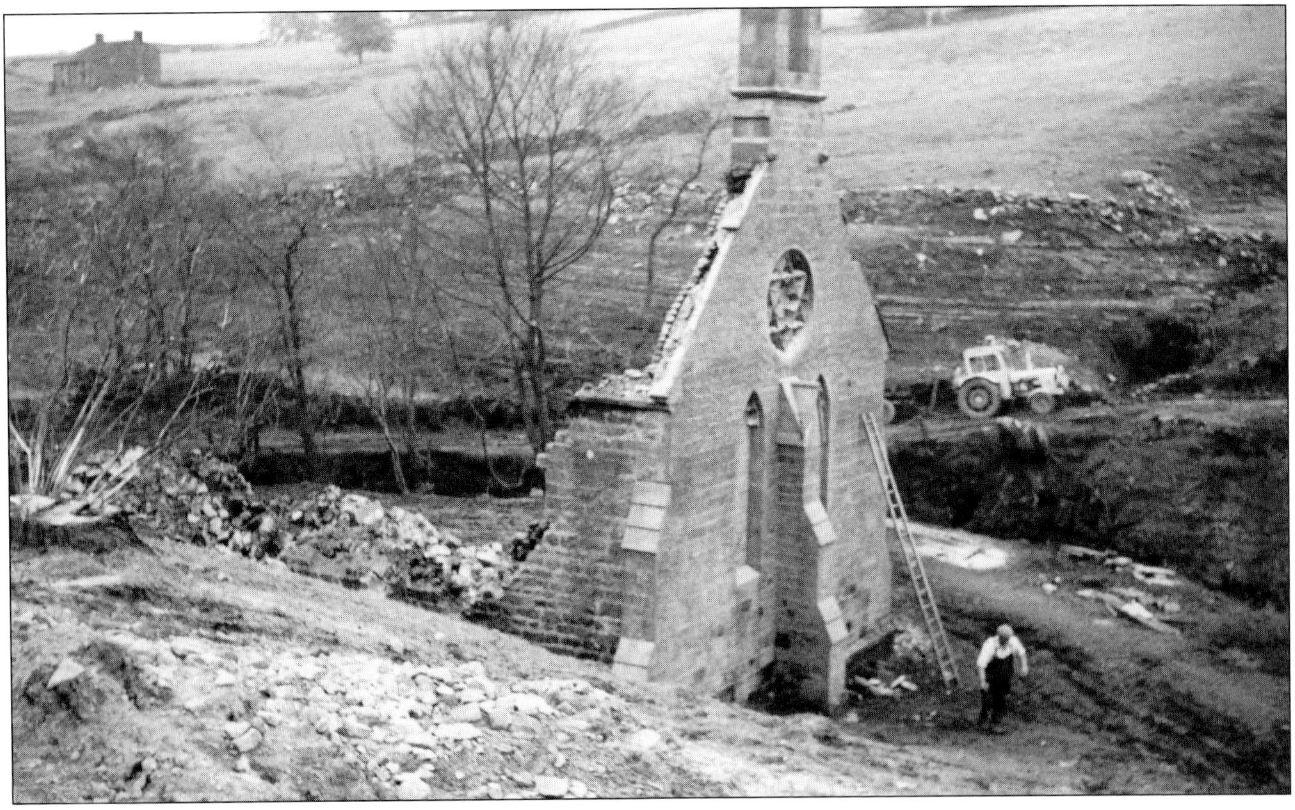

Demolition of Holy Trinity.

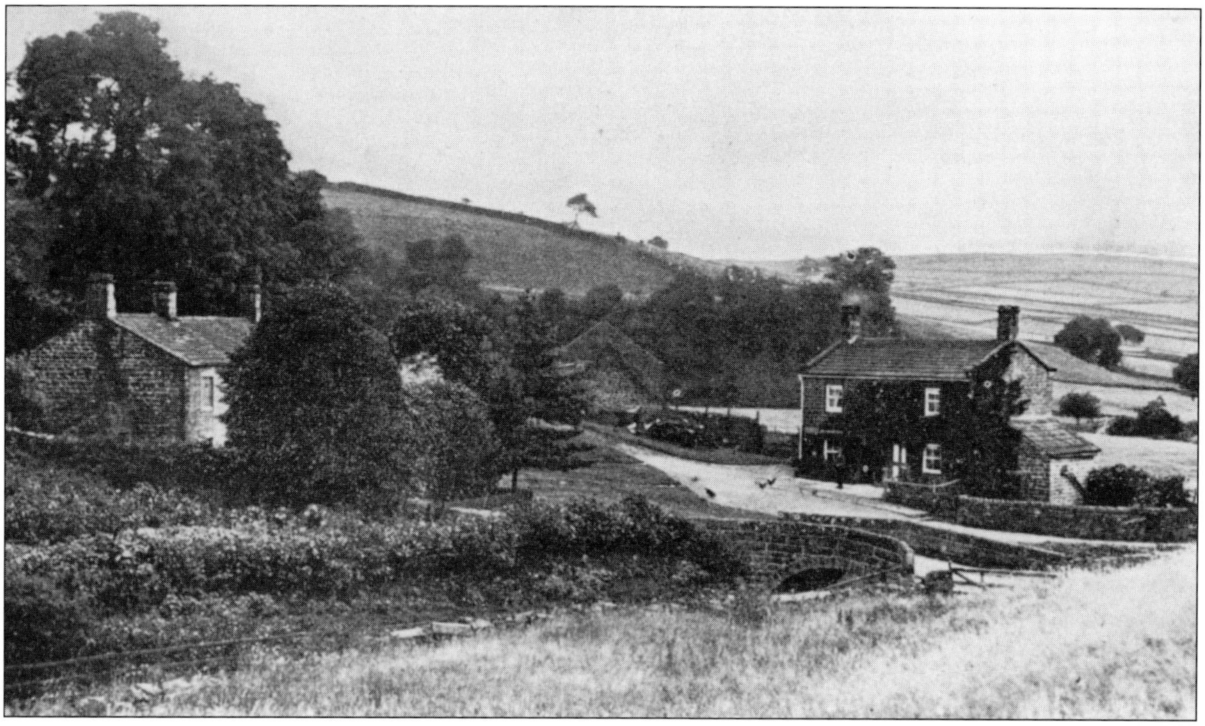

Low Green Post Office and cottages. This was also the site of the Butcher's Arms run by Molly Horsman, who provided lunches for shooting parties, and some empty cottages in one of which, known as the Postman's Rest, Bob Worthington, the valley postman from Dacre Banks, ate his midday meal. Initially his round of the valley was on foot, a toot on his bugle at Moorhouse Hill announcing his imminent arrival although in 1901 on the occasion of the death of Queen Victoria, he simply shouted loudly 'she's gone.' After getting a bike, from which he often fell, he took care to carry a bottle of unspecified liquid which he reckoned cured 'inside bruises'. In 1901 the post office was kept by John and Annie Jeffrey. John was also a clogger and shoe repairer. Later it became the home of Will Waite and his wife.

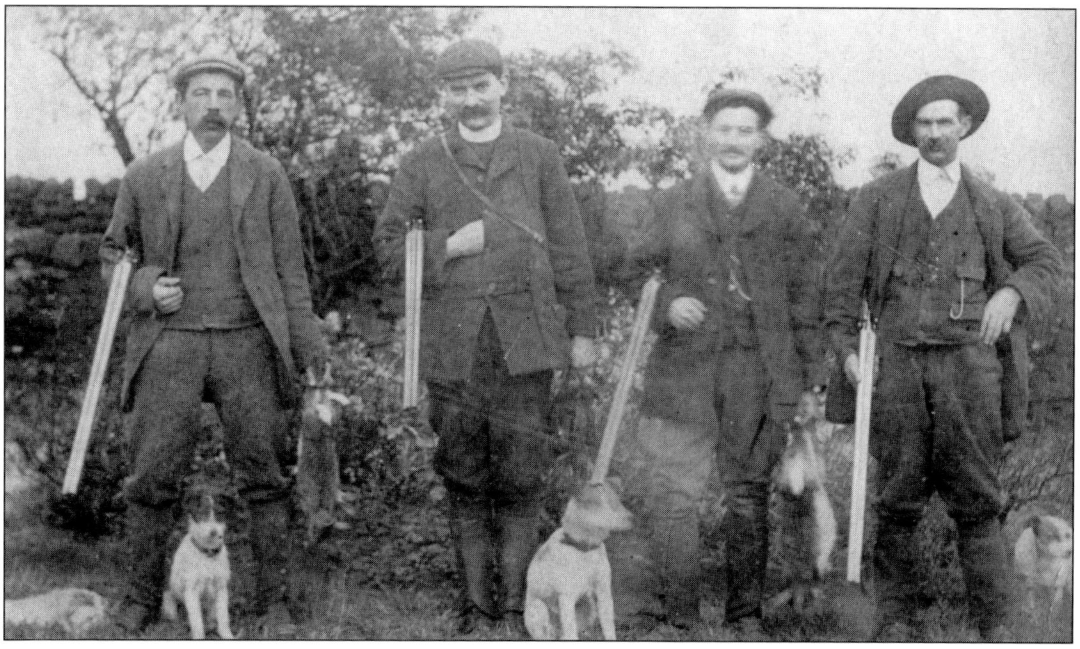

Rabbit Shoot with the Rev. George Elliott.

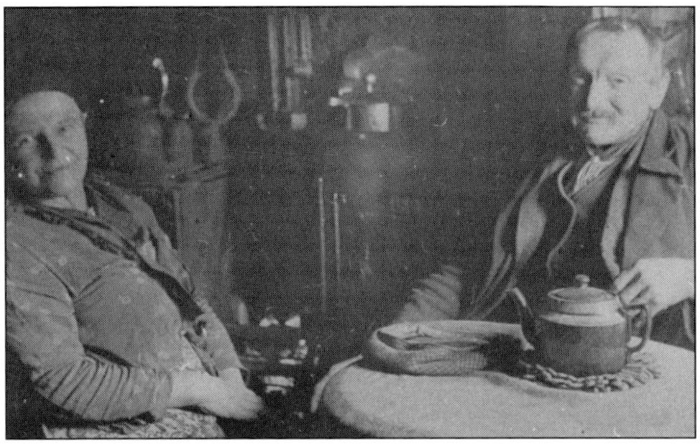

Mr and Mrs Will Waite. Will, a stone mason who also acted as verger and cleaner, tramped many miles to follow his trade while Mrs Waite looked after the shop where she sold only stamps. She was known not only for her wooden leg, acquired as a result of a childhood accident, but also for her vast collection of every kind of clock, 'Grandfathers, Grandmothers ... carriage, bracket, cuckoo, alarm ... ticking away and chiming the hour', and a polyphone which was popular with the local children. She was also famous for her ability to handle birds, a robin becoming her 'daily companion ... ' while 'linnets and goldfinches perched on her person ... [and] within the house lived a friendly owl'. Mrs Waite died in 1953 aged sixty-nine.

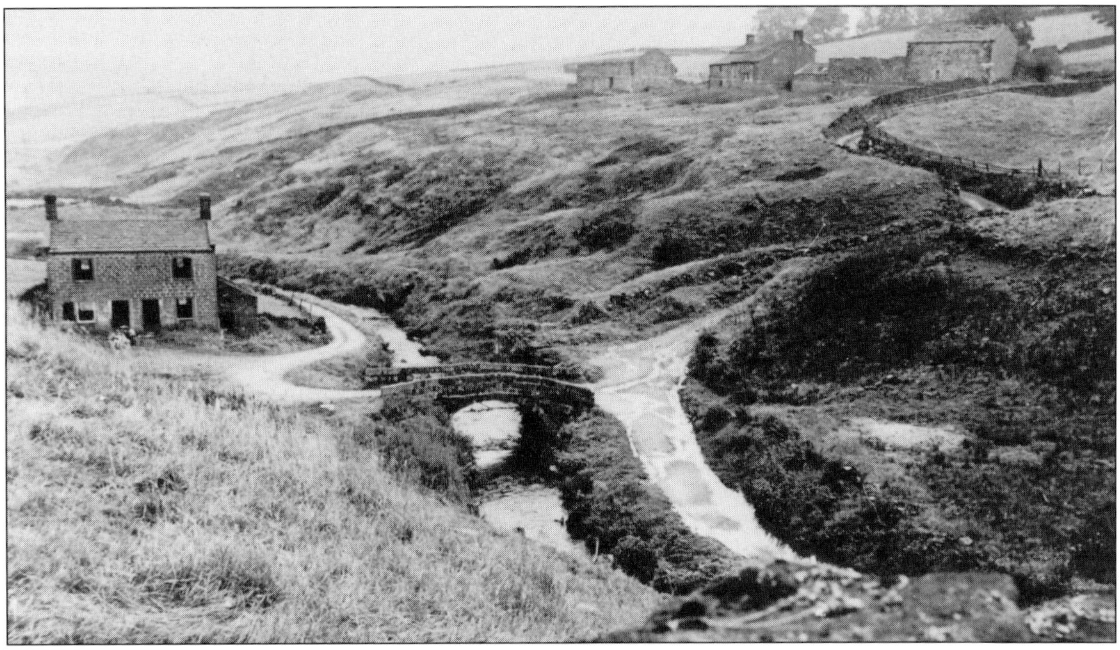

Low Green Bridge, Post Office, Gibb House Farm and Corkscrew Lane. In the Second World War both the church and post office were used by troops for target practice.

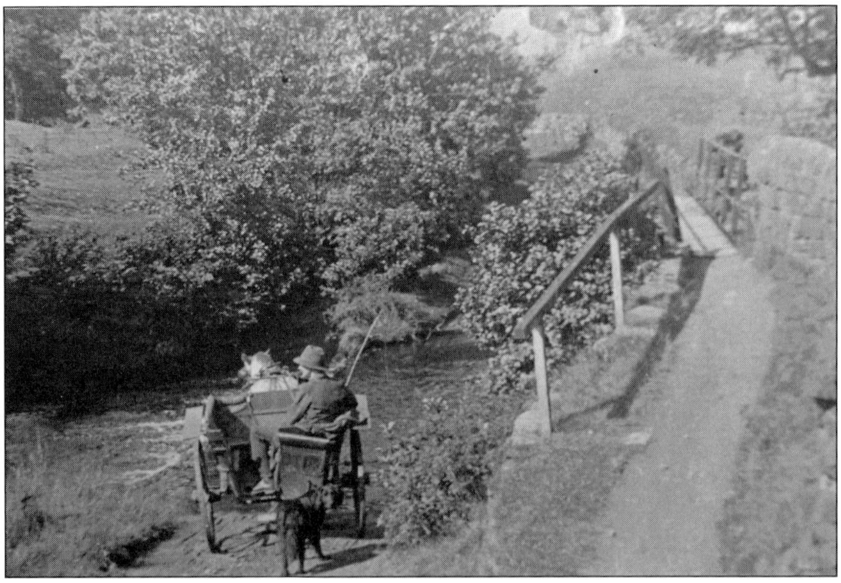

Beckfoot Bridge. This part of the valley, known as 'the meeting of the waters,' was at the confluence of the Washburn and the Capelshaw Beck. Prior to the creation of the reservoirs, the Washburn often ran high and fast and consequently the many valley bridges required frequent attention. In 1825 following a flood at Beck Foot, twelve shillings and sixpence was spent carting away the broken bridge and supplying new wood, bolts and nails.

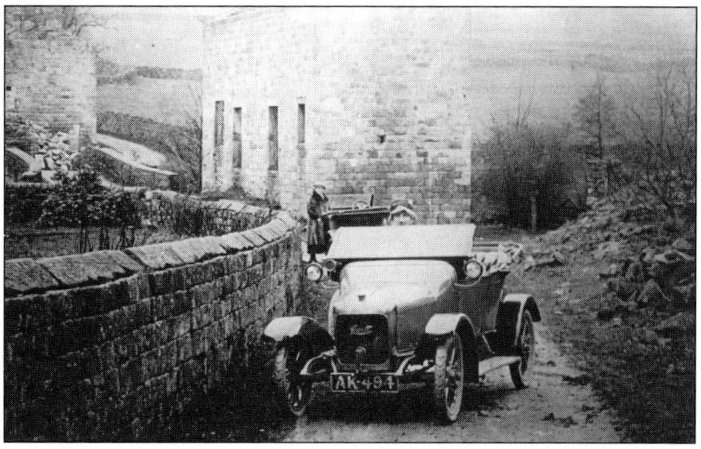

The car stands on an area known as 'The Strand'. Low Mill Bridge is to the rear.

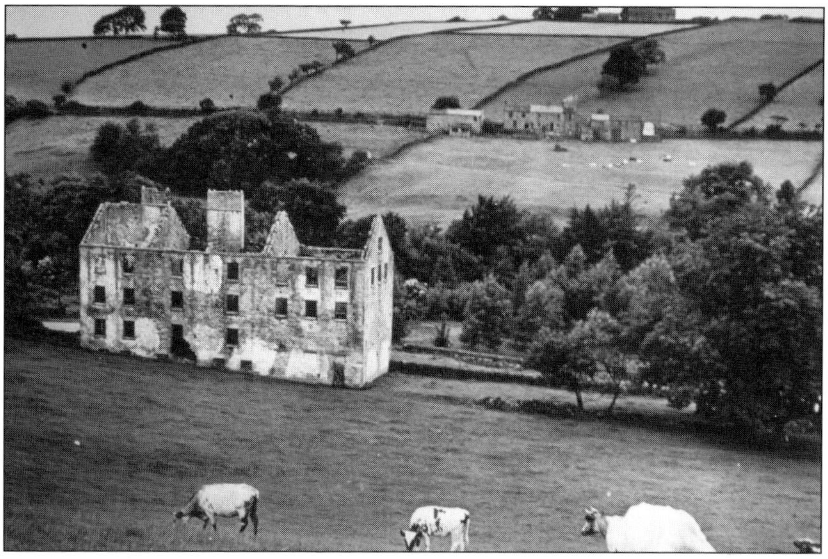

Low Mill Warehouse and Murgatroyd's Farm.

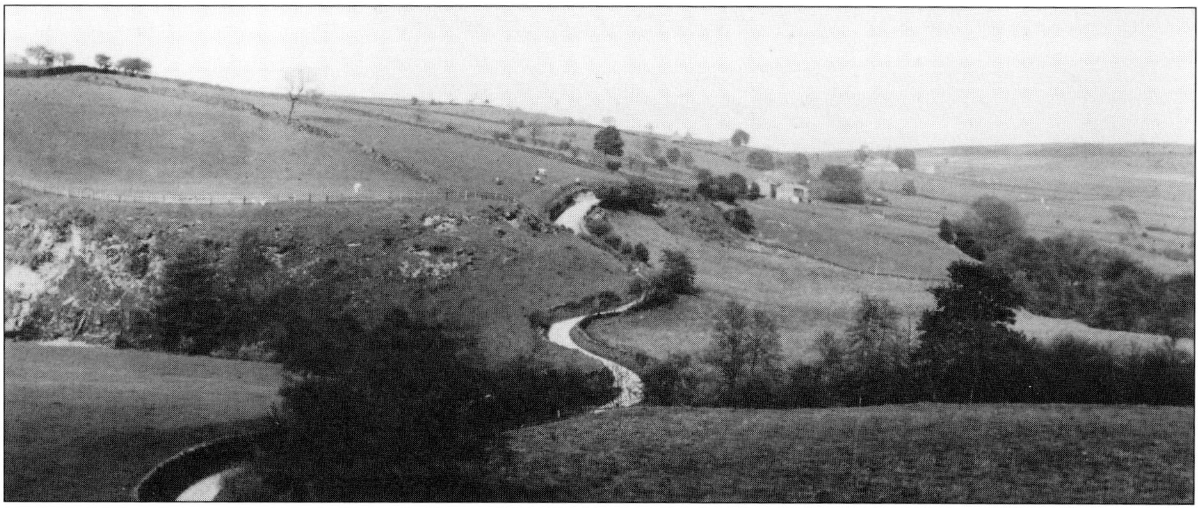

Scot Lane between Low Green and Thruscross. Beyond the bridge was Scot Lane, probably an old drove road along which thousands of sheep and cattle would have been driven from the Upper Dales as well as Scotland annually in earlier centuries, and in that way acquired its name. In 1648 'a Scotish man, John Priestley' was buried at Fewston, and a map of 1853 also shows the site of a 'Scot's grave' alongside the lane. The presence of a nearby shop and also an inn would have proved an attraction to the drovers. At Scot Lane House, Robert Wigglesworth ran a shop for thirty years and later Harold Murgatroyd and his wife Elsie ran a shop for thirty years. The bank on the left was known as the 'Laddie Pits' where poor quality coal could be obtained.

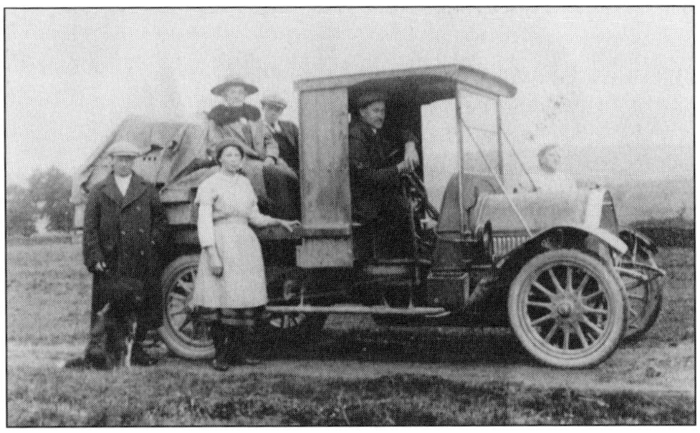

Robert Wigglesworth – Thruscross carrier –1915.

In the early twentieth century only two people in the upper valley, the vicar and the land agent, owned cars. The only other means of transport was on horseback or via a carrier such as Robert, or Harold Murgatroyd who started a transport business with a bus locally known as 'the flying hen coop' in which he transported livestock such as calves in sacks at the same time as the passengers.

At the end of Scot Lane stood the Gate Inn. Built in 1699 by the Hardisty family, the pub had an inscribed lintel bearing the date and the initials 'JH' for John Hardisty. In 1822 Ninian Proctor was the licensee but in 1877 John Peel took over and remained for forty five years. 'A quiet man of rare anecdote and good humour' with 'never a black mark' he was also tough and hardy,

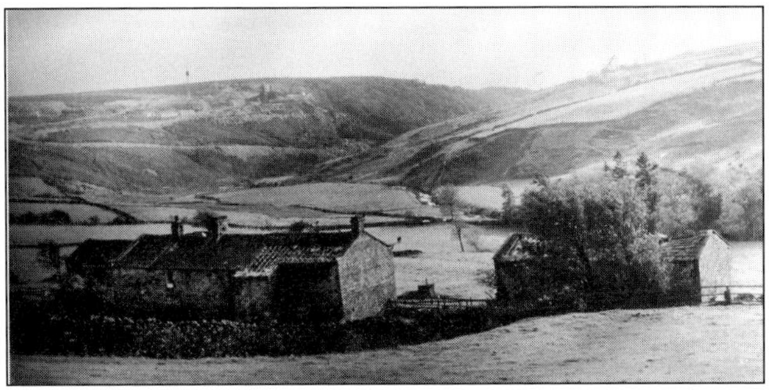

Rear view of Scot Lane buildings.

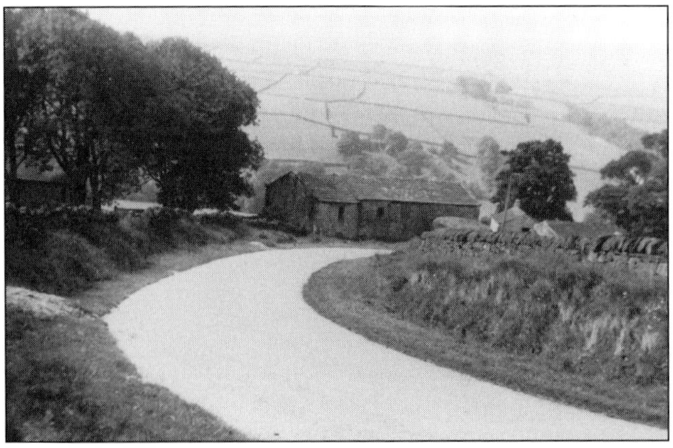

Gate Inn and smithy.

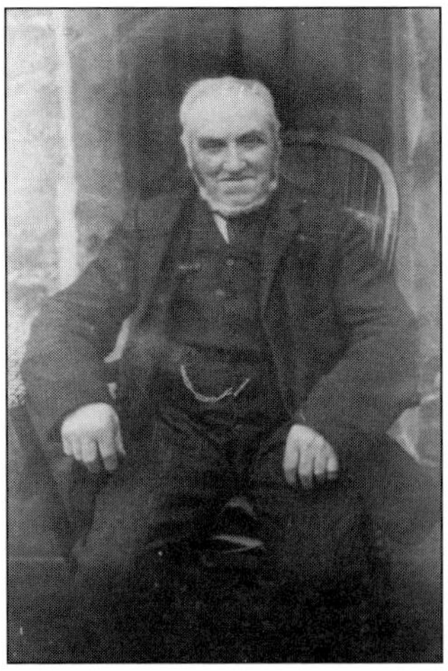

John Peel (c.1836-1923).

rough weather making little impression on his constitution. Returning soaking wet from the fields, he sat before the fire to dry off and if the clothes remained wet the next day, put them back on boasting he had 'never been badly in his life'. He died while feeding his cattle in 1923 aged eighty-seven. His daughter, Sarah (Sally) Ann took over the inn until her own death in 1942 aged eighty-six.

In the 1950s the Simpson family took over, despite having had no previous experience of inn keeping, and Mrs. Simpson became known for providing a 'grand lunch'.

GATE INN SIGN

The inn had no bar and seats were placed around the edge of the room. Beer was brought up from the cellar. The West End Women's Institute met in a separate room. The well-known sign was made in 1876 by David Petty of Fewston, the cost born by labourers working on the construction of Fewston Reservoir. It bore the words 'This gate hangs well and hinders not, refresh and pay and travel on.'

THE SMITHY

Next door to the Gate Inn was East Gate House and the smithy owned by Christopher, or Kit, Horsman who with his wife Martha (Heaton) had six sons and two daughters. The youngest son, Sydney, born in 1894 at Low Mill cottages lived in the valley all his life except for three years during the First World War, carrying on the forge until there was insufficient work.

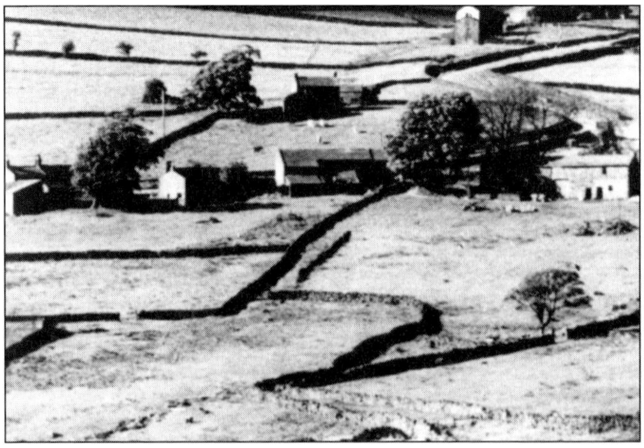

East Gate House, Gate Inn, smithy and shop.

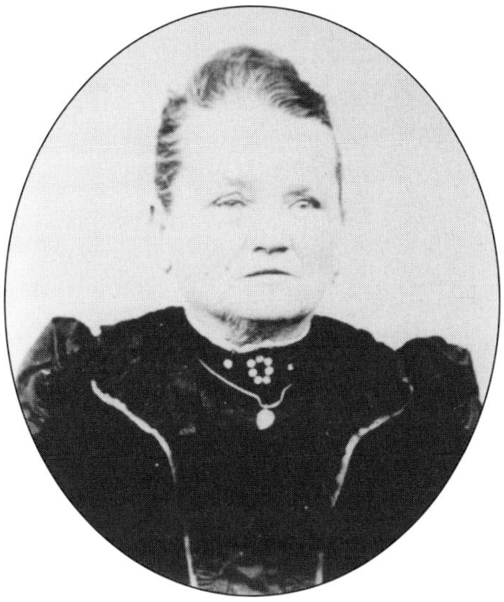

Sarah Peel (c.1857-1942). Daughter of John.

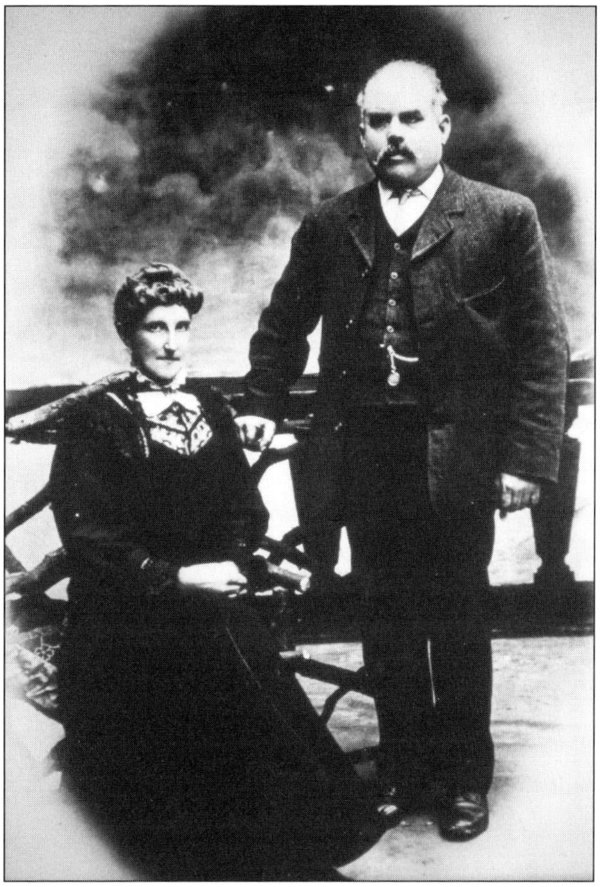

Kit and Martha Horsman.

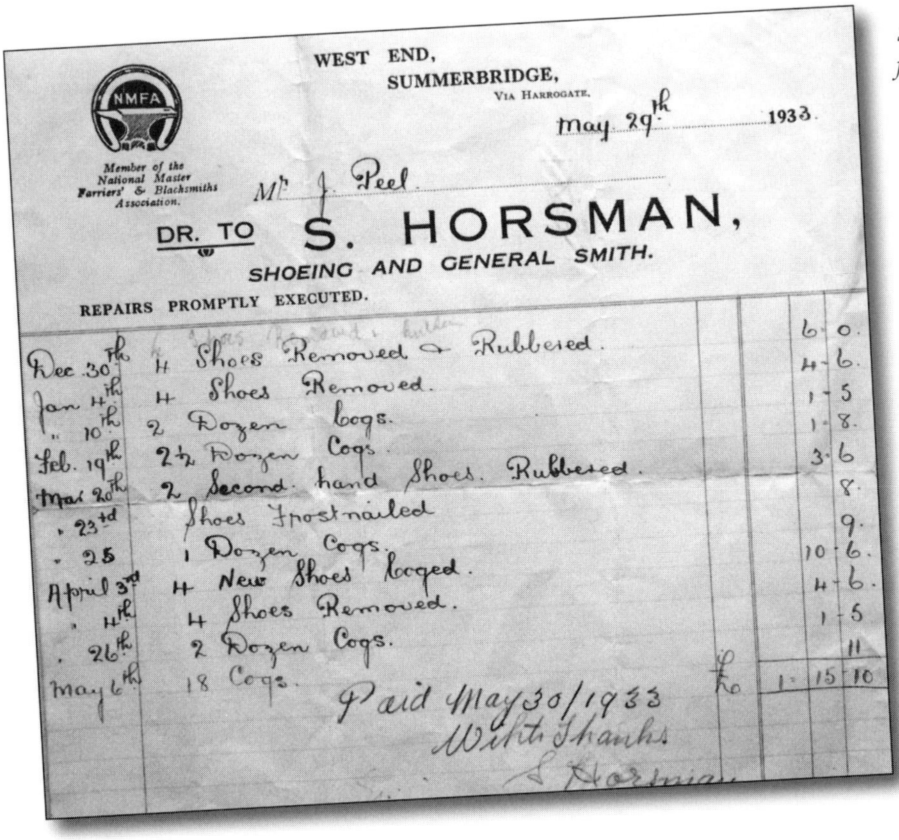

WEST END,
SUMMERBRIDGE,
VIA HARROGATE.

May 29th 1933.

NMFA

Member of the National Master Farriers' & Blacksmiths Association.

Mr J. Peel

DR. TO S. HORSMAN,
SHOEING AND GENERAL SMITH.
REPAIRS PROMPTLY EXECUTED.

			6. 0.
Dec 30th	4 Shoes Removed & Rubbered.		4-6.
Jan 4th	4 Shoes Removed.		1-5
" 10th	2 Dozen Cogs.		1-8.
Feb. 19th	2½ Dozen Cogs.		3-6
Mar 20th	2 Second hand Shoes. Rubbered.		8.
" 23rd	Shoes Frostnailed		9.
" 25	1 Dozen Cogs.		10-6.
April 3rd	4 New Shoes Coged.		4-6.
" 4th	4 Shoes Removed.		1-5
" 26th	2 Dozen Cogs.		11
May 6th	18 Cogs.	£	1-15-10

Paid May 30/1933
With Thanks
S Horsman

Sidney Horsman's bill for shoeing.

THRUSCROSS GREEN

North west of the Gate Inn a small and isolated cluster of houses forms the area known as Thruscross Green. Here Peter Nelson (1823-1900) lived at a farm formerly known as Pete's Yard.

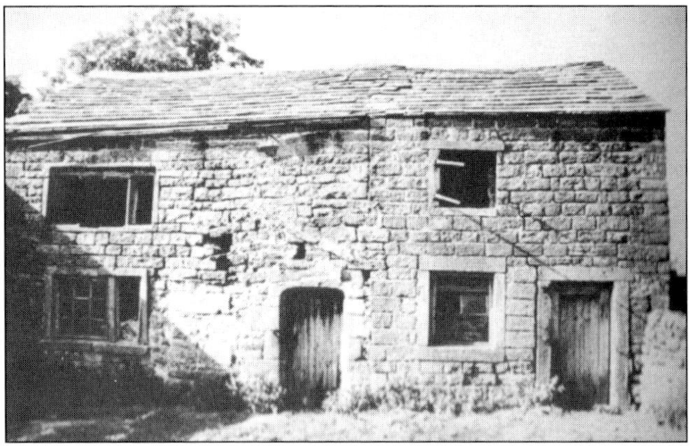

Pete's Yard.

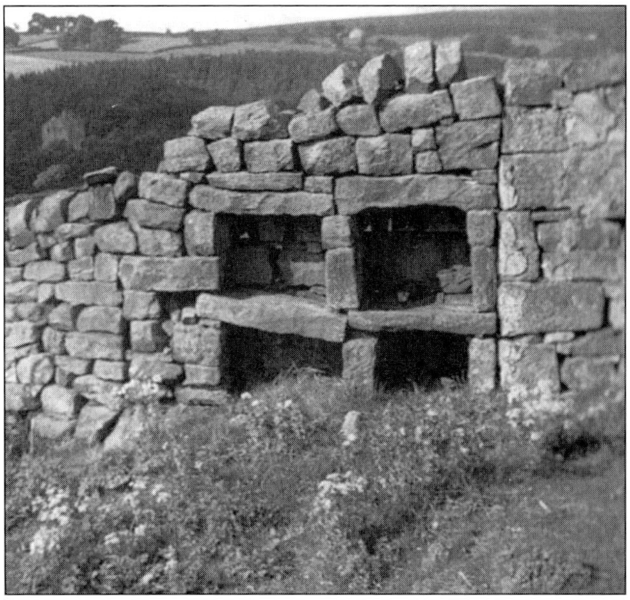

Bee boles, Thruscross. The boles would have contained a wicker 'skep' or round basket in which to house the bees. Several families in the area are known to have kept bees, among them Thomas Richardson of Thruscross whose inventory of 1692 shows that he left 'a parcel of hives of bees'.

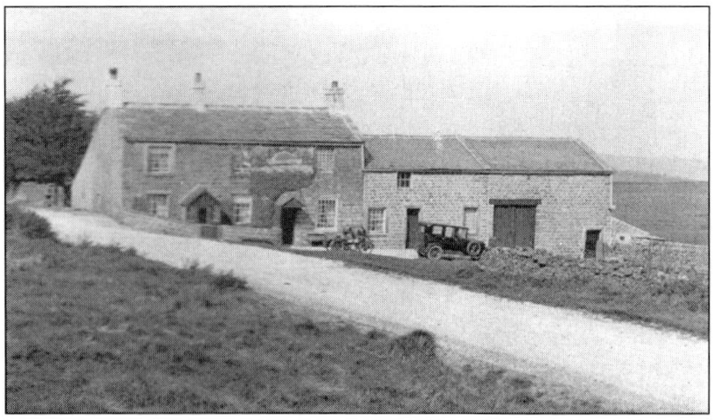

Stone House Inn.

His father, also Peter, had previously farmed at Clogger Lane on the opposite side of the valley. In about 1854 while digging peat on Pock Stones Moor, Peter discovered the murdered body of a cattle dealer, Stephen Carnil or Carlisle, who some years previously had disappeared from Woodhouse near Bolton Abbey with £500 in his pocket.

STONE HOUSE INN

Originally a farmhouse owned by William Abbott the Stone House Inn has had several landlords, among them John Emsley who also kept a shop and served as a blacksmith. The best known landlord, Jesse Peel, senior, and brother of John, was born at the inn in 1839. Initially apprenticed to his father, a wheelwright, he later worked from 4 am to 9 pm at Westhouse Mill where he was paid £20 a year. When the mill closed he left to seek employment elsewhere but returned in 1869 to take possession of the inn and to install a brewing plant. He remained at the inn for fifty-four years. In 1870 he married Sarah Elizabeth Proctor and raised a large family. Only once did he travel out of the valley – to Leeds, where his horse refused to pull its cart, obliging Jesse to unyoke in the middle of Briggate.

For several years during the late nineteenth and early twentieth centuries, Robert Spencer of Littondale, who every year drove a thousand sheep from Wharfedale to the East Riding, made the Stone House an overnight stop.

Jesse had considerable musical talent with an ability to play several instruments including the violin, and for many years he was leader of the Fewston Brass Band consisting mainly of members of the Peel family, which met twice weekly in a building later converted into the Fewston Reading Room. This may have been the small two-storey building the remains of which are now in a private garden at the foot of Hardisty Hill. On fine days the band practised outside to the annoyance of one farmer who complained bitterly that they were putting his cows 'off milk'.

Among their regular musical engagements was the annual Timble Club Walk, sabotaged one year when some members of the committee engaged another band, so that for the first and only time in the history of the Walk, there were two competing bands. In 1859, after the Fewston Band disbanded, Jesse joined the Birstwith Band, on one occasion travelling to York to play where to his horror he found a public execution taking place outside the Minster.

Like the church and the chapels the inns were the focus for much of the social life of the valley. Popular events included a tea party with a maypole, sports, whist drives, a 'sit down supper' and fortnightly

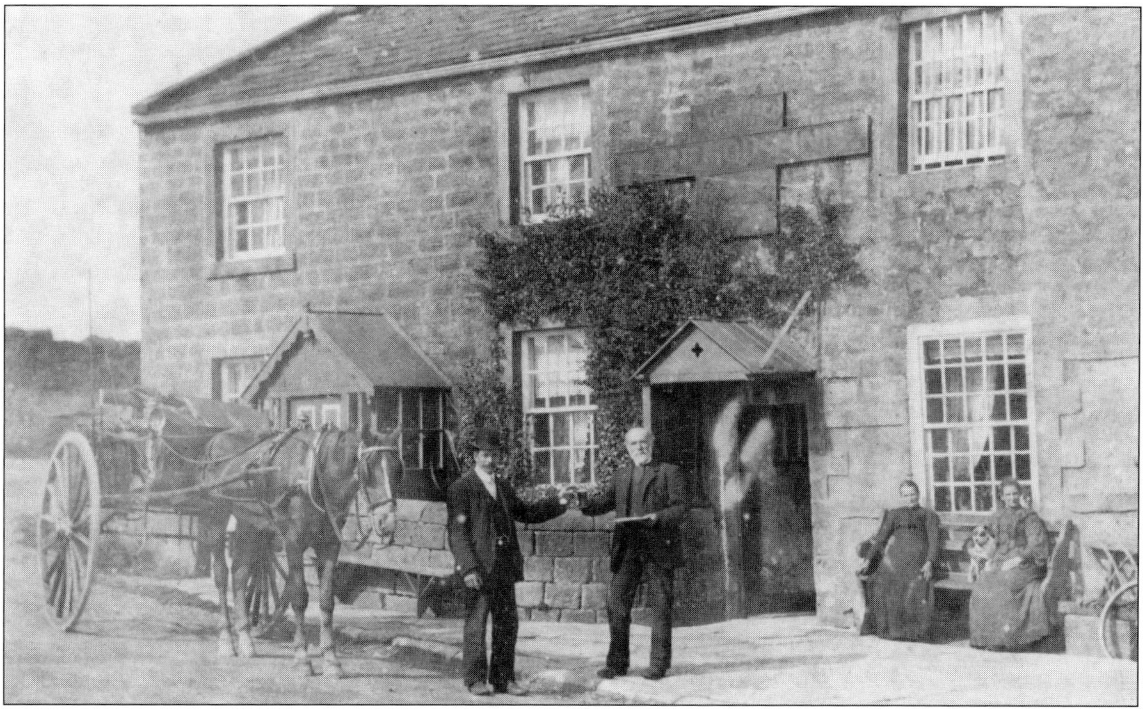

Jesse Peel serving a customer.

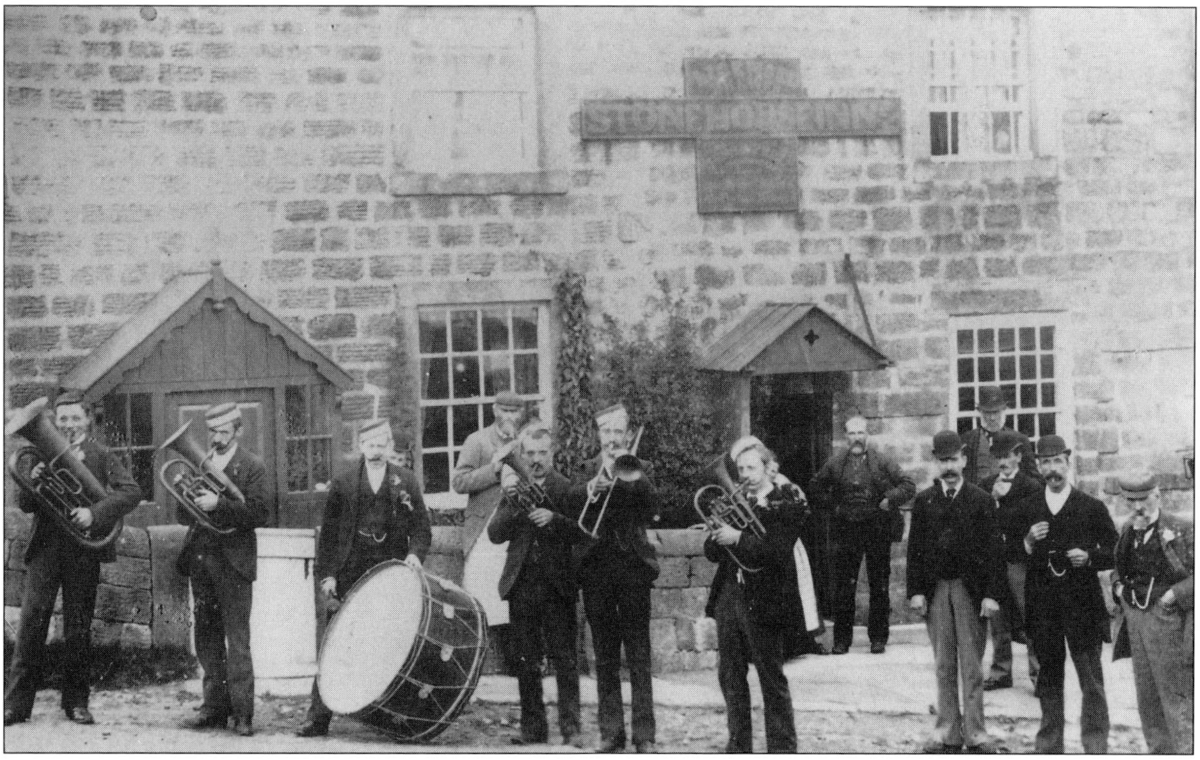

Stone House Band.

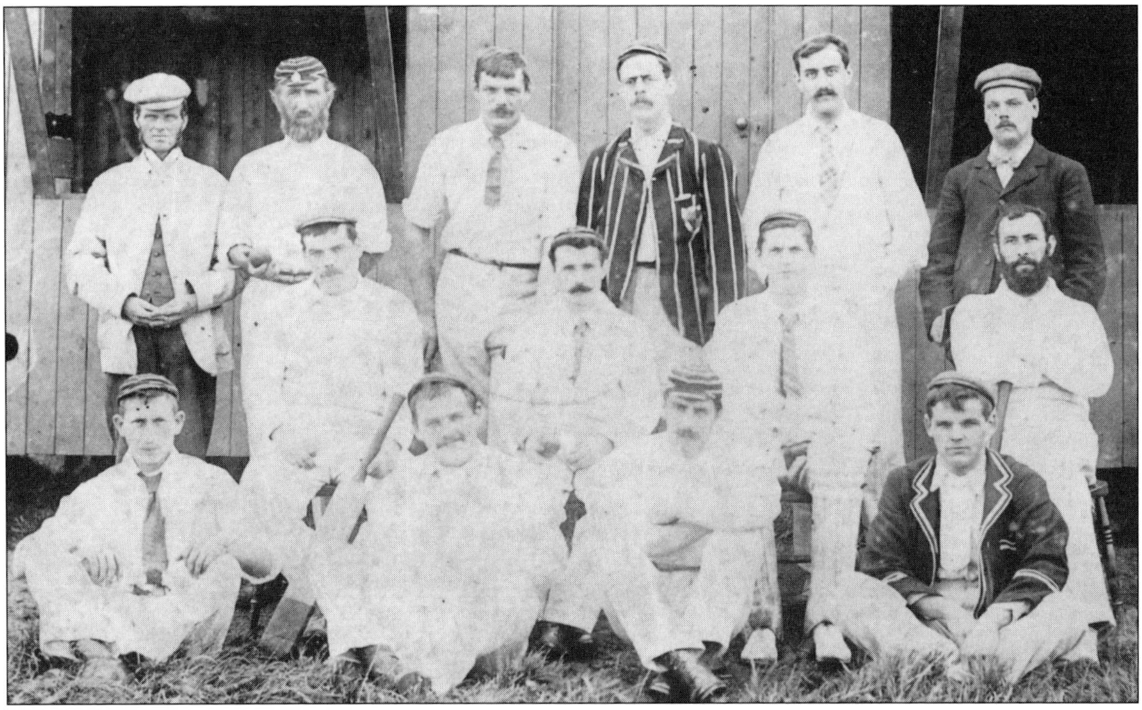

Thruscross cricket team.
'I really don't know how they played [the pitch] was as steep as could be.' Ethel Peel.

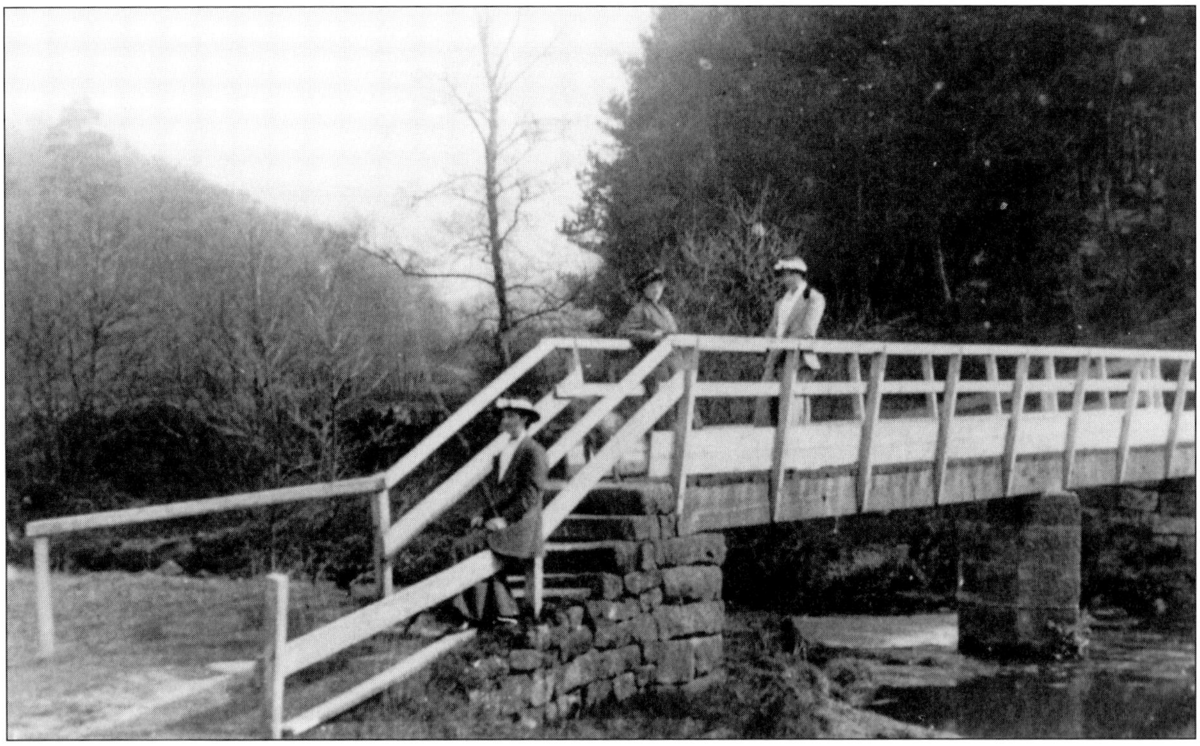

Mogington Bridge. The bridge spanned the river to the south east of the Gate Inn.

dances held at the Stone House which often continued into the early hours and were a particularly popular feature of valley life for which local musicians, especially fiddlers, were much in demand for the favourite 'Pop goes the weasel.'

Willie Hardy of Fewston, the lame schoolmaster and musician was often pressed into service, having to be carried to and from his home at Fewston on the back of some stalwart resident.

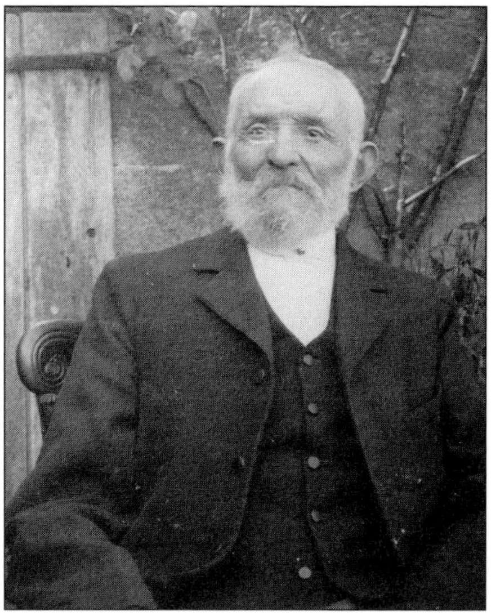

Willie Smith Laycock – Jubilee singer. Born at Silsden c.1842 Willie farmed at Dukes Hill, West End and was known as the Jubilee singer at Holy Trinity, Thruscross.

Among other activities at the Stone House were meetings of the Womens Institute, a free gift club, an East Monday walk, darts and dominoes, whist drives and bridge and, in the shooting season, a beaters' supper for which an extension was granted. In 1902 the Coronation Sports were held in a field near the inn. In summer there was also cricket, for which the sloping Thruscross Green provided an unlikely pitch. For away matches the team often travelled long distances by waggonette.

Opposite the Stone House Inn at the head of Street Lane was the rocky outcrop known for some unspecified reason as Maukin's Cross, or locally, as Bilberry Top. Further south and on the right of the lane are the houses known as Ratten Row. It has been suggested that 'Ratten' may derive from 'retting' or the softening of flax, an initial process in the preparation of yarn for spinning into linen. Equally however, its origins may derive from the tanning industry. An inventory of the goods of John Gill of Ratten Row in 1681 includes the entry 'barke for tanning with'.

From Thruscross, Breakes Fold Lane crossed the valley while Corkscrew Lane and Clogger Lane united at Low Green Bridge. Clogger Lane is said to have been named from the noise of the worker's clogs as they passed on their way to Patrick's mill. On one occasion a horse became so frightened by the noise made by the clogs that it caused a trap to overturn killing one of the occupants. Now all three lanes lead only to the reservoir's edge.

THE VALLEY AND ITS TEXTILE PAST

A woollen cloth industry has existed in the Yorkshire valleys from the thirteenth century. In the early sixteenth century, Robert Ward obtained a licence to

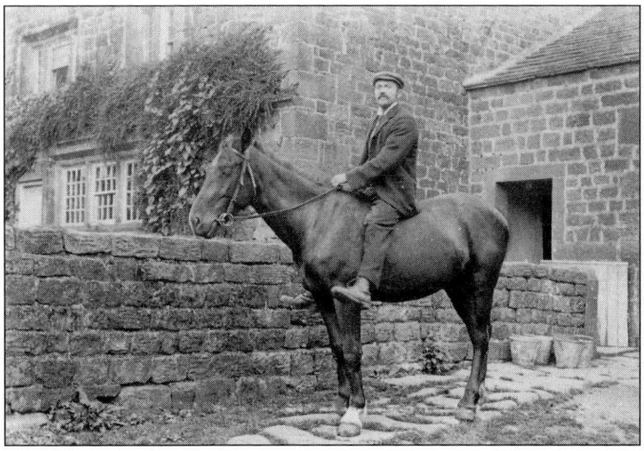

Joseph Everard Peel of Redshaw Hall, West End c.1872-c.1969 Many of the Peels had large families. Joseph and his wife, Annie , were the parents of ten children. When the seventh, Edith, was born in a heavy snow storm in November 1915, Joseph rode his horse to Dacre 5 miles away, to fetch the doctor.

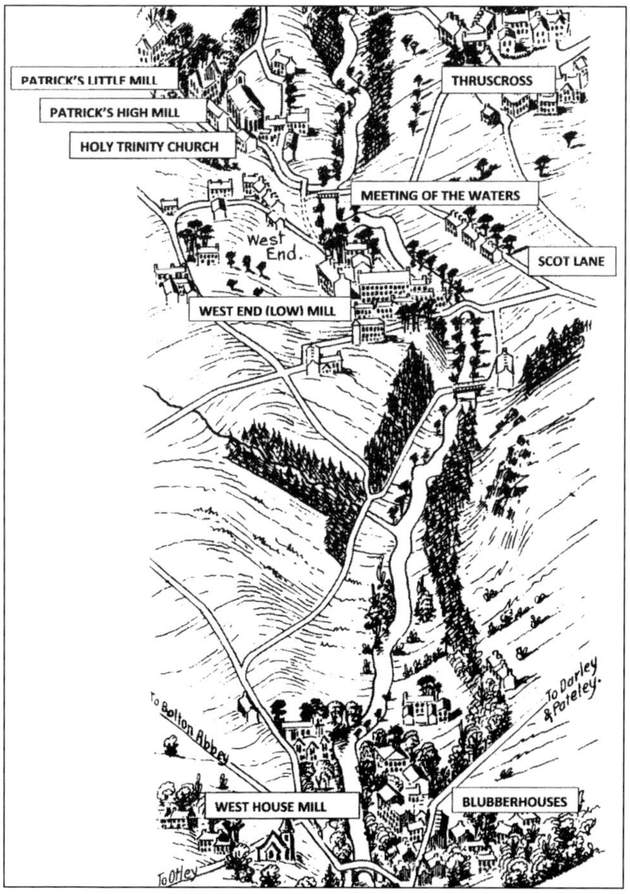

Pictorial map of valley and mills in Upper Valley.

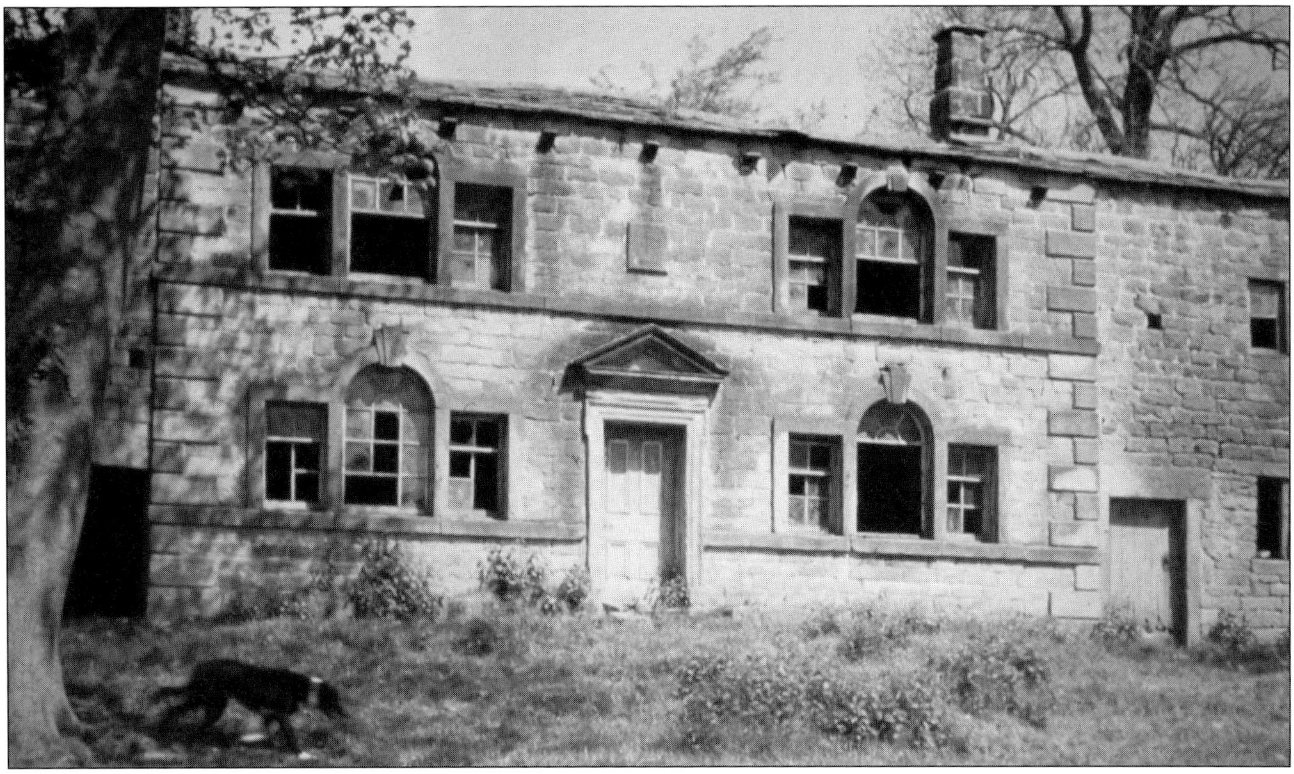

Duke's Hill House.

build a fulling mill on the Washburn, probably at Blubberhouses. Fulling allowed the warp and weft fibres to compact thereby producing a superior cloth. This mill changed hands twice, latterly to Hugh Frankland, a London clothier and son of William Frankland who had been granted the manor of Blubberhouses in 1562.

In the upper reaches of the valley many farmers practised a dual economy with a small-holding of land, a few cattle, some sheep and the home spinning of wool; at least one farm, Lane Head, had a spinning chamber. Some of these men became quite wealthy; when Richard Pullein of Hill House died in 1625 the value of his estate was £73.15s.0d. An inventory of his possessions included more than fifty sheep, cattle and horses, a loom, clothier's shears, tenters, a spinning wheel, several pounds of wool and blanket yarn, and four pieces of woollen cloth.

DUKE'S HILL HOUSE

Duke's Hill house was built c.1765 for Stephen Hudson who has been described as a "shopkeeper" and it has therefore been suggested that he may have been the owner of a weaving shop. However in the mid eighteenth century a man of this name also kept a general store in Blubberhouses where, in addition to groceries, he offered items of haberdashery such as ribbons, lawns, buckram, braid and whalebone. A leghorn hat was priced at 1/1d. and a pair of worsted hose at 2/4d. In 1715 'Maizey Swaine paid twelve shillings for a scarlet cloak'. The opulence of this house may therefore reflect the success of one or both of these enterprises. At some time the house was also said to have been the home of a member of the Walker family who owned some of the five mills which formerly lined the valley.

In the late eighteenth and early nineteenth centuries the textile industry moved away from a domestic economy to industrialisation, and a chain of five mills sprang up along the northern valley, initially for the spinning of cotton. The first, Low Mill at West End, an old corn mill, was bought in 1791 for £530 from Samuel Hardisty by a consortium consisting of John Walker, a silver plater (son of William Walker, a publisher), his father in law Joseph Hardcastle, a grocer, Richard Holdsworth, a maltster, and Robert Thomson, a joiner, all from Otley, together with William Maude, an ironmonger. Built alongside the old mill and equipped with a single large wheel, the precise diameter of which is the subject of some debate, Low Mill, which later changed to the spinning of flax due to a greater demand, was able to spin 250 bundles a week, its ninety workers housed in thirteen nearby cottages. With the longest continuous use of any mill in the valley it changed hands many times before being taken over by Thomas Gill in 1868 who ran it in conjunction with Dacre Banks mill for the spinning of hemp and jute, and the production of rope and twine

So successful was John Walker at Low Mill – in 1796 its value was estimated to be in the region of £4550 – that in 1800 he built a second mill initially known as

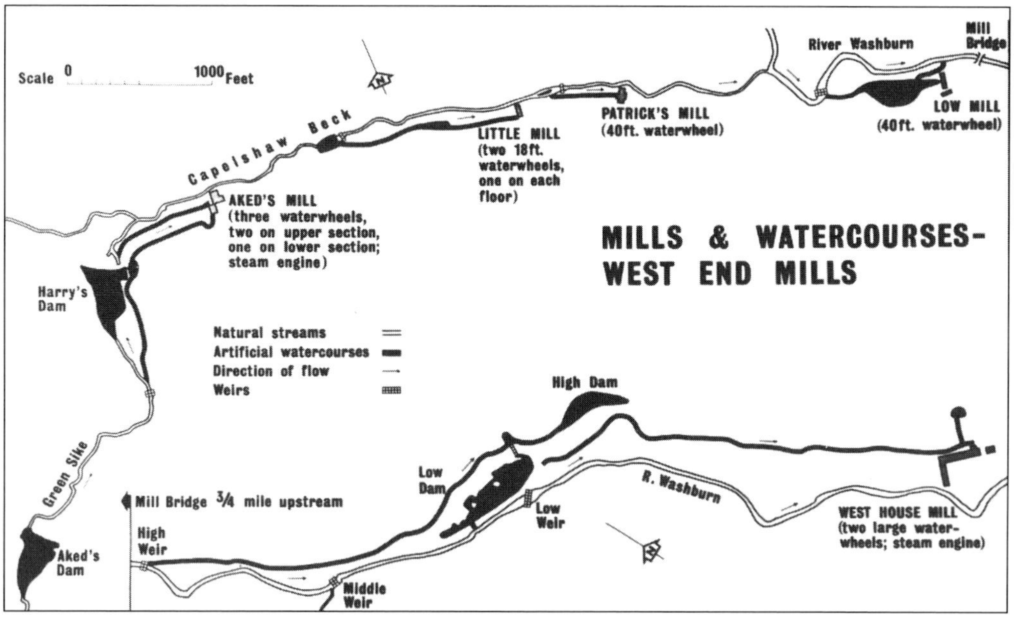

Mills and watercourses of the Upper Valley.

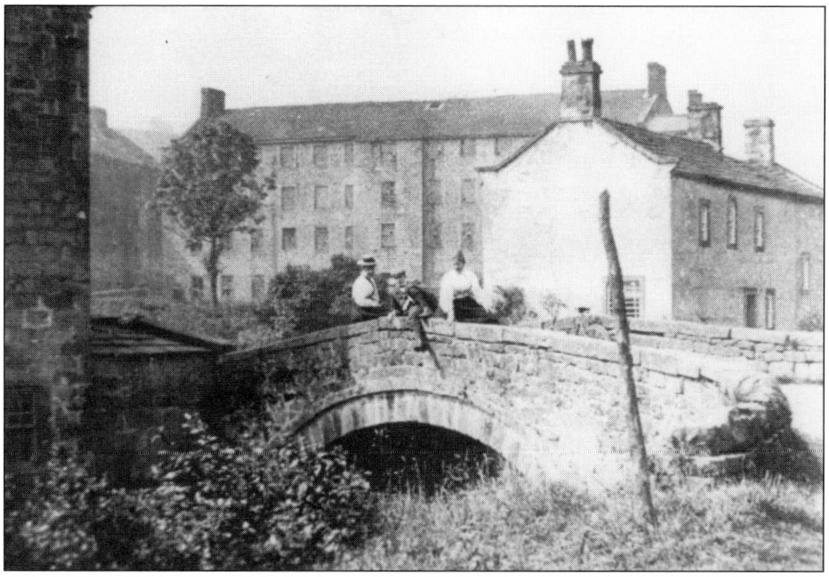

Street Lane Bridge, mill manager's house on right, mill beyond. Left: *Ethel Gill,* Right *– Alice Maud Mary Gill – the boy Raymond, gassed in an accident at the mill died aged forty-two. Thomas Gill took over the mill in 1868. Originally trained as a mill mechanic and patenting one of his own inventions, he lived in the manager's house. He died in 1880, and in 1901 Low Mill was compulsorily purchased by Leeds Corporation as part of their reservoir scheme.*

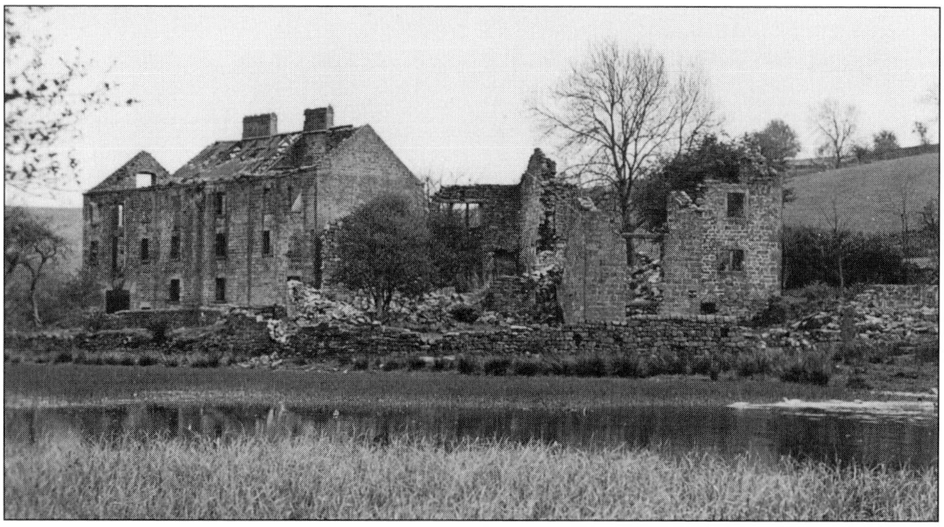

Low Mill – ruined warehouse.

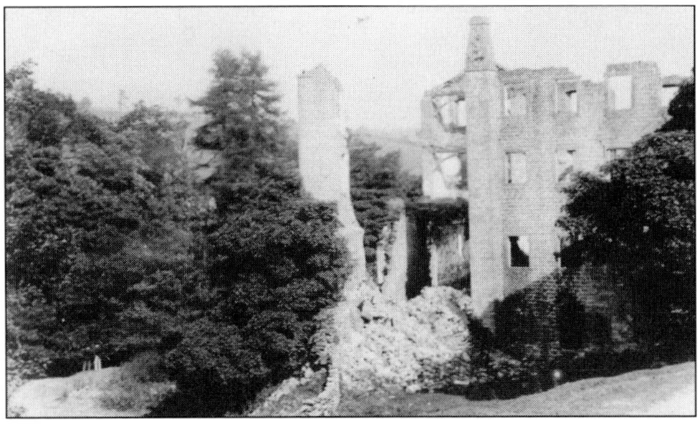

Ruins – Patrick's High Mill (also known as Patrick's Mill).

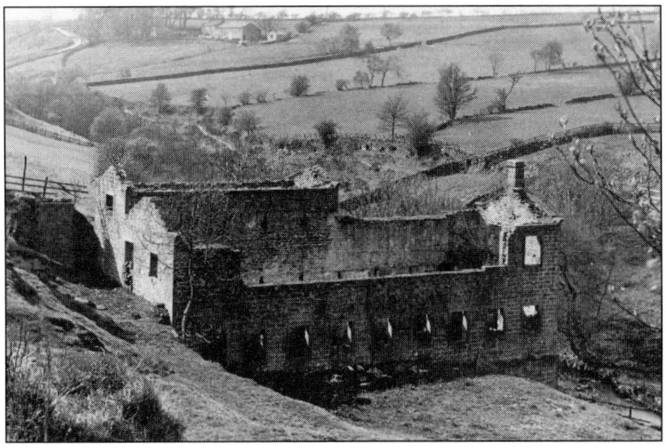

Ruins – Patrick's Little Mill.

High Mill, (not to be confused with Aked's [High] Mill) further upstream which had four floors and a huge wheel which when working is said to have caused the building to rumble and shudder alarmingly. In 1803 the mill had thirty workers and 516 spindles. In 1812 Walker transferred the tenancy of High Mill to his manager at Low Mill, John Patrick, and the former then became known as Patrick's Mill or Patrick's High Mill. In 1822 John Patrick bought both this mill, and also (Patrick's) Little Mill further up the valley running the two together. A two-storey building, it is said to have had two large waterwheels and five to six hundred spindles for flax and tow. Between them these two mills had a work force of 120 operating more than 2000 spindles. Both ceased textile production in 1838 although Little Mill later became a saw mill

In 1809 yet another mill for the spinning of flax was left to John and James Aked of Halifax by their father, William. Before the establishment of John Patrick's High Mill, Aked's mill had been named High Mill because of its position at the head of the valley; later it became known locally as Aked's Mill. On nearby moorland the brothers created Harry's dam and Aked's dam which supplied the two storey mill via two long leats and a 75 foot drop to three waterwheels, two upper and one lower. By 1836 the mill had 1000 flax spindles but in 1838 the enterprise suffered financial difficulties and the building burned down, whether by accident or by design is not known. It was however rebuilt and renamed Croft House Factory. A steam engine was installed in 1841 but in 1845 it ceased the production of textiles for good.

As a young man, the writer J. B. Priestley escaped from the uncongenial toil of work with a Bradford wool firm to discover the joys of hiking in the valley at weekends. Many years later, returning from the trenches of France, he took to cycling around his old haunts, and it was during this time that he recalled 'a deserted village with two small factories, and several rows of cottages, all completely uninhabited', where he had once eaten his sandwiches in a roofless cottage surrounded by gaping doorways beside a grass-grown street. Long afterwards he was quite unable to locate Low Mill but always felt that even in war torn France he had never seen such 'a complete picture of desolation'. Between 1811 and 1891 the population of Thruscross parish fell from 610 to 219.

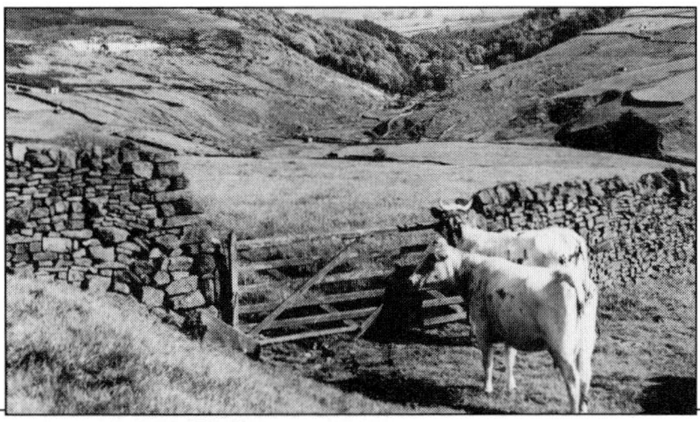

View south from Thruscross before reservoir.

West End – deserted village.

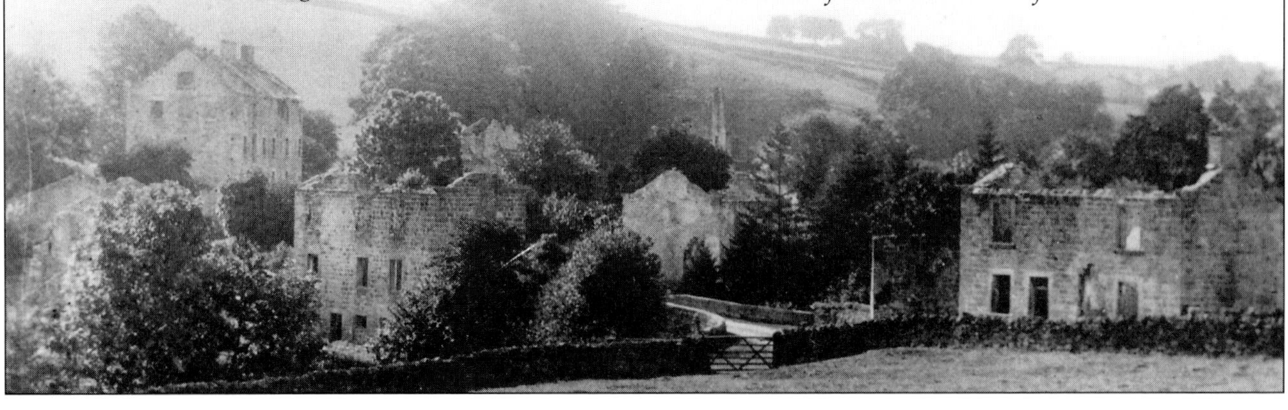

Chapter 3

The Middle Valley

The middle section of the valley includes the old townships of Blubberhouses, Fewston, Clifton with Norwood, and Timble Great. At Blubberhouses, where the A59 crosses the River Washburn as it enters Fewston Reservoir, the buildings straddle the main road. This township once housed the largest textile mill in the valley with its two apprentice houses.

In about 1797 a group of men with considerable experience of the textile trade including Thomas Colbeck, William and John Holdsworth, William Ellis, and Jacob Wilks of Knaresborough had begun to spin flax at Westhouse Mill on the site of the old Blubberhouses corn mill. A five-storey building with a steam engine and the first power looms in the

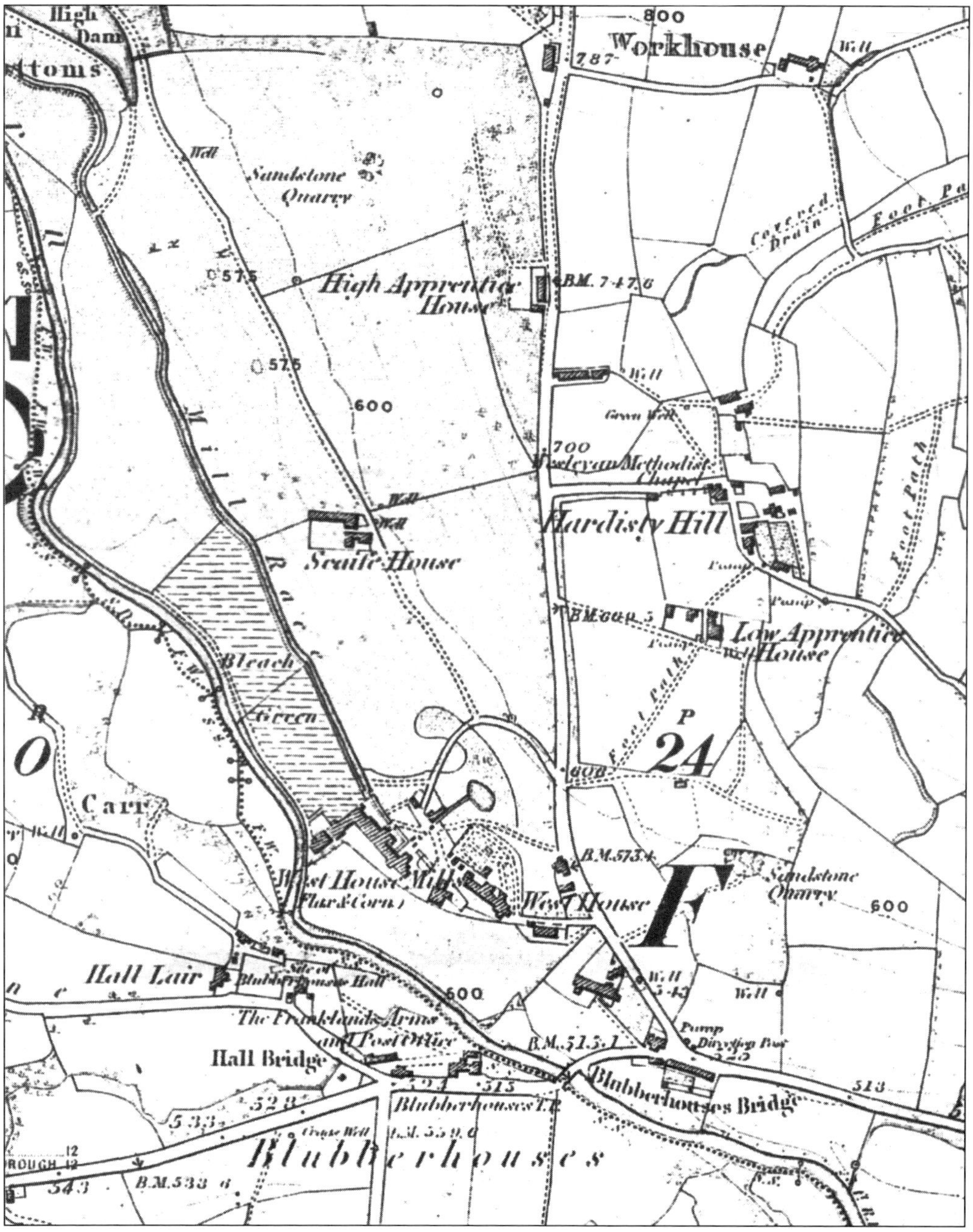

Area around Blubberhouses.

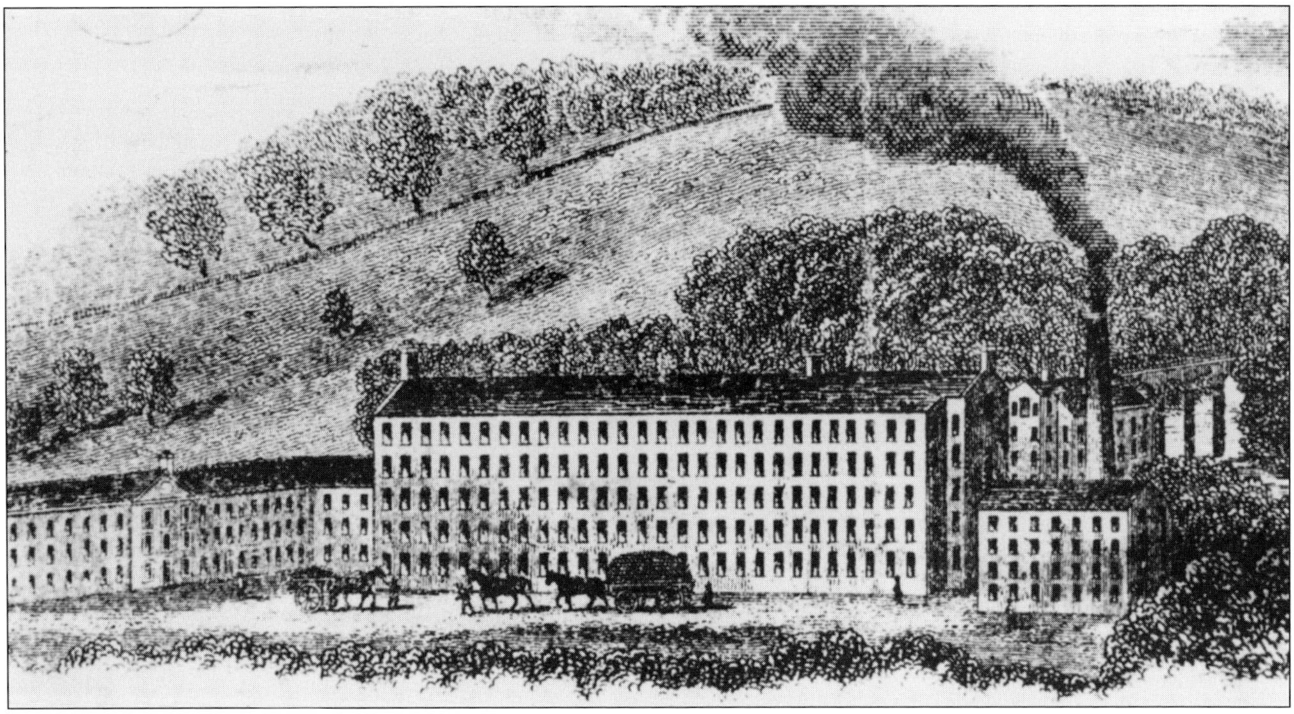

Sketch of Westhouse Mill, Blubberhouses.

Plan of Westhouse Mill showing probable use of buildings.

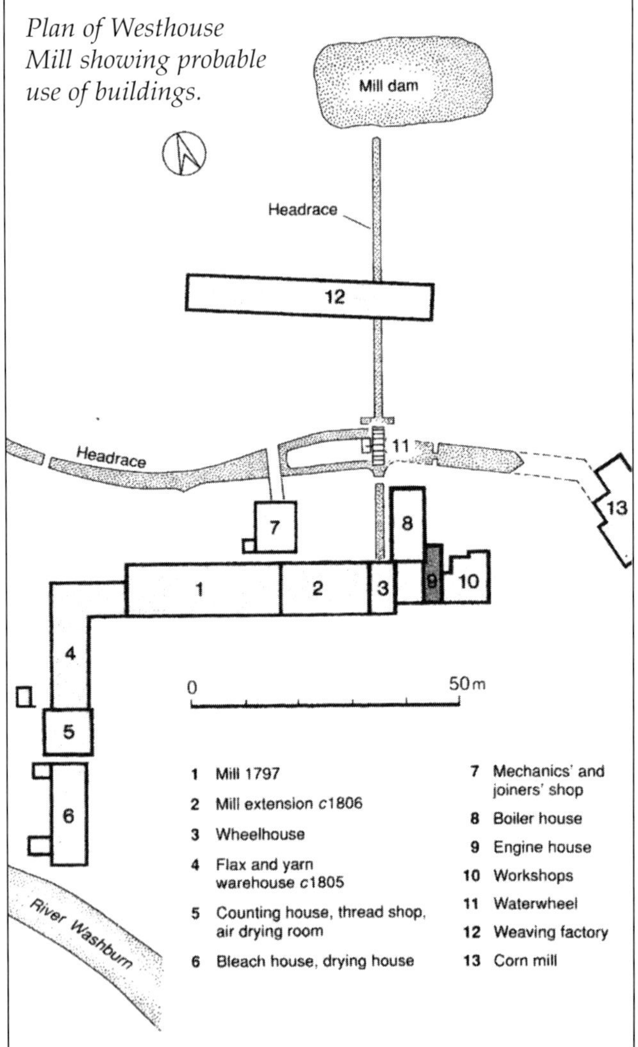

valley, it had a large amount of land, an impressive system of watercourses and ancillary buildings including a weaving shop, counting, bleaching and drying houses.

Unfortunately in 1840, after a promising start during which time it doubled in size, the mill suffered many setbacks in trade due to a combination of factors including the Napoleonic wars, isolation from coal and transport links, the relocation of factories to the cities, and changing market forces. In 1816 the company went bankrupt and the mill became the property of the Skipton bank, Chippendale, Netherwood and Carr, who had to pay debts of £85,000 as well as being responsible for a £2400 mortgage. Faced with the possibility that they would be unable to find a buyer they eventually restarted production, and by the 1830s, after a brief resurgence in trade the work force rose from about 140 to 200. In

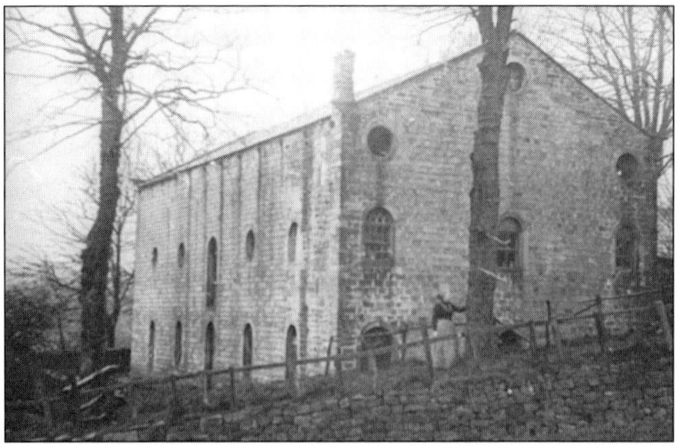

Westhouse Mill barn.

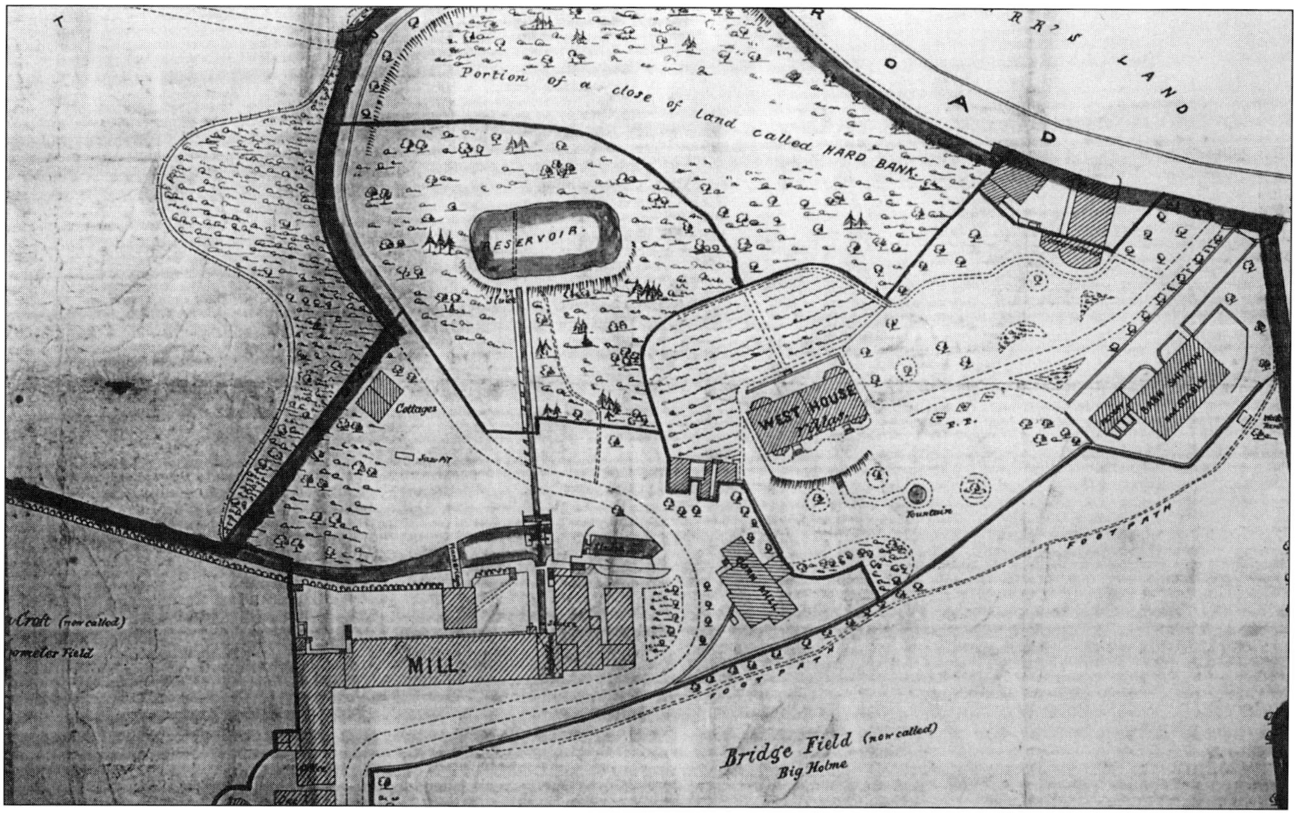

Plan of Westhouse Mill, dams, race and buildings in relation to surrounding landscape.

1839 ownership was vested in Christopher Netherwood, Jnr, and John Carr, Jnr, who later sold out to Netherwood for £5000 payable at the rate of £1000 per annum. He installed gas lighting and lived on the site. The mill, equipped with two waterwheels, one of iron and 39 feet in diameter, the other of wood and 33 feet in diameter, was said to be capable of containing 14000 spindles producing approximately 1500 bundles of yarn weekly.

Unfortunately in 1840 matters took another downturn with the introduction of continental tariffs on the importation of linen yarn, and by 1843 Netherwood's overdraft on the Craven Bank at Skipton amounted to £35,000 with a mortgage of £5000, a debt so large that the company's title to the Forest of Knaresborough had to be surrendered.

In 1850 a buyer for the mill was finally found but, like subsequent purchasers including Crowthers of Halifax who opened it as a silk mill, they had little if any success, and the mill finally closed in 1870 when it was bought by Leeds Corporation who demolished it, using the stone in the construction of Fewston Reservoir.

The collapse of the textile industry in the valley brought great hardship to the area. In 1841 the population of Fewston parish, which included the whole of the upper valley, was 850; ten years later it had sunk to 399 and most of the cottages at Low Mill were empty. By 1891 the population of Fewston parish was 233. Although it has been said that the creation of the reservoirs 'ripped the heart out of the valley' they were in fact only a contributory factor.

FLAX AND CORN MILLS,

AT WEST HOUSE, NEAR OTLEY, YORKSHIRE,

WITH NEW MACHINERY,

AND

ESTATE CONTAINING ABOUT 547A. 2R. 31P.,

BE THE SAME MORE OR LESS,

TO BE LET,

EITHER IN ONE LOT OR IN FARMS TO SUIT TENANTS.

TO BE LET, WITH IMMEDIATE POSSESSION,

ALL THAT VALUABLE STONE-BUILT WATER-POWER

FLAX MILL, CALLED WEST HOUSE MILL,

IN THE TOWNSHIP OF FEWSTON, IN THE COUNTY OF YORK,

Capable of containing 14,000 Spindles; also all the New and Valuable MACHINERY in the said Mill, all of which has been put into it within the last four years, and has been made by the first Machine Makers in Leeds; the said Machinery at present is spinning from 1400 to 1500 bundles per week, ranging from 10 leas to 120 leas. Also all the POWER LOOMS in the said Mill for Weaving Linen, all of which have been purchased within the last four years. The Mill is driven by two powerful Water Wheels, one of iron, about 36ft. in diameter, and buckets 10ft. broad, the other of wood, about 33ft. in diameter, and buckets 11ft. broad. Also a valuable STEAM ENGINE of about 30-Horse Power, to be used in case of scarcity of water, which is of very rare occurrence, not more than about two days having been lost during the last summer, noted for its excessive drought. Together with large and convenient FLAX and other WAREHOUSES and DRYING HOUSES; in fact, the Premises are replete with every convenience calculated for carrying on the flax business upon a large scale.

Also THIRTY-SEVEN COTTAGE HOUSES

Situated conveniently near to the said Mill, and at present occupied by the work people. Also

SEVERAL GOOD AND SUBSTANTIAL FARM-HOUSES,

With the LAND adjoining, containing 547A. 2R. 31P. be the same more or less, in a ring fence, a considerable part of which is in high cultivation, well protected with ornamental Woods and Plantations, and will be let with the Mill, if desired, or will be divided into lots. Also all those

NEWLY-ERECTED BLEACH WORKS,

Conveniently situated near to the said Mill, and constructed upon the most approved system for Bleaching.

Westhouse Mill – sale particulars.

CHILD LABOUR IN THE MILLS

The staffing of large mills in rural locations was always difficult and it was necessary to look further afield for an adequate labour force. This need fortuitously coincided with an escalating birth rate and a five-fold increase in the cost of poor relief which placed a huge financial burden on the large towns. The answer to the difficulties of both the employers and the Overseers of the Poor was therefore to transfer large numbers of paupers from the overburdened towns to the rural mills.

These apprentices were usually acquired either through an agent, a newspaper advertisement, or by direct approach to a city parish on payment of a premium by the mill master – usually between two and four guineas. Young children were the preferred form of labour, not only because they were cheap, unaccompanied, and therefore a captive force, but also because their small stature ensured their hands were at the correct level to twist together the slivers of yarn. Once the offer of an apprenticeship was accepted, after seven years they became the permanent responsibility of their new parish. Refusal of an offer meant the withdrawal of parish relief.

HIGH APPRENTICE HOUSE

Between 1803 and 1814 at least 49 girls and 30 boys, often but not always orphans from the London parishes of Shoreditch, Lambeth and Southwark as well as Hull, were apprenticed to Colbeck, Ellis and Wilks at Westhouse Mill for 'weaving and flax dressing'. Conditions were hard. The children, usually aged between seven and eleven, began work as doffers removing full bobbins and replacing them with empty ones, and at Westhouse they were eventually trained for weaving and flax dressing. Their hours were from 6 am until 8 pm and up to the age of twelve they were paid between one shilling and sixpence and two shillings and three pence per week. There were five holidays a year; Christmas, Easter, Whitsuntide and Shrove Tuesday, plus a day for Pateley Bridge Feast.

Colbeck, Ellis and Wilks are said to have been renowned for the brutal treatment of their apprentices. (See poem on p.47.) It is certainly known that in some mills children making mistakes at the spindles causing lumps to form in the yarn were beaten by their supervisors, but when officials of the Health and Morals Apprentices Act, who included William Vavasour, squire of nearby Weston, inspected Westhouse in 1802 no evidence of any ill treatment could be found. In fact the officials reported that the mill was whitewashed and well ventilated and that the boys and girls had separate sleeping quarters in two 'prentice' houses on Hardisty Hill, in which they slept no more than two to a bed. The children were not required to work at night and received new clothes every year.

It would be interesting to know if the managers concerned had received prior warning of the officials' visit for the memories of Robert Collyer, who began work in the mill as a doffer in 1832 at the age of eight, were very different. Then the children 'were rung in at six in the morning and out at eight in the evening with an hour for dinner and rest ... if we got chance to sit down for a few moments when the overlooker was not round with his leathern strap to lay on our small shoulders we were in luck ... the result of this was that the weaker children were ... crippled.' It has also been stated that 'at West End ... not far from the main road from Harrogate to Skipton lie the remains of an old woollen mill operated by water power to which hundreds of children were sent by magistrates, and as they died at their looms their bodies were thrown into a pit dug on the opposite side of the road.' This mill may have been Westhouse although from the late eighteenth century the mill was spinning flax rather than wool.

All this was in spite of the fact that in 1802 the first Factory Act had restricted the hours of employment for apprentices to twelve hours a day. In 1833 another Factory Act reduced the number of hours still further, although many employers still contrived to avoid compliance. However in about 1809, a Sunday School was established in Fewston by the employers at Westhouse, and a Fewston day school return of 1815 records 'one private Sunday School appropriated to the instruction of parish apprentices bound to the spinning manufactory of Messrs. Colbeck, Ellis and Co. to the number of 500 boys and girls.' Such provision was ahead of its time for it was not made compulsory until 1833.

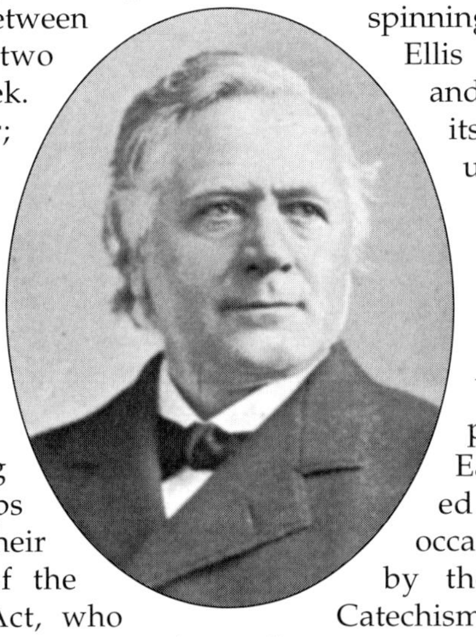

Robert Collyer.

In 1868 William, or Willie, Hardy taught the youngest factory children all day, and the half-timers in the afternoons, one of his teaching aids being a hieroglyphic Bible with pictures illustrating the Word of God. Each Sunday the children also attended Fewston church where on one occasion a local worshipper, impressed by the way in which they said the Catechism, gave them a guinea to share.

One of Willie's pupils, Robert Collyer, was the son of Samuel Collyer, a blacksmith or mechanic at Westhouse whose own father Robert, a sailor in Nelson's fleet, had been lost at sea leaving his widow with four small children. Unable to rear her family alone his wife was left with no option but to

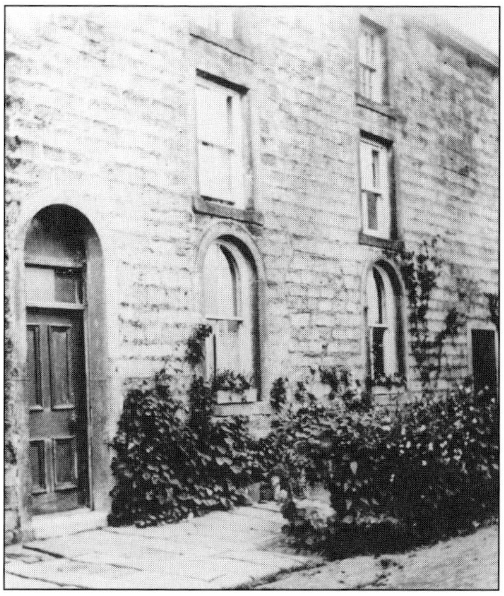

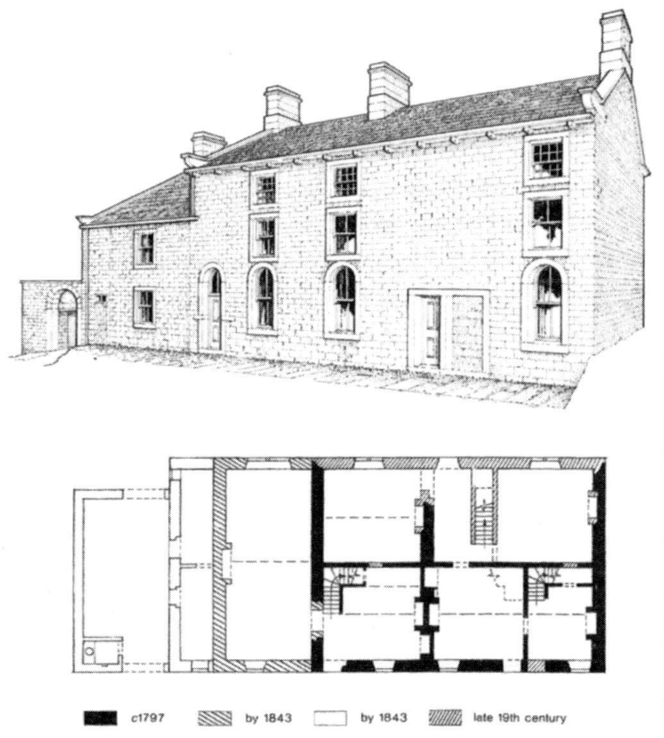

High Apprentice House for Boys, right: *an elevation and plan of the building.*

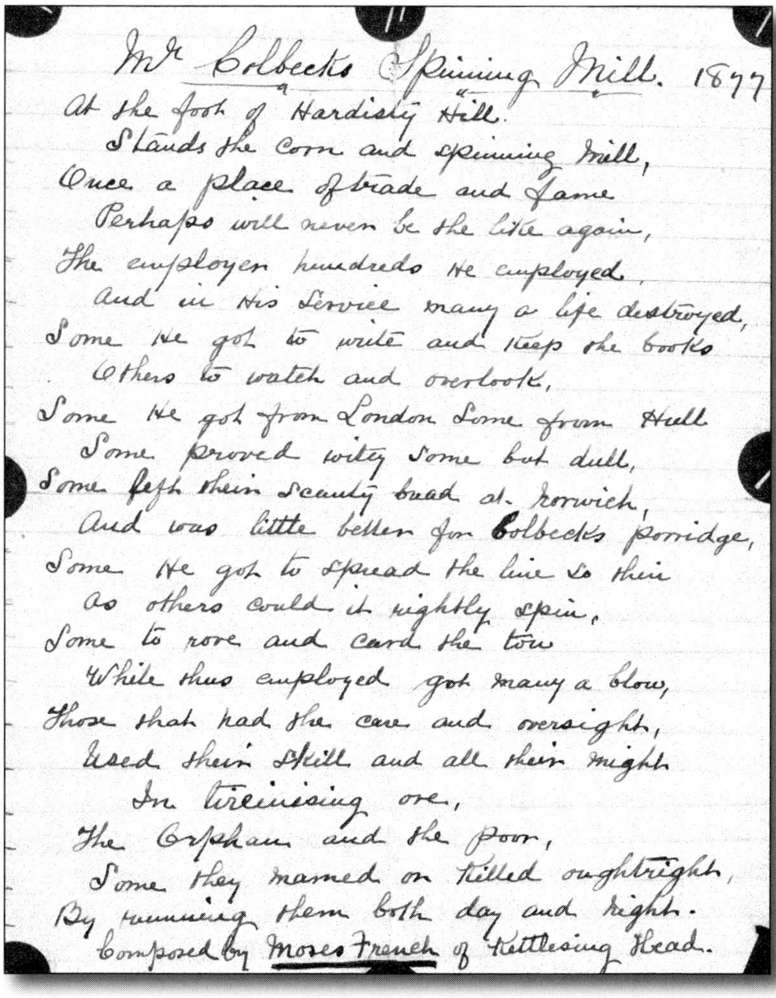

Mr Colbecks Spinning Mill. 1877
At the foot of Hardisty Hill
Stands the Corn and spinning Mill,
Once a place of trade and fame
Perhaps will never be the like again,
The employer hundreds He employed,
And in His Service many a life destroyed,
Some He got to write and keep the books
Others to watch and overlook,
Some He got from London Some from Hull
Some proved witty some but dull,
Some left their scanty bread at Norwich,
And was little better for Colbeck's porridge,
Some He got to spread the line so thin
As others could it rightly spin,
Some to rove and card the tow
While thus employed got many a blow,
Those that had the care and oversight,
Used their Skill and all their might
In tireinsing ore,
The Orphan and the poor,
Some they maimed or killed oughtright,
By running them both day and night.
Composed by Moses French of Kettlesing Head.

Poem by Moses French. Moses, a farmer at Kettlesing Head, was born in 1801.

give them up, and Samuel had been one of the many pauper apprentices sent to Blubberhouses in 1807 from the parish of St George's, Southwark in London.

Robert was born at Keighley in 1824 and brought up at Blubberhouses in a cottage adjoining the mill, where he remained until 1839 when he left for Ilkley to become apprenticed to a blacksmith, John Birch, whose wife Frances was a Blubberhouses girl. Here Robert became self-educated, reading widely in such works as the *Encyclopaedia Britannica*, *Macauley's Essays* and *The Pilgrim's Progress*, and in 1849 he became a Methodist local preacher. A year later he married and emigrated to America, settling near Philadelphia where he continued both to practise his trade and his preaching.

Disenchanted with Methodism he became a Unitarian, moving to Chicago to begin work as a missionary among the city's poor. In 1859 he was ordained, becoming pastor to the Unity Church, but in 1871 that church was destroyed in the great fire of Chicago. Robert pledged to remain until the church had been rebuilt, remarking that the congregation would not find a cheaper parson because if funds ran short he could make as good a horseshoe as any smith in Chicago.

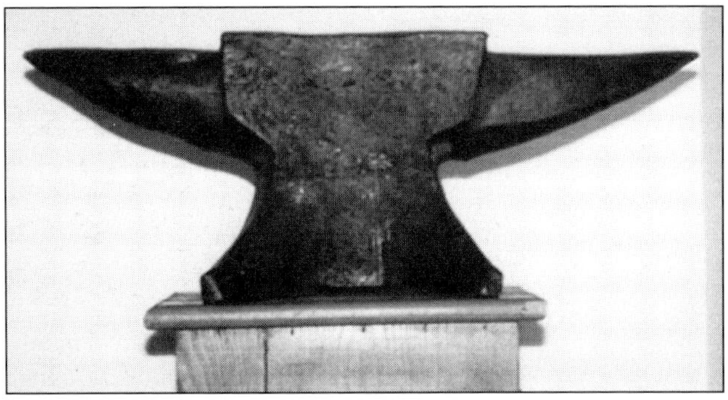

Robert Collyer's anvil.

An inspired preacher, and a popular and widely known priest in America, in 1879 he moved to New York where he became pastor to the Church of the Messiah. He visited England in 1865, 1871 and 1878, but during a further visit in 1898 an attempt to speak in Fewston church was turned down, the rector stating that he had 'no authority to allow it.' Robert continued to live in New York until his death in 1912. The new church in Chicago, now the Second Unitarian Church, still stands, and contains the bell from

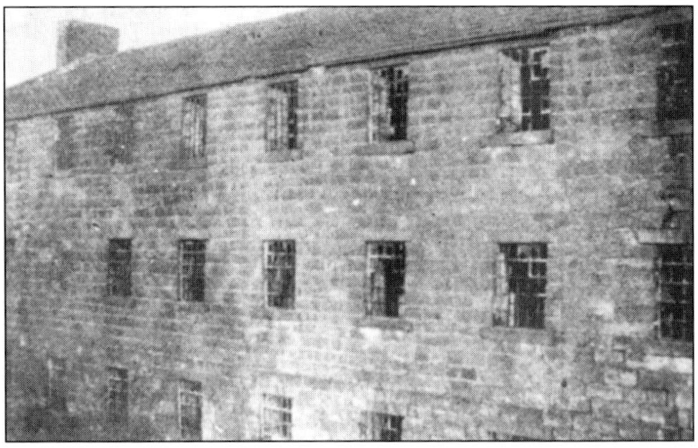

Workhouse, Hardisty Hill, Blubberhouses.

Westhouse which once summoned him to work each morning as well as the anvil on which he served his apprenticeship in Ilkley.

In 1827 Fewston parish borrowed £600 to erect a workhouse on Hardisty Hill a few yards beyond the High Apprentice House. After the formation of the Wharfedale Poor Law Union in 1834, an elected Board of Guardians oversaw Washburn parish. In 1867 the Fewston workhouse was sold, still owing more than £300 of the original loan. A suggestion that it should be converted into accommodation for the reservoir navvies was abandoned, the vicar of Fewston arguing that work on the reservoirs was not imminent, that conversion costs would be prohibitive, and that 'knowing the general nature of men engaged as excavators, we fear the house may be made the scene of the greatest licentiousness' adding that 'the township was not willing to run the risk of such disgrace and guilt'. The workhouse was sold at auction for £165 in 1868 to Matthew Gill of Blubberhouses when it still held twelve aged paupers. It is believed that it was demolished in the 1950s.

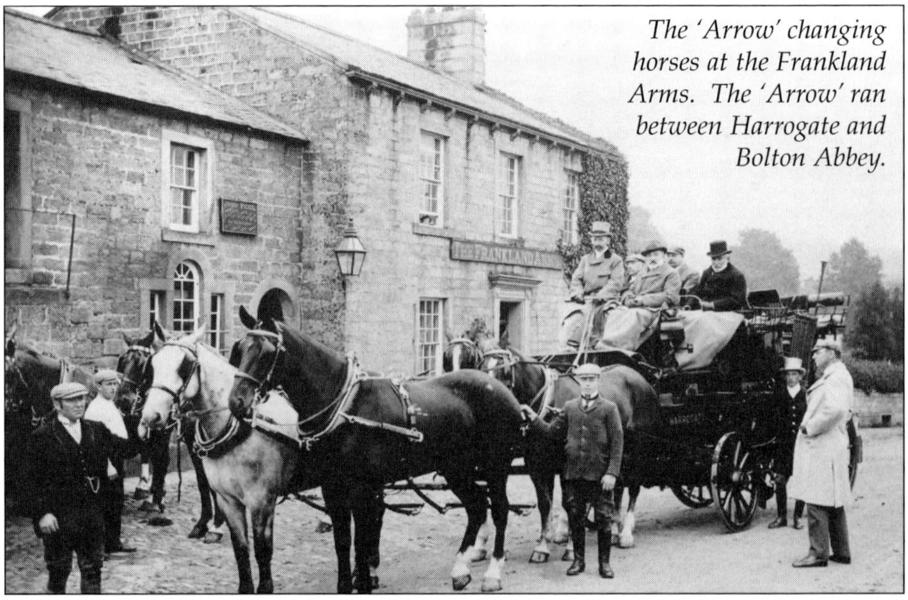

The 'Arrow' changing horses at the Frankland Arms. The 'Arrow' ran between Harrogate and Bolton Abbey.

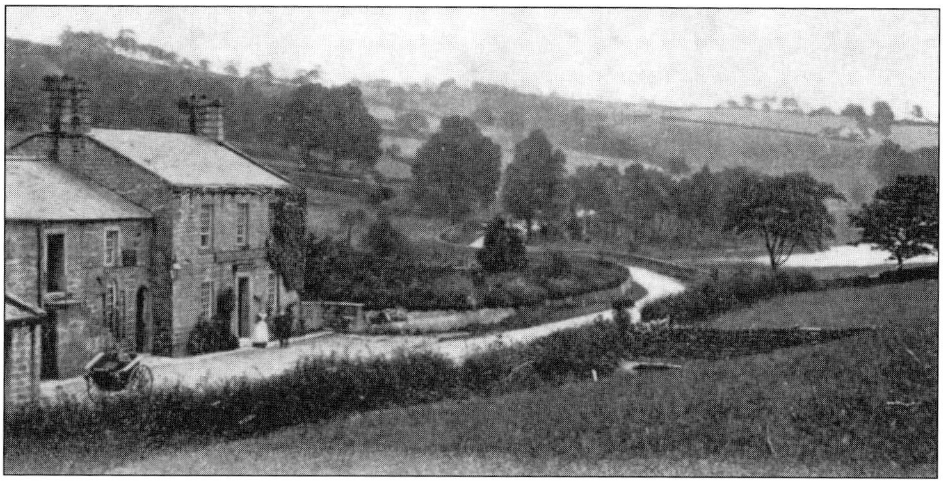

The Frankland Arms, Blubber-houses, and the old road to Harrogate.

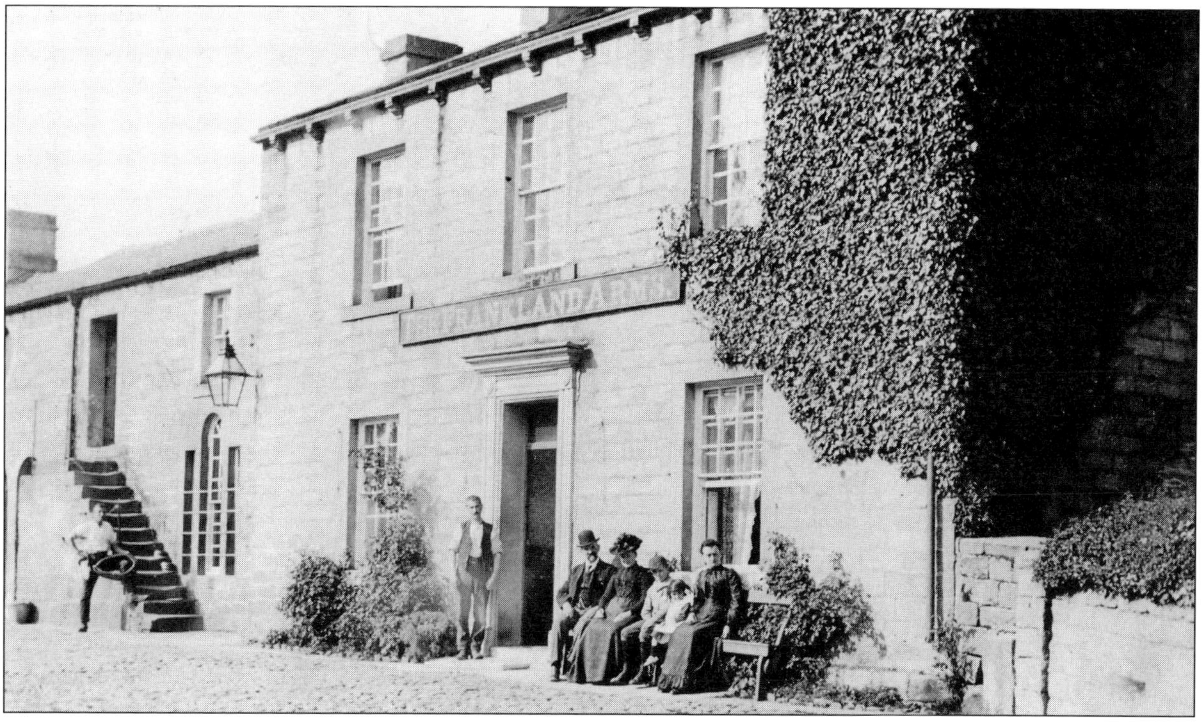

The Frankland Arms. Formerly the Anchor and Dolphin it was built by Robert Frankland early in the nineteenth century to serve workers at Westhouse Mill. There were several landlords including John Gill in 1837 and Isaac Maud who in 1888 served John Dickinson of Timble when he called for three whiskies. In 1863 on the occasion of the marriage of King Edward VII the owners of the mill provided a banquet at the inn at which Jesse Peel played his violin. By 1897 John Peel was the landlord, advertising the inn as a 'good place for cyclists' and having 'large airy bedrooms ...Visitors boarded at 6 shillings per day'. The inn closed in 1903 and was demolished in 1907 when John Dickinson and his nephew, George Archer, drove to 'look at old buildings of the late Frankland Arms with a view to using them for the new Fewston cemetery chapel in Meagill Lane'.

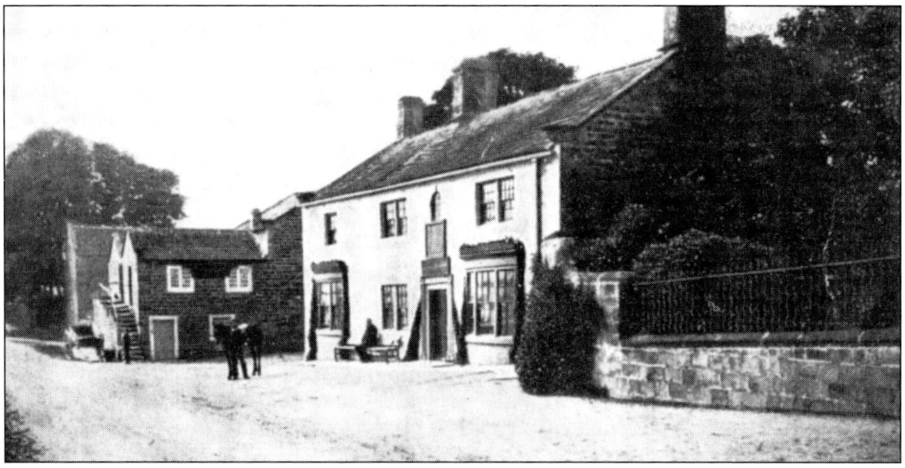

Hopper Lane Hotel. The inn was also known as the Blacksmith's Arms when the landlord was Thomas Ward between 1822 and 1881. After attending his funeral in 1886 John Dickinson wrote that he had 'spent many pleasant and social hours with him ...a man of superior education and intelligence ... a remarkable, active, careful man in his younger days when the Hopper Lane was a great posting house.' He also added that as a bachelor his friend had '... none of the sympathies surrounding his dying bed which might have been had he married.' In 1909 Dickinson recorded 'How changed is the old Inn since his death ... [his] genial social receptions are still green in my memory'. In 1912 the landlord was Daniel Neville and in 1917 Mrs Mary Demaine took over.

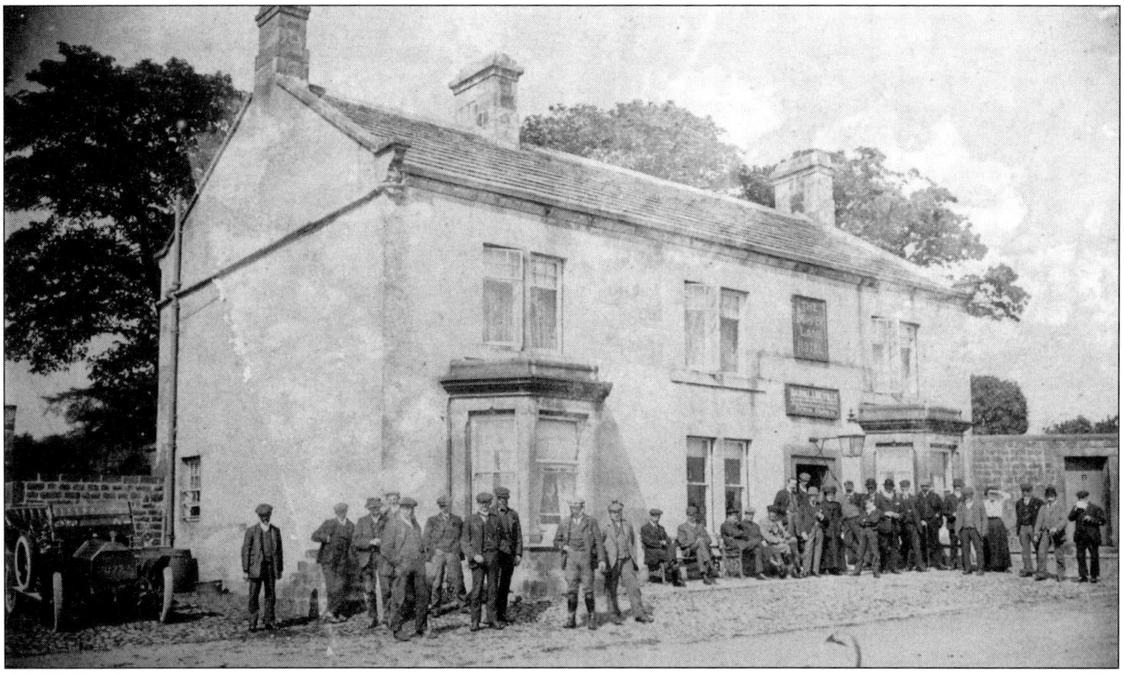

Rent day at Hopper Lane Hotel c.1910. After paying their rent local farmers had a meal at the landowner's expense.

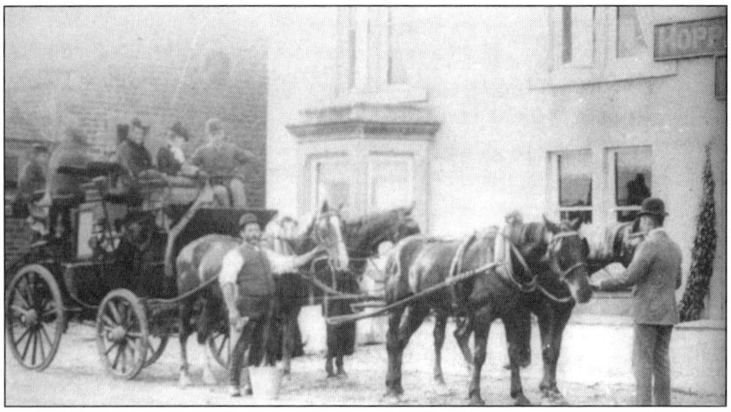

Stage coach at Hopper Lane Hotel.

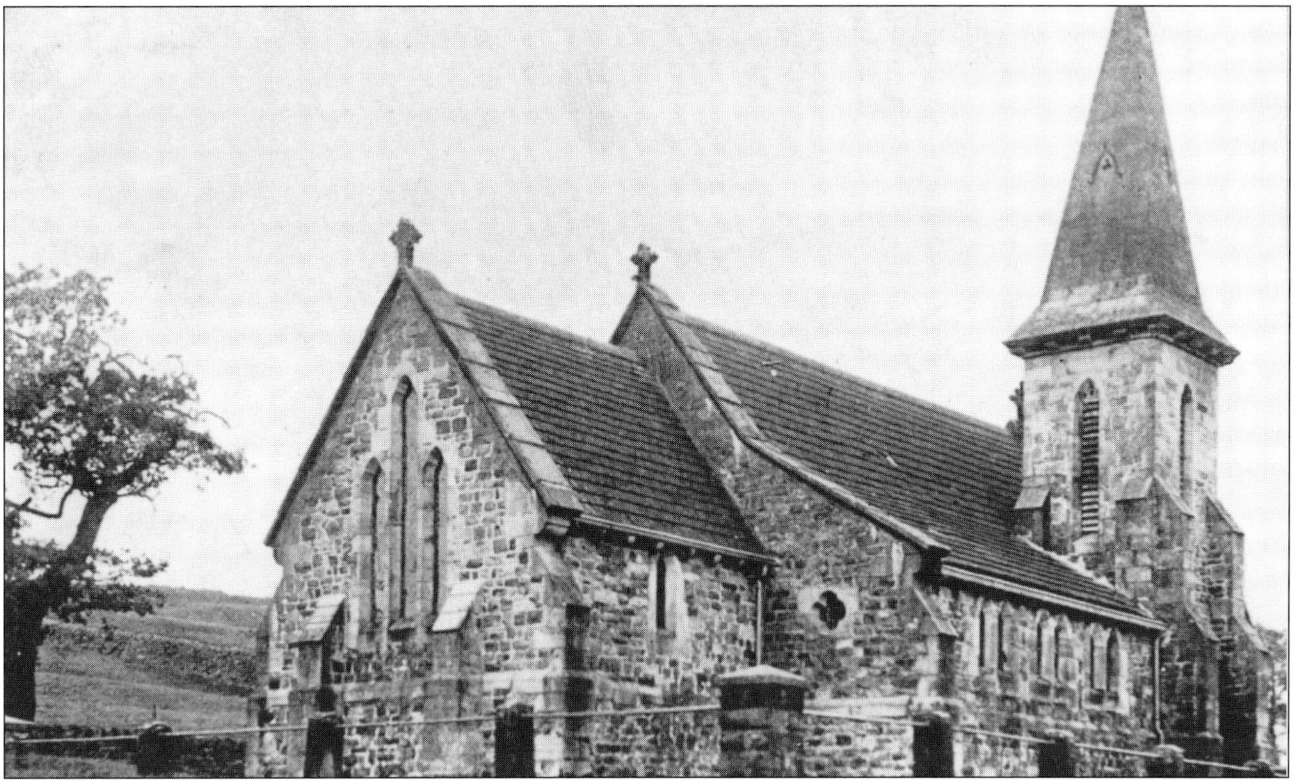

The church of St Andrew, Blubberhouses.

The church was built in 1856 at the instigation of Lady Emily Anne Payne Gallwey (formerly Frankland Russell) wife of Sir William Payne Gallwey whose principal estate was at Thirkleby, near Thirsk. A chapel of ease, it was intended to enable the Blubberhouses workers to worship without undertaking the long walk to Fewston. Endowing the church with £30 per annum she made it a condition that the parishioners would provide a cart-load of fuel to heat it during the winter months.

The architect employed was Edward Buckton Lamb (1805-1869) known as the 'Rogue Architect' because of his advocacy of the architectural style of 'true Gothic' said to be based on Anglo-Venetian and early French designs. This style was part of an attempt to combine medievalism and modernism with traditional forms, new materials, pointed arches and plate glass, all very popular in the 1860s. A recurring feature of such churches was a tall spire topping a central tower and an altar fully visible from the nave. This style was also used by the more famous architect William Butterfield, who designed a number of prominent churches including All Saints, Margaret Street, London, and the chapel of Balliol College, Oxford. Lamb also designed four other Yorkshire churches in the same style – at Sowerby, Bagby, Healey and Aldwark – all of which are on former Frankland land in North Yorkshire.

The stone was quarried at Pace Gate near Bolton Abbey, and the building work supervised by Lady Emily's estate manager John Gill, who died in 1864 aged sixty-six. 'In memory of his valuable service' a tablet was placed in the chancel by Lady Emily. The church was consecrated on the 24 September 1856. The altar rail belongs to the seventeenth century and the pews, each of which bear a Roman numeral, are said to have come from the old church at Thirkleby.

In the late nineteenth century the church was apparently well attended by the reservoir navvies, one of whom started a Sunday School held in one of the Westhouse Villas which formerly stood on the opposite side of the valley and eventually became Skaife Hall.

The hall occupied land behind a row of cottages on the site of Westhouse Mill. In 1898 it became the country home of William Johnson Galloway and his mother

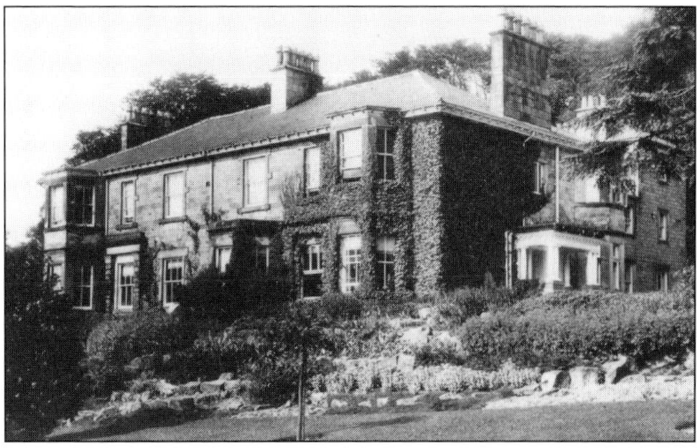

View of Skaife Hall formerly Westhouse Villas.

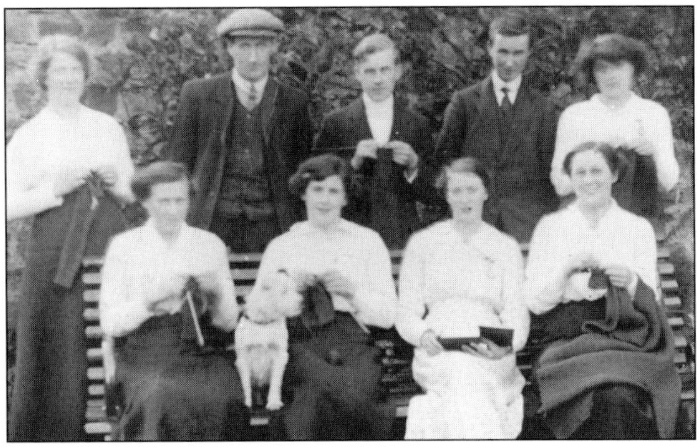

The staff at Skaife Hall.

when they moved from their home at West End. Born in 1868, Col Galloway was a partner in an engineering and boiler making firm and a director of the Great Eastern Railway Company. Between 1895 and 1906 he served as MP for Manchester South West. An Honorary Colonel of the East Lancashire Regiment Royal Engineers, he also held positions with the Ministry of Information and the Foreign Office.

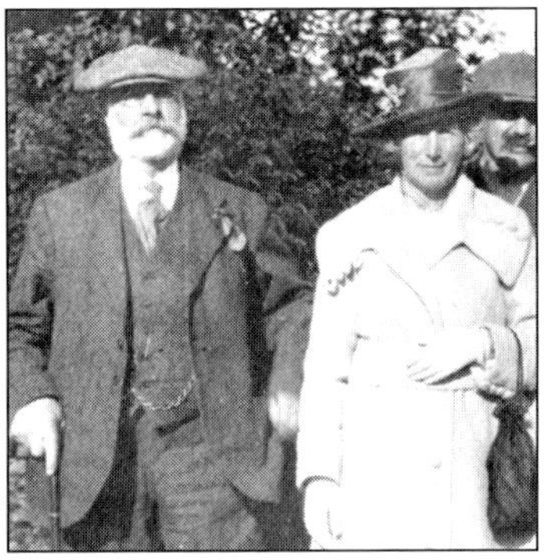

Col Galloway with his mother.

As well as taking a keen interest in music and writing two books on the subject, Colonel Galloway was an enthusiastic cricketer who established a cricket ground and bandstand in front of the hall where he organised an annual cricket festival inviting some important cricketing personalities of the day.

The Colonel's mother, Mary Ann Hall Galloway, was particularly active in the social affairs of the valley; in 1909 the pair entertained 150 tenants and friends to tea served in a marquee. The church contains a memorial to Mary Ann who died on the 11 April 1922 aged 82. In 1924 the house was sold, but before moving to London, Galloway hosted a garden party for three hundred people. He died in 1931 and the house was later demolished.

BLUBBERHOUSES HALL

In 1267 when Robert the Forester granted land at Blubberhouses to the Canons of Bridlington Priory he ordered them 'to enjoy their Manor', an instruction which does not necessarily imply the presence of a house but may relate only to the land. However in 1562, following the Dissolution of the Monasteries, 'the scite and mansion of the Hall' was granted by the Crown to Thomas Wood, gentleman, and William Frankland, and the estate remained in the hands of the Franklands until the 1840s when it was divided among the daughters of the late Sir Robert Frankland Russell, one of whom was Lady Emily Anne Payne-Gallwey.

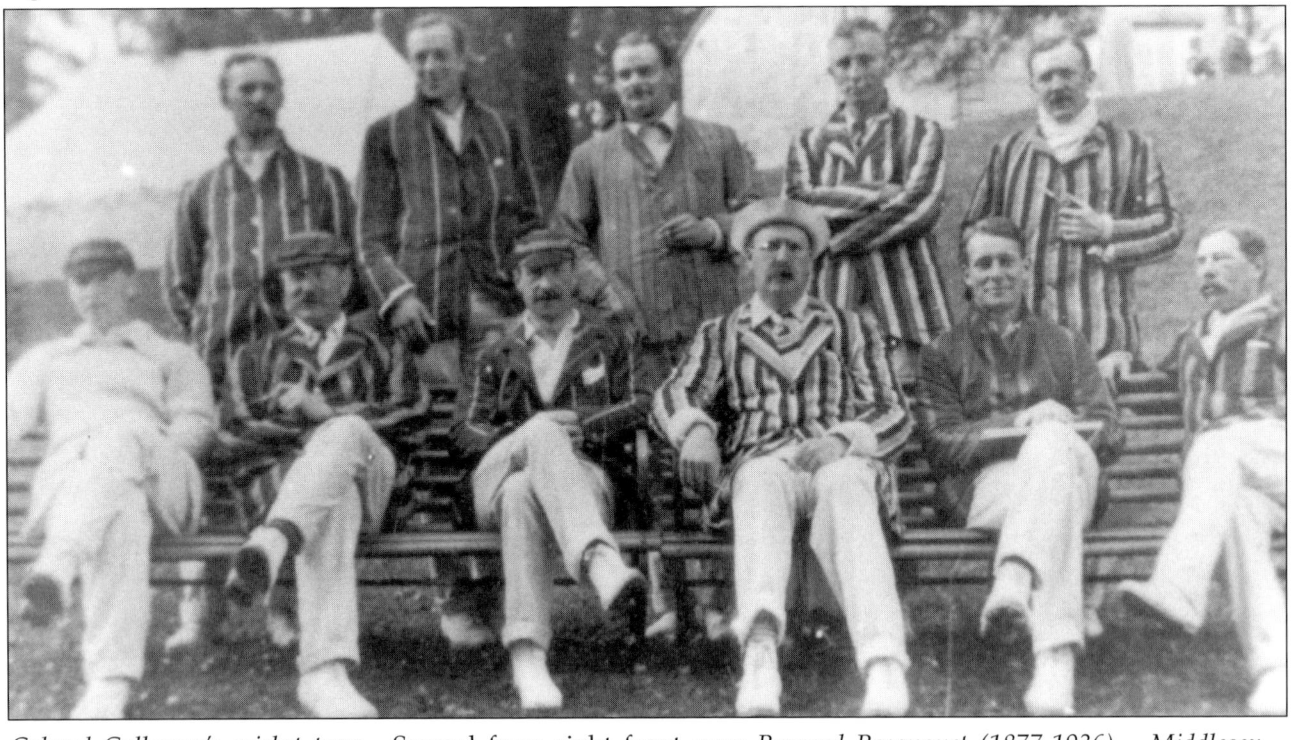

Colonel Galloway's cricket team. Second from right front row: *Bernard Bosanquet (1877-1936) – Middlesex – invented the googly.* 4th from right on front – *Humphrey Gilbert (1886-1960) Worcestershire – a fast bowler known as 'the express merchant'.*

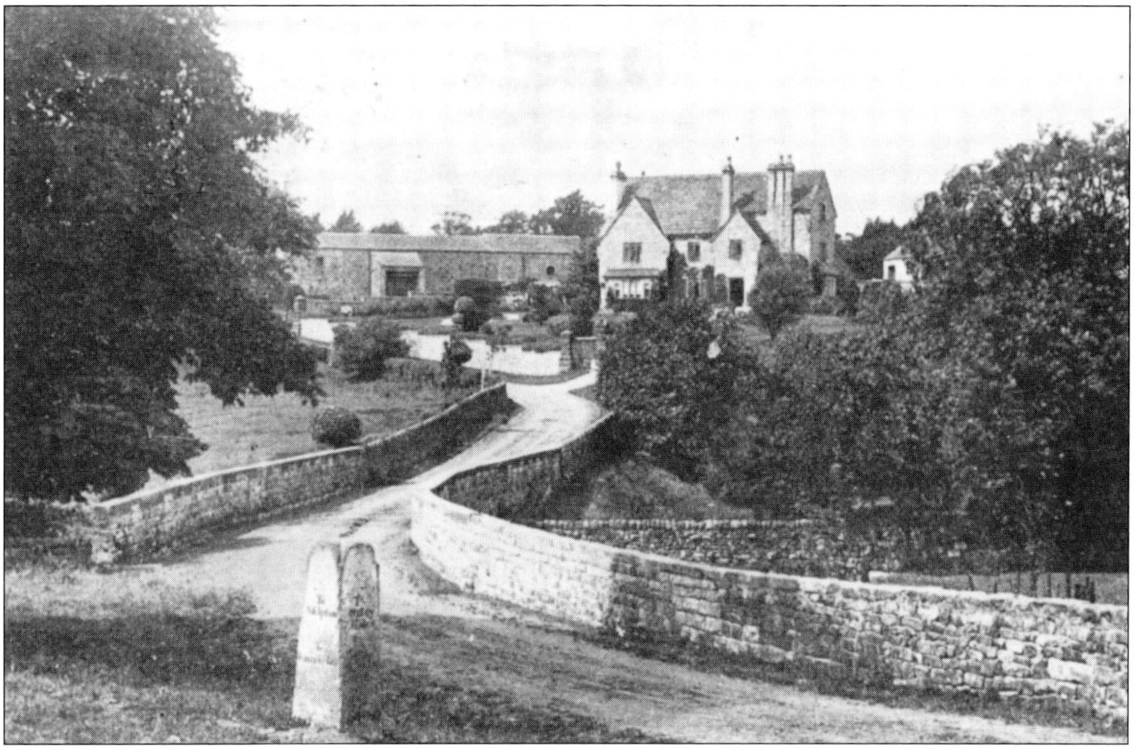

Blubberhouses Hall and the Old Road to Skipton.

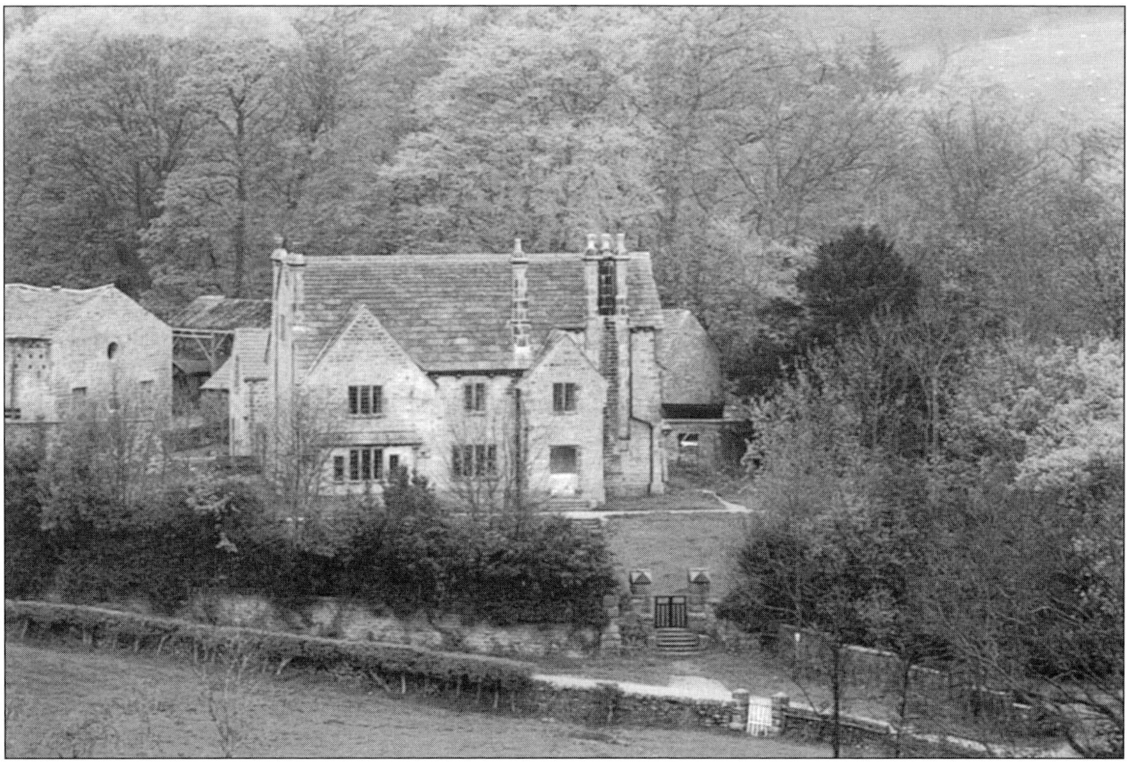

Blubberhouses Hall.

In the mid nineteenth century Lady Emily commissioned Edward Buckton Lamb to build a shooting lodge for her nephew, Thomas de Grey, 6th Lord Walsingham, and the house was constructed on an Elizabethan plan by John Gill. A formidable shot, Walsingham is credited with accounting for more than a thousand head of grouse between dawn and dusk on Blubberhouses Moor. He was also a noted entomologist. He died childless in 1919 six years after Lady Emily and three years after her son. In September 1914 her only grandson, William Thomas Payne-Gallwey born in 1881, a captain in the Grenadier Guards, was reported missing presumed killed in action at the Battle of the Aisne. The house was afterwards occupied by her steward, Matthew Gill before coming known as Venture House, a centre for Scouts. Now fully restored it is once more a private home.

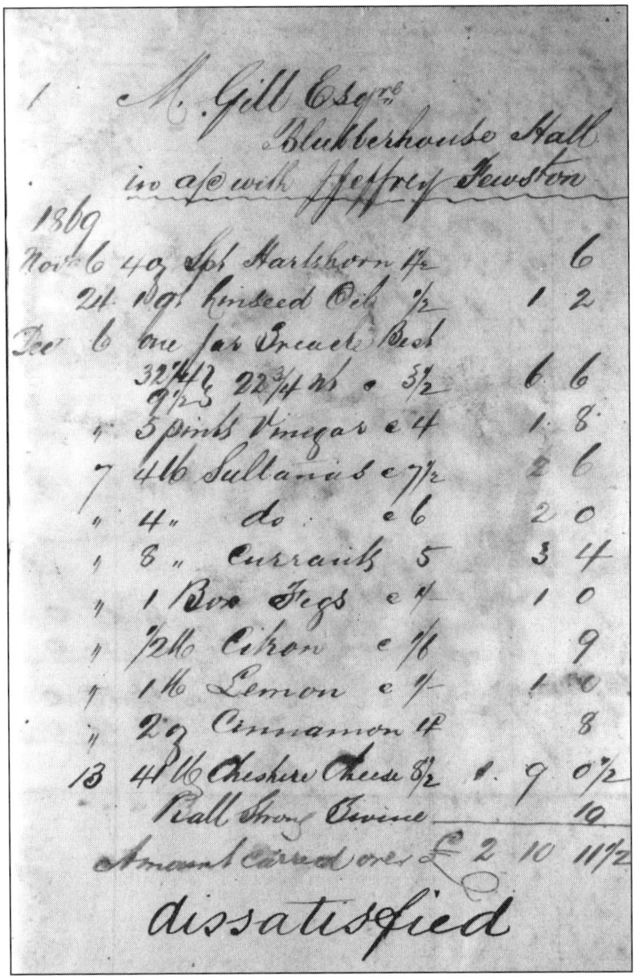

M. Gill Esqre
Blubberhouse Hall
in a/c with Jeffrey Fewston

1869			
Nov 6	4oz Spt Hartshorn 1½		6
21	1qt Linseed Oil ½	1	2
Dec 6	one Jar Treacle Best 32¼lb 22¼ lb @ 3½	6	6
"	5 pints Vinegar @ 4	1	8
7	4lb Sultanas @ 7½	2	6
"	4 " do @ 6	2	0
"	8 " Currants 5	3	4
"	1 Box Figs @ 1/-	1	0
"	½lb Citron @ 1/6		9
"	1lb Lemon @ 1/-	1	0
"	2oz Cinnamon 4		8
13	41lb Cheshire Cheese 8½	1 . 9	0½
	1 Ball Strong Twine		10
	Amount carried over £2	10	11½

dissatisfied

1869 account between Matthew Gill and Jonathan Jeffrey. History does not relate who was dissatisfied, or why.

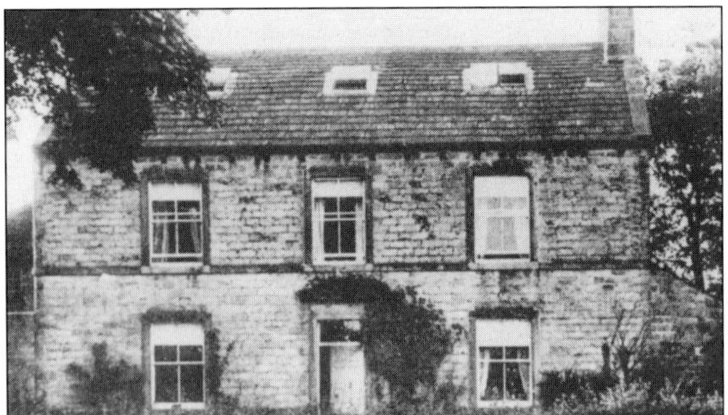

Manor House, Blubberhouses (SW of Blubberhouses church).

MANOR HOUSE

If a manor house ever existed in Blubberhouses perhaps it was situated on this site. However, the present house dates only from the late nineteenth century. It was once the home of Charles Powell, farmer and director of Wharfedale Farmer's Auction Mart, and his wife, Edith. Two of their five children also served in the First World War, one son, Percy, being killed in action in France. The Powells left the house in 1942.

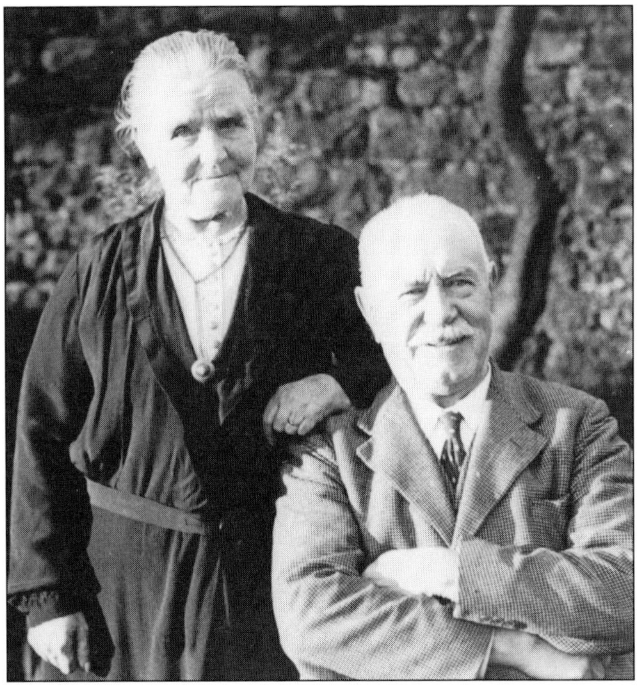

Charles and Edith Powell.

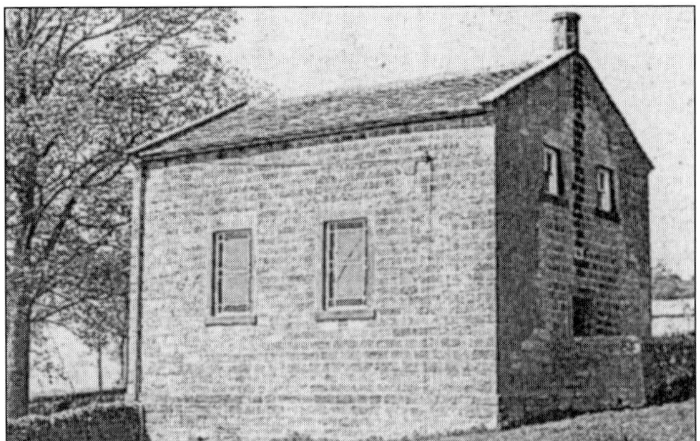

Hardisty Hill Wesleyan Methodist chapel.

HARDISTY HILL WESLEYAN METHODIST CHAPEL

Although there is said to have been a Congregational meeting house on Hardisty Hill served in the nineteenth century by students from Airedale College, no trace of this building remains.

In 1838 land was acquired from Joshua Yeadon of Plompton for the building of the Methodist chapel which was intended to accommodate a congregation of a hundred. Twelve trustees were appointed and the superintendent minister was the Rev. James Fowler. In 1887 the chapel was the scene of a great circuit gathering. A small dilapidated building beside Hardisty Hill, now in a private garden, and known locally as the 'reading room' may have been the chapel's Sunday School. It contained several religious works including the Christian Miscellany, Bible commentaries and picture books including the *Tenth Doctrine of Hades.* Less challenging perhaps were the *Sunday School and Preachers Magazine, Children's Friend* and books by Mark Twain. Open for half an hour on Sunday afternoon, non-members paid one shilling and six pence yearly, scholars one shilling a year. There was a penny fine for books not renewed or returned after fourteen days, and any book damaged had to be made good.

HIGHWAYS AND BYWAYS

Prior to the eighteenth century most of the roads in the country were little more than rutted tracks. The first attempt to rectify this situation came in 1555 when an Act of Parliament placed the responsibility for the repair and maintenance of highways on their parishes. This was a considerable burden in terms of both finance and labour, every adult male householder being required to spend four days a year on the task, increasing to six days in 1583. Where roads were damaged by too many horses and waggons, parishioners found the duty particularly costly and irksome. In 1637 George Booth of Snowden appeared at Knaresborough Quarter Sessions charged with planting 'at Tymble in the King's highway there, leading from the town of Tymble to the market town of Leeds, certain pales and fences and dug a ditch ... so that the subjects of Our Lord the King cannot pass there with their horses and carriages.' In 1687 William Ward of Haverah Park left to the 'poure folks in Fewston parish three shillings and four pence 'to repaireing of the hieways.'

In 1658 when a levy of forty six shillings and eight pence was laid on the parishioners of Thruscross, the Constable denied responsibility demanding that if the repairs were not carried out the Blubberhouses parishioners should be fined £10. In 1681 the situation arose yet again when a fine of £30 was levied at Skipton for non-repair of the same bridge. Eventually Thomas Gill and George Taylor, inhabitants of Thruscross, undertook to carry out the repairs, for which £12 was collected from the parishioners.

In Thruscross township in 1831 Stephen Hardisty,

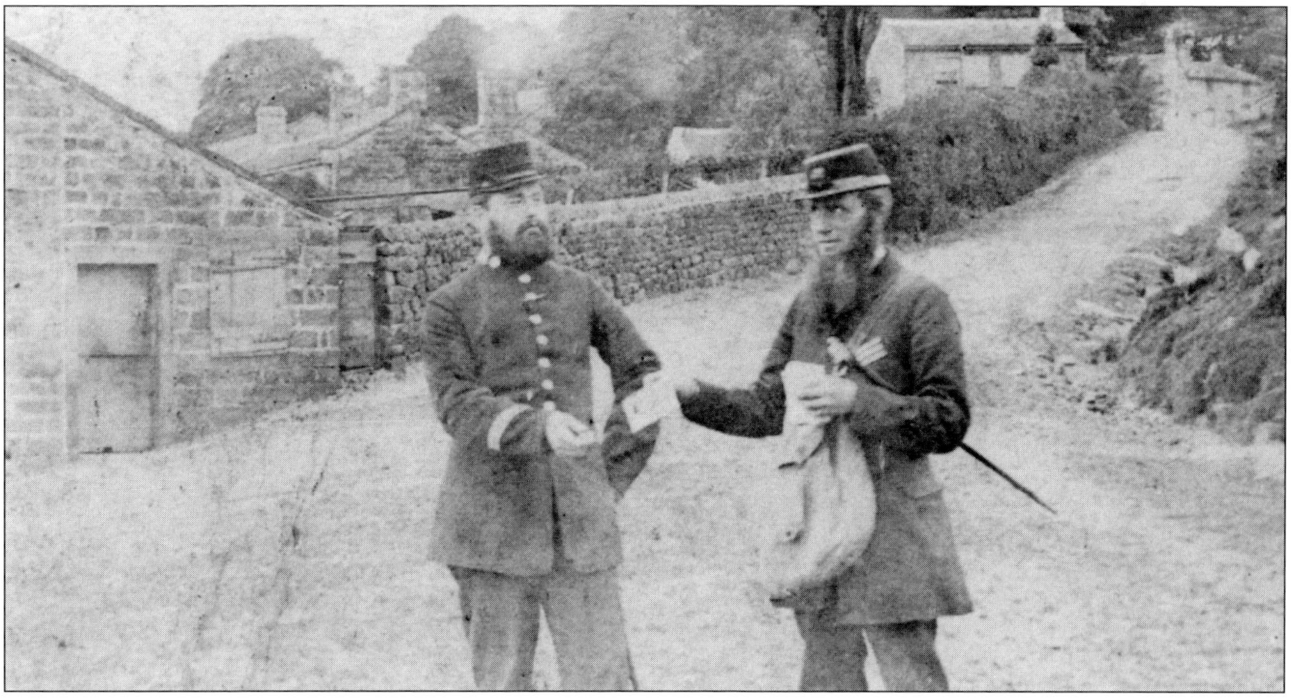

Postman and policeman at Hardisty Hill. The small building visible between the cottages is believed to have been the Reading Room.

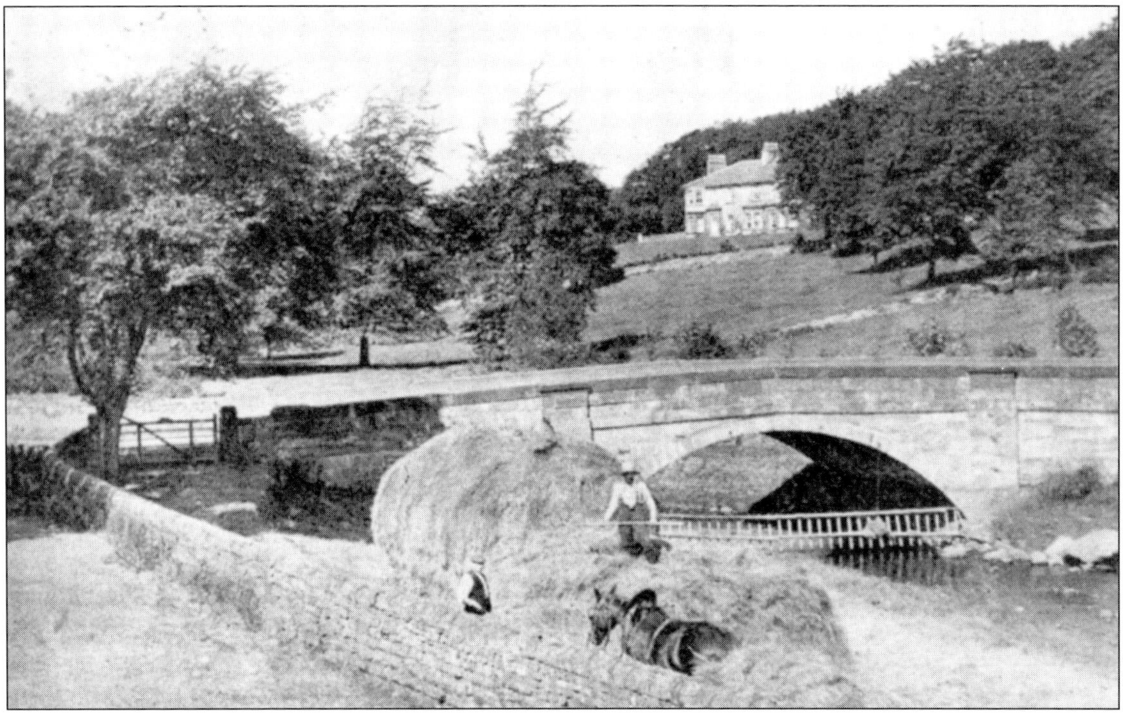

Hay making at Mylne Bridge, Blubberhouses. Mylne Bridge was so called because of its proximity to the corn mill, later Westhouse Mill.

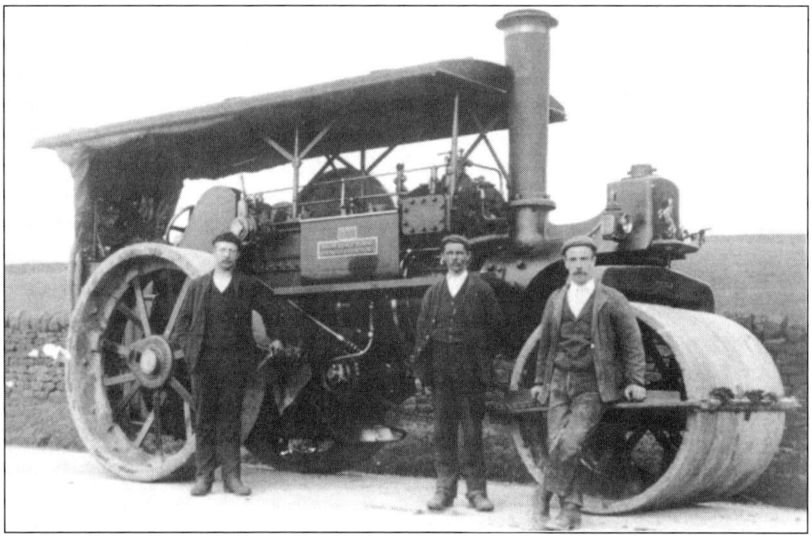

Road repair gang. Three local men, Joseph Firth, Tommy Hunter of Bland Hill, and Charles Newall of Fewston with an Aveling and Porter steam roller c.1905.

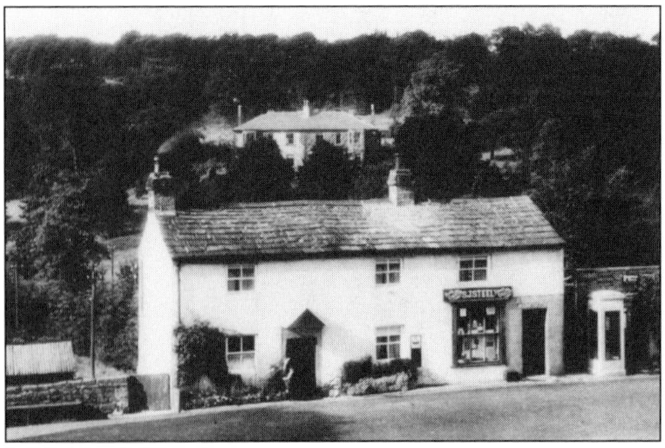

Blubberhouses Toll House and Post Office. Towards the end of the seventeenth century Parliament created the first Turnpike Trusts consisting of prominent local landowners acting as Trustees who managed routes around the country. In 1777, coinciding with the enclosure of the Forest of Knaresborough, the Skipton to Harrogate road was turnpiked. Users were charged at strategically placed toll houses and the money raised provided funds for the creation and repair of roads.

Thomas Halliday, George Parker and Thomas Holmes each spent eleven days working on the roads for which they received one shilling a day. Two unpaid highway surveyors appointed as overseers were fined by local judges if repairs were not completed satisfactorily. Between 1860 and 1862 repairs to the highways in Thruscross township alone cost a total of £188. This system continued until the Turnpike Trust expired in 1876; in January of that year allowances of £28.10s were made to Blubberhouses, £16 to Fewston, £3 to Norwood and £1 to Timble Great. The eventual expiration of the Turnpike Trust resulted in the sale of many toll houses including that at Blubberhouses for £138 in 1835. It was later demolished. Thereafter the highways were maintained by the Wharfedale Rural Council.

From the 1870s Jonathan Jeffrey kept a grocer and druggist's shop in Blubberhouses. By the 1890s this had been acquired by Joseph Renton, grocer and postmaster who walked daily to Low Mill to leave mail at Sarah Jeffrey's shop. With his daughter Sarah, a dressmaker, he remained at the shop until the 1930s when it was taken over by Sarah. There were no house deliveries. The postman delivered from Otley and people called for their mail. The wall letter box covers the place where the toll bar lever was situated. Despite a spirited effort to retain the post office it was demolished for road widening in the 1960s.

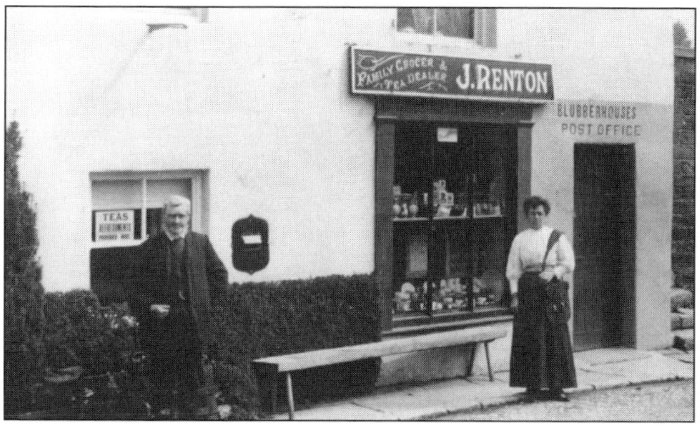

Sarah Jane Eliza (Renton) Steele outside her shop.

CRAGG HALL

Actually a large farmhouse, the hall was situated beside the Harrogate-Skipton road near the head of Fewston Reservoir. It may have been built as early as the sixteenth century when the Manor of Blubberhouses was granted to Thomas Wood of Timble and William Frankland of Fewston. In 1638 the Franklands conveyed it with thirty acres of land and three adjoining farms to the Rev. Henry Fairfax of Newton Kyme, brother of the second Lord Fairfax, General of the Forces in the North and uncle of the third Lord Fairfax, Lord General of Parliamentary Forces in the north during the Civil War, and also known as 'Black Tom'.

Following Henry's death in 1665 the house passed to Edward Robinson of Swinsty Hall who in 1716 sold it with the land for £600 to Stephen Parkinson. Born in 1678, the son of Thomas Parkinson of Denton near Ilkley, he was a yeoman farmer, breeder of horses and owner of a tanning business in the tanyard below the hall. In 1718 he sold hides at sixteen shillings and six pence each to Edward Hudson of Fewston. The tanyard remained until 1850. Stephen, who also planted an extensive orchard at the hall, died in 1766 and the house was then occupied by four successive Thomas Parkinsons, one of whom was the Vicar of North Otterington, near Northallerton, and author of *Lays and Leaves of the Forest*, a collection of local historical and literary essays published in 1882.

Cragg Hall.

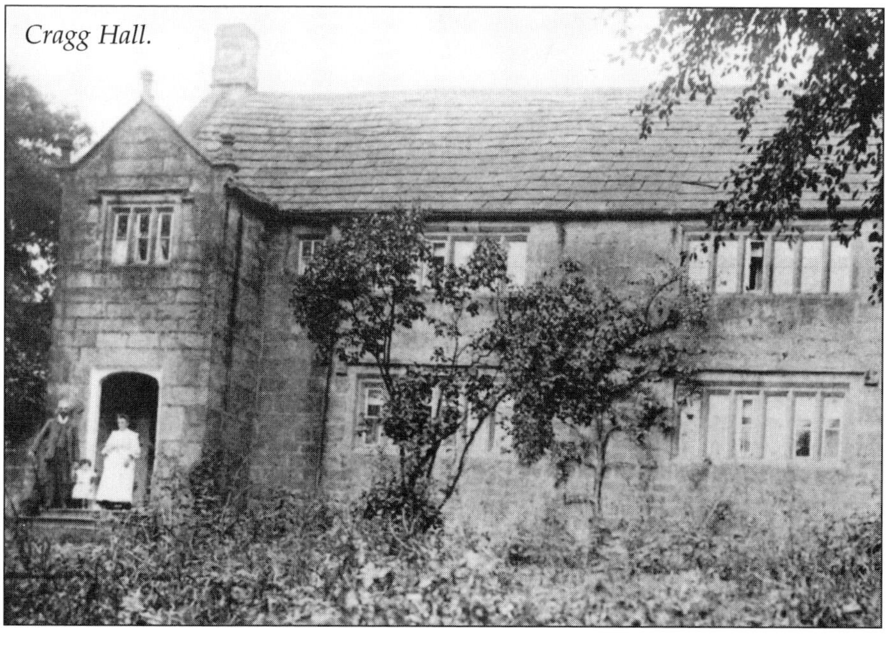

The house has been the subject of several wild theories concerning the identity of a seventeenth century intruder, perhaps even the King, who it has been supposed hid in the chimney at the time of the Battle of Marston Moor. If an intruder was indeed present, it was certainly not the King, who at the time was in Oxford and it seems far more likely that it was in fact a simple burglar.

In the late nineteenth century the house was used for lodging navvies working on the reservoirs. Later it was let to farming tenants including the Watkinson family who lived there from 1893-1910.

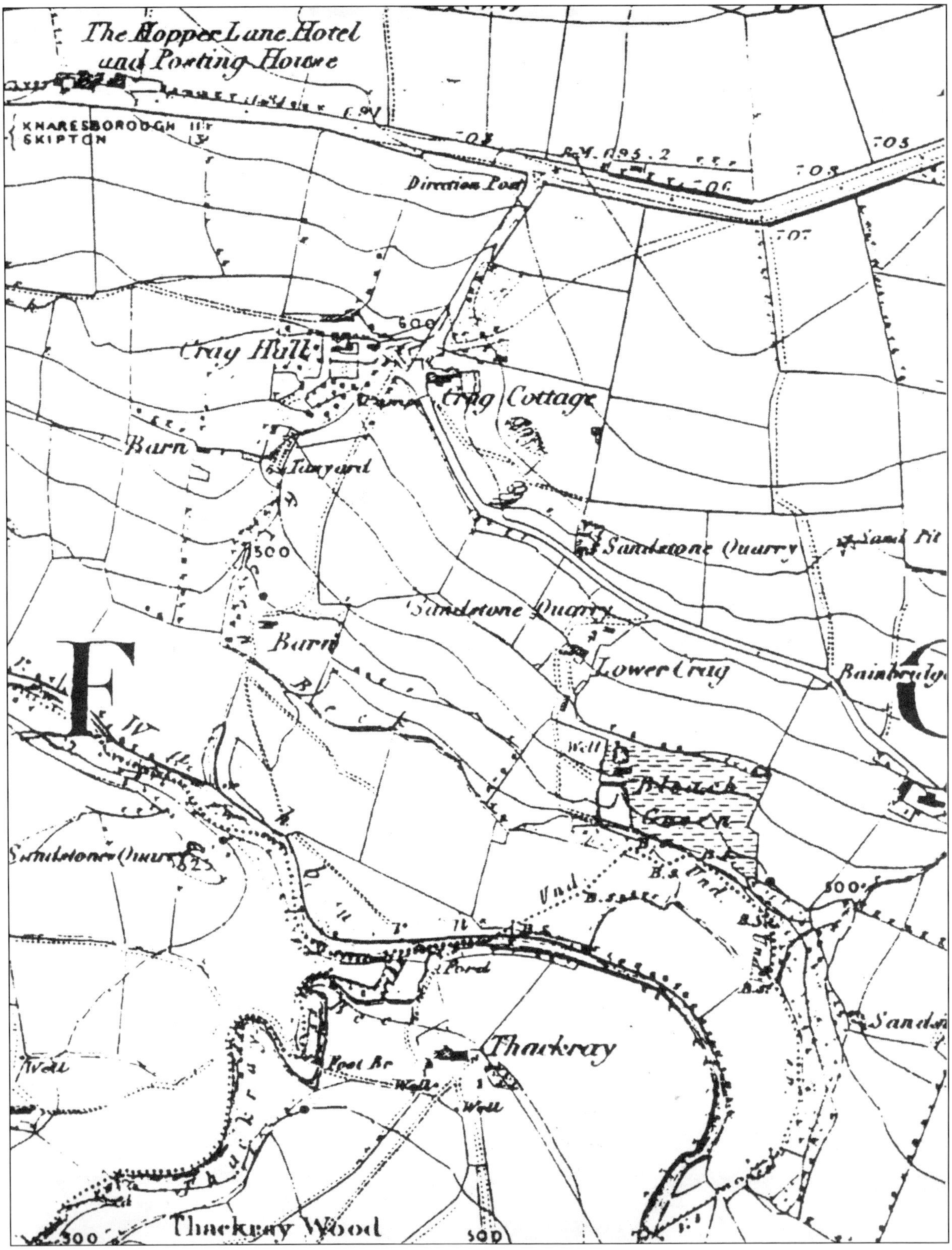

Cragg Hall and Thackray before the reservoir. Note the Hopper Lane Hotel and the A59 at the top of the map, Cragg Hall and the settlement of Thackray.

The house was demolished by Leeds Corporation in 1912 when it was said to be 'practically a ruin' only the front walls remaining. In the late 1950s the stone was transferred to Huby, near Harrogate, and used in the construction of a house. It has been suggested that a door of the house is now the south-west door of Fewston church. (See page 67)

THE LOST HOUSE OF THACKRAY

Described as 'a long, low thatched dwelling with three sets of mullioned windows' it was probably named after the Thackray family. Now under Fewston Reservoir it stood near the confluence of the Thackray Beck with the Washburn. From the fourteenth century it was in the hands of the Pullen family, influential valley land holders. When one member of the family, Richard Pullen died at West End in 1554 his assets apart from his house and land included twenty four cattle, three horses, 118 sheep, 8 stones of wool, agricultural implements, a loom and eight pieces of pewter

SCHOOLS OF THE MIDDLE VALLEY

In the mid-eighteenth century John Jeffrey left an endowment for a school in Brame Lane, Norwood. In 1757 William Hobson was paid eight shillings and sixpence for building work. In 1769 Timothy Ellil (or Ellis) of Brame Hall Farm, Fewston also gave money, the interest from which was to pay for the teaching of 'eight poor children in the English tongue.'

In 1813 a dame school was established at Toad Hole beside the church at Fewston. 'Supported by subscription ... for the education of poor children within the township' of which there were said to be one hundred and fifty to two hundred within 2 miles, one of the teachers was a daughter of the vicar, probably Isabel Gwyther, 'a tall and gracious lady of dignified appearance, with lovely blue eyes and wavy hair in the prime of life. The scholars looked upon her with reverence and awe. She had many a hard battle to fight ... for cleanliness ... but generally proved victorious. The grand secret was that she loved her scholars and they loved her. Many of her pupils came from homes that were crude and rough, and where luxuries were scanty, but she was always labouring to make their lives brighter and happier.'

All the children were taught the 'three Rs' and those whose parents could afford to pay a little more also learned grammar, geography and history. Over the fireplace a 'history map' showed pictures of all the Kings and Queens of England with their dates. The schoolroom was described as 'a big square room, lighted by two windows facing south with an east facing main door. It extended over two cottages, one of which was occupied by a saddler's shop, the other by a waggoner. Immediately inside was a small bowl and 'leather sponge' for washing, the water coming from 'a small sunk well across the road.' Opposite the school 'a man of independent means' and his wife, known as 'the tidy couple', sold soft fruit from their garden, probably at Ivy Cottage.

The Elementary Education Act of 1870 provided for the creation of Board Schools, run by a local school board, funded from local rates and government money. The School Board District of Fewston, also covering Blubberhouses, Great and Little Timble, was formed with seven members in 1878, and a school established on land in Buskey Dike Lane bought from Stephen Beecroft by the United Schools

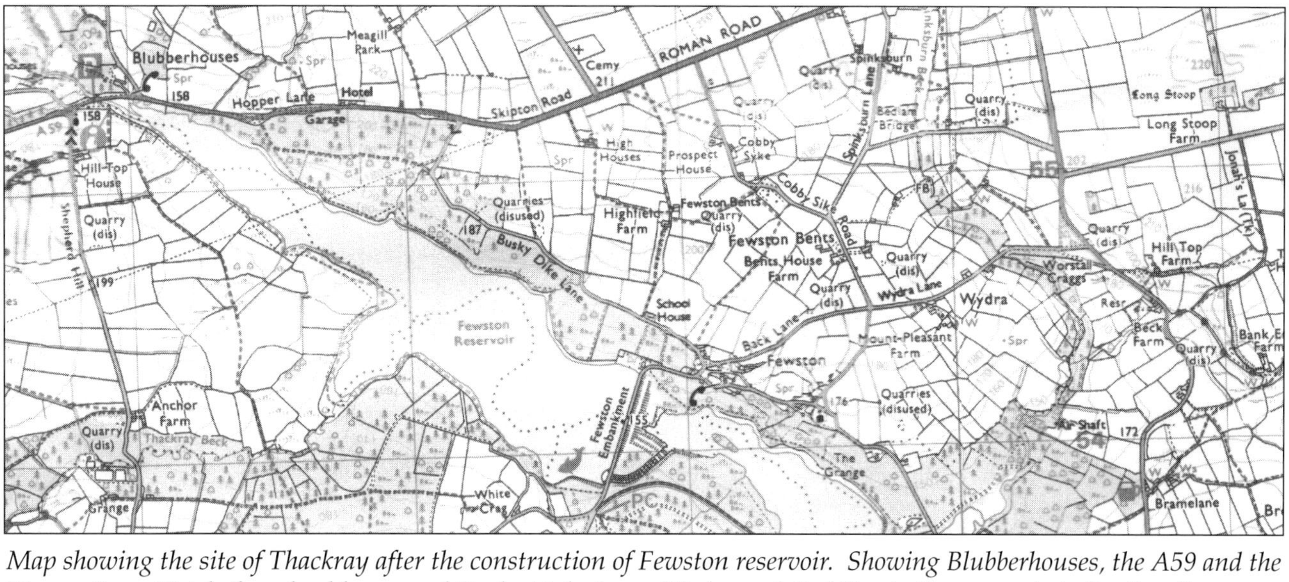

Map showing the site of Thackray after the construction of Fewston reservoir. Showing Blubberhouses, the A59 and the Hopper Lane Hotel; the school house and Busky Dyke Lane; Wydra; a dotted line in the reservoir indicating the course of the river; and an inlet on the south bank (in which there is a boundary stone) near the site of Thackray.

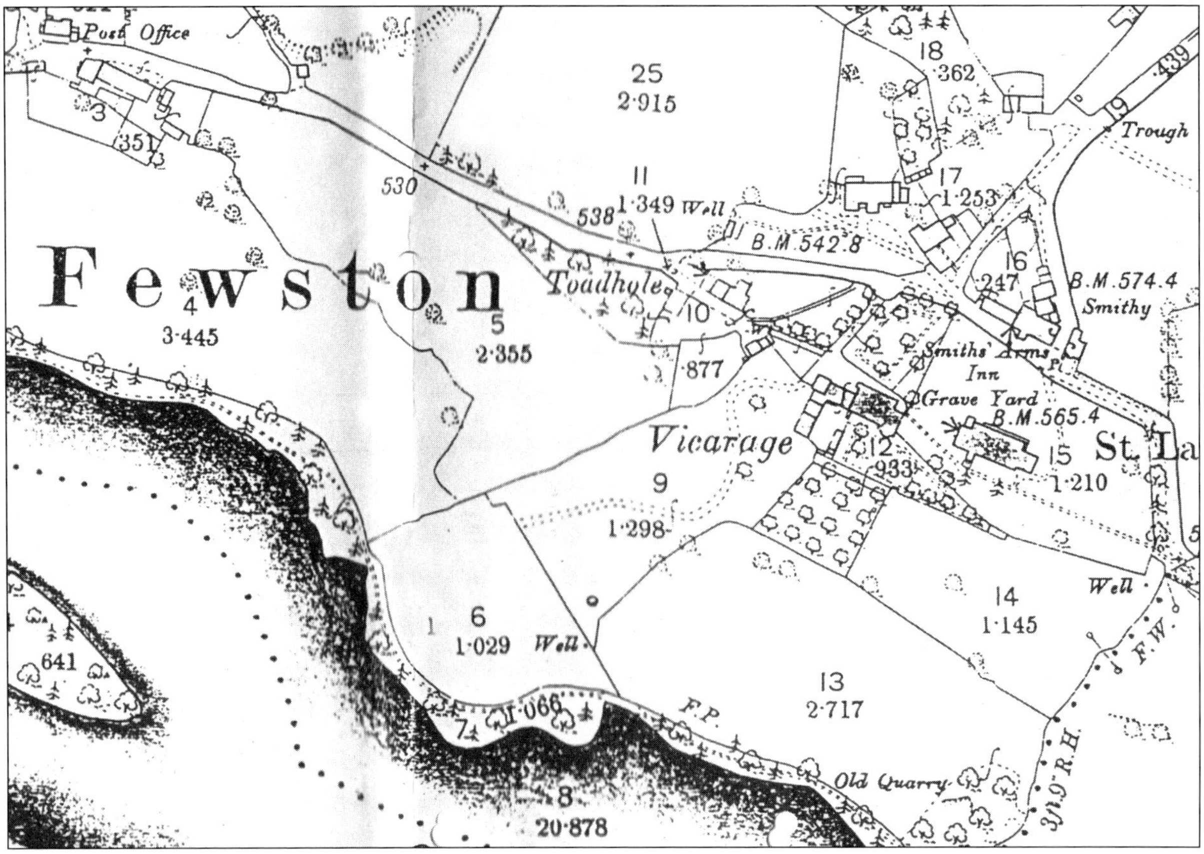

Map of Fewston showing Toad Hole, church, vicarage, smithy, Smith's Arms and the post office.

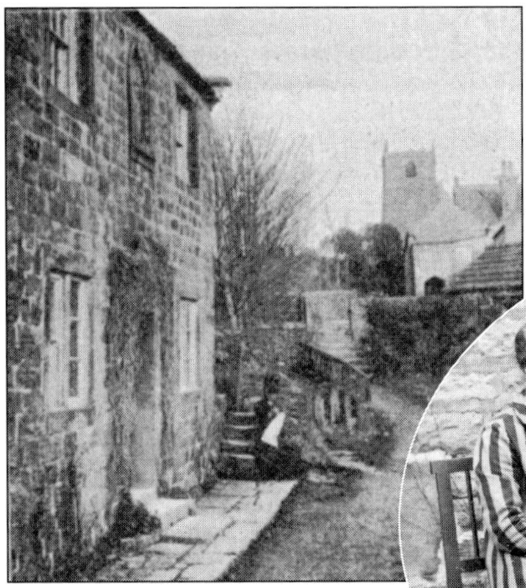

Toad Hole.

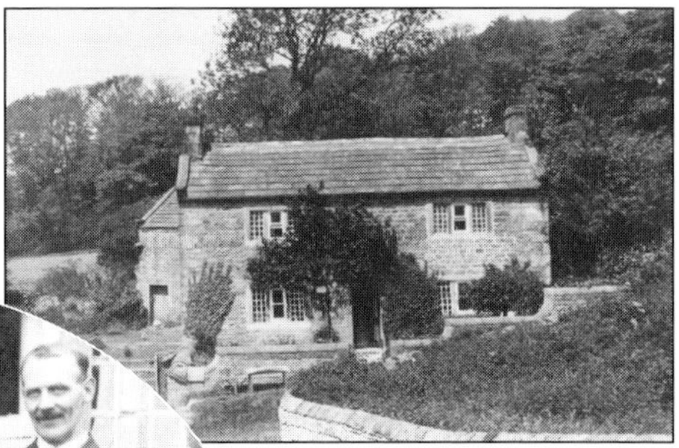

Ivy Cottage.

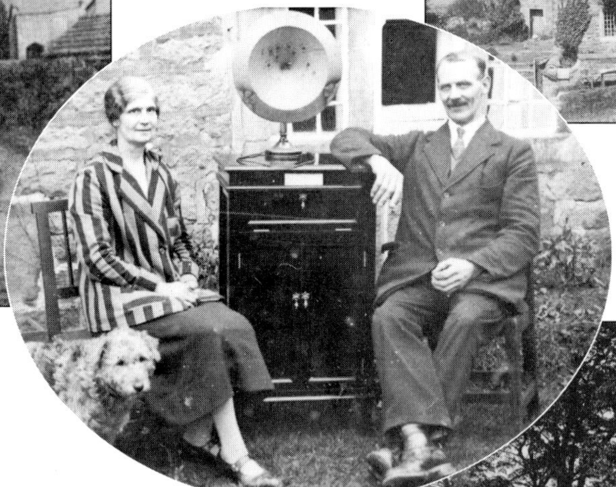

P.C. Cross and his wife at Ivy Cottage.

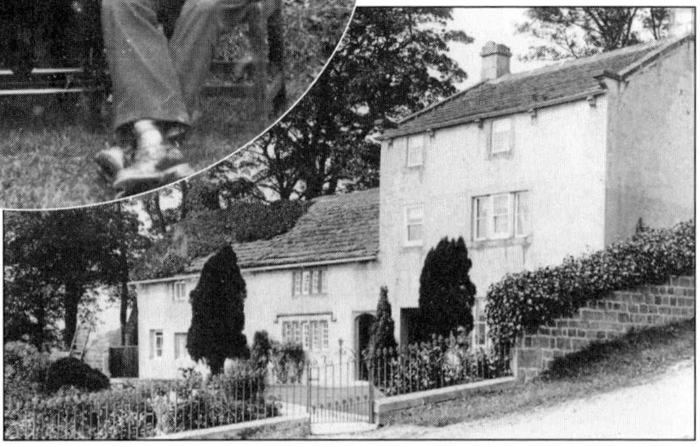

Right: *Grove House, Fewston. Now demolished it was the home of Joseph Helliwell, a teacher at Fewston Board School, his daughter, May, also a teacher at the school, and another daughter, Dorothy, who taught at Timble School.*

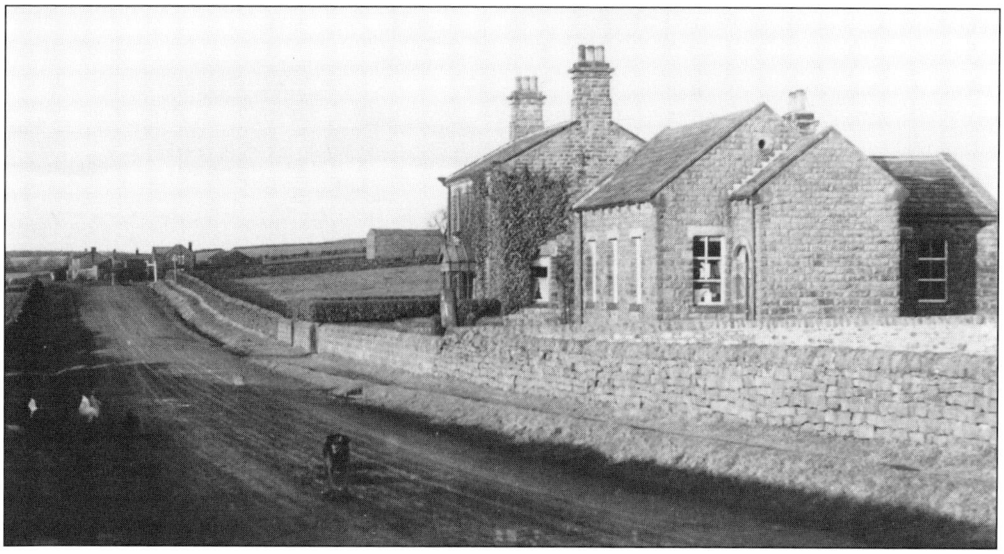

Norwood National School and School House, Bland Hill. In 1811 the Church of England was instrumental in the formation of National Schools. In 1833 the National Society started to pay annual grants for the establishment of a school in every parish providing instruction in religion, reading, writing and arithmetic. In 1875 a schoolhouse was built at Norwood on land purchased from the Duchy of Lancaster. The school closed in 1991 and is now a private house.

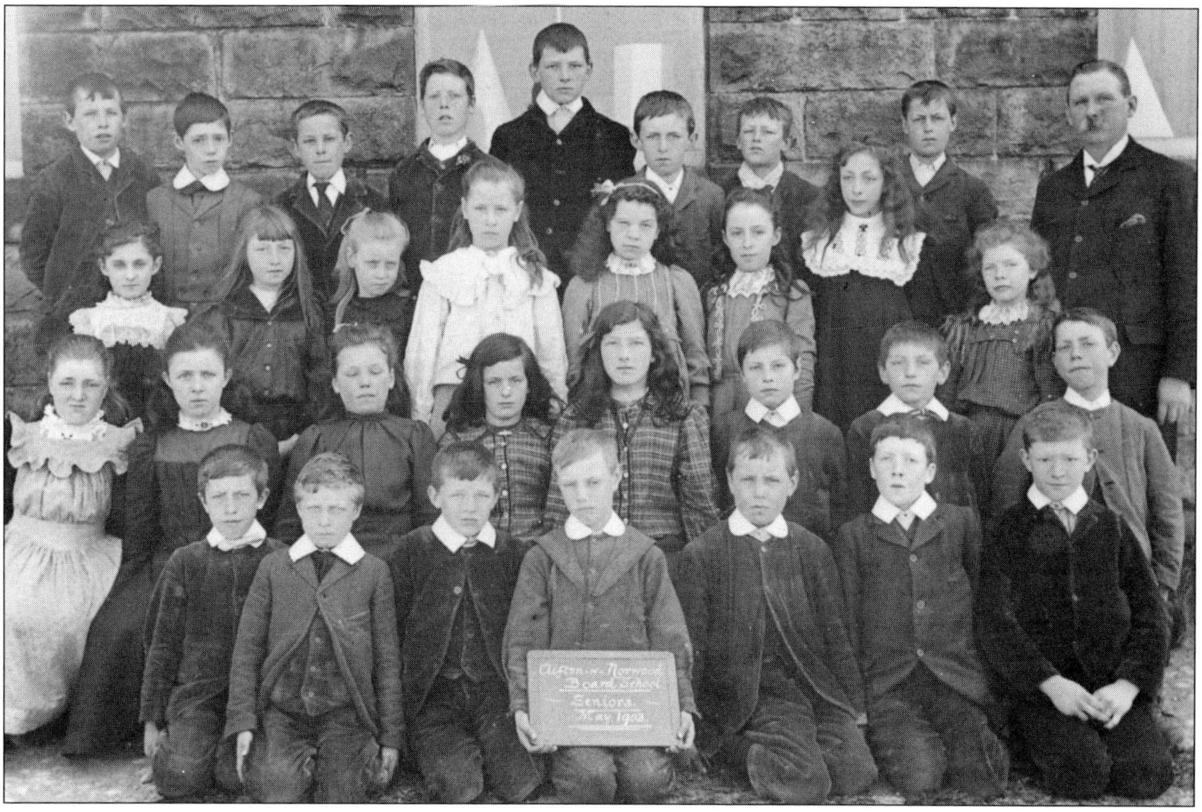

Among the many teachers was William Mackenzie.

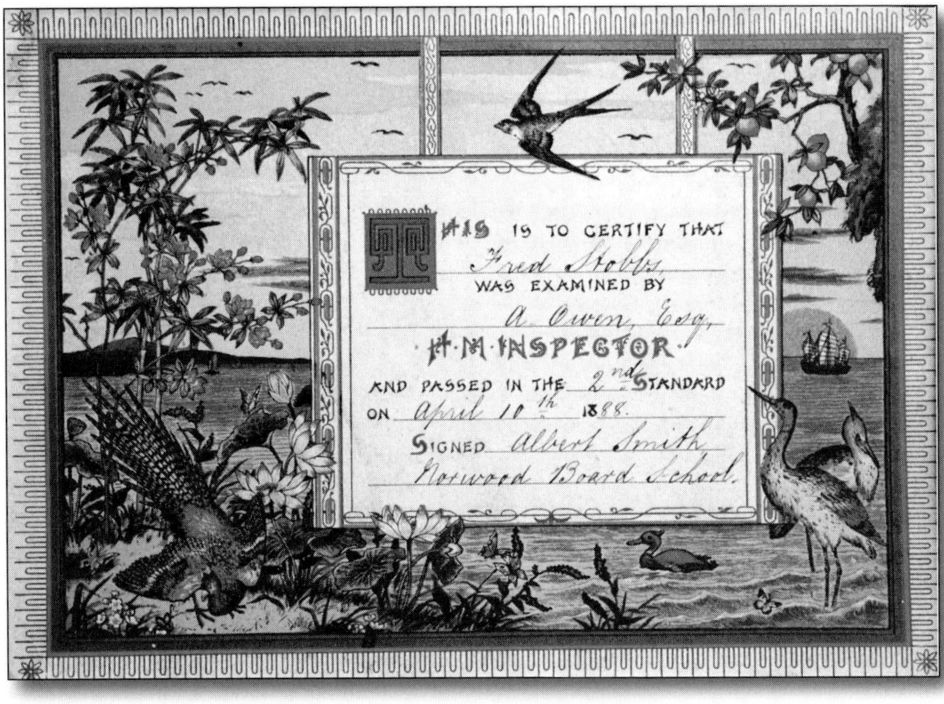

THIS IS TO CERTIFY THAT Fred Stobbs WAS EXAMINED BY A. Owen, Esq. H.M. INSPECTOR AND PASSED IN THE 2nd STANDARD ON April 10th 1888. SIGNED Albert Smith Norwood Board School.

School certificate – Fred Stobbs 1888.

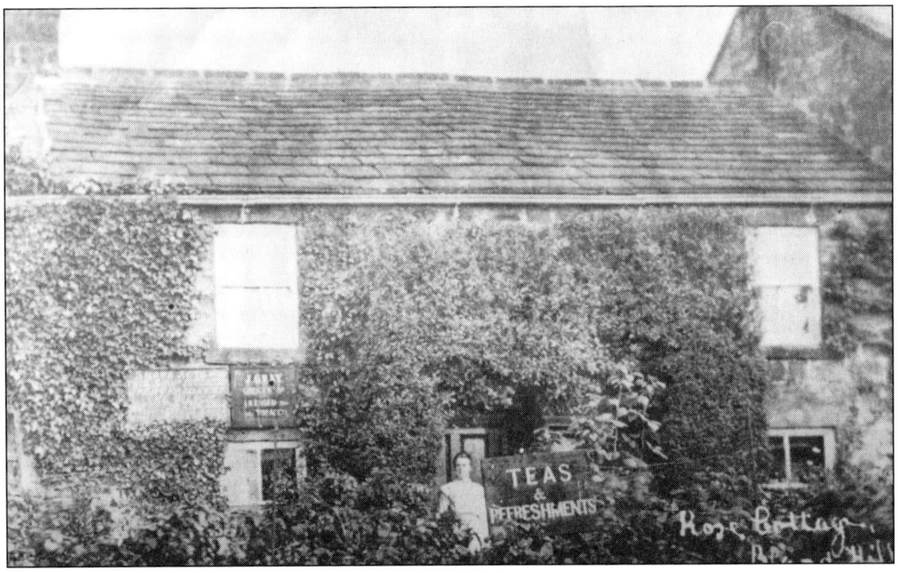

Rose Cottage, Bland Hill. In the 1920s this was the home of Sarah Barrett and her sister, Lily. As well as taking in lodgers and providing teas for walkers and cyclists, Sarah also cleaned at the school and was very vexed when a pupil exploded a tin of Epsom salts on top of the stove causing her a great deal of work.

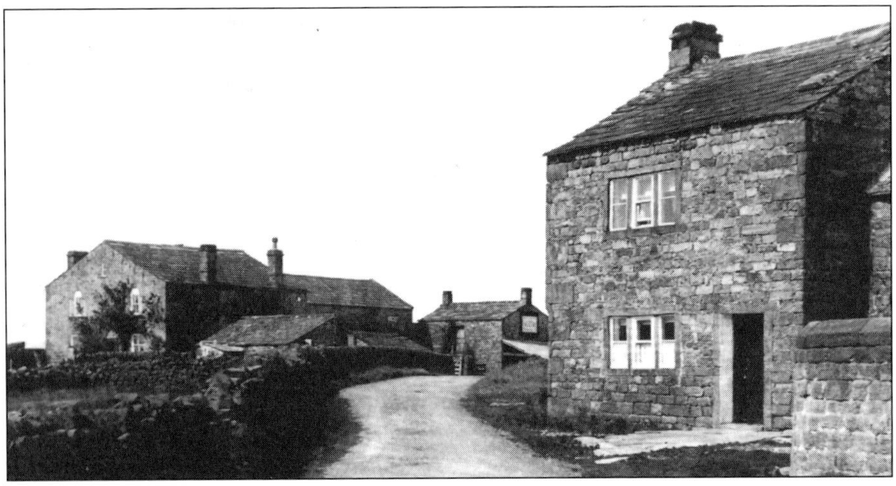

Bland Hill Cottages and forge with sign.

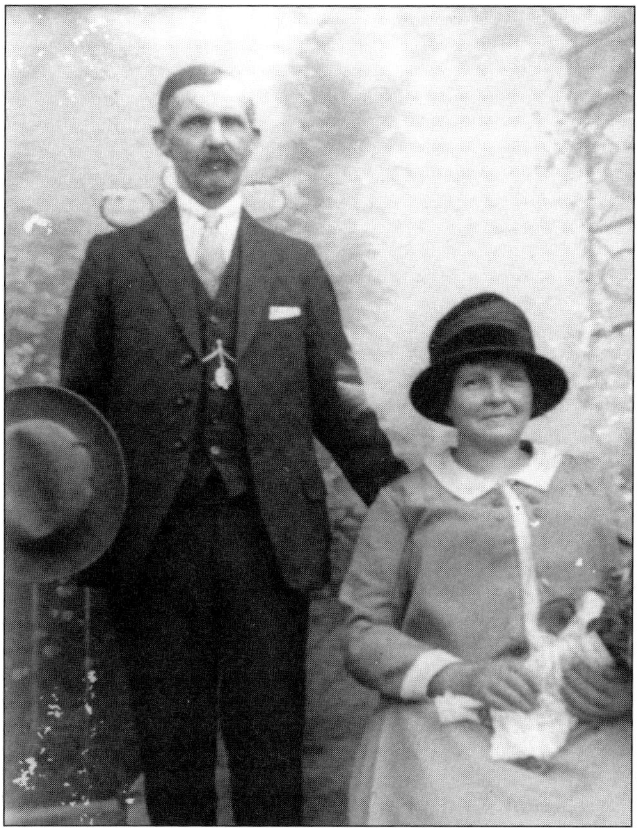

Tommy Hunter and Sarah (Barrett) on their wedding day. Sarah married Tommy Hunter who worked on the roads. When Tommy went to arrange the wedding, the vicar at Fewston told him that he had 'stolen a pearl from his congregation'. Both he and Sarah were most upset, afterwards having to be reassured that the comment was in fact a compliment.

Board. Charlie Petty became Clerk to the Board and School Attendance Officer, better known locally as 't'kid catcher'. John Dickinson was the builder. Charging a small fee for each pupil these schools were initially intended for children between the ages of five and ten; by the turn of the century the leaving age had risen to twelve.

In September 1878 John Dickinson, the diarist and builder of the school, 'dressed up very smart' and went to the school to hear the Rev. Robert Collyer give a lecture on the subject of 'Fewston in 1620 and Edward Fairfax', considering it 'a masterpiece of pathos and eloquence'.

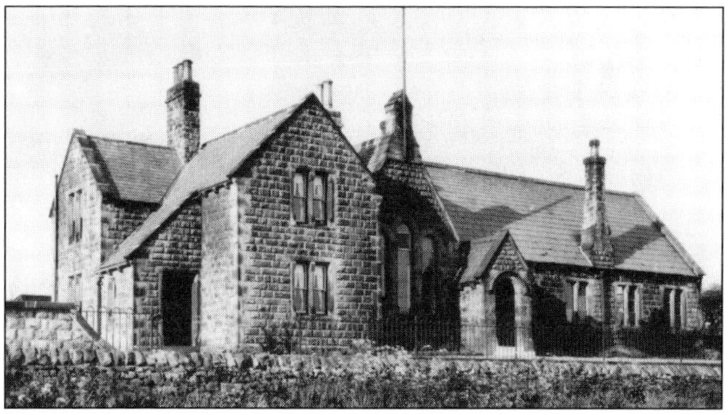

Board School, Busky Dyke Lane.

By the time the school closed in the late 1960s there had been several headmasters including Joseph Helliwell, William Cornelius Benton and Henry Bottomley, and in 1881 the twenty-eight-year-old unmarried James Holmes, who died of typhoid fever tended only by Mrs Dickinson, the mother of John, no one else daring to go near for fear of infection. Between 1889 and 1893 the head was William Thomas Whittaker, followed in 1897 by Walter Bartle.

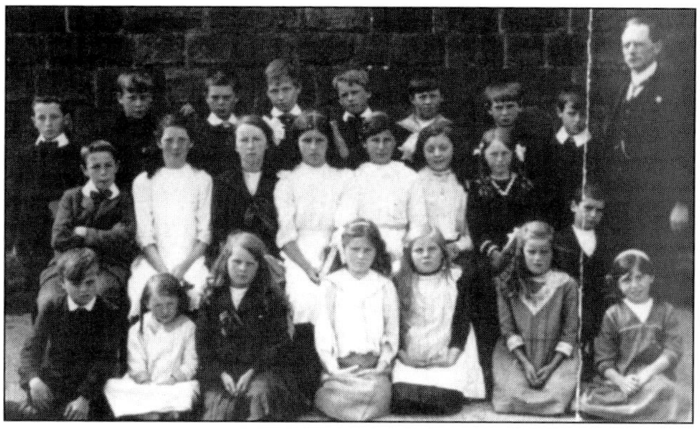

Fewston Board School pupils with their teacher, Harry Ford Mitchell.

A STORM IN A TEACUP

On 5 January 1892 John Dickinson made the following entry in his diary. 'Wrote piece for Otley paper in reply to article in last week's paper which has caused much talk about Fewston'. The article in question concerned a 'school entertainment' in the Board School given by the master, Mr Whittaker, and the scholars, reported in the local newspaper by someone other than the usual correspondent.

There had, it seemed, been a good attendance, the performance was "highly creditable" and the proceeds were to provide an outing in the summer. Credit was given to Mrs Beecroft of Hill Top, Fewston who provided refreshments free of charge, and the account ended with the statement that the occasion's 'success ... [was] very largely due to Mr. Whittaker's especial talent and perseverance in training his youthful performers.' No mention was made of anyone else connected with the concert.

Subsequently there appeared in the local paper an anonymous letter in which the writer complained about the report, having apparently assumed that it had been written by Mr Whittaker himself. 'How does Mr Whittaker make out that there is no honour due to anyone but himself and Mrs A.B. ... the coffee woman' he asked. After all, he argued, there were others who deserved more praise including 'Miss Thackwray, who not only lent her piano but presided at the same ... [and] what about the decoration ... by the sewing mistress?' The correspondent ends 'I would sooner have paid a shilling to see the decoration than have paid 6d. to hear Mr Whittaker's husky voice'.

This letter was followed by yet another, this time from Mr Jerome Petty accusing the letter writer of spite and malice, and challenging him to put his name to any subsequent correspondence. At this point John Dickinson intervened. 'Your correspondent, who so spitefully complained of the distribution of praise, is entirely wrong in charging Mr Whittaker.' Praising him for his efforts he concludes 'it is well known that there is not a person in the district who can sing a comic song as well.' As for Mrs Beecroft, 'she richly deserved all that was said in her praise as the bright, happy faces of the children testified.'

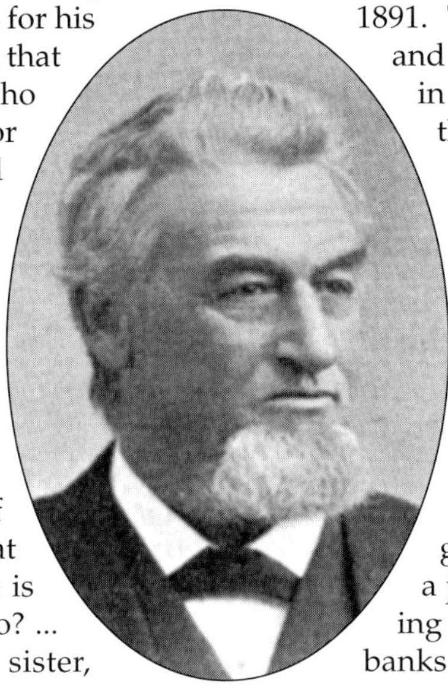
Robinson Gill.

At this point Mr Whittaker himself felt obliged to 'take up the cudgels' on behalf of Mrs Beecroft. 'If Mrs. Beecroft ceases to bestow her generosity in such a manner on account of the insult so ignominiously hurled at her, will [he] repair the loss, or if he is not a bachelor, allow his wife to do so? ... Let [him] imagine his wife, or sister, providing school children with refreshments, and then ... be termed the "coffee woman".' He also added that as one of the 'decorators' of the hall, it would have been 'imprudent' for him to have proposed a vote of thanks to himself. Finally he challenges the anonymous author to send him the shilling promising that he will not disclose his identity but will acknowledge receipt through the press.

The letter signed 'Wm. Thos. Whittaker, Board School, Fewston, 5 January 1892' had the following postscript from the editor. 'If any reply is forwarded by our anonymous correspondent, he must now send his name and address for publication.' There was no further correspondence.

THE SCHOOLS AT TIMBLE GREAT

In 1778 at the time of the enclosure of the Forest, 'a parcel of land' amounting to about 2 acres was awarded to the 'poor at Fewston and the school of Timble Great'. In 1815 this school was presumably that referred to by the vicar of Fewston as the 'antient school' held 'in a cow house', probably an outbuilding at Timble Ridge Farm. Run by Edward Marshall, it was for a time attended by Robert Collyer in 1817.

A second school situated in the building which is now the Wesleyan Methodist chapel, received a grant of £22, the remainder of the funds being raised by public subscription. Most of the building work was done by local farmers and the first schoolmaster was Willie Hardy succeeded by Edward Marshall and afterwards by John Robinson of Knaresborough.

THE ROBINSON LIBRARY AND FREE SCHOOL, TIMBLE GREAT

The third school was founded by Robinson Gill in 1891. The son of William Gill, a stonemason, and a former Miss Robinson, he was born in 1829 the eldest of five sons educated at the Dame School at West End and then at Timble.

In 1851 he was apprenticed to his father, a blacksmith and former pauper apprentice. Robinson left his mark on at least one house in the valley – a stone at Shaw Hall, Low Snowden bearing his name and the date 1848. Four of the Gill sons, including Robinson, eventually emigrated to America where he worked as a journeyman mason, eventually becoming the owner of two stone yards on the banks of New York's East River where he is said to have employed 300 men. Astonishingly he also became the President of two New York banks.

On the 15 August 1889 he called on John Dickinson to 'talk on the question of him building and endowing a reading room for Timble' in gratitude for everything given to him in his early life. The building was intended to serve as a free school, a social centre and a library in the hope that others would be able to rise as he had. In addition to endowing the building, Robinson also provided £100 worth of books.

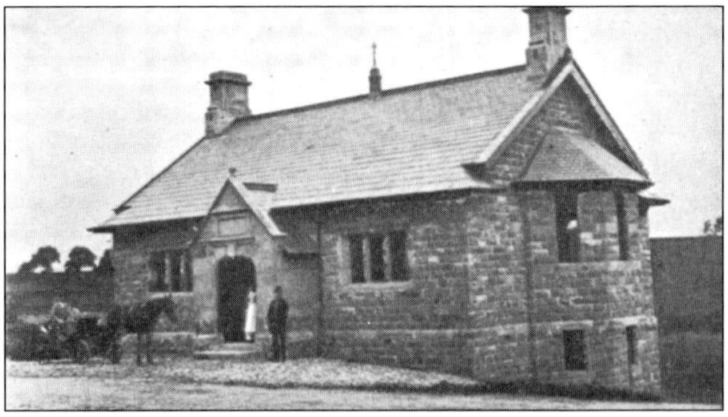
Robinson Library.

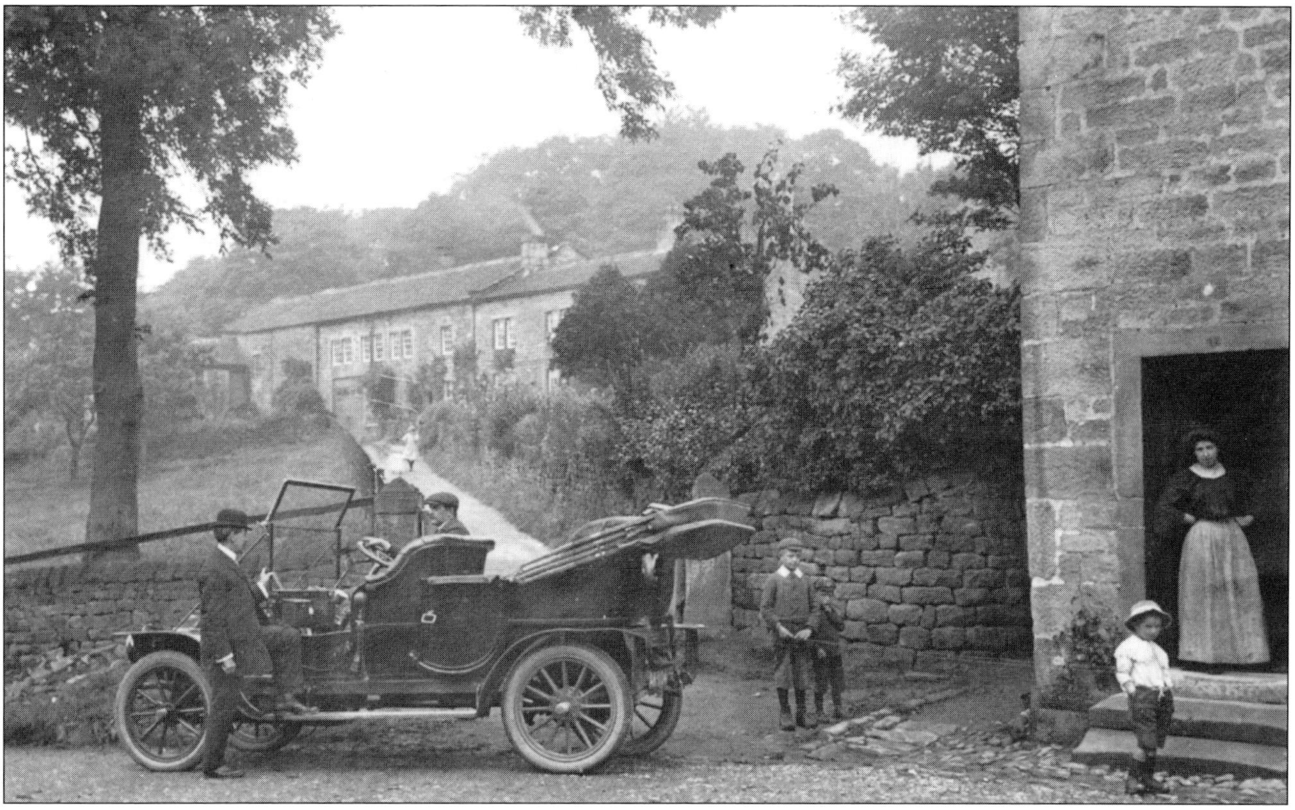

Bridge Cottages, Blubberhouses. One of these cottages was the home of the Gill family.

The school was built at a cost of £861.8s, by John Dickinson who also became one of the first trustees and on the 2 August 1892 the Robinson Library and Free School at Timble for the residents of Timbles Great and Little, together with Low Snowden, was opened by Robinson, recorded by John Dickinson as 'a great day for Timble'. After the ceremony, at which Robinson apparently delivered 'a noble and eloquent discourse', both he and Robert Collyer dined at John Dickinson's home. 'We felt it an honour to have Mr. Gill, the large-hearted philanthropist, and [Robert] Collyer, the man of brain and genius in our humble abode.'

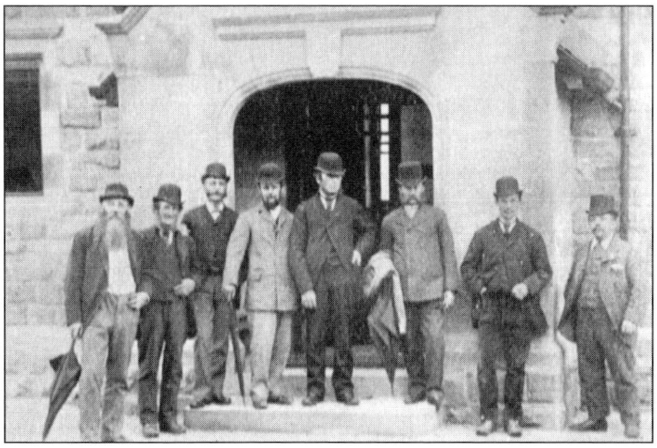

Trustees of the Robinson Institute. John Dickinson who described himself as 'small boned, ten stones, heavily whiskered but who shaved only his chin' may be the third man from the left.

The school began with sixteen pupils, the first head teacher and librarian being Mrs Ellen Elizabeth Barnes who received a salary of £40 per year. In addition the building became the centre for a host of social events including billiards, bagatelle, whist drives, reading, debates and a children's Christmas concert. Unfortunately within five years the school ran into financial trouble when the company in which the endowment fund was invested suffered severe financial difficulties. Robinson having by that time died, the trustees approached Robert Collyer, and a wealthy member of his American congregation generously gave the school $2000 allowing it to continue until 1932 when the children transferred to Fewston School, a move initially opposed by villagers because transport provided for the children at Low Snowden, was not extended to those at Timble Great.

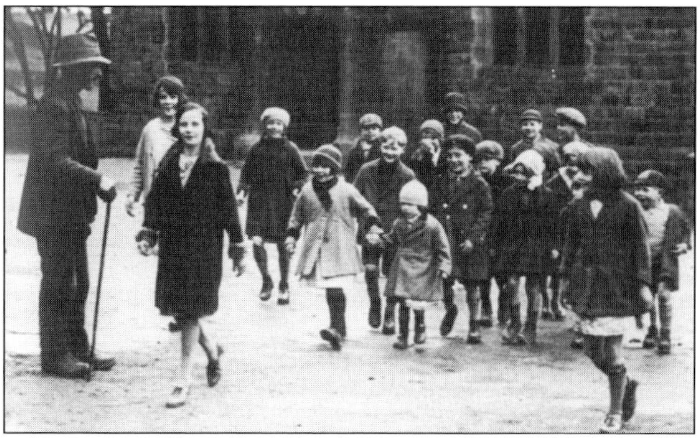

Strike at Timble School.

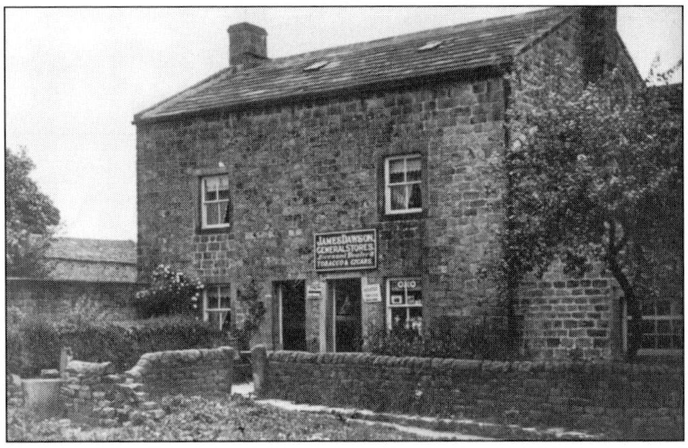

Dawson's shop, Timble Village.

Indeed one villager, George Marjerrison, brought the children 'out on strike' in a successful protest.

WILLIE HARDY/HARDISTY – A VALLEY SCHOOLMASTER

By far the best known of the Washburn schoolmasters Willie Hardy, or Hardisty as he was also known, began teaching in the 1820s. Born in 1808 in the house of Joshua Hardisty, the parish clerk, he was the son of Joseph Hardy and Grace also a teacher, perhaps at the Blubberhouses Dame School. At the age of two Willie became paralysed for no apparent reason, saying that he went to bed well and next morning was unable to walk. Probably because his disability precluded most other forms of employment, he began his teaching career early continuing until his death, and is said never to have missed a day's work.

Initially he taught in a thatched cottage at Fewston, possibly at High Bents Farm, the home of Jerome and Jane Petty, launching three of his pupils, Robinson Gill, the Rev. Robert Collyer and the Rev. Thomas Parkinson on distinguished careers. This suggests that he was not among those disabled teachers described in 1846 by an inspector of schools as being 'neither intended by nature nor fitted by art for the situation in which they are placed.' Over a period of fifty years he taught at various locations in the valley.

Willie's principal teaching aids seem to have consisted of a long stick with which he could chastise any pupil, a ruler often thrown at any boy who was misbehaving, and a three-wheeled chair in which he propelled himself around the room. His salary was made up of the three, four or six pence a week he charged each boy, his income supplemented by tax collecting and helping the local farmers. He was also responsible for surveying the township and naming the owners or occupiers of each field. An accomplished musician, his violin playing was in great demand at local feasts and fairs to which a friend carried him piggy-back fashion, often over miles of moorland, to play at dances for a halfpenny a dance. According to John Dickinson, 'A man of sound, practical knowledge, and a most industrious and competent teacher' he died in 1879 aged seventy-one.

THE CHURCH OF ST MICHAEL AND ST LAWRENCE, FEWSTON

It is believed that there have been at least three churches on this site and the early dedication to St Michael suggests that Christian worship may go back many centuries. Although there is no record of a church at the time of the Domesday Survey in 1086, this does not mean that one did not exist. The base of the tower has evidence of a church on the site from at least the Norman period.

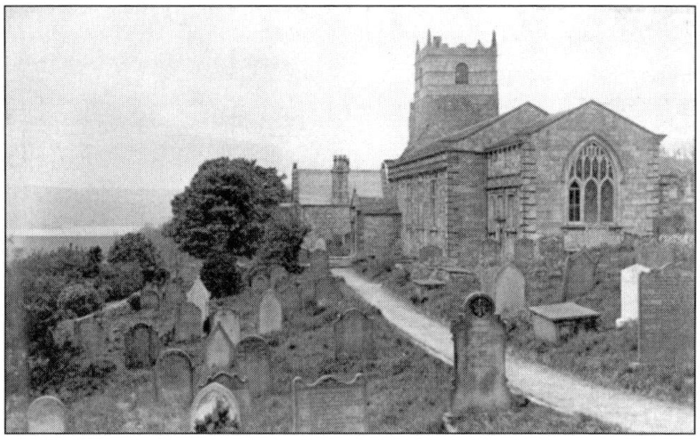

Church.

The first recorded rector of Fewston was William Plesitz in 1234, and in 1280 Edmund, Earl of Cornwall, cousin and lieutenant of Edward I, granted the advowson (the right to appoint a priest) to the Trinitarian Friars of St Robert's Friary, Knaresborough. In 1318 the Friary was destroyed in a Scottish raid, but in 1344 the advowson was recovered by Edward III and his wife, Philippa, obtaining a licence for the friars to claim the parish tithes and other endowments of the church. Despite the fact that the Friary was surrendered in 1538, Fewston continued to be served by one friar, Robert Gibson, until at least 1545 when the tithes of the church amounted to £10.10s.0d a year. Afterwards these rights passed into private hands.

The sixteenth-century church is said to have had a nave, chancel, west gallery, north aisle and clerestory, misericords, a three decker pulpit, a marble monument to Edward Fairfax and what was described as a 'patterned vault.' A chantry of 1521 was dedicated to St Mary the Virgin, and in the will of George Pullen of nearby New Hall dated 1557, money was left to pay for this 'so long as there is a priest synging at our Lady Aulter at Fuston'. The words 'so long' are probably an indication of the uncertainty which must have surrounded the church during the religious upheaval of the mid sixteenth century.

The Pullen family, long established in the valley, supplied at least one priest for the church, John, in 1571. However by 1575 it seems that the church was not in good condition for the chancel windows were reported to be 'in greate ruyn and decaye'. In 1635 a private 'stall, seate or pew' was granted to Elizabeth Brearey, widow of John Brearey of Scough Hall, and to Charles Fairfax and Mary his wife, daughter and heir of John. The pew was said to be 'two yards long and four feet in breadth ... situate in the east part of one little quier, cell or dormitory ... commonly called the Lady Quier, or Little Quier.'

In 1637 orders were issued that an 'auncient church way for goeing, riding and carrieing corpses ... from the towne of Timble unto the Parishe Church of Fuiston ... be laid open, and sufficient gaites and stiles be maid by all and everie of the owners or occupiers of the landes ... in and over their severall walles and fences ... upon paine of every person or persons making defaulte herein to forfeit to the quenes Majestie the sum of xxs.' [20 shillings.]

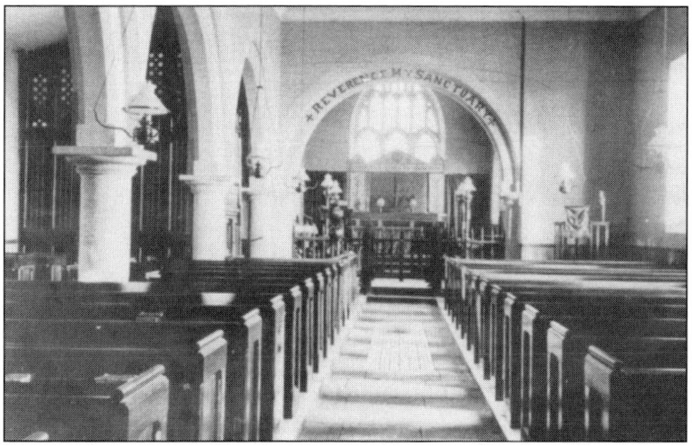

Church – interior.

With the exception of the tower, which was extended in 1809, that church was destroyed by fire in 1696, and the present church, Perpendicular in style, was built in 1697. Grade II starred by English Heritage it has several unusual features. Firstly, it is one of only a few seventeenth century churches in Yorkshire and as such is said to be of outstanding national importance; secondly, it was built in the medieval style with a nave and clearly defined chancel, rather than on the more usual rectangular plan of the period and thirdly, its classical construction is unique among churches in the area, suggesting that the design may not have been influenced locally.

The stone shaft beside the interior tower arch is believed to date from the twelfth century and the font with its Jacobean oak cover from the late seventeenth century. The Royal Arms are of George III and the catechism boards probably belong to the eighteenth century.

It has been suggested that the south west door originally belonged to the demolished Cragg Hall but no documentary evidence has been found to confirm this claim. However the description of 'a stout oak studded door with nuts and bolts ... planks double and fastened together by considerable large shield-headed nails' certainly describes the present door at Fewston which consists of a once more elegant outer section of which the decorated hinges appear to be an integral part. A middle section of stout vertical planks and an inner section of horizontal planks serve the dual purpose of strengthening and enlarging it. Although the outer sections of the door would have needed enlargement to fit the church doorway, it seems probable that this modification was made in its previous location because the door has a 'spy hole' about 5 inches by 6 inches, a structure that would not be needed in a church door. This opening, which is now sealed, penetrates all three sections suggesting a domestic purpose. The story that the door was marked with 'bullet holes' accords with the presence of numerous small holes around the 'spy hole', some containing metal fragments which may have been made by lead shot.

It was believed initially that the south east door, formerly visible only on the exterior, was purely ornamental, but removal of the chancel panelling in 2012 revealed that it did indeed give access to the chancel, and that the base of the door was level with that of the old chancel beneath which two Fewston vicars, the Rev. William Carmalt and the Rev. Thomas Bolland were buried in the early eighteenth century.

The church has undergone several restorations, most notably in the early nineteenth century when the tower and north aisle were raised at an estimated cost

Fewston Parish Magazine.

FEBRUARY, 1911.

Extracted from the Parish Church Register and Old Vestry Book :—

1830.

Half-year's Accounts

	£	s	d
The Stove pipes reparing	1	5	7
Ling, and leading	0	3	0
John Wilkinson for Bell Ropes	1	10	0
Letters postage	0	3	0
Christopher Watson for Church cleaning, lining washing, oill etc.	1	10	10
Ringers half years Salry	2	2	0
Allowance to the same	0	8	0
Violin reparing	0	14	0
To persons extinguishing the fire in Church	0	4	0
John Ward's Smith Bill	0	5	8
Allowance at Accounts making	1	4	0
4	9	10	1
Each Township's Share =	£2	7	6¼

(Fewston, Blubberhouses, Norwood, Timble Great.)

Thomas Parkinson, John Beecroft, William Myers, John Moorhouse, Churchwardens.

Half-yearly account for church 1830.

of £750. In 1844 following the arrival of the Rev. John Gwyther further alterations were carried out including the erection of a west gallery to provide another fifty seats. However in 1884, during yet another restoration, this was removed together with the old pulpit and box pews, the latter being replaced with those now present. In the mid 1980s there was a fourth major restoration of the church fabric.

The church has six bells, four cast by Thomas Mears of London in 1808 and restored in 2001; a further two were added in 2010. The clergy stall is in memory of William and Myra Hill who had a connection with the valley, and the hymn board is in memory of Harry Simpson Gooch, a popular lay reader. The main altar, replacing an old table, was presented to the church in 2009 by the Friends of Fewston Church, as was the wooden cross in the Lady Chapel in 2012. In 2010 part of a stone cross was discovered when the old hearse house at the north-west corner was demolished to create the Washburn Heritage Centre. This has been incorporated in the new cross which now stands outside the centre.

The graveyard contains several curiosities. Most famous is the stone opposite the porch recording burials of the Ridsdale family on the 30 February 1802, as well as on the 29 February 1823, which was not a leap year. Another stone records the displeasure of the Lister family when Ann, widow of George of Timble Great, was refused burial in the family vault in 1897 because the graveyard had been closed by the Home Office the previous year. The stone records the 'perceived omission of the churchyard authorities'. On the 2 October 1908 after prolonged negotiation, a new graveyard was opened a mile north of the church at Meagill Lane although it does not appear to have been consecrated until 1910.

SOME VICARS OF FEWSTON AND THE VICARAGE

After the Dominican order at Knaresborough ceased to provide rectors for Fewston, the Archbishop of York in 1351 ordained that a vicar should be appointed, and that 'a competent mansion' should be provided.

It is not known when the first vicarage was built but in 1786 it was said to contain 'three bays' 27 feet long by 13½ feet wide, with two rooms to a floor. There was also said to be 'a closet, a milk house and two stone-built chambers covered with straw and ling thatch.' In the Victorian period a large wing was added to the original house. Fanny Dickinson, the wife of John, remembered the gardens as 'pictures of beauty.' Near to the house, and possibly attached to it, was a three-bay stone barn thatched with ling. A stone trough, which remains, was probably adjacent to this barn. (See p.60.)

Surrounding the church were approximately 24 acres of glebe land stretching southward from the village and the cottages at Toad Hole, as far as the River Washburn. In 1536 this land brought in an income of approximately £11.6s.6d a year for the maintenance of the priest. He was also eligible for half of the rental income from two further sizeable portions of land elsewhere in the valley.

In 1900 following the construction of the reservoirs, the writer J. S. Fletcher noted considerable subsidence which had begun to occur on the hillside around the church.

'The stranger finds an exploration of the village productive of strange sights and curious surprises. Here he meets with some ancient houses gabled and timbered, the walls of which are cracked and split from top to bottom; there he comes across another which has so far removed from its original position as to challenge comparison with the Leaning Tower of Pisa; further on he will find himself gazing on a third, which after various crackings and bendings, has finally collapsed in a heap of ruins.'

In the vicarage it was said that 'there was scarcely a wall or ceiling ... that was not cracked' and that the vicar's summerhouse, 'on the knoll at the bottom of the lawn' was 'gradually slipping from its moorings'. In 1927 when the vicar of Austwick, Aubrey Cunliffe Sutcliffe, became vicar, a member of his old congregation remarked that 'Mr Sutcliffe is going to an outlandish place where the vicarage has been condemned and he is going to lodge in two or three rooms in a house owned by Leeds Corporation.' Despite this, the house was still occupied in the 1930s when it was the home of an artist who in the Second World War eventually moved to live at the Timble Inn and the Sun Inn. Following an appeal a new vicarage was built on land nearby given by the Corporation, now the privately owned Fewston House. This building served the parish until 1967 when it passed into private hands.

In all a total of thirty five vicars have served the church at Fewston, most leaving little trace of their existence. In 1504 the then vicar, Friar Thomas Parysh, was 'assaulted during Divine service' by Henry Wilson of Fewston. In court it was revealed that Wilson had failed to pay the customary mortuary, or sum of money from the estate of the deceased, to the vicar. As a result Parysh suspended him from attending church whereupon Henry reportedly called him 'a false friar' and shook an axe

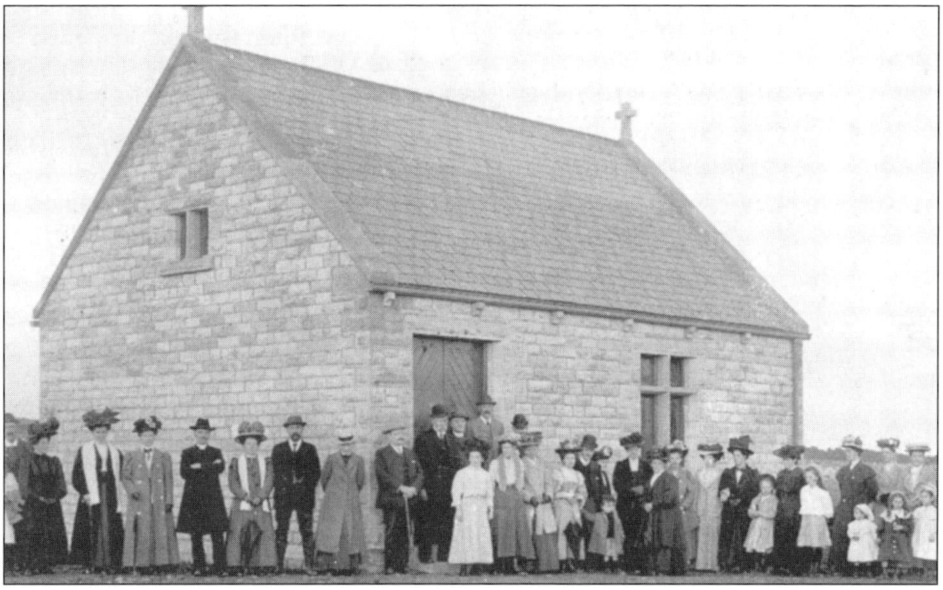

Consecration of new Fewston burial ground at Meagill Lane. 19.4.1910 'a lot of folks turned up and the ceremony was quaint and interesting' John Dickinson. Among those attending were the Bishop of Ripon, and the vicars of Fewston, St Margaret's, Ilkley, Thruscross and Hampsthwaite.

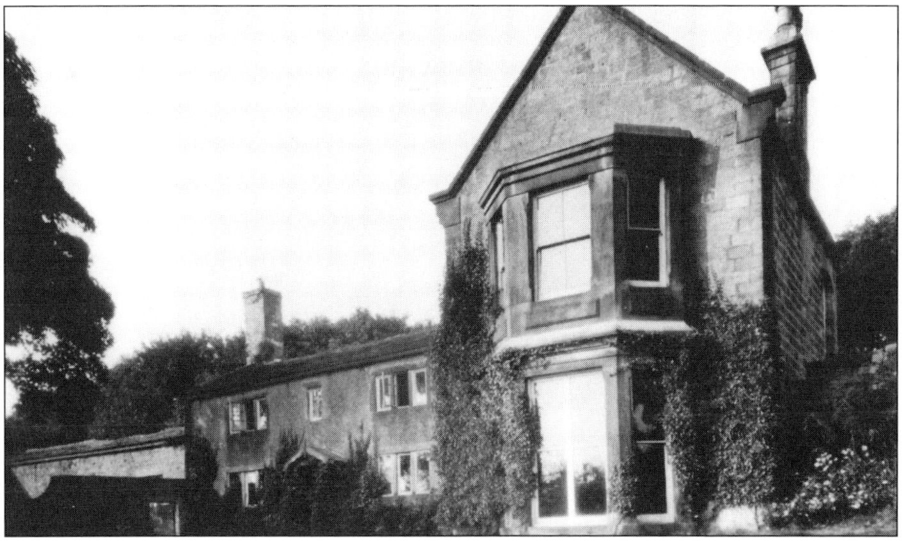

The Old Vicarage.

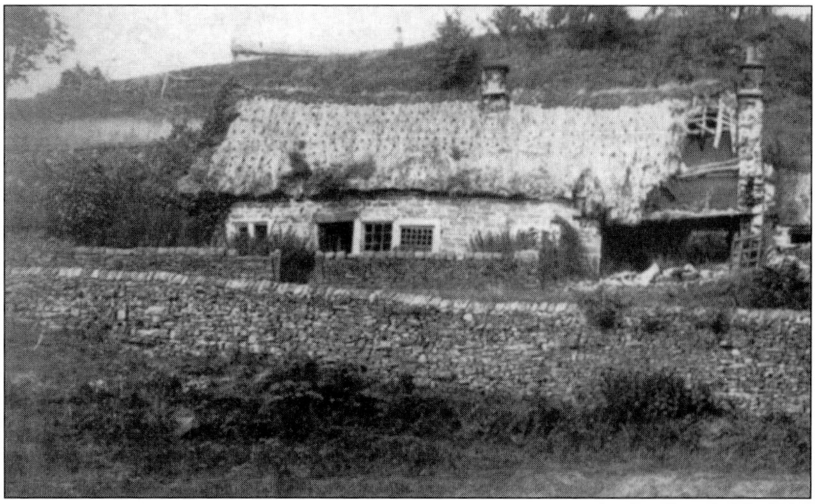

Benson House, Fewston. One of the buildings damaged by subsidence.

in his face saying 'If thou suspend me, I shall give ye with this axe that thou shalt suspend me no more.' Informed by Parysh that he would not do 'divine service and ye be in the kirk' Henry replied 'Thou art a false curate, and whoremaster.'

Another sixteenth century vicar, John Pullen, was accused of allowing an alehouse to be kept in his vicarage, and of 'frequenting the company of another man's wife'.

Contrary to popular belief church attendance in the past was not always regular. In 1743 Thomas Burton reported that he had begun to 'Catechise in Lent ... when I can get any Children to come before me, but the Parishioners are very slack in sending [their] Children.' Nor had matters improved in 1764 when his successor, John Whinnerah commented 'The parishioners do not send their children and servants to be catechised as I could wish.'

In 1790 Mr Whinnerah was succeeded by Christopher Ramshaw. Born c.1761 Christopher was the son of Richard of Scorton, North Yorkshire and had held a curacy at Thurcroft in South Yorkshire before serving as vicar of Fewston between 1790 and 1843. In 1804 he married Elizabeth Curtis of Otley with whom he had seven children. Dying at the age of eighty-two in 1843 he had perhaps been unable to serve his parish adequately in his later years for a letter from the Lord Chancellor to his successor, John Gwyther, states that the 'living was much neglected by your predecessor.'

Beside the church porch is the imposing table tomb of the Rev. John Gwyther, '28 years Vicar of the parish'. John, born in Bristol in 1801 and educated locally, was a graduate of St John's College, Cambridge, and the unfortunate subject of a short story published in *Blackwood's Magazine* of 1857 entitled 'The Sad Fortunes of the Rev. Amos Barton' by George Eliot, the pen name of Mary Anne Evans. Before being appointed to Fewston he had served a curacy at Chilvers Coton in Warwickshire, where Eliot was baptised. Known for drawing her characters from real life, she had used him as her model for Amos Barton, a man of 'strong views' whose chief 'sin' seems to have been a certain lack of tact in the introduction of reforming measures resented by his parishioners. John's eldest daughter recognised the resemblance to her father, and following a letter from him to the editor, Eliot, who had believed the clergyman to be dead, was obliged to send him a letter of apology. John's first wife, Emma Wilson, died leaving him with seven children, and in 1849 he married a local girl, Mary Ann Hobson, with whom he had a further nine.

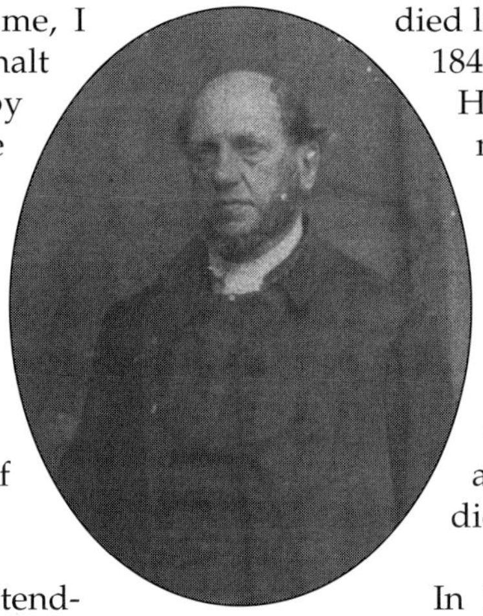
The Rev. John Gwyther.

Fanny Dickinson described John as 'one of the best [vicars] Fewston has ever had. A sound practical man of good ideas, a clever preacher and half doctor; all the parish went to him in times of sickness for medicine and advice, which was given gratis.' John died in 1873 aged seventy-two.

In 1873 John Gwyther was followed by John Marks Ashley 1828-1909. Born the son of Henry Ashley, a lawyer, at Langham Place, London in 1828, his family later moved to Greenhithe, Kent. Educated at King's College, London and the Royal College of Chemistry, between 1848-1855 John became a lecturer in Chemistry at the Hunterian School of Medicine, the foremost eighteenth century private school of anatomy. Ordained priest in 1858, in 1866 he married Ellen (née Tibbits) at St Mary's, Greenhithe. Before coming to Fewston he held two curacies, at Swanscombe, Kent and at St Peter's church, Brighton. In 1873 he moved to the fashionable St Peter's church, Vere Street, London, now the Marylebone Chapel, once considered 'the most beautiful edifice of its class in the metropolis', but for unknown reasons stayed for only two years before moving to Fewston and a dramatic change in his lifestyle.

Ashley wrote many works on theology, including the 'Commentary on St Paul's Epistle to the Ephesians', and also some poetry, but his academic disposition is said to have rendered him unsuitable for the life of a country cleric in a remote parish. 'He is a fine classical scholar and can talk well, but that is not what is wanted here' remarked John Dickinson in 1899. He did however succeed in teaching two boys from the village school Latin and Greek, one of whom was perhaps his son, Cyril, who became a clergyman and who, on at least one occasion, returned to preach at Fewston. John's powerful and successful sermons brought large congregations from the valley and beyond, his last 'farewell sermon being very affecting ... the vicar wept and so did we. Twenty seven years is a long time, and we had known him closely.' The couple had three sons and a daughter, Edith, who with her mother organised popular musical gatherings in the valley. John died at Malvern in 1909 aged eighty.

THE VOICE OF DISSENT

The Quaker movement founded by George Fox in the middle of the seventeenth century usually took hold in remote areas where it could develop unhindered by manorial or religious control. The movement appealed in particular to the upper working classes, or 'middling sort', who were disillusioned by the religious turmoil of the sixteenth and early seventeenth centuries.

In Yorkshire the movement was divided into fourteen monthly meetings, the Knaresborough meeting encompassing the Washburn Valley where it apparently had only a small following.

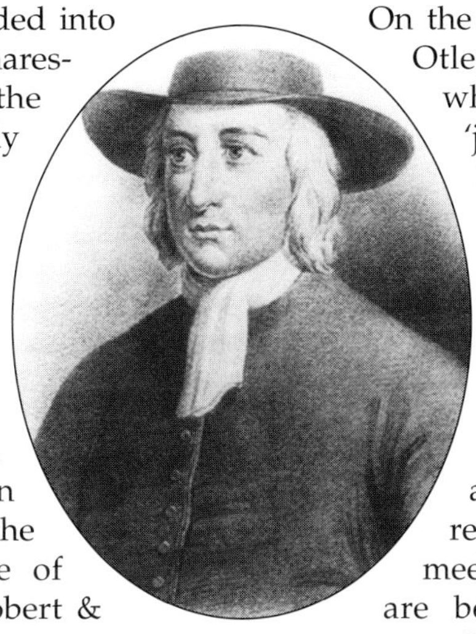

George Fox.

Quakers were routinely distrained, often heavily, for a variety of transgressions including the holding of illegal conventicles, which in 1664 and 1665 were probably held in the home of Jeremiah Wilson of Timble. In the early 1670s several families in the valley were actively involved in the Quaker movement including those of William Bradley of Timble Little, Robert & William Smith of Fewston, Nicholas Pawson and Thomas Pape of Farnley, John Bainbridge of Lindley and, in Thruscross, the Moores and the Simpsons of Redshaw Hall. In 1682 John Barber of Leathley was committed to prison for four months for meeting at Weston on the edge of the valley although it was later reported that he 'was never at any such meeting ... nor was there any meeting there for ye space of Eight Years and Upwards.' In 1679 William Hill, a farmer of Ratten Row at Thruscross requested burial in 'the burying place of Hardcastle Garth', the Quaker burial ground over the hill in Nidderdale.

Not until the introduction of the Toleration Act in 1689 were licences for meeting introduced, one being granted to Jeremiah Smith of Fewston. In 1721 a similar licence was granted to Christopher Rhodes at 'a house called Sorbyland' now Sourby Farm, Timble.

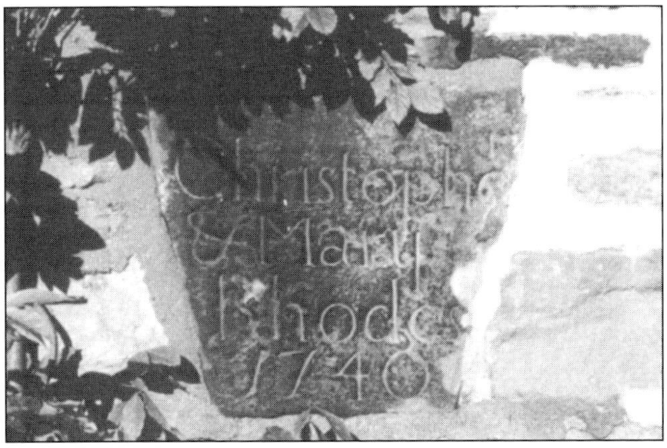

Stone at Sourby Farm inscribed 'Christopher and Mary Rhodes 1740'.

By 1743 and 1764 the Archbishop's visitations show that there were then only three Quaker families in Fewston parish, and it seems likely that the powerful message of John Wesley was already taking over.

METHODISM

On the 6 July 1761 John Wesley preached at Otley before travelling on to Fewston where he found 'one or two more' people 'just ripe for receiving all the promises'. Like Quakerism, Methodism had a particular appeal for a working class population, and by 1763 a small class of eight, six of whom were involved in textile production, became established at Bramley Head. A further thirty seven Methodists were also living at Fewston and Norwood, and by 1764 the Vicar of Fewston reported that about a dozen were meeting at two houses in the parish which are believed to be Elsingbottom Farm, Lindley, and Norwood Hall, home of the Smith family.

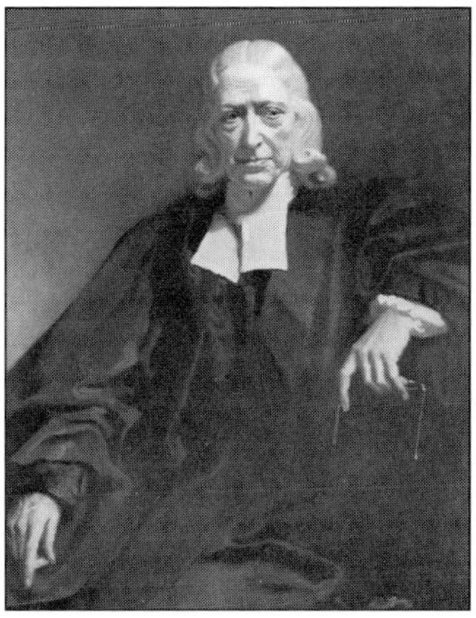

John Wesley.

In July 1772 Wesley again passed through the valley en route for Nidderdale, staying 'at an inn on the moors near Fewston [where] I spoke to the old man, as my wife did to the woman of the house. They both appeared to be greatly affected. Perhaps providence sent us to this house for the sake of these two poor souls.' It is possible that this inn, perhaps no more than a drinking shop, may have been at Moorcock Hall beside the old road between Otley, and Dacre in Nidderdale.

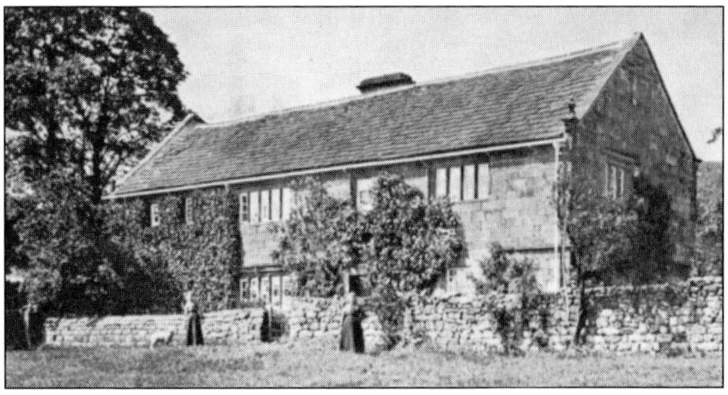

Norwood Hall.

A Deed of Covenant dated 1821 gave permission for John Hardcastle to sell an original meeting house in order to erect a chapel at Fewston. Built in 1825 at a cost of £150 it was first licensed for public worship in 1855. In 1891 Leeds Corporation conveyed the freehold plot to the chapel trustees, and in May 1945 it became part of the Methodist Conference. The chapel closed for worship in 1961 and is now a private house.

A popular occasion in Methodism attracting large numbers of people was a love feast. In 1758 this was conducted at Fewston by the Rev. Thomas Pawson who began with the hymn *'Come, and let us sweetly join Christ to praise in hymns divine'*. The congregation then sang Grace, and pieces of special love feast cake, basically a yeast mixture which differed according to the area, were passed around with a two handled cup of water for which the congregation gave thanks. Testimonies followed, some delivered by 'hearers' reading from the scriptures, reciting a verse, or a hymn. The full service lasted two hours – longer at a special anniversary. Admission to the love feast was by a ticket issued every quarter and checked at the door to ensure validity. If lost or forgotten, admission was at the discretion of the preacher who had to provide written permission.

Itinerant preachers such as 'Halleluiah Tommy'who preached at Fewston on 10 November 1895 served most, if not all, of the valley chapels, although such men were possessed of varying degrees of skill. On the 8 September 1895 John Dickinson reported that Johnny Burnill who preached at Timble was 'a man of considerable natural ability but ... no scholar' and on 20 September 1896, after a sermon from 'an illiterate preacher', remarked that 'such men fill a gap that would otherwise be empty.' A month later on 25 October matters had not improved, Dickinson reporting 'only a poor preacher and I don't feel much benefited.' Others were more able and favourably received. 'Preacher C.J.F. Atkinson whom we had to tea. A very nice fellow.' This may have been the Otley solicitor, and author of *Recollections from a Yorkshire Dale* published in 1934.

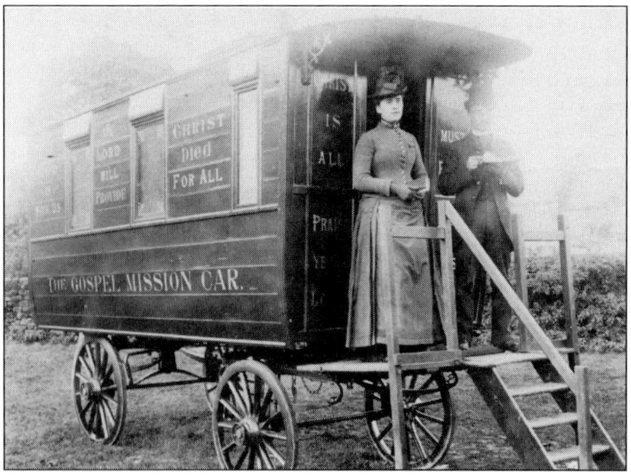

On 31 March 1889 John Dickinson 'went to Fewston Chapel to hear Mr & Mrs Bradford who are visiting places with a mission car.'

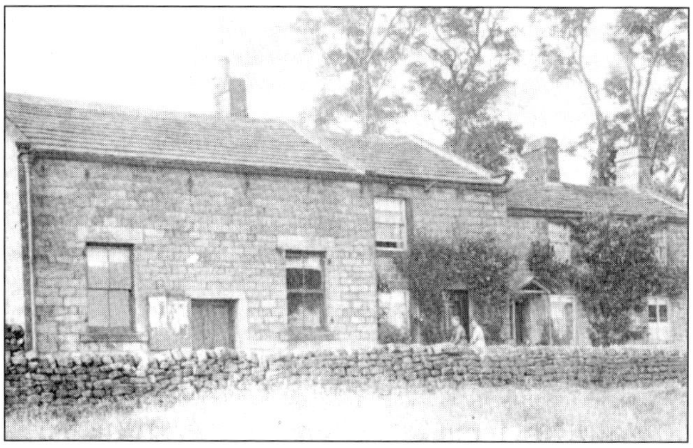

Timble Wesleyan Methodist chapel and chapel house.

At Timble the chapel was built in 1835 with the aid of a government grant of £22, the remainder being raised by public subscription. Building work was done by the farmers free of charge. As there were then few Wesleyan Methodists in the village, the Primitive Methodists initially sent a preacher, and a pulpit was provided by mutual agreement. This situation later changed when the Primitive Methodists declined to hold services unless the chapel was made over to their Conference, and thereafter the Wesleyan Methodists established themselves in the building. Warmed in winter by a stove, the chapel accommodated around fifty people. In 1889 John Dickinson attended a love feast here 'About thirty came from Otley and Timble. Perhaps 40 spoke of their experiences'. By the 1930s the chapel was fully under the aegis of the Methodist Conference. On the immediate right is the Chapel House once the home of John Dickinson's mother-in-law 'Aunt Mary' which passed to John who by then was living in Otley. The cottage was used by him and his wife as a holiday home or for occasional overnight visits.

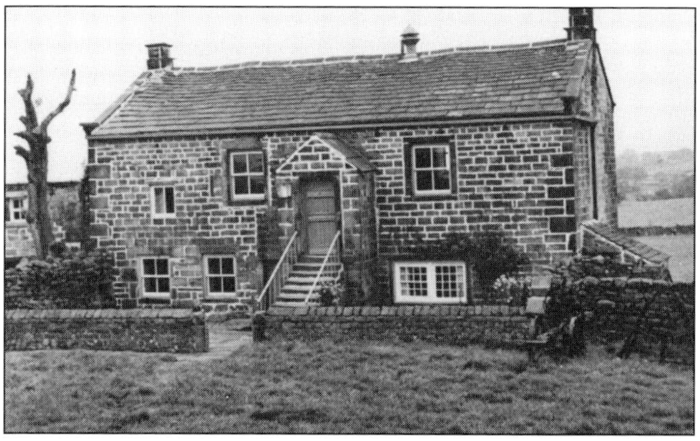

Brown Bank Wesleyan Methodist chapel, Norwood.

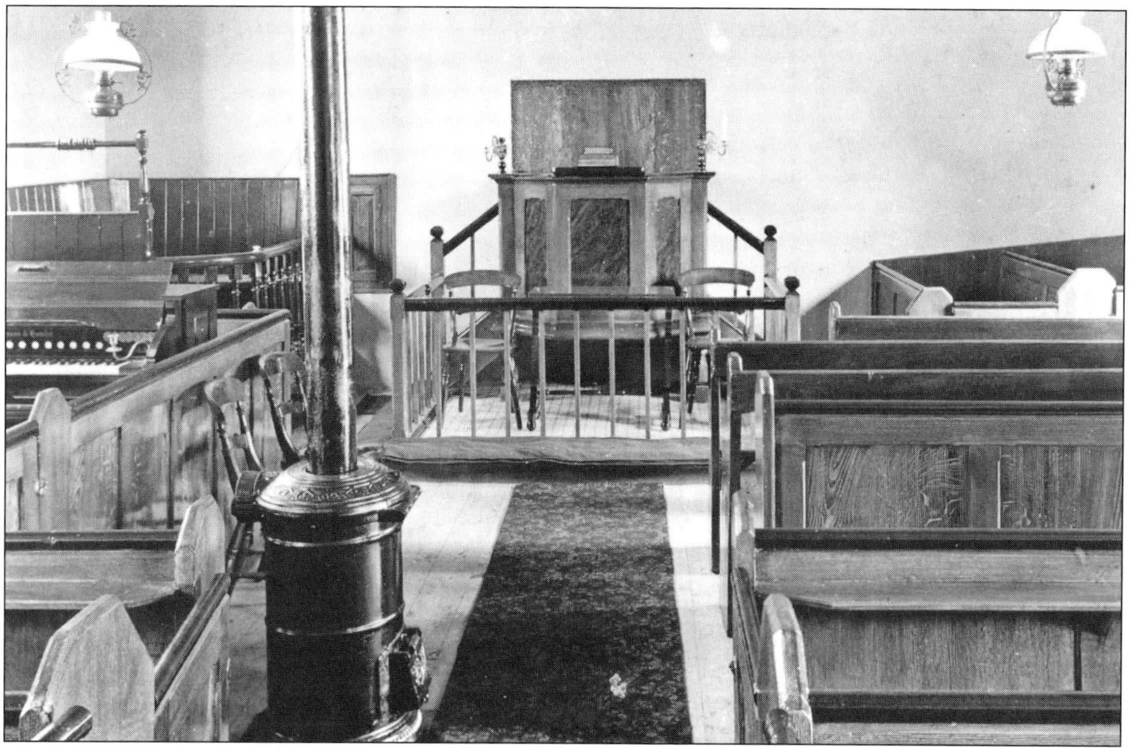

Brown Bank Chapel was founded by Robert Bramley in the first half of the nineteenth century but closed for worship in 1884. The chapel was situated on the upper floor, the ground floor providing accommodation for the caretaker and a Sunday School.

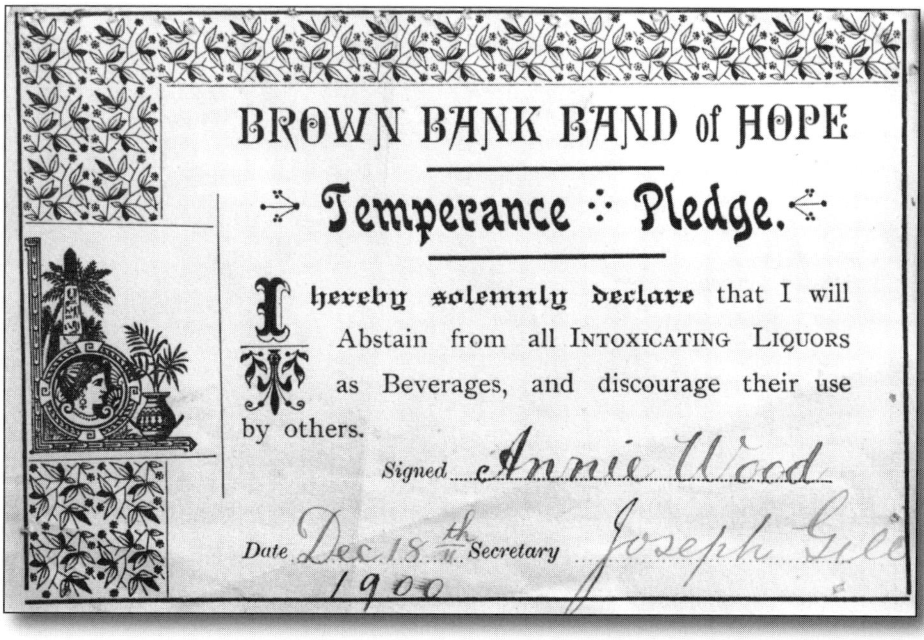

BROWN BANK BAND of HOPE

Temperance ∴ Pledge.

I hereby solemnly declare that I will Abstain from all INTOXICATING LIQUORS as Beverages, and discourage their use by others.

Signed Annie Wood

Date Dec 18th 1900 Secretary Joseph Gill

The Band of Hope was a temperance organisation founded in Leeds in 1840 which advocated complete abstinence from all alcohol for life. The promise to do so by signing the pledge was intended to strengthen the resolve.

Norwood Wesleyan Methodist chapel. Built at a cost of £2000 on land which had been donated, the chapel opened in 1925. As well as meeting at Norwood Hall, in the past it is believed that Methodists may also have met at Elsingbottom Farm.

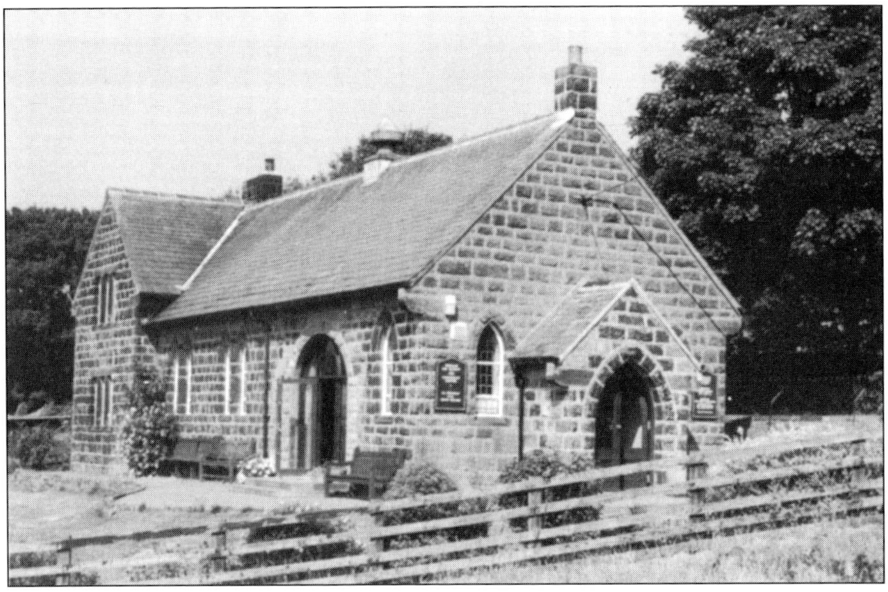

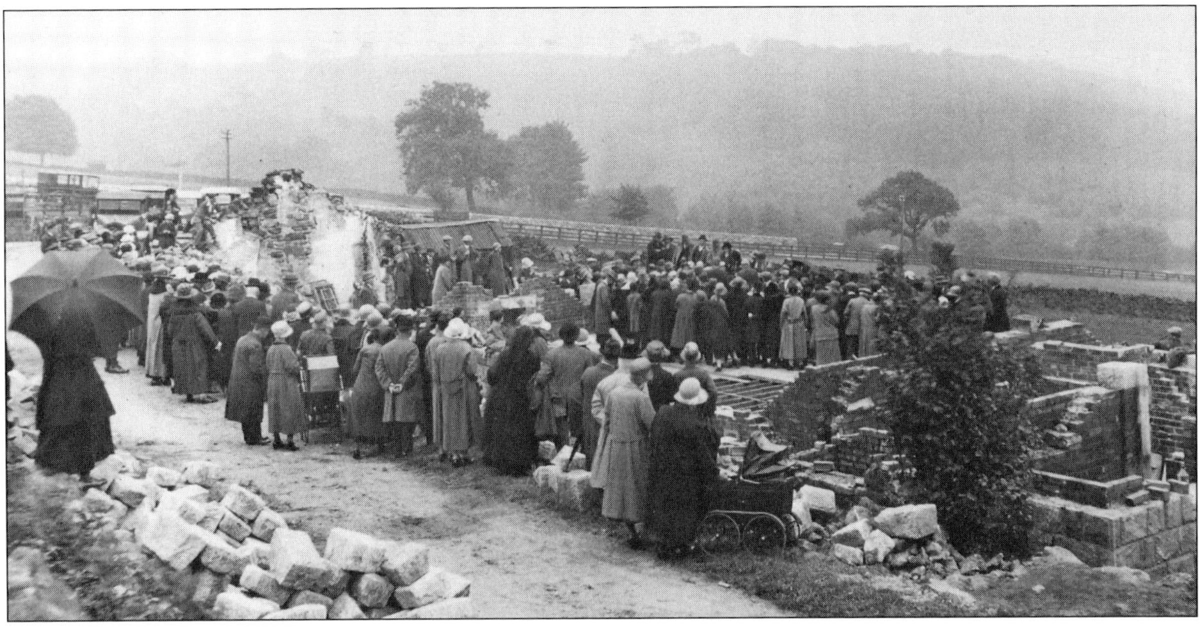

Laying of foundation stone at Norwood Wesleyan Methodist.

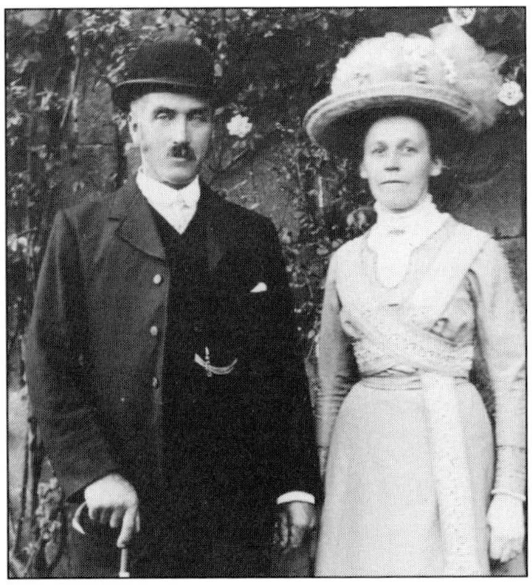

Samuel and Mary Shepherd of Norwood chapel.

Membership of the valley chapels always fluctuated according to the fortunes of the mills but even before the last of these closed down in the 1880s, much of the population had moved away to seek employment in the expanding towns, or even overseas, and Methodism in the upper valley dwindled rapidly. The Norwood chapel which now doubles as a Christian Retreat Centre and the chapel at Timble are today the sole survivors of Methodist worship in the valley.

OLD FEWSTON BRIDGE AND CORN MILL

In 1640 'the bridge commonly called Fewston Bridge ... standing over a river called Washburne, in the parish of Fewston, was presented att the general Quarter Sessions att Skipton to be in great decay. Ferdinando, Lord Fairfax and Ingram Hopton, Esq., two of the Justices ... have viewed the same, and doe certify that the summe of forty five pounds will build a bridge there.'

This bridge was also the site of the ancient soke mill belonging originally to the lord of the Manor to whom all payments would have been made. In practice, however, many mills were leased to tenants who were charged for grinding based on the amount ground.

In 1407 a 'John Milner took Fosteton Mill paying four shillings'. In 1433 John Polayne (Pullen) visited Knaresborough Castle 'to ask to hold the water mill at ffuston' for ten years at an annual rent of forty shillings', for which permission was granted. Four years later, his wife Elizabeth, now a widow, also visited the Castle 'to pray the tenure of the mill.' The tanyard immediately next to the mill may also have been worked by the Pullens for in 1574 a John Pulleyn of Norwood is said to have followed his father's trade of tanner. The Pulleyns certainly worked a tanyard near Folly Hall 2 miles away. By 1822 the miller at Fewston was Aaron Hardcastle who was succeeded by Nancy Moon in 1837, and then by Joseph Moon. Joseph, a bachelor who in 1901 lived at Prosperous House in Fewston where he was known for wearing buckled shoes and knee breeches, also owned mills elsewhere in the North and East Ridings. When Fewston Mill was demolished to make way for the reservoirs, he moved to Topcliffe Mill near Thirsk. He was buried in the churchyard of Bolton Priory.

In 1891 John Dickinson visited 'all that is left of the Moons at Fewston ... formerly 'a family of the first note in the busy village ... now the corn mill is swallowed by the waterworks [and] the trade has passed away.'

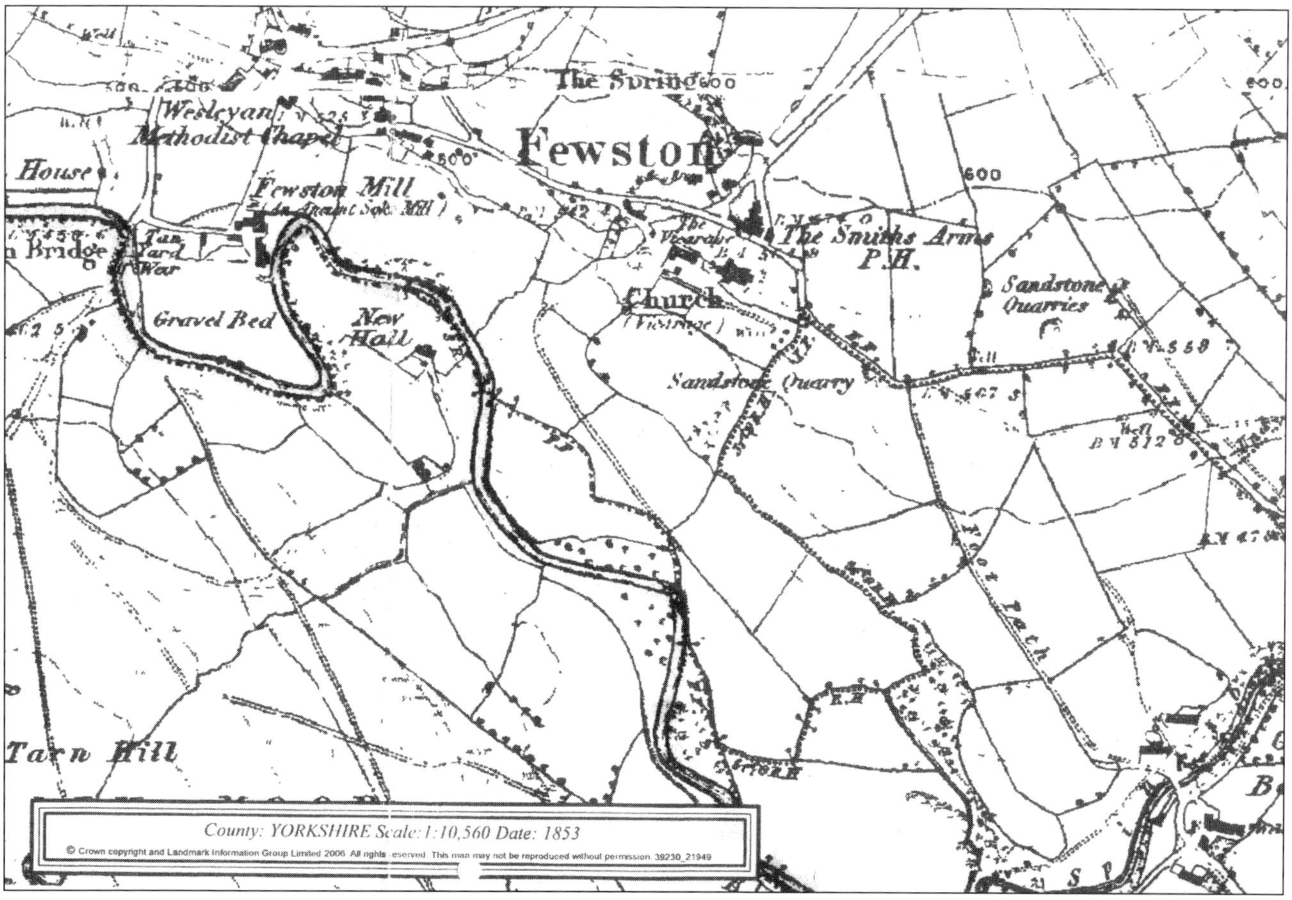

Area around Fewston including New Hall, the Methodist chapel, the mill, the tannery and the Smith's Arms. The original course of Spinksburn Beck is shown in the bottom right hand corner.

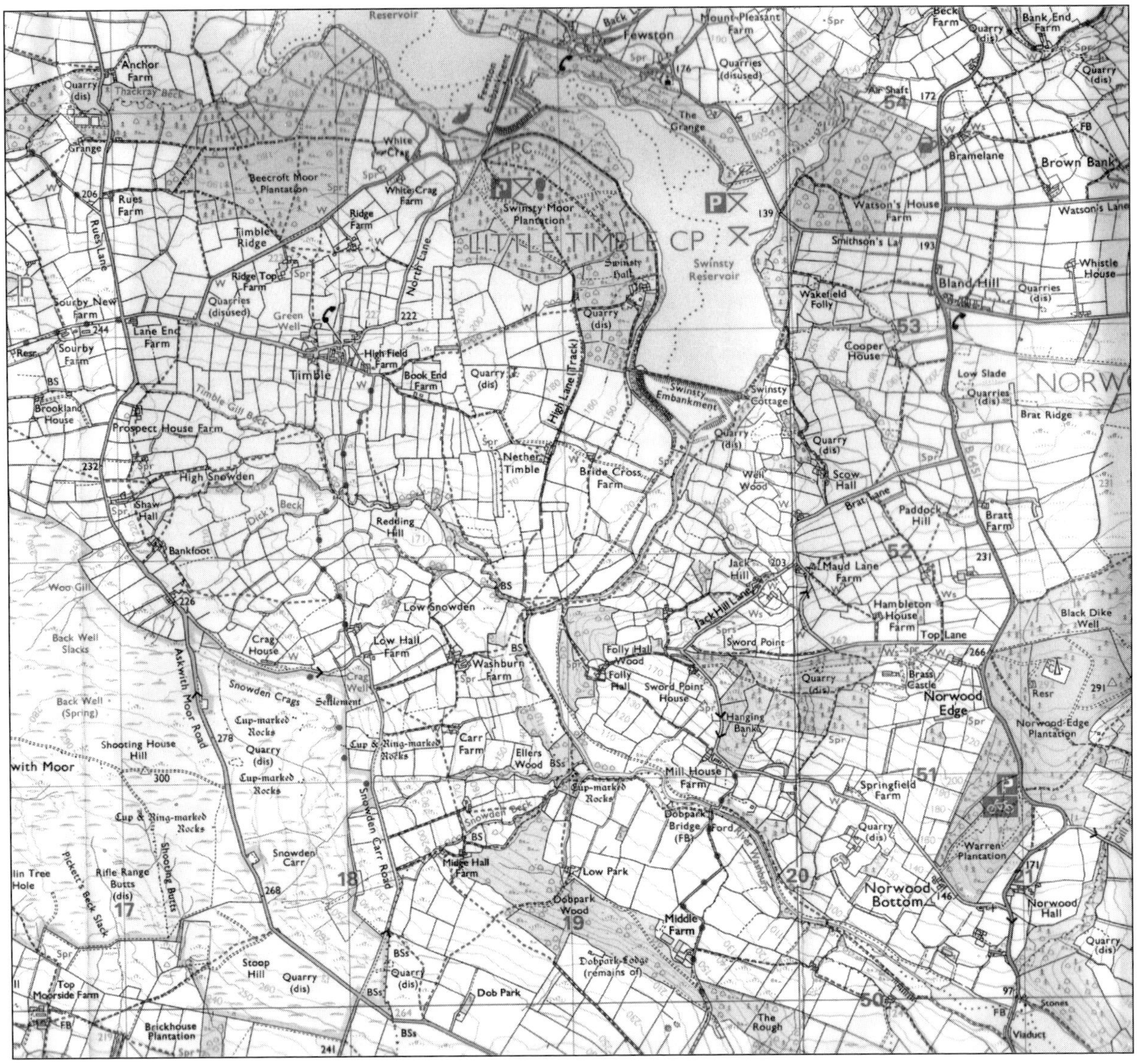

The area south of Fewston after the bulding of Swinsty Reservoir. The course of the Washburn is marked by a dotted line in the reservoir. The Spinksburn Beck which ran under Spinksburn Bridge at Wydra north of Fewston joins the Washburn at a point near the lagoon and the Stack Point Car Park on the east side of the reservoir. This map also shows Dob Park Bridge, Folly Hall, Jack Hill, Norwood Hall, Scow Hall, Shaw Hall, Snowdon, Swinsty Hall, Sword Point, Wakefield's Folly and Washburn Farm.

THE SMITH'S ARMS

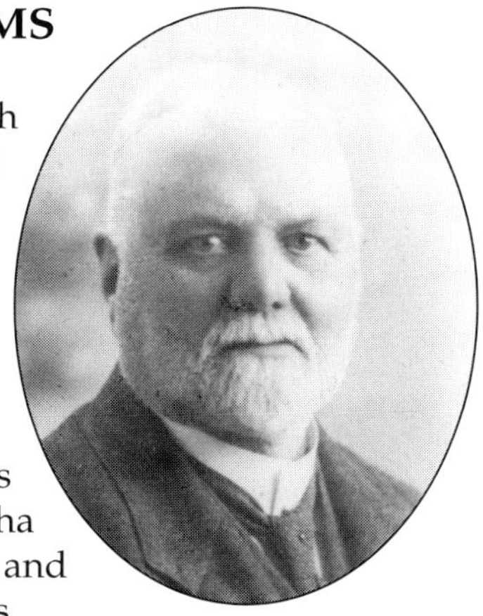

Edmund Worsnop.

Almost opposite the north gate of the church, in 1822 the The Smiths Arms was in the hands of Stephen and John Ward who was also a blacksmith. In the 1850s and 1860s it was known as the Mason's Arms after its then landlady, Mrs. Martha Mason, but between 1877 and 1881 a Thomas Mason is said to have been the licensee of both the Smith's Arms and the Mason's Arms. Between 1889 and 1897 when David Petty was the licensee it was a regular port of call for John Dickinson. In 1896 he arrived 'to find a chimney sweep inside who was very unruly and finally was ordered out by D[avid] Petty, the landlord... After getting out he commenced smashing the windows.' A later landlord was Edmund Worsnop.

CRAGGS MILL

Famed for the quality of its oatmeal throughout Nidderdale and Wharfedale the mill was later taken over by Isaac Barker, followed by his son, Tom. Following Tom's death in 1911 it continued under his son, Willie, but in 1910 the property with 6 acres of land was compulsorily purchased by Leeds Corporation for £3000, and the mill was demolished in 1936. The Barker family then moved to Wydra and the mill closed in 1939. Willie Barker died in 1951.

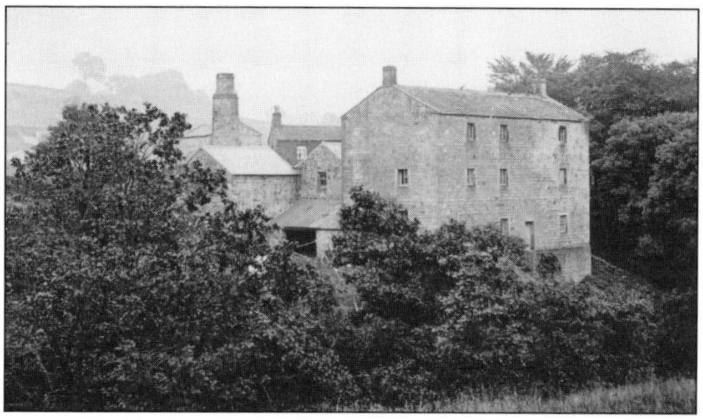

Craggs Mill. Situated on the Spinksburn Beck, below Wydra bridge, the mill was built in the 1820s of stone from the nearby Craggs Quarry. The first miller appears to have been William Hardisty known locally as 'Goose' Hardisty because of the geese he kept. When the water supply was inadequate, power was provided by a steam engine which consumed a ton of coal a day transported from the station at Darley in Nidderdale. The millstones were of French Burr.

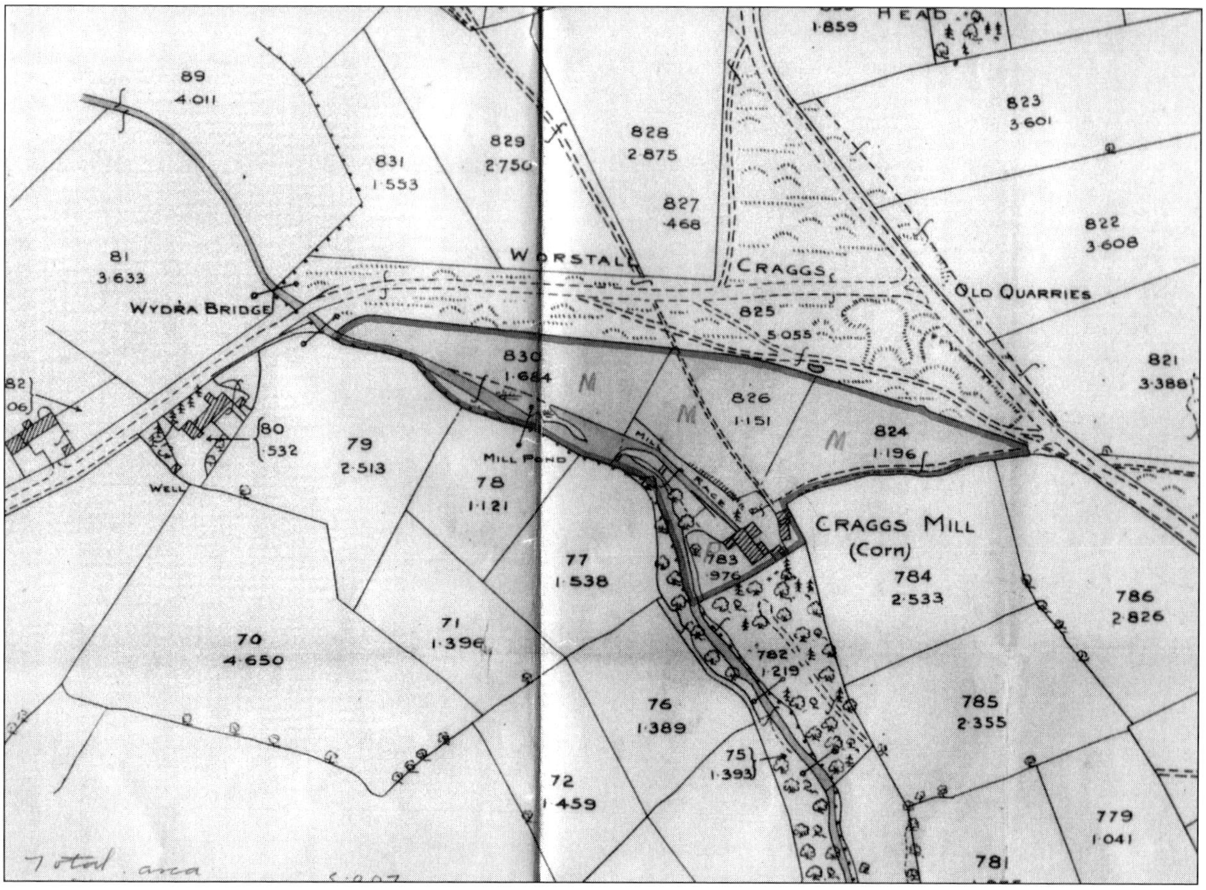

Plan of site of Craggs Mill and dam.

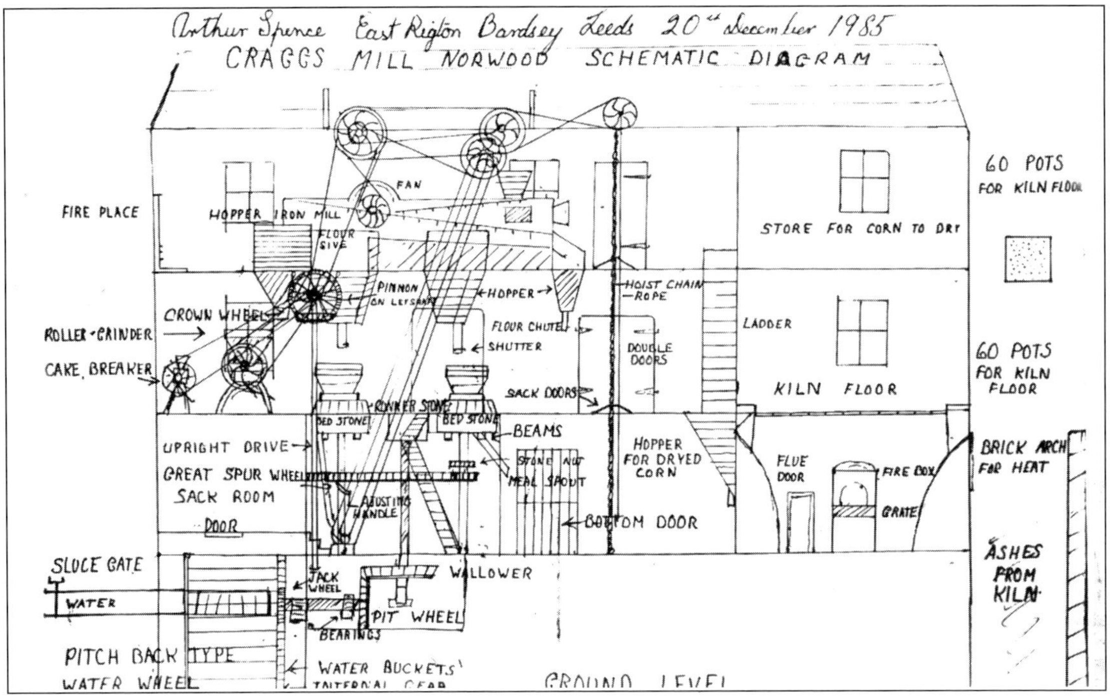

Sketch of Craggs Mill by Arthur Spence.

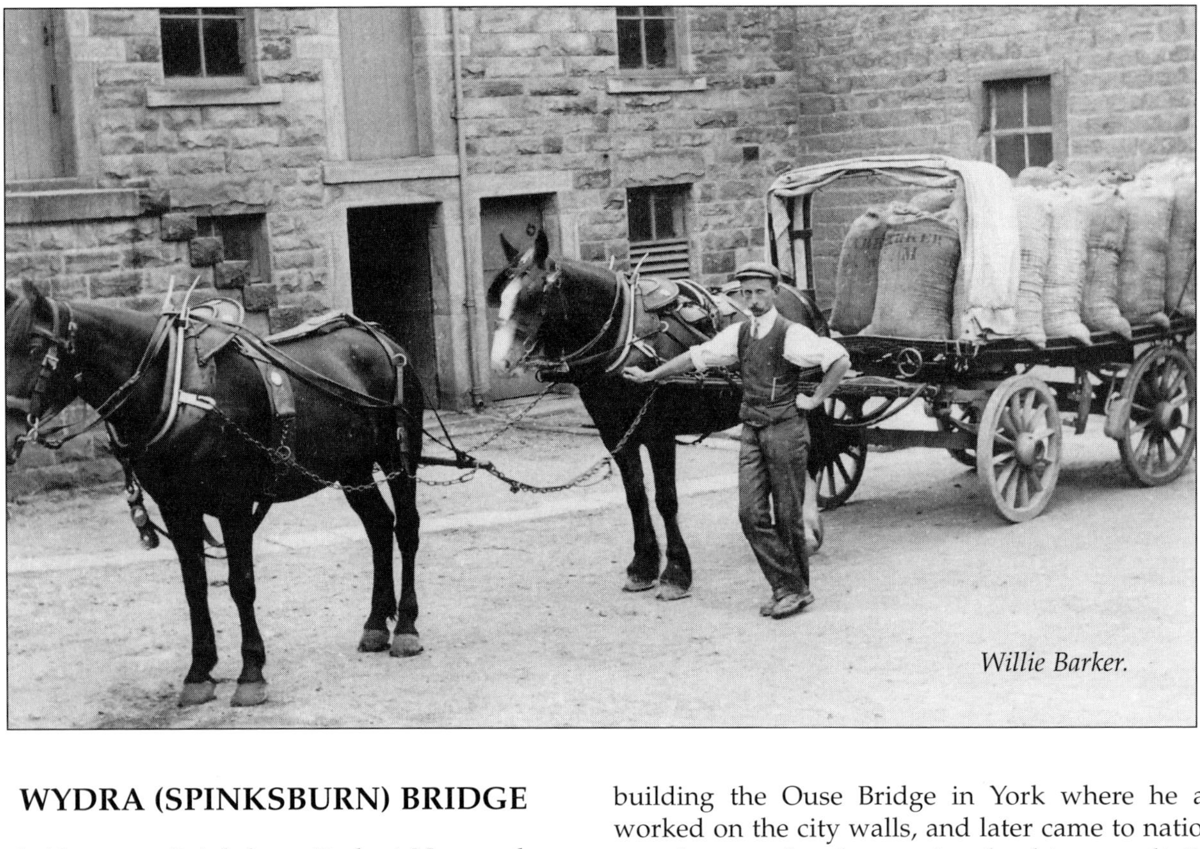

Willie Barker.

WYDRA (SPINKSBURN) BRIDGE

The bridge over Spinksburn Beck at Norwood was widened between 1809-10 at a cost of £392.14s.10d. by Hiram Craven, stonemason, civil engineering contractor and millowner in Keighley. The eighth of twelve children of John Craven, stone mason of Colne in Lancashire, Hiram was responsible for building the Ouse Bridge in York where he also worked on the city walls, and later came to national prominence when he was involved in consultations over London Bridge. Married with eight children, several of whom eventually joined him in the business, he died in 1821 after falling from the roof of an Edinburgh to London coach while crossing Sunderland Bridge.

THE SUN INN

The Sun Inn near Brown Bank was built in 1771 and was probably a farm house originally. One of the early landlords, Mr Turner, was the grandfather of David Spence, tailor, of Timble who is said to have been the only man in the valley able to read, villagers assembling to hear him read 'news of Bonaparte and Wellington.' Between 1893 and 1917 the licensee was Mrs Hannah Hobson.

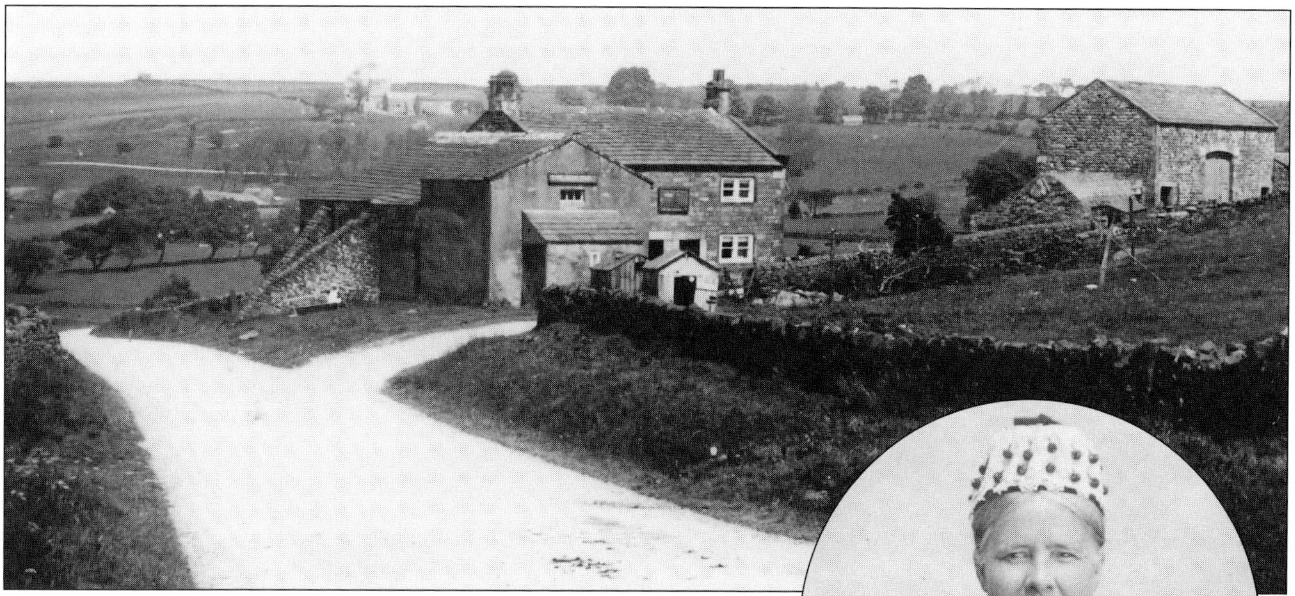

The Sun Inn, Norwood.

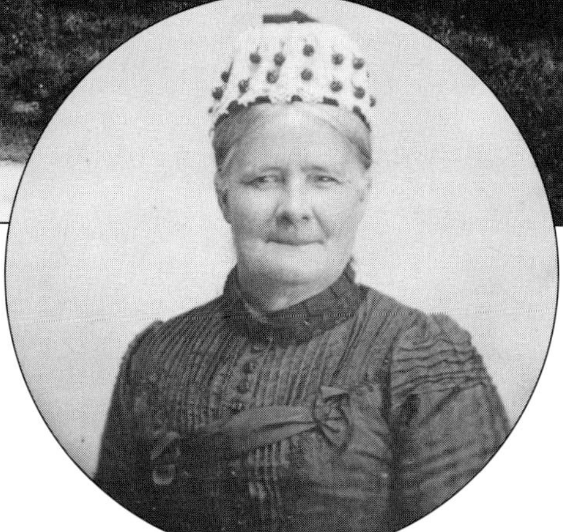

Mrs Hannah Hobson, landlady of the Sun Inn.

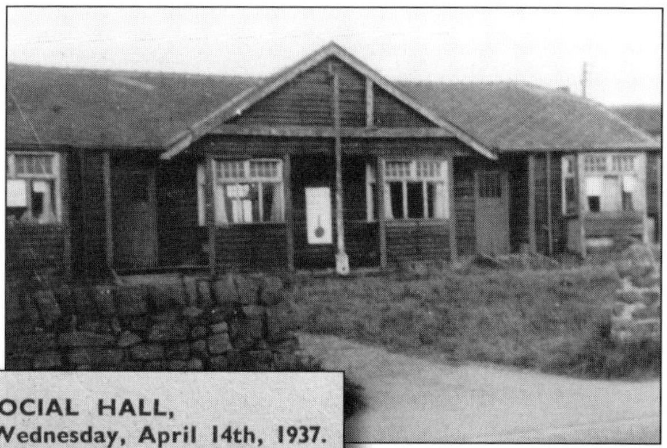

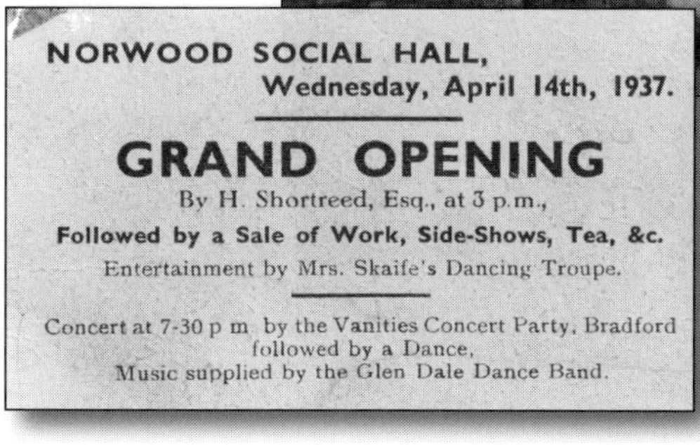

NORWOOD SOCIAL HALL,
Wednesday, April 14th, 1937.

GRAND OPENING

By H. Shortreed, Esq., at 3 p.m.,
Followed by a Sale of Work, Side-Shows, Tea, &c.
Entertainment by Mrs. Skaife's Dancing Troupe.

Concert at 7-30 p m by the Vanities Concert Party, Bradford
followed by a Dance,
Music supplied by the Glen Dale Dance Band.

Norwood Village Hall. The old hall consisted of two houses used by navvies during the building of Scar House Reservoir in Nidderdale. Brought to the valley by Stephen Beecroft and Walter Brownridge in 1936, it has now been replaced by the present hall on the same site.

The Seven Stars, Norwood. First licensed in 1869 it stood on the west side of the road between Bland Hill and Beck Farm and was a popular watering hole for drovers on their way to market. Run by James Marston in the late nineteenth century it also provided lodging for navvies working on the reservoirs. In 1884 John Dickinson found it 'a poor wretched inn and all dirty.' Closed in 1907 it was demolished in the 1920s.

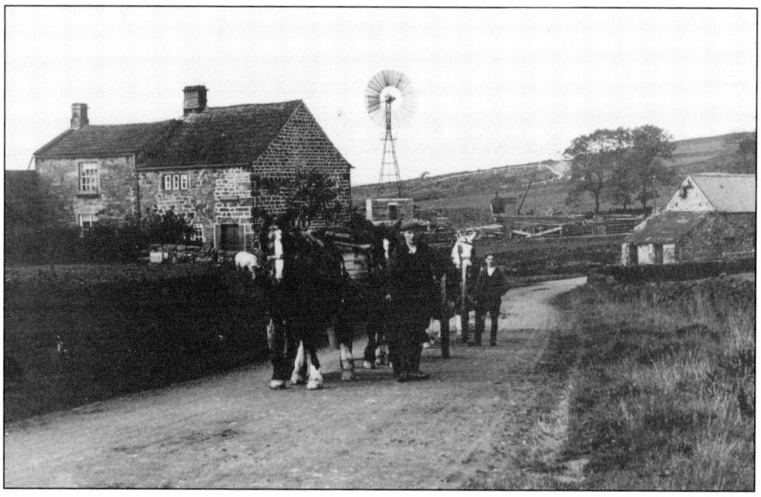

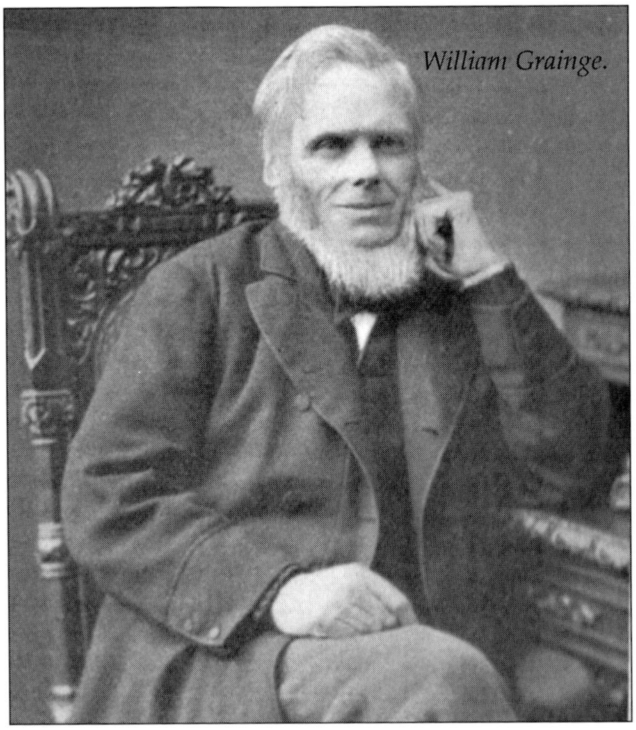

WILLIAM GRAINGE – THE VALLEY HISTORIAN 1818-1895

An antiquarian and poet as well as a competent historian, Grainge was born into a farming family at Castiles Farm between Laverton and Kirkby Malzeard. Leaving school at the age of twelve to work on the farm, on his father's death in 1845 he moved to Boroughbridge to work as a clerk in a solicitor's office, remaining for the next fifteen years while studying and writing.

In 1859 he published *The Vale of Mowbray: a Historical and Topographical Account of Thirsk and its neighbourhood* and in 1860 he moved to Harrogate, beginning a business as a bookseller and stationer. The following year he published his *Guide to Harrogate* followed by the *History of Knaresborough* in 1862. Among his later works is the *History and Topography of Harrogate and the Forest of Knaresborough* published in 1871. His final book, *The History & Topography of the town-ships of Little Timble, Great Timble and the hamlet of Snowden in the West Riding of the County of York* was written with the help of John Dickinson. The book was published in 1895 shortly before Grainge's death in the same year.

JOHN DICKINSON – THE WASHBURN DIARIST 1844-1912

John Dickinson was born in Timble Great, the youngest child and second son of John Dickinson, a stone mason, and Mary Dickinson, the local 'handy-woman' who delivered the new and laid out the dead. The valley roots of the family go back at least to the sixteenth century when a William Dicconson farmed in the Forest. Little is known of John's early life but it is likely that he received his education at Timble School. In his thirties he began to keep a diary which he continued with some gaps until his death in 1912, and the account of his varied professional and social life in nineteen surviving diaries which begin in 1877 gives an invaluable glimpse of valley and village society.

The aim of John's diary was 'to supply such matter as it can for the historian to draw upon' and it is undoubtedly a rich vein. We learn of his attending church twice on Sunday, of hearing a 'good sermon' at Fewston, of visiting the navvy camp for a service and of attending the local Methodist chapel to hear a variety of local preachers. He attended chapel anniversaries, dropped in at Bolton Priory to find the Duke of Devonshire, up from Chatsworth for the shooting, at morning service, and enjoyed watching Lord Walsingham and 'an Italian duke' play cricket at Blubberhouses. He visits the local agricultural shows and the village feasts at Timble and Fewston, and spends evenings in the pub playing his concertina. In 1902 he is impressed by his first ride in a car declaring 'these motorcars ... must become the thing of the future'.

Although primarily a builder by trade, John derived much of his income from a huge variety of jobs, mostly held simultaneously, including that of small-time farmer, pork salter, insurance agent and trader in such diverse commodities as tea, paraffin, hay and manure. Other jobs were those of rate collector, insurance agent, vaccination officer, local authority building inspector, parish councillor, rain gauge attendant, way warden, waterworks superintendent for Timble, Overseer for the Board of Guardians, and occasional teacher at Timble School. A trustee of the Robinson Memorial Hall in Timble, and Secretary to the local Friendly Society, he was also frequently called upon to contribute articles to the local newspaper. His role as Registrar of Births, Marriages and Deaths over a wide area of lower Wharfedale, a position held by his father before him, involved tramping many miles to remote farms in all weathers, recording events of happiness and sadness. This position he regarded as one of his more lucrative jobs; in 1912 he recorded with some satisfaction that the issuing of two death certificates and the registering of a birth on a single day had brought him the then considerable sum of seven shillings and six pence.

Towards the end of his life John had registered the deaths of many of those with whom he had grown up, and these entries are often accompanied by small pen portraits. 'Poor Willie ... a quiet industrious harm-less fellow' or, 'Stephen was about my age ...

we were schoolboys together.' There was also Nellie, 'a healthy fresh-looking girl thirty years ago whom I, in my wayward youth, walked out with.' In fact John enjoyed a somewhat racy youth pursuing several girls with varying degrees of success, describing one as his 'mistress' while simultaneously looking elsewhere because he was 'in great want of a loving wife'. Eventually in 1889, aged forty-five he married a cousin, Fanny, 'a jewel of virtue' and their first and only surviving child, Dorothy, was born in 1891.

Despite frequent complaints about the state of his health, John's energy was prodigious. He often walked 6 miles to Pool, arriving by eight a.m. to register a birth or death, and sometimes worked all day 'leading stone' which left him too tired to sleep at night. Despite declaring gloomily on his thirty-seventh birthday in 1881 that he 'expects soon to go downhill', thirty years later and a year before his death, he walked a roundabout route of 17 miles from Otley to his home in Timble.

In his capacity as the local registrar, John was also responsible for organising the local census taken in

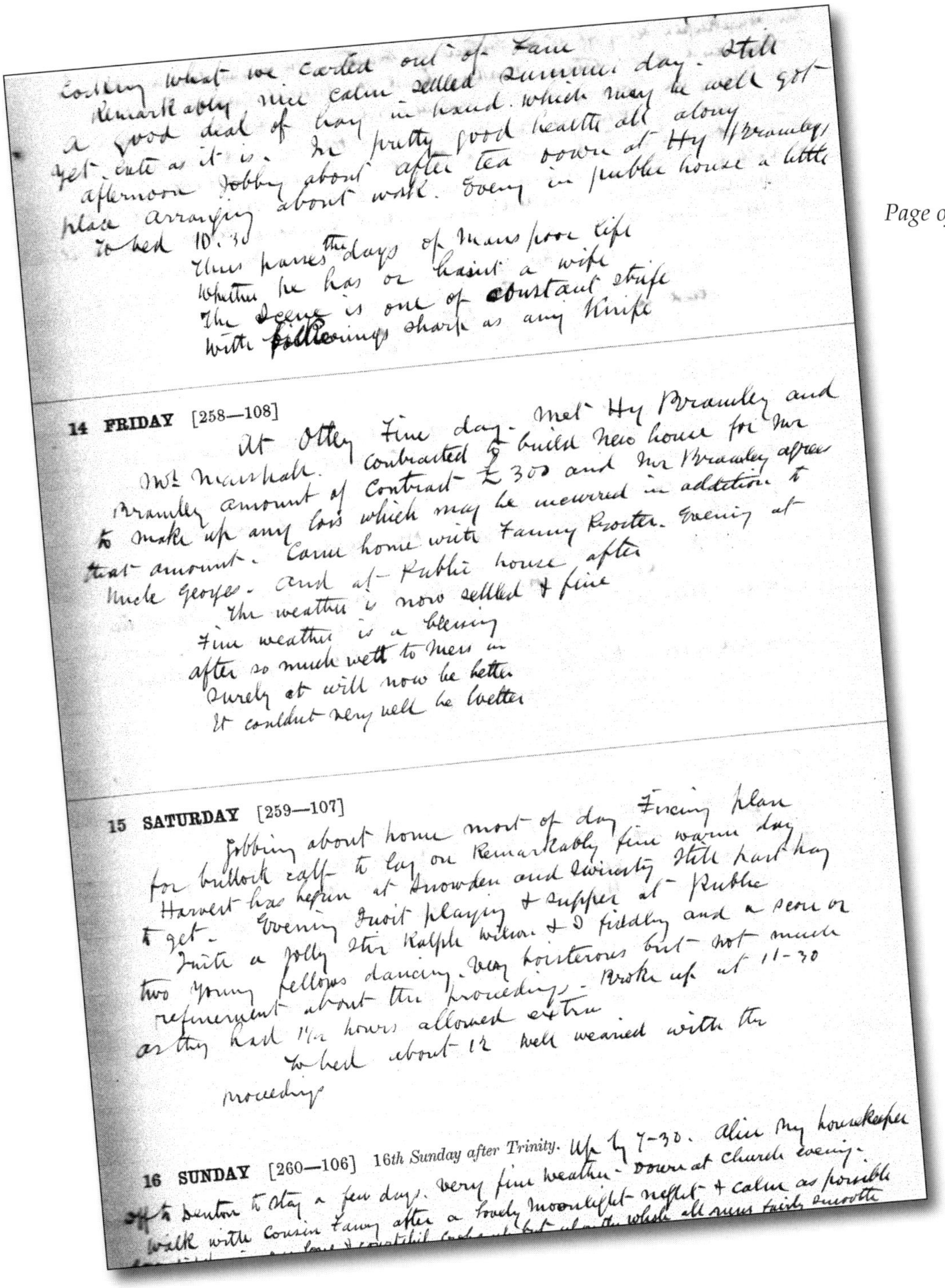
[illegible] what we carted out of [illegible]. Still Remarkably nice calm settled summer day. a good deal of hay in hand. which may be well got yet cute as it is. In pretty good health all along afternoon Jobbing about after tea down at Hy Bramley's place arranging about work. Evening in public house a little To bed 10.30

Thus passes the days of mans poor life
Whether he has or hasnt a wife
The scene is one of constant strife
With [illegible] sharp as any knife

14 FRIDAY [258—108]
At Otley Fine day. Met Hy Bramley and Wm Marshall. contracted to build new house for Mr Bramley amount of Contract £300 and Mr Bramley agree to make up any loss which may be incurred in addition to that amount. Came home with Fanny [illegible]. Evening at Uncle Georges. and at Public house after

The weather is now settled & fine
Fine weather is a blessing
after so much wett to mess in
Surely it will now be better
It couldnt very well be wetter

15 SATURDAY [259—107]
Jobbing about home most of day. Fixing plan for bullock calf to lay on. Remarkably fine warm day Harvest has begun at Snowden and Swinsty. Still hard hay to get. Evening Quoit playing & supper at Public Quite a jolly stir Ralph Wilson & I fiddling and a score or two young fellows dancing. Very boisterous but not much refinement about the proceedings. Broke up at 11-30 as they had 1½ hours allowed extra To bed about 12 well wearied with the proceedings

16 SUNDAY [260—106] 16th Sunday after Trinity. Up by 7-30. Alice my housekeeper off to Denton to stay a few days. Very fine weather. Down at Church evening. walk with Cousin Fanny after a lovely moonlight night & calm as possible [illegible] whole all runs fairly smooth

Page of John's diary.

England and Wales every ten years. He found this 'a very bothering business' involving much time and effort. 'I have to arrange the districts at once' he reported on the 6 October 1910, and on the following day visited his twelve enumerators two of whom, to his surprise, were women. Two of the men were local schoolmasters. By the 7 March 1911 the schedules were ready for distribution to the heads of every household who were required to list the details of everyone under their roof on a specific night.

John did not always approve of the quality of the enumerator's work. 'Some ... have made bad work' he reported on the 11 April 1911 and one 'left without carrying out his duties' adding darkly 'he will think better of it later – if not I shall have to report him.' He found the 1911 census especially difficult, doubting the accuracy of the information obtained and remarking that many incomplete returns must inevitably occur' – a cautionary note for present day researchers. Eventually the details required by the Registrar General were checked, the figures meticulously entered, and John was able to declare that the information was as 'complete and accurate as possible'. After the details had been posted off, the twelve enumerators shared the sum of £22.15s.4d.

Despite a deep affection for his home village he gradually became disenchanted with it, lamenting in 1899 that there were too many tourists, and that 'people seem crazy about ... holidays'. He also felt that 'the tone of the village is going down' finding it 'a hot bed of envy, hatred, and malice as is usual in country villages'. Eventually factors including increasing age and ill health persuaded him to move to Otley where he built a large house for himself and his family.

In 1912 John died in hospital from a perforated duodenal ulcer and as he had wished was buried in the new Meagill Cemetery at Fewston. His funeral was not without drama. Arriving in heavy rain the cortege found the grave completely waterlogged, causing the interment to be postponed for two days.

EAST END MANOR, NORWOOD

This Grade II listed house lies to the east of John o' Gaunt's castle and consists of two storeys and three bays dating from the latter part of the sixteenth century with a nineteenth century bay to the left.

The inner front door of the house is heavily fortified and the porch was added in 1625. The initials 'RA' on the lintel are believed to refer to Robert and Anne Parker who lived at the house in the early eighteenth century. Their daughter, also Anne, married into the Bramley family thereby acquiring Swinsty Hall near Timble.

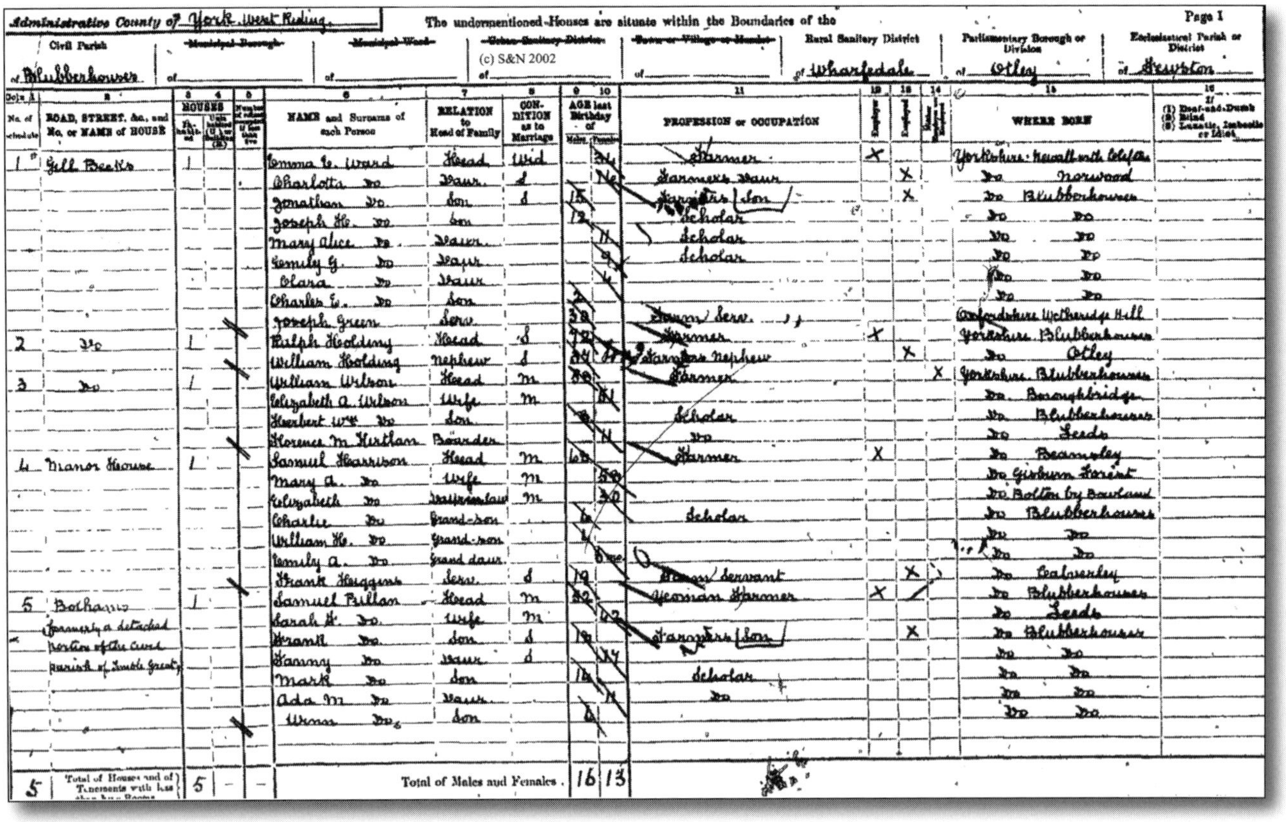
Administrative County of York West Riding. The undermentioned Houses are situate within the Boundaries of the — Page 1

Civil Parish of Blubberhouses | Municipal Borough of | Municipal Ward of | Urban Sanitary District of | Town or Village or Hamlet of | Rural Sanitary District of Wharfedale | Parliamentary Borough or Division of Otley | Ecclesiastical Parish or District of Fewston

(c) S&N 2002

No. of Schedule	Road, Street, &c., and No. or Name of House	Houses: Inhabited	Houses: Uninhabited (U) or Building (B)	Number of rooms if less than five	Name and Surname of each Person	Relation to Head of Family	Condition as to Marriage	Age last Birthday of Males	Age last Birthday of Females	Profession or Occupation	Employer	Employed	Neither Employer nor Employed	Where Born	(1) Deaf-and-Dumb (2) Blind (3) Lunatic, Imbecile or Idiot
1	Gill Beck	1			Emma E. Ward	Head	Wid		34	Farmer	X			Yorkshire: Hewarth with Clifton	
					Charlotte Do	Daur.	S		16	Farmer's Daur		X		Do Norwood	
					Jonathan Do	Son	S	15		Farmer's Son		X		Do Blubberhouses	
					Joseph H. Do	Son		12		Scholar				Do Do	
					Mary Alice Do	Daur.			11	Scholar				Do Do	
					Emily G. Do	Daur.			9	Scholar				Do Do	
					Clara Do	Daur.			4					Do Do	
					Charles E. Do	Son		2						Do Do	
					Joseph Green	Serv.		38		Farm Serv.				Oxfordshire Wetheridge Hill	
2	Do	1			Ralph Holding	Head	S	72		Farmer	X			Yorkshire Blubberhouses	
					William Holding	Nephew	S	34		Farmer's nephew		X		Do Otley	
3	Do	1			William Wilson	Head	M	38		Farmer			X	Yorkshire Blubberhouses	
					Elizabeth A. Wilson	Wife	M		31					Do Boroughbridge	
					Herbert Wm Do	Son		8		Scholar				Do Blubberhouses	
					Florence M Hirtlam	Boarder			11	Do				Do Leeds	
4	Manor House	1			Samuel Harrison	Head	M	63		Farmer	X			Do Bramley	
					Mary A. Do	Wife	M		58					Do Gisburn Forest	
					Elizabeth Do	Daughter-in-law	M		30					Do Bolton by Bowland	
					Charlie Do	Grand-son		6		Scholar				Do Blubberhouses	
					William H. Do	Grand-son		4						Do Do	
					Emily A. Do	Grand daur.			8 mo					Do Do	
					Frank Higgins	Serv.	S	19		Farm servant		X		Do Calverley	
5	Bothams formerly a detached portion of the civil parish of Timble Great	1			Samuel Pullan	Head	M	52		Yeoman Farmer	X			Do Blubberhouses	
					Sarah H. Do	Wife	M		42					Do Leeds	
					Frank Do	Son	S	19		Farmer's Son		X		Do Blubberhouses	
					Fanny Do	Daur.	S		17					Do Do	
					Mark Do	Son		14		Scholar				Do Do	
					Ada M Do	Daur.			11	Do				Do Do	
					Wm Do	Son		6						Do Do	
5	Total of Houses and of Tenements with less than five Rooms	5	–	–	Total of Males and Females			16	13						

Page of John's 1911 census return.

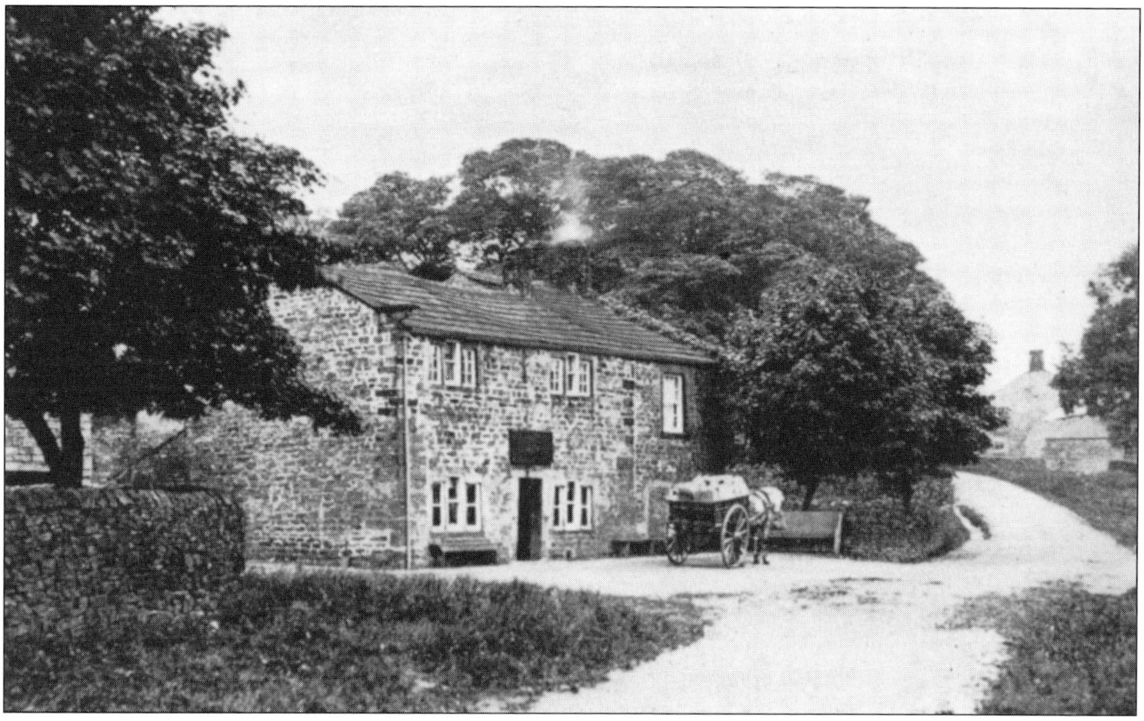

Timble Inn. Once a favourite haunt of many walkers and cyclists and very much at the heart of village life, for many years it was owned by members of the Lister family beginning with James, born in 1787, who lived into his nineties. He was succeeded by his son, also James, whose widow, Mrs Ann Lister took over in 1888 when John Dickinson reported that 'business seems poor and not likely to do her much good'. John was a frequent visitor at the 'public', enjoying a whisky, and in 1891 meeting the public hangman, James Berry of Bradford 'a jolly sociable figure ... Can tell a good story'.

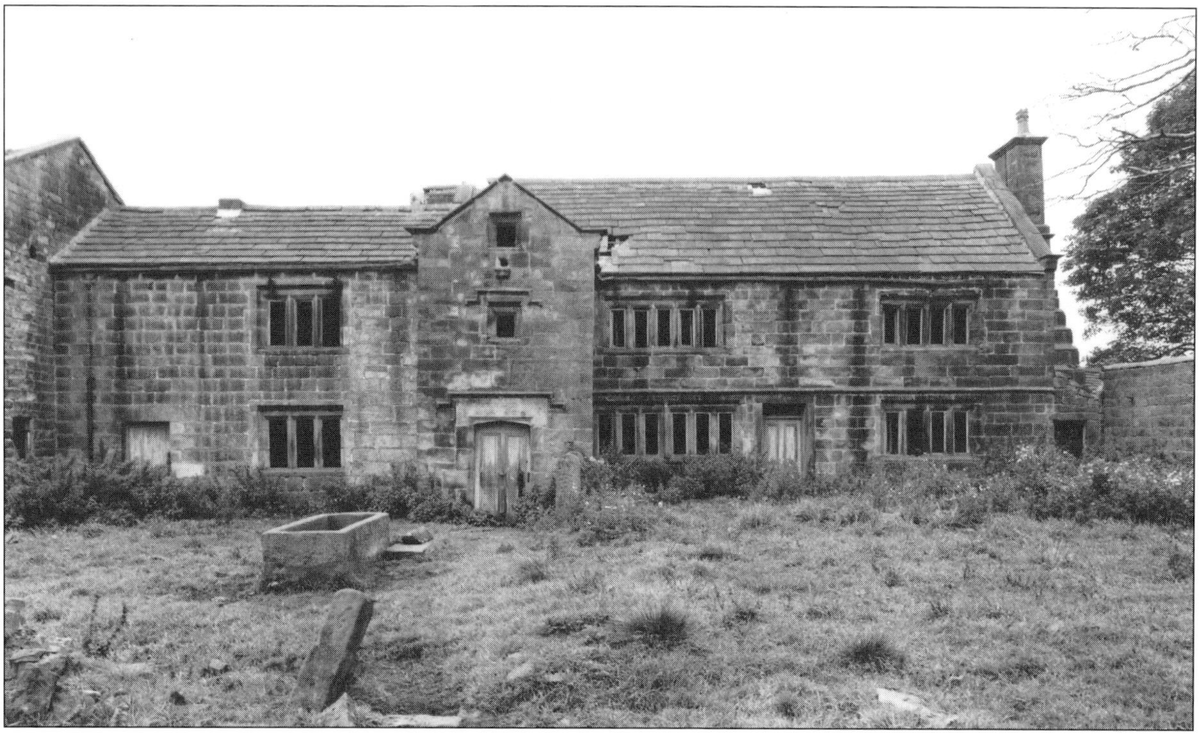

East End Manor, Norwood.

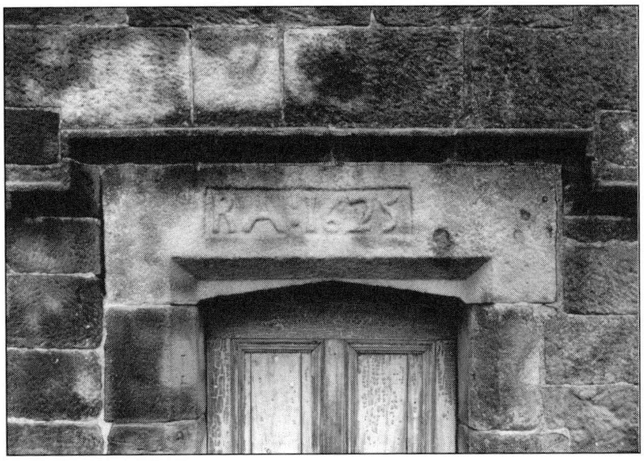

Inscribed lintel.

The first owner of the house, John Jeffrey, died in 1577 the evidence of his will suggesting that he was a man of some means. As well as several items of brass and pewter there were also monetary bequests, some of which amounted to a few pounds, and included 'Five shillings for the amendment of Witheray [Wydra] bridge and the church waie from my house to the churche.' In addition to several cows and a number of sheep he also left a loom, shears and woollen combs indicating that he practised a dual economy of agriculture and textile production.

By the mid nineteenth century East End was the home of John Bramley, a 'gentleman' farmer with 68 acres of land. Said by John Dickinson to be 'the wealthiest man in the district but one of the plainest and homeliest of men ... somewhat eccentric but most honest ... in his dealings.'

After his death in 1889, his son, the bachelor John Moorhouse Bramley, moved to live at Swinsty Hall. Until 1894 the house was occupied by William Darnbrook but later became a ruin. In the 1950s a tramp known as 'Blackout' lived in a stone structure in the grounds perhaps used originally for storing peat or potatoes. Now restored, the house is in private hands.

SWINSTY HALL

This Grade I listed house was built in 1575 by Ralph Wood of Timble Little and Henry Sotell of North Grange for their children, Francis and Ellen, at the time of their marriage. An indenture states 'that the said Francis shall by the Grace of Almighty God, marry and take to wife Ellen Sotell ... and the said Ellen will thereunto condycende and agree.'

From the early fourteenth century the Woods of Timble had been influential in the area, Walter, the son of John del Wode doing homage to the Archbishop for lands he held at Timble while in 1504 another Walter acted as a witness for Sir Robert Plumpton in a law suit. In 1537 a Walter Wood of Timble owed the nuns of the Priory at Esholt near Bradford thirty three shillings for his child's board for a year and a half.

The house stands on a sloping hillside and consists of three parts. The main section is of three storeys with a storeyed porch and stepped lights. Together with the glazing and the fact that some of the window glass is dated 1627 suggests that this part of the house was remodelled in the seventeenth century.

The west wing, or Old Hall, is an attached and recessed two storey range with two bays which may predate the main building. To the rear and attached

Exterior with outbuildings.

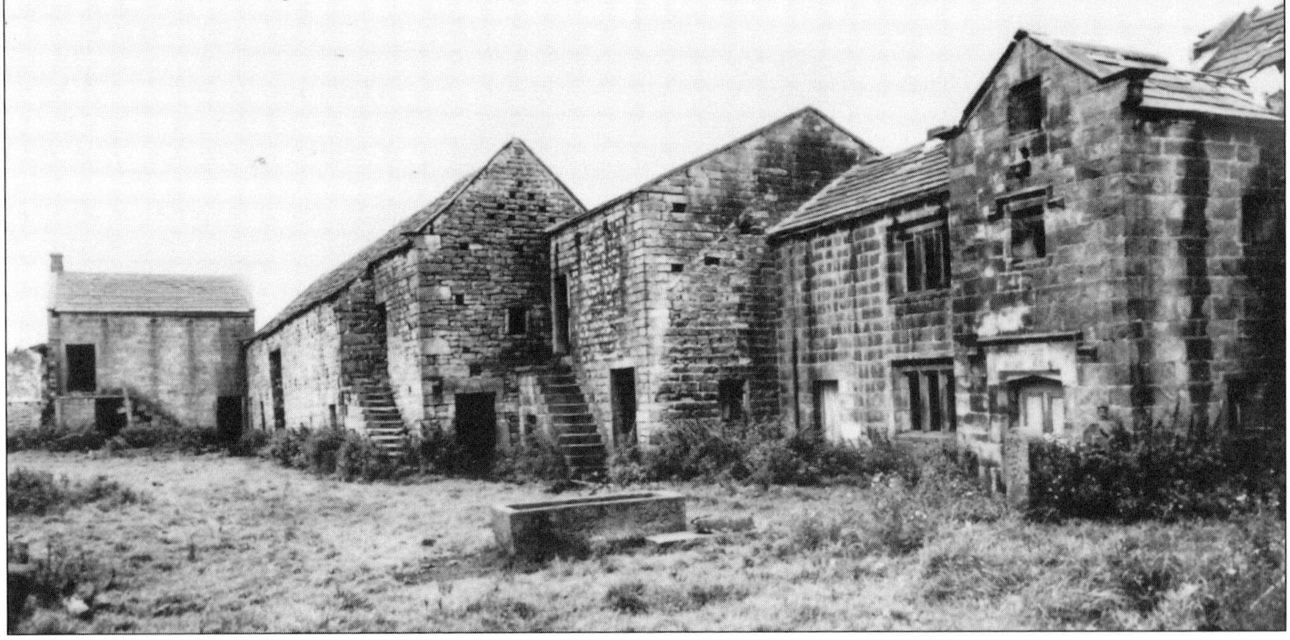

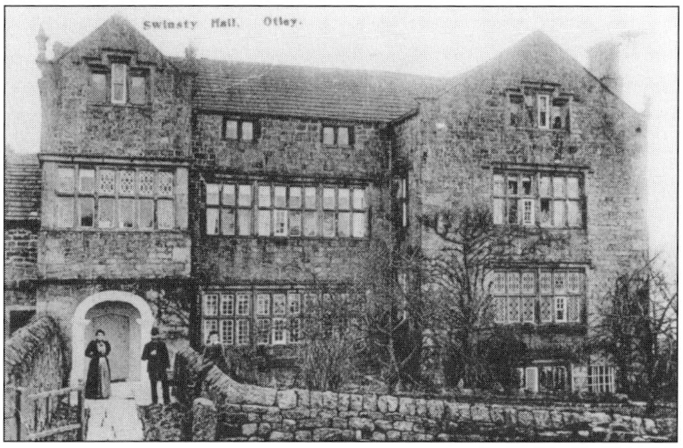

Swinsty Hall.

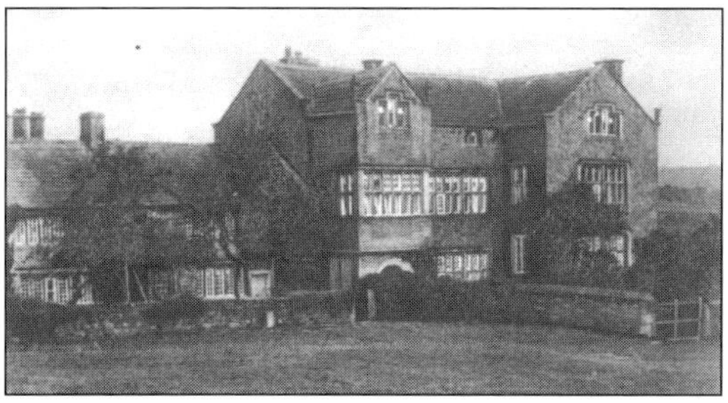

Swinsty Hall showing west wing.

at right angles to the west range, there is a three bay, possibly service, range.

Unfortunately for Francis and Ellen the house became something of a poisoned chalice. Unable to keep up the payments, Henry Robinson, a Lancashire yeoman of considerable wealth, foreclosed and completed the building of the house in 1637. On his death in 1639 the inventory of his goods listed a considerable amount of livestock including more than three hundred sheep and some sixty cattle. No doubt his 'shopp' with its extensive collection of spinning and weaving equipment together with 'thirty stone of wool' also contributed greatly to an estate of £744.14s. The house passed to the ownership of his son, John, whose birth is commemorated on an oak screen in the chamber parlour.

The house has since had many residents including John Moorhouse Bramley 'a straight forward and self-taught man,' 'something of a scholar' who drew up wills for the locals to whom he was known as 'Moorhouse the will maker' and remembered for 'never making a crooked one'. He lived in the house with his much younger housekeeper prompting John Dickinson to remark enigmatically 'man and maid together are a mixy quantity ... fresh and buxom she ... seems destined to remain with him to the end either as wife or housekeeper, I cannot even guess which.' In fact the couple eventually married in 1900.

In later years the house, which had become the

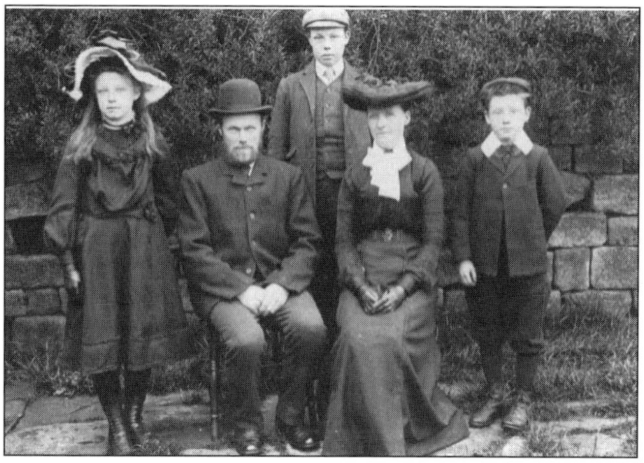

The Holmes family.

property of Leeds Corporation, was divided into four separate dwellings and tenanted by farming families including Miles and Sarah Holmes (pictured above) with children from left, Annie, Albert and Joe.

In 1902 one of the tenants was the agent for the Leeds Corporation, Captain Edward Marcus Attwood Wakefield who came from a distinguished family. Born in 1877 in Middlesex his gt. gt. gt. grandparents were prominent Quakers, his gt. gt. grandfather a cousin of the Quaker reformer, Elizabeth Fry, and his grandfather related to Edward Gibbon, author of *The History of the Decline and Fall of the Roman Empire.* Soon after arriving at Swinsty, Edward married into a wealthy Sussex family and a presentation was made to the couple by the Washburn Tenant Farmers Association. With his wife and two children he remained at Swinsty until 1909 when the family moved to Pontefract. Wakefield's Folly [see p.76], a ruined farm on the opposite bank of the reservoir, has no connection with Captain Wakefield taking its name from Henry Wakefield, a farmer of 28 acres.

In 1925 the hall attracted illustrious visitors when King George V and Queen Mary visited while staying with their daughter, Princess Mary and her husband Viscount Lascelles at Goldsborough Hall near Knaresborough. The Princess, having visited the hall for a meet of the Bramham Moor Hunt, persuaded her parents to visit the house which they did secretly. Very few people apparently noticed the royal party as they walked the last hundred yards to the hall to be welcomed by the then occupiers, Alfred Pope, the Corporation's head forester and his wife, and shown around the house.

Alfred, who served with the Warwickshire Regiment in the Boer War, was the first English university graduate in forestry. 'A great countryman,' in later life he became a contributor to the radio programme 'Diary of a Countryman.' He and his wife were renowned for their hospitality, and the hall became a popular venue for the annual general meeting of the Leeds City Waterworks. He also had a fearsome reputation as a driver, travelling along the narrow lanes at speed, even in fog, in his 1927 two seater Morris. In later years other tenants of the hall included the harpsichordist Malcolm Cuckston. The house was sold by Leeds Corporation in 1992 and elegantly restored by a new owner.

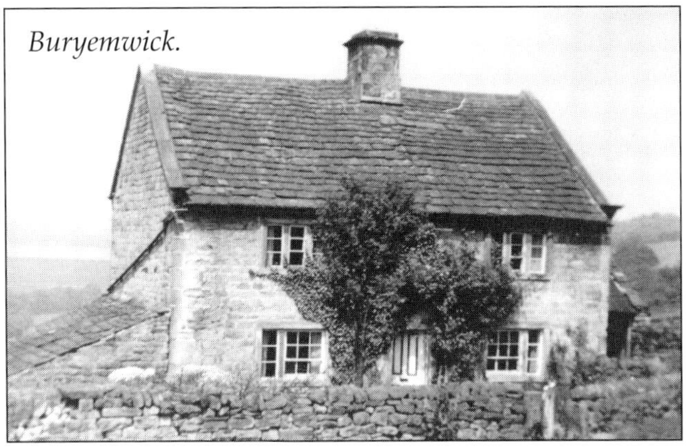

Buryemwick.

BURYEMWICK

The name of this house has given rise to several theories, the most common of which is that because it is located in an area known as Sword Point (see p.76), it was the scene of a Civil War skirmish. Furthermore it has been suggested that its name is derived from the need to bury the dead quickly, 'wick' in the Yorkshire dialect meaning 'lively' as in 'look lively'. In fact there is no evidence that such an event occurred either here, or elsewhere in the valley, during the Civil War period. It is more likely that the name 'Sword Point' is derived from 'Elseward', an old name for the area, and a nearby feature of the landscape which comes to a point bounded by three lanes. The derivation of 'Buryemwick' remains open for debate.

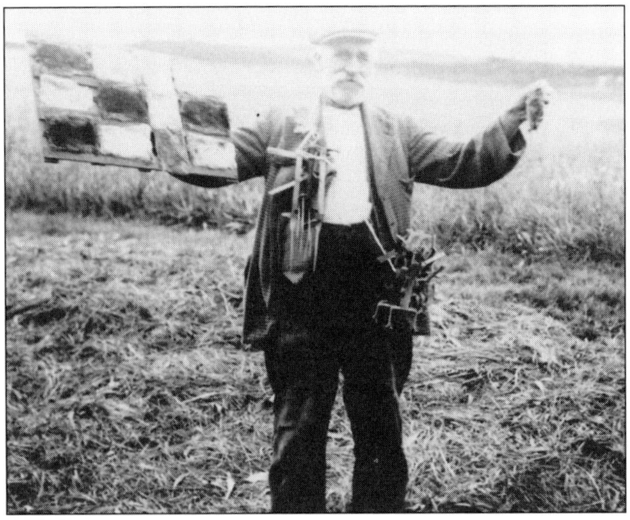

Tom Hebden, mole catcher, of Salt Pie Farm with pelts.

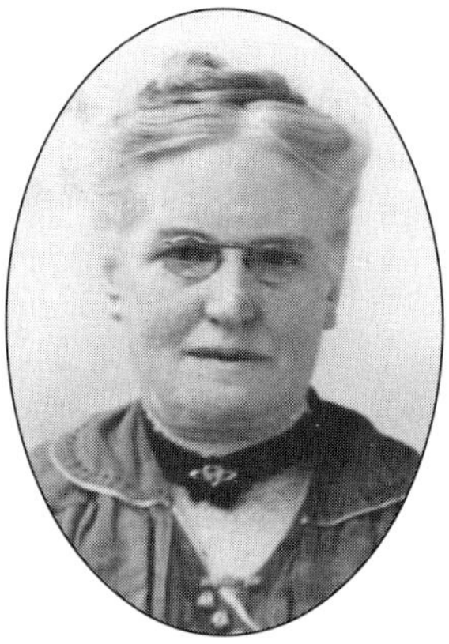

Miss Edith Worsnop of Salt Pie Farm 1920's. Born in Hunslet, Leeds, Edith took over the tenancy of Salt Pie in 1927. She farmed poultry and goats until her death in 1962 when she left her personal belongings to her niece, Mary Hannah (Polly) Hebden, and her stock and equipment to Fewston church.

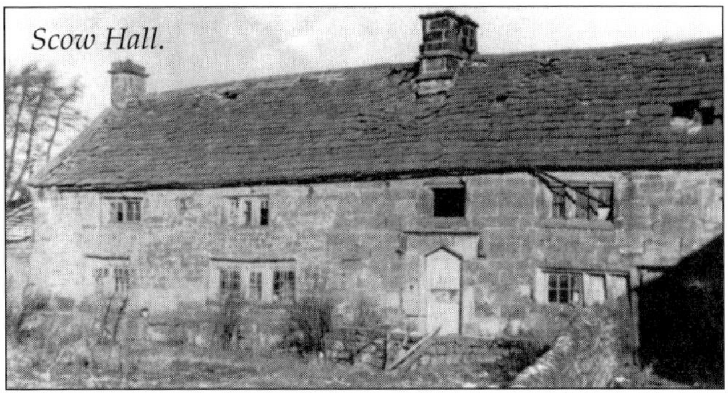

Scow Hall.

SCOUGH (SCOW) HALL AND THE FAIRFAXES

Dating from the sixteenth century Scough is the oldest Grade II* house in the valley. With a timber frame encased in stone it consists of two storeys and five bays with mullioned windows to the ground floor. Originally occupied by John Beckwith who died in 1588, it then passed to his son-in-law, John Brearey, who died in 1613 and was buried in the churchyard at Fewston. In 1625 his daughter, Mary, married into the Fairfax family who lived at Menston.

In 1612 Sir Ferdinando Fairfax, the Parliamentary General, briefly lived in the house with his family; three of his children, Elizabeth, Mary, and Charles who was killed at Marston Moor, were all born in the house. A fourth child, Tom, the third Lord Fairfax, and Cromwell's second-in-command during the Civil War, known as 'Black Tom', was born at Denton Hall just outside the valley. Ferdinando's daughter, Mary, became the wife of George Villiers, the 2nd Duke of Buckingham.

In 1715 the house became the home of William Wilkinson, and in the 1730s passed by marriage to the Fawkes family of Farnley. Some additions were made to it in the nineteenth century and in 1900 it became the property of the Leeds Corporation and was tenanted by a number of farming families.

Eventually the house became a ruin but was bought and restored in the middle of the last century and is now in private hands.

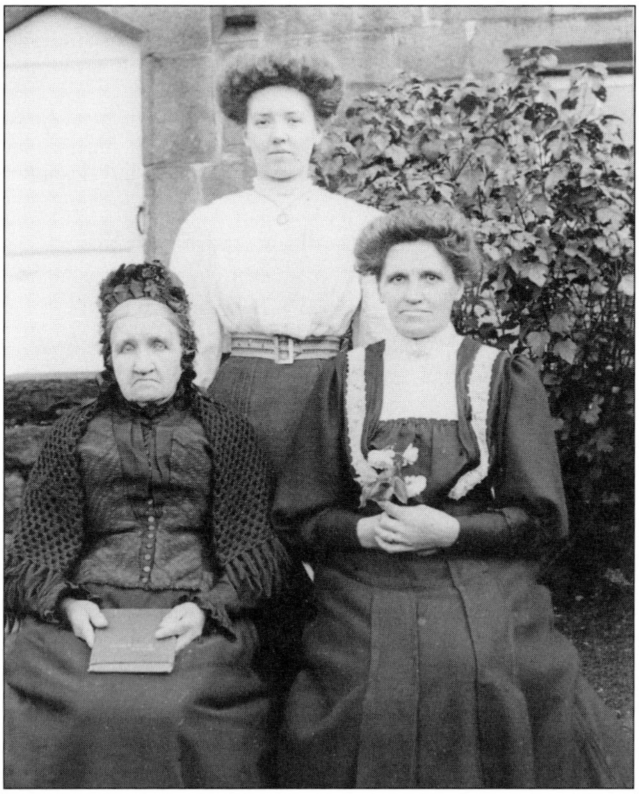

Three generations at Scow. Left *Mrs Annie Wood, her daughter Mrs Mary Driver b.c.1864* and behind, *Mrs Annie Bradley b.c1889.*

It is interesting to speculate on the ownership of about thirty silver coins found only yards from the house in 1892 by Joseph Steele, of Sword Point. Belonging principally to the period 1553-58 they had been walled up in the crevice of a 'large crag in a rough piece of ground'.

THE 'WITCHES' OF NEWHALL (NEW HALL)

In the fourteenth century Newhall was the site of the original timber framed house which belonged to the Wood family. This was subsequently sold to the Pullens who had a tannery on a 5-acre plot known as Skinner Flatt. In 1577 the house was bequeathed to John Pullen, the vicar of Fewston, who was connected to the Fairfax family and in 1597 it passed to them, eventually becoming the home of Edward Fairfax.

The house stood 'immediately below and to the south of the village of Fewston' with its 'back towards the brook Washburn on the north, and the front towards the steep rise of the hill on the south' below the church (see p.75). Like Cragg Hall it was not as grand as its title suggests, being described as of 'humble appearance, a square two storey south-facing building with a grey slate roof, two rooms in length and two in breadth.' It also had narrow windows with stone

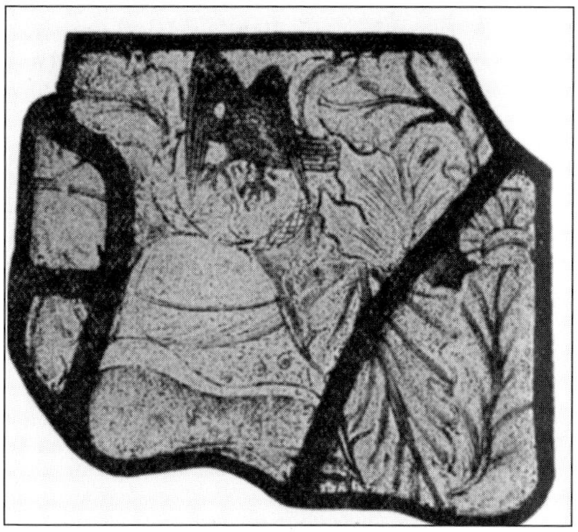

Crest of the Pullen family. This pane from a window showing a pelican pecking its breast, a symbol of piety, was removed from the hall when it was demolished in the nineteenth century, and taken to Tatefield Hall at Beckwithshaw. It is now in private hands elsewhere.

mullions at least one of which contained stained glass bearing the heraldic shield of the Pullen family. There was a porch with a stone bench, a large hall and parlour (both of which had fireplaces), and the parlour was filled with 'green boughs in summer'. Outside there was a back and front courtyard, 'a garden with alleys', a 'milk house' and a 'turf stack'.

Edward Fairfax (1575-1635) was a poet, and the illegitimate son of Sir Thomas Fairfax (1521-1599) chiefly known for his acclaimed translation of Tasso's poem 'Jerusalem'. In 1601 he married Dorothy Laycock of Leeds by whom he had six children, two of whom, Ellen and Elizabeth, he believed had been bewitched by a group of local women. The so-called 'bewitching' apparently took the form of hallucinations or trances in which the girls, whether awake or asleep, experienced bizarre 'dreams' involving local people known to them. It is said that they also suffered episodes of blindness, deafness and lameness, as well as loss of consciousness. Convinced that these were genuine manifestations of 'enchantment' their father eventually accosted one of the women he believed to be guilty. Not surprisingly the accusation was denied but she and several other suspected women were taken before the local justices and tried at York Assizes. Supported by local people including the then vicar of Fewston, Nicholas Smythson, all were acquitted. For some time after the trial the hallucinations continued but eventually both girls apparently made full recoveries and both subsequently married.

An adequate explanation for these episodes has never been offered. Their father, an intelligent man, was genuinely convinced that his daughters had been bewitched. Perhaps this idea was fostered by the widespread belief in witchcraft at the time, allowing fear and concern for his daughters to over-ride his common sense. Or perhaps the attacks were due to a physical cause. A modern medical opinion is that the girls may have been experiencing genuine hallucinations due to fungal, or ergot poisoning, derived from eating 'mushrooms' or musty rye bread.

Edward Fairfax died in 1635 and is said to have been buried in Fewston church although this cannot be confirmed because of a break in the parish records. Newhall was subsequently occupied by Mary Bramley who married James Kent of Tatefield Hall, Beckwithshaw in 1847, and in 1851, by Thomas and Elizabeth Stubbs. In 1860 when a wall was demolished a gold ring was discovered with the words 'After consent ever content' engraved within the band. Seven years later Leeds Corporation compulsorily purchased the property and demolished it completely in 1900.

SHAW HALL, SNOWDEN

The hamlet of Snowden lies to the east of the Otley-Blubberhouses road. From the latter part of the fourteenth century this area has been associated with the Newsome family whose descendants were instrumental in building the hall in the early seventeenth century. In 1687 the house was extended and a porch added which covers the join. Beside the porch there is a rounded projection, perhaps the base of a stair turret suggesting that the porch may originally have had two storeys. The door lintel is inscribed 'JN 1687' and the house also bears the inscription 'R. Gill 1848' for Robinson Gill, one of the builders. At some stage it is believed that the house may have been divided into two or three dwellings.

The house was the home of Thomas Newsome who was born in 1739 and died aged ninety-four in 1833, and his wife Mary, who died in 1849 aged ninety-five. Said by John Dickinson 'to have been a man of wealth and high social position' Thomas also owned several other adjoining farms and lived well, keeping 'a good table'. The Newsomes had three daughters and five sons. Although four of the sons never married they were said to be 'fine, stalwart fellows...well mounted ... creating something of a stir when they rode to Ripley Fair'. Unfortunately they all appear to have been rather strange. Robert, who continued to live at Shaw, was 'the tallest and most portly but at the same time the most ignorant and childish'; Richard was said to be the most intellectual but regularly drank sixteen pints of beer at the Timble Inn, stopping on the way home to sleep off the effects; Joseph was a good farmer but suffered from religious mania, and Henry, the youngest and an eccentric, became increasingly rich every time one of his brothers died, eventually regarding himself as a member of the landed gentry. He also owned the Snowden corn mill beside Timble Gill which he is said to have preserved with a 'kind of reverence'. After his death in 1881 the

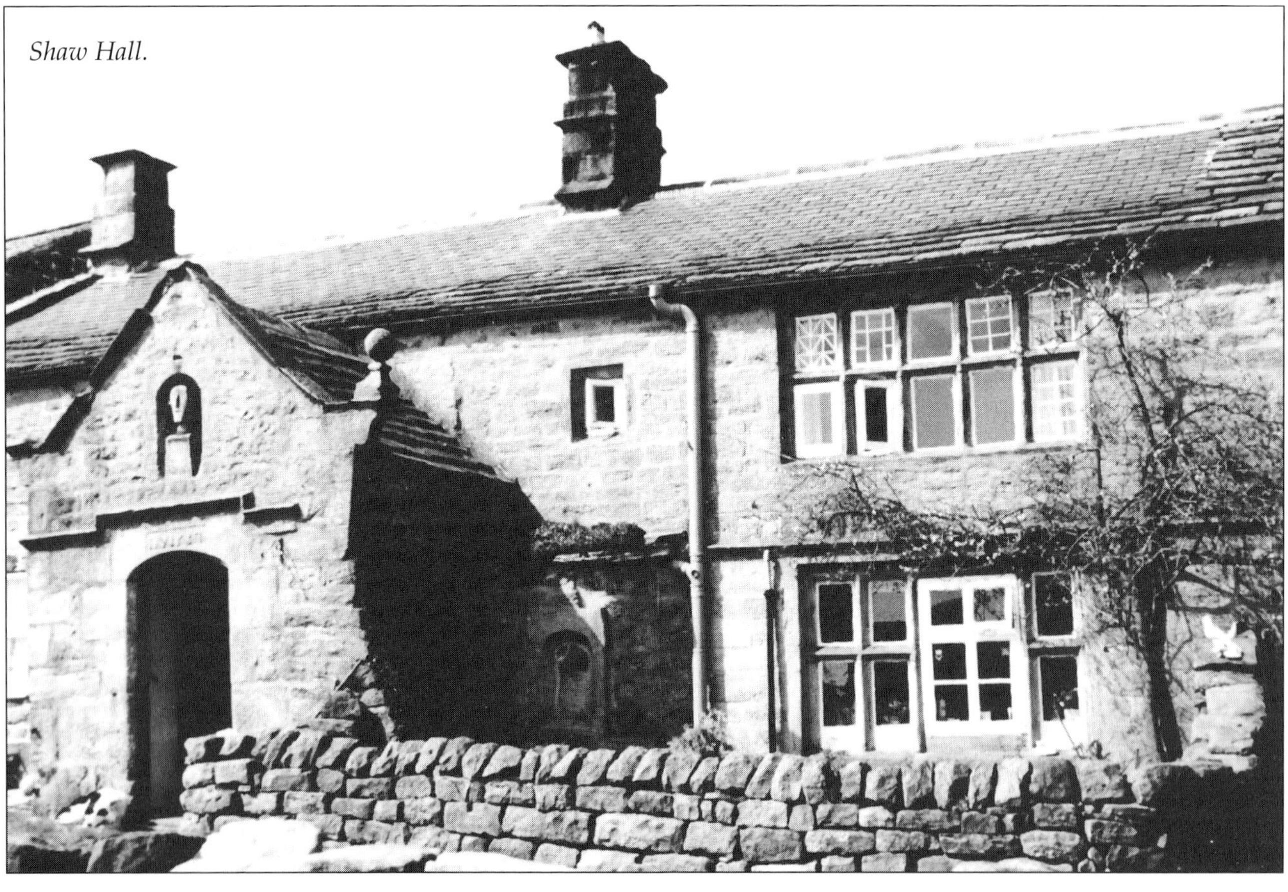

Shaw Hall.

mill became the property of the Dawson family of Weston near Otley, and was demolished in 1884. It had run for more than sixty years when it was said to have 'made good oatmeal'.

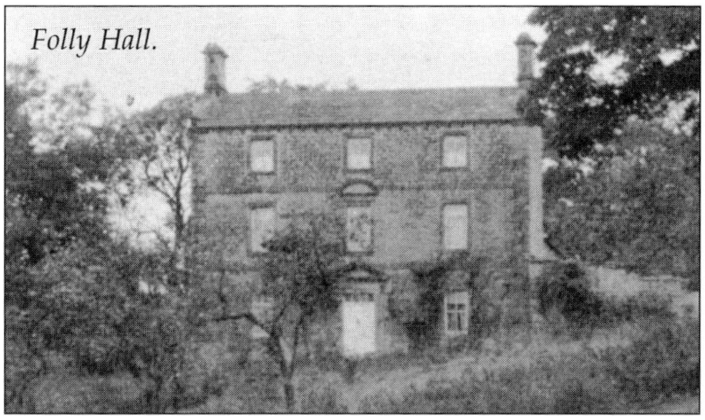
Folly Hall.

FOLLY HALL

Originally this was the site of a house occupied by the Pulleyne family of farmers and tanners but the present three storey house was built in 1757 by Samuel Smithson, a farmer, who could not afford to live in it. In this way it is said to have gained its name. The house has two staircases, one of stone, and on either side of the front door stone carvings of the rose of England and the thistle of Scotland.

GRANNIE DIBB AND FARMHOUSE TEAS

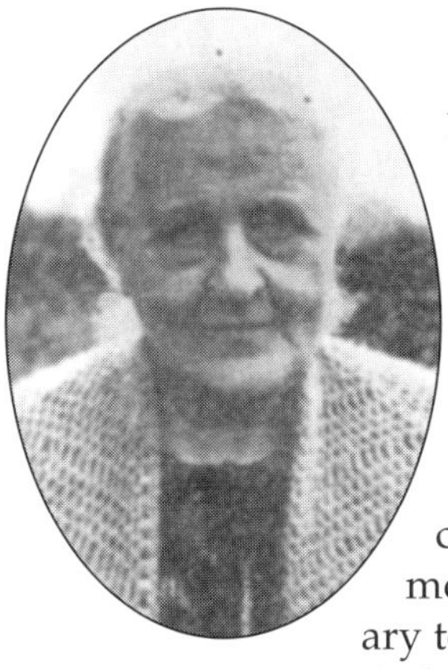
Left: *Ruth Dibb.*

One of the best remembered residents of the valley, Grannie Dibb of Washburn Farm, Snowden (see p.76) was known to many weary and hungry walkers and cyclists for providing accommodation and serving legendary teas during the first half of the twentieth century.

Ruth Dibb was born at Timble Great in 1866, the daughter of Lister and Mary Holmes who later farmed at Braim House, Norwood. She attended Fewston School in a room above cottages at Toad Hole beside the church where she was taught by the vicar's daughter. Married to Bolland, born at Weston in 1863, the couple went to live at Snowden in about 1900. He had attended Askwith School a mile beyond the valley boundary to which he and other children from Snowden walked. In deep snow they were carried through drifts on the shoulders of men whose clothes, in the days before waterproofs, often froze. Bolland often played truant, once saving his 6d.

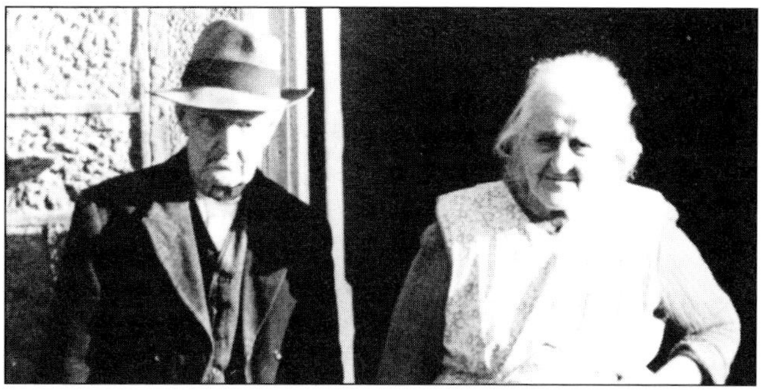
Bolland and Ruth Dibb.

school money until he had amassed 7s.6d, and hiding it for safety in a wall at Washburn Farm – so successfully that he was never able to find it.

The couple had a large family of seven children, five sons and two daughters, but standards at Washburn Farm were always high. The guests' teas were served on tables with freshly washed, ironed and starched cloths. All the baking was done at night when everyone else was asleep, and at weekends and in school holidays the children, and later grandchildren, were called upon to help out with the washing up, while Grannie cooked and served. Despite the fact that the farmhouse was not especially large it was not unusual for groups of fifty or more to arrive in need of refreshment. Among those who visited were members of the Leeds College of Commerce Rambling Club who particularly remembered Mrs Dibb's Christmas dinners. When one of the party married in 1938 he received from her the present of a beautiful tablecloth. Grannie Dibb died in 1960 but is still fondly remembered far beyond the valley.

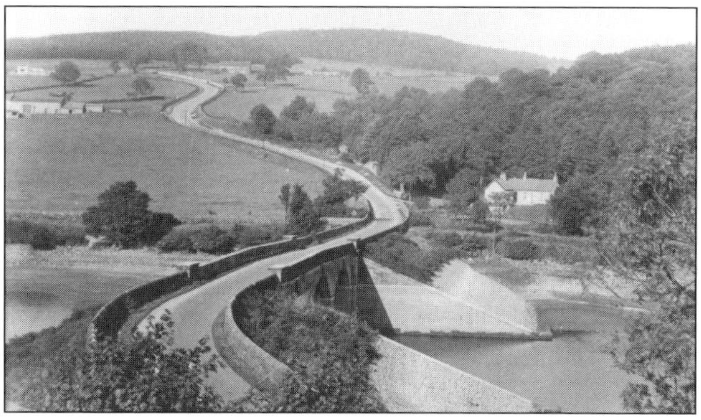
Norwood Edge 1920s looking north to sunny Bank Farm and Norwood Hall.

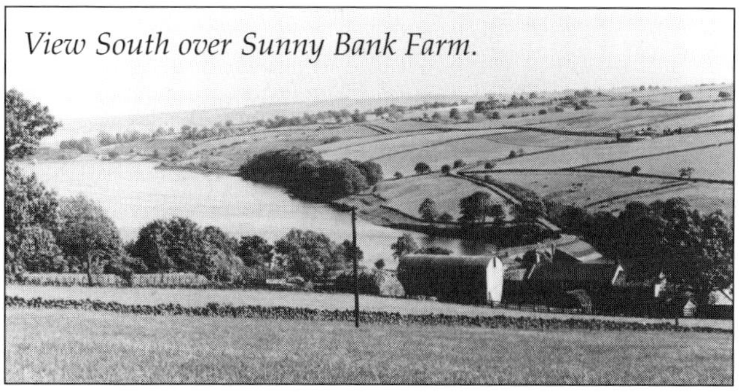
View South over Sunny Bank Farm.

Chapter 4

The Lower Valley

From the mid eleventh century ownership of this part of the valley has been divided between a number of landlords including the King, the Archbishop of York, the Cistercian monks of Fountains Abbey and several lay landlords, among whom were the Percies, Lindleys, Brandlings, Palmes, Hitches and Maudes, and the Fawkes family at Farnley who remain.

The four principal areas of settlement are the three villages of Farnley, Leathley and Stainburn and the hamlet of Lindley, north of Leathley, all of which lie in the most fertile and productive part of the valley. In the mid nineteenth century both Lindley and Leathley encompassed a thousand acres of arable and pasture land and were surrounded by a further thousand acres of moorland. Today the land is devoted almost entirely to pasture.

In 1672 Lindley had an estimated population of just over a hundred but it now consists of little more than a few farms, one of which, Lindley (Hall) Farm, was once the home of the Lindley and later the Palmes families who would have celebrated mass in a private chapel, since demolished. In 1719 the hall was bought by the Fawkes family of Farnley and has been much altered. It is now a working farm. Four alms-houses formerly stood nearby. The mill which once stood on Hensan's Beck to the south east of the hall may have belonged to the Lindley family in the eleventh century. In 1861 the miller, Richard Lamb also held 20 acres of land. The beck joined the River Washburn to the south.

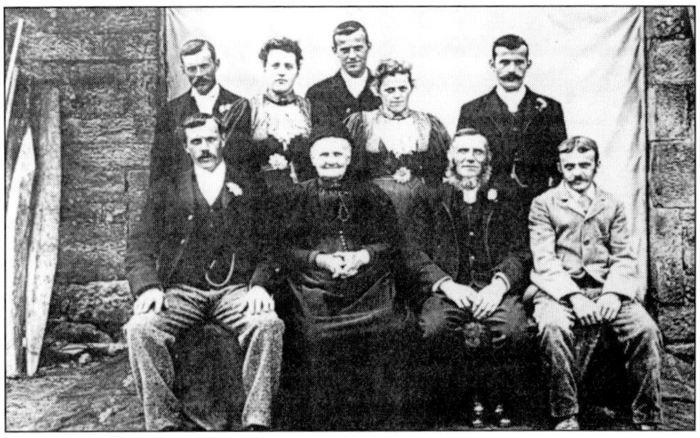

The Smith family at Middle Farm, Dob Park.

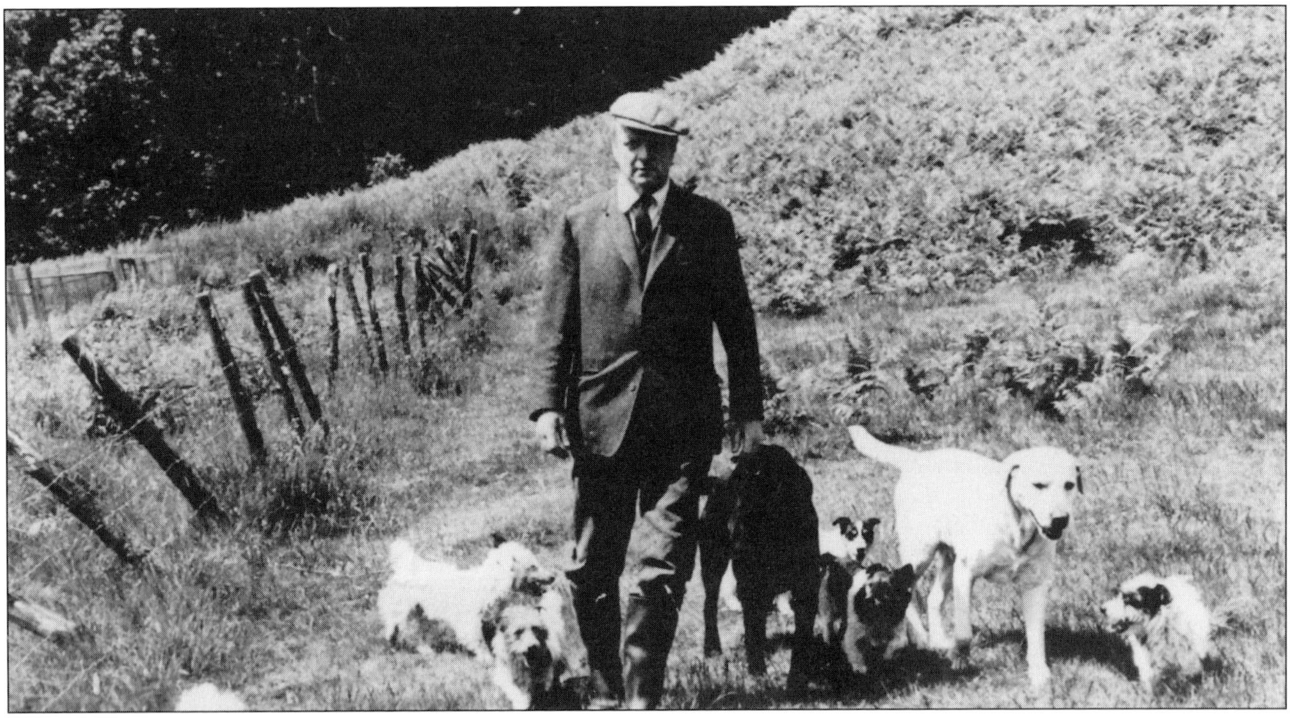

Alf Forder – Lindley gamekeeper and 'a true countryman' c.1955.

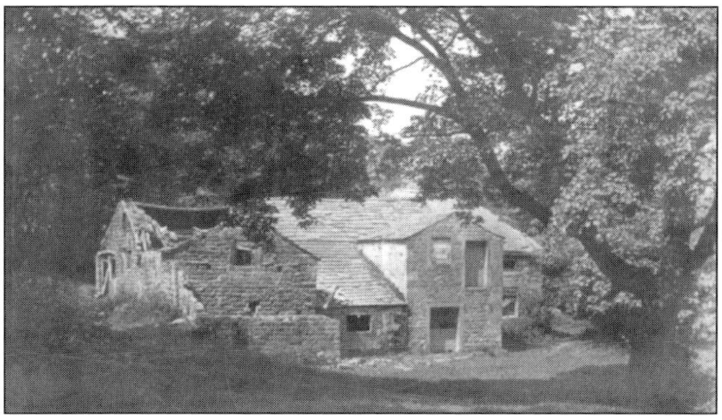

Dob Park Mill.

DOB PARK MILL

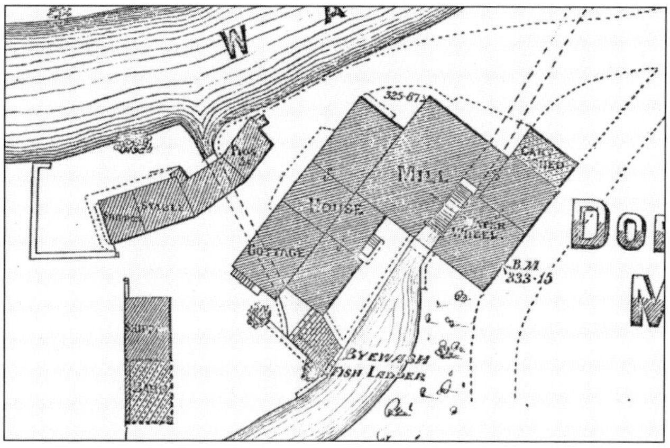

Dob Park Mill – plan.

Built by the Vavasour family in the mid seventeenth century the mill was later conveyed with the rest of Dob Park to the Hitch family of Leathley. By the 1780s it belonged to the Hardcastle family of Hampsthwaite. In 1806 the mill and two islands of land were sold by Henry Hardcastle to William Thornton of Dob Park, who in 1840 was succeeded by his son Matthew.

A plan of the mill shows a coke cellar and furnace at ground level with a drying kiln and grinding chamber containing three pairs of stones on the first floor – two pairs for removing the husk, and a pair of smaller stones for making flour. The wheel was approximately 14 feet in diameter. The Thornton's living accommodation was attached to the mill. William's grandson, John William, who inherited the mill, eventually left in order to farm.

By 1897 the mill was partially roofless and deserted, its land compulsorily purchased by Leeds Corporation. There then followed a lengthy dispute between the Thorntons and the Corporation over the amount of financial compensation due, the Corporation claiming in their defence that as there was 'no trade for old-fashioned country corn mills the mill was no longer a going concern' and therefore worth little.

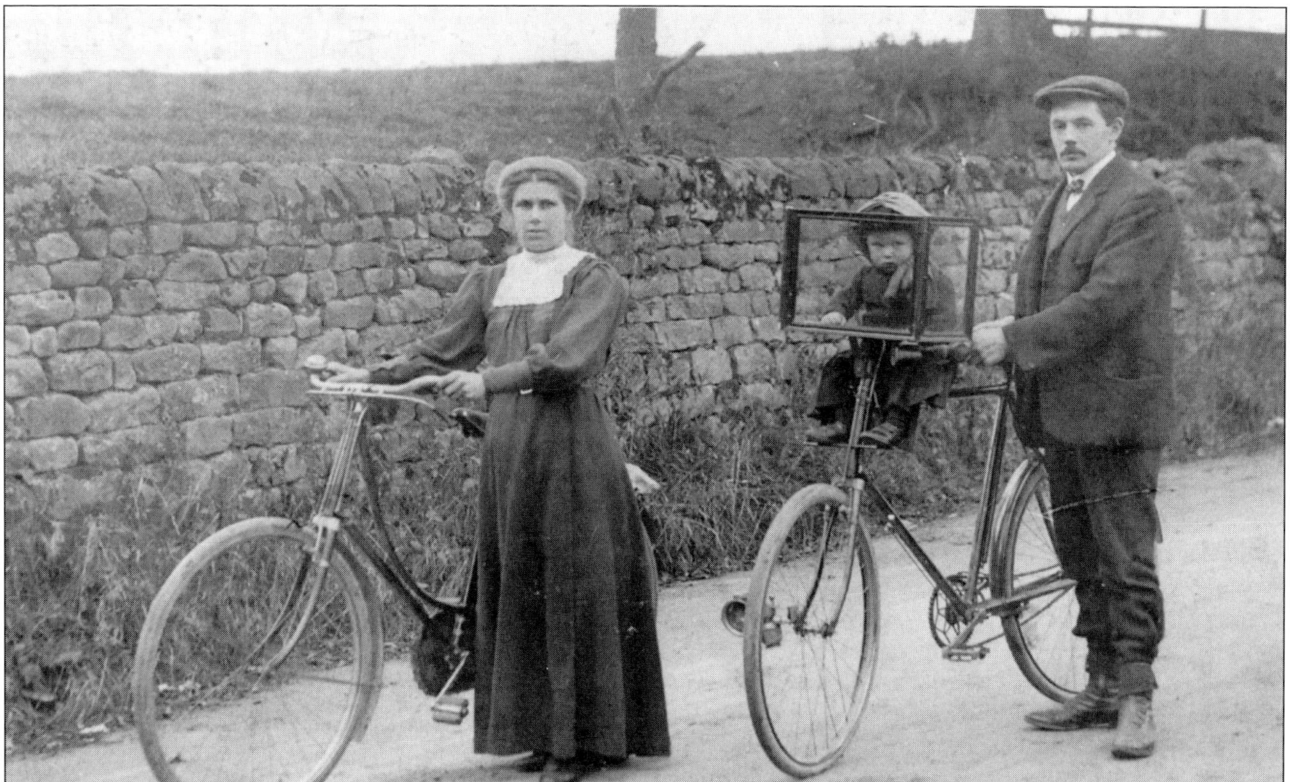

Anthony and Lizzie Thornton with Jimmy. Anthony Thornton was the son of John William.

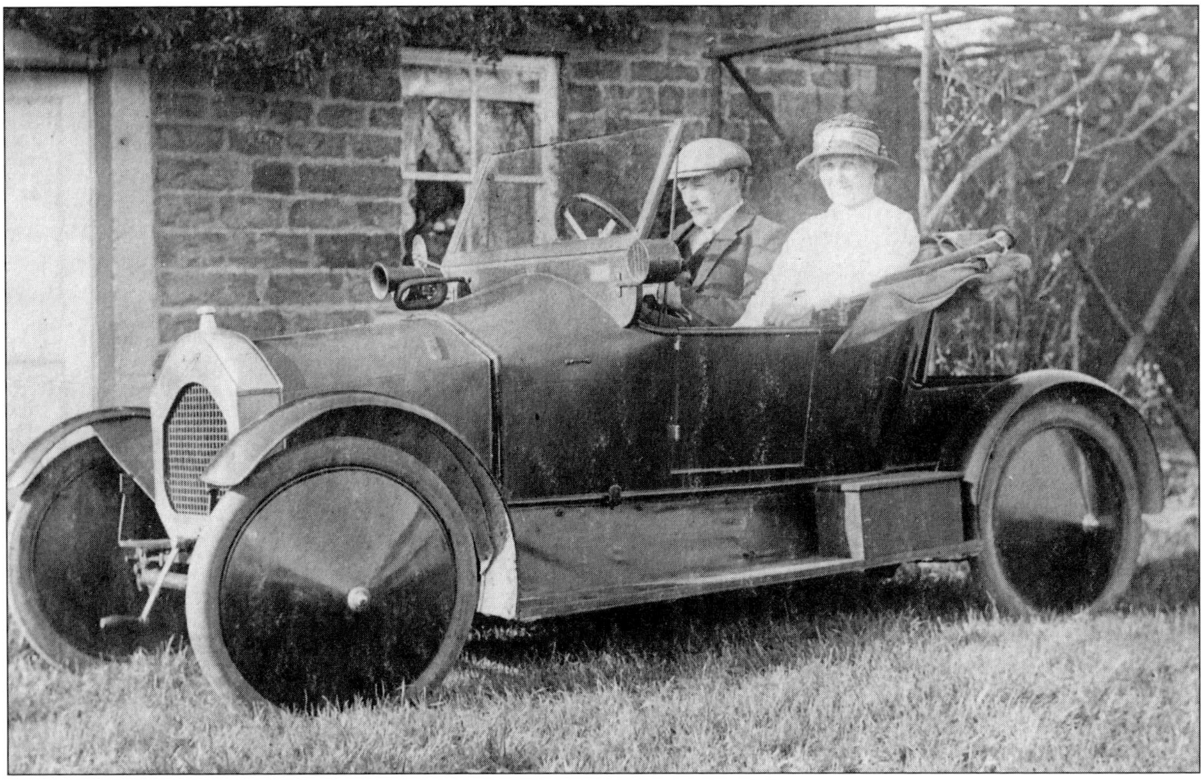

Anthony and Lizzie at Pear Tree Farm.

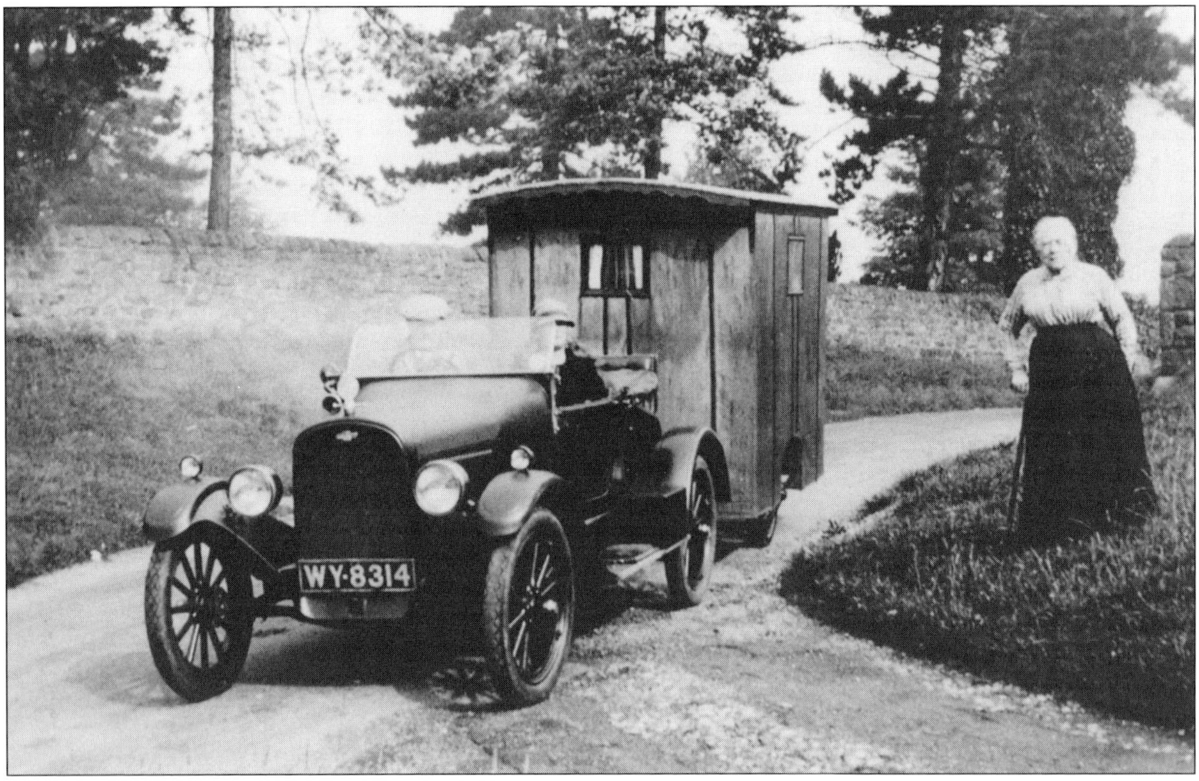

The Thorntons – camping style 1920s.

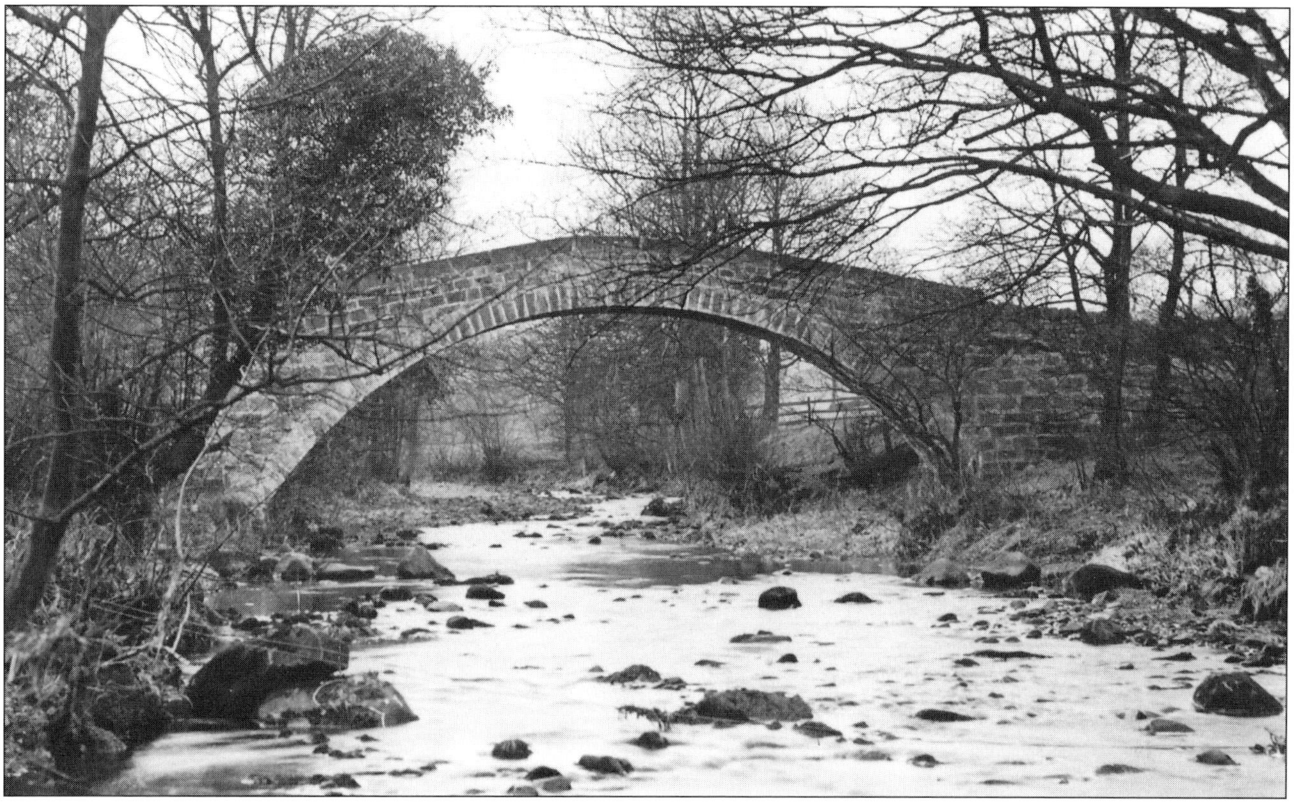

Dob Park Bridge.

DOB PARK BRIDGE

The first reference to a bridge over the Washburn occurs in 1560 when the packhorse bridge provided a link to the old trade route between Otley and Nidderdale known as Psaltergate. Until the eighteenth century salt, a vital commodity for the preservation of meat, was transported to the area from the north-east coast. In 1658 the parishes of Fewston and Weston were summoned to appear at Wetherby Quarter Sessions for the non-repair of the bridge, and ordered to carry out the repairs before Michaelmas 'on pain of £20'. Fewston refused saying that the bridge was out of their parish, while Weston, in whose parish it lay, also refused saying they had no use for it. In 1659 both parishes were therefore indicted at Skipton for non-compliance and Fewston, found guilty, was ordered to repair it before Michaelmas.

By 1738 the bridge was stated to be 'so ruinous it must be rebuilt' at a cost to Fewston of £50 for stone, towards which the justices at Pontefract granted £16.13.4. In 1767 a disastrous flood caused the river to rise six feet in an hour, destroying both it and also Lindley Bridge. The present bridge was rebuilt in 1768-69.

In 1807 a legal battle occurred involving Wm. Thornton, the miller at Dob Park, who requested that the route to the mill be indicted as a carriage road – thereby providing an improved surface – and also the removal of toll gates. This was contested by Weston parish and in an attempt to save the expense of litigation, Wm. Vavasour offered Thornton a road of his own which he turned down. The case eventually went to trial at York, and after a hearing lasting almost twelve hours, Vavasour triumphed '... much to the disappointment and confusion of our perjured enemies, thus they expend for nothing a large sum of money and lose their road several times over I offered them for nothing – perverse and mischievous villains!' Thornton and his associates then collected money and appealed for a new trial, in the meantime tearing down the new toll gate, pulling up posts and insulting Vavasour and his lawyer as they rode over Dob Park Bridge, all to no avail as their application was refused.

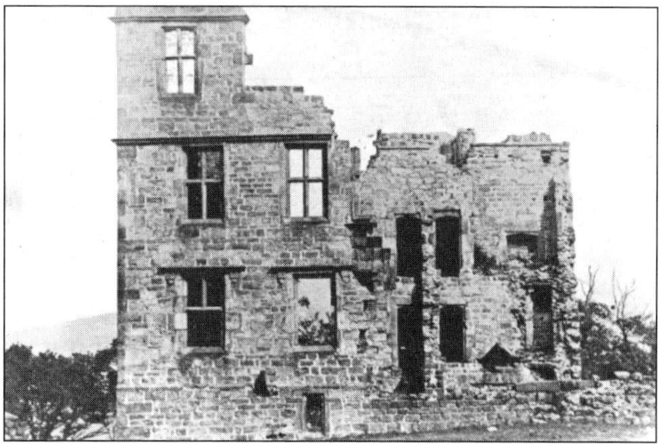

Dob [Dogge] Park Lodge.

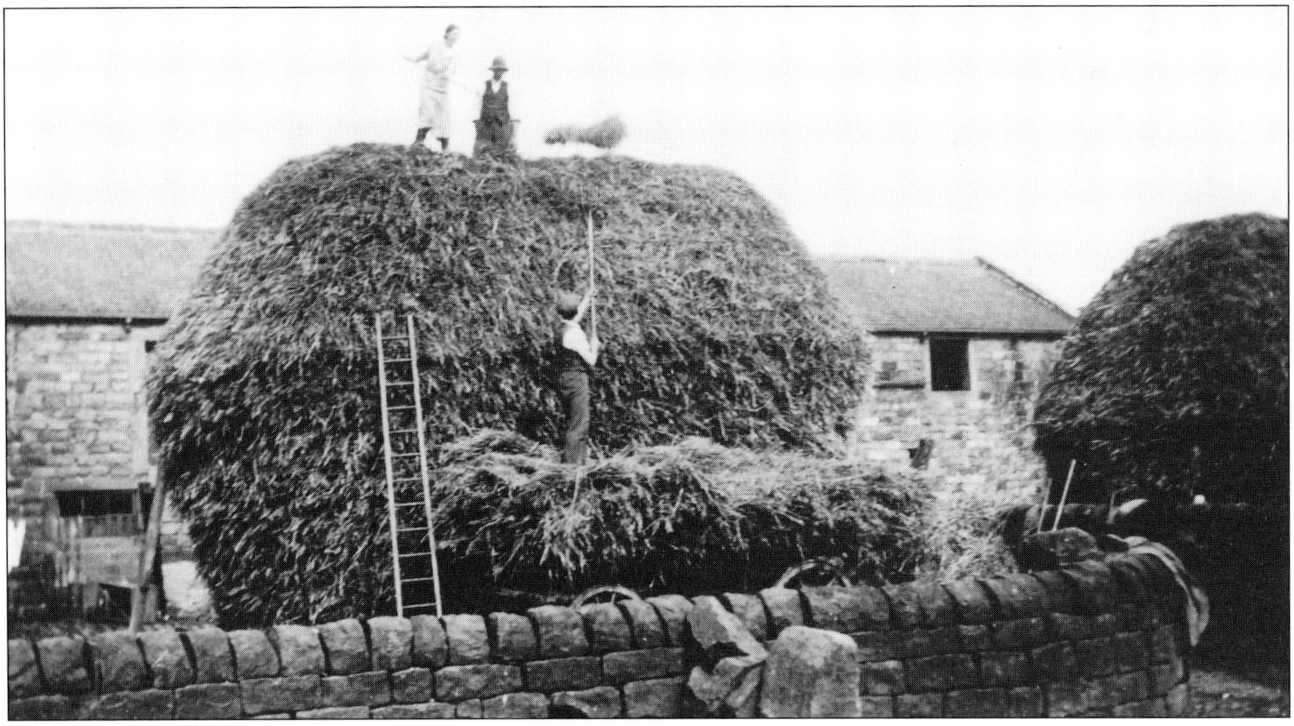

Building a corn stack at Haddockstones Farm, Farnley.

DOB [DOGGE] PARK LODGE

Built in the early seventeenth century on land emparked by the Vavasour family of Weston, the area is widely known today as Dob Park appearing as such in a sixteenth century document, although registers of the seventeenth century contain references to both 'Dob' and 'Dogge' Park. The latter name has given rise to the theory that the lodge may once have been connected to the Royal Forest and used for keeping hounds, or as a venue for 'dog courts where owners of 'unlawed' dogs were held to account. However, the lodge was never part of the Royal Forest. A four storey building once containing five hearths, it has a shield with three quoits, part of the arms of Lancaster, under one window. In 1671 the lodge was the home of Walter Hitch a member of a Leathley family who sold it in 1789 after which it fell into disrepair. A story that the lodge was once connected to Lindley Farm by a tunnel has no foundation.

FARNLEY HALL AND THE FAWKES FAMILY

'A place where great genius was loved and appreciated'
John Ruskin

The Fawkes association with the Washburn Valley has lasted for more than six centuries since William Fawkes was Lord of the Manor of Farnley in 1290. In 1382 the Manor passed to John Fawkes, an innkeeper and tanner in the village. In the fifteenth century a John Fawkes served as a Steward of Knaresborough Forest, and in the sixteenth century two members of the family were sword bearers to the Lord Mayor of London. In the seventeenth century the infamous Guy Fawkes was a distant relative. In the nineteenth and twentieth centuries two members of the family were involved in political life, Walter Fawkes as MP for Yorkshire in 1806, and Frederick Fawkes serving as MP for Pudsey and Otley in 1922. Other members of the family have also served as High Sheriffs and Deputy Lieutenants of the county.

From the late eighteenth to the early nineteenth century, Farnley was at the centre of a great estate regarded as one of the major English land holdings with 20,000 acres of pasture, woodland and moorland in West and North Yorkshire and Northumberland amassed largely as a result of advantageous marriage, inheritance and wise management. From 1819 a policy of consolidation saw the sale of more distant holdings and by 1872 the estate encompassed more than 11,000 acres including in the valley Leathley, Lindley, Stainburn, Norwood with Clifton, Fewston, and Farnley with its 500-hundred acre park. In the late nineteenth century land was compulsorily purchased by Leeds Corporation for the creation of Lindley Reservoir.

The Grade I listed Hall consists of two wings, one dating from the early seventeenth century, and the other, the late eighteenth century.

The later wing with a canted central bay, Doric frieze and cornice, and balustraded parapet dates from

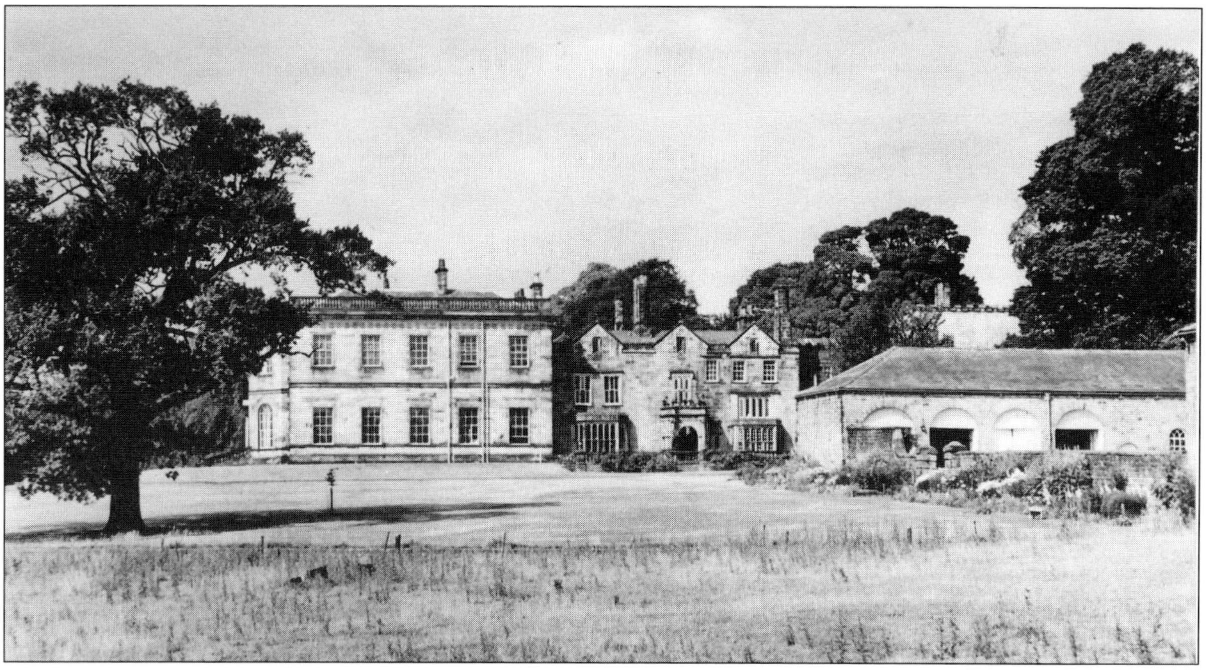

Farnley Hall – Elizabethan and Georgian wings.

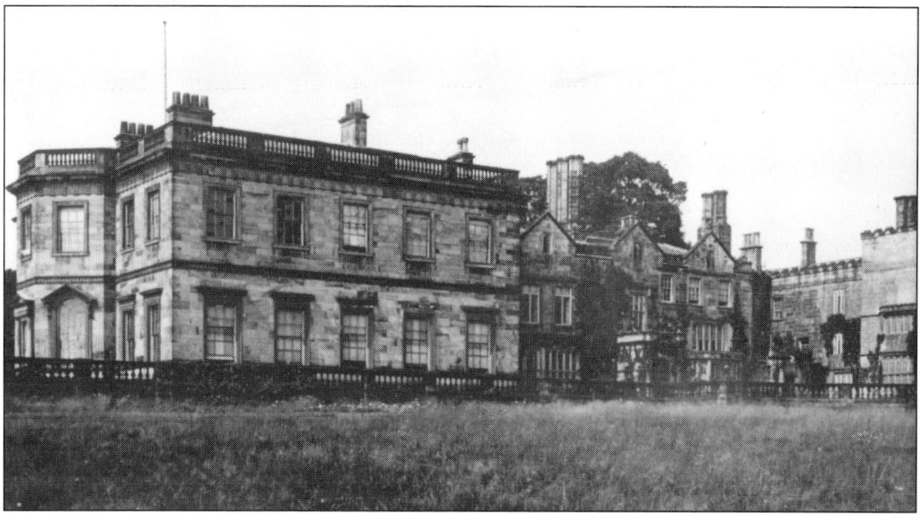

Farnley Hall.

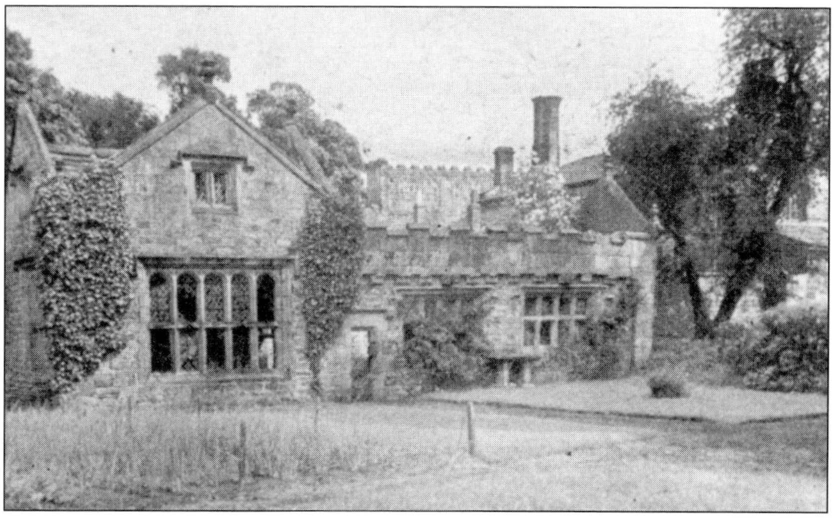

Farnley Hall – Elizabethan Wing – rear with stone table.

1786, and is by John Carr of York. A third wing built in the Victorian period was demolished in the late 1980s.

Members of the family have always been great benefactors, the best known example of which was their patronage of the landscape artist, Joseph Mallord William Turner. Turner was a close friend of Walter Ramsden Hawksworth Fawkes [1769-1825] and for almost twenty years from 1808, a frequent and popular visitor to Farnley, especially during the shooting season. A room was kept for him where the children of the family were welcome to watch him paint. Fawkes commissioned many of Turner's paintings, especially those of birds, the house, and the surrounding countryside. Other famous guests were the artist Thomas Girtin and the poet John Ruskin, another admirer of Turner's work. Ruskin and his wife were present in December 1884 when Ayscough Fawkes, a descendant of Walter and his wife, entertained Prince Leopold, the son of Queen Victoria, and Princess Helena his wife, the Duke and Duchess of Albany, all of whom were visiting the Leeds Music Festival.

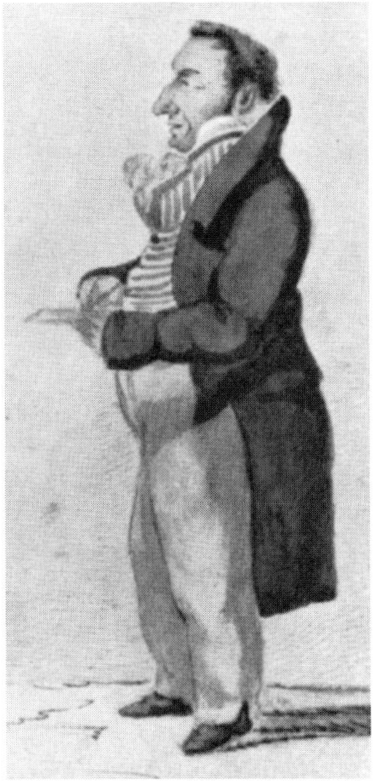

Caricature of J. M. W. Turner 1775-1851.

In the early nineteenth century the house received a number of additions from other family houses including a fireplace engraved 'CF' for Charles Fairfax and a stone gateway and table.

The table is said to have 'formerly stood in the Orchard of Menston Hall', widely assumed to be the house also known as Fairfax Old Hall in Menston. Three miles from Farnley it was the home of Charles Fairfax, son of Sir Thomas Fairfax of Denton, and brother of Ferdinand, General of the Forces in the North. It has, however, also been suggested that the table may have come from Low Hall which stood at the opposite end of Menston village and was the home of Richard Rhodes, a kinsman of Fairfax, who in 1685 demolished the house to build a new house.

Wherever the table was originally situated, it is thought that on 30 June 1644, just before the Battle of Marston Moor, Oliver Cromwell, other Parliamentary leaders and Charles Fairfax met around it. Despite the fact that Charles Fairfax and the Rhodes family of Low Hall were related, it seems unlikely that Cromwell and his group, especially as it included

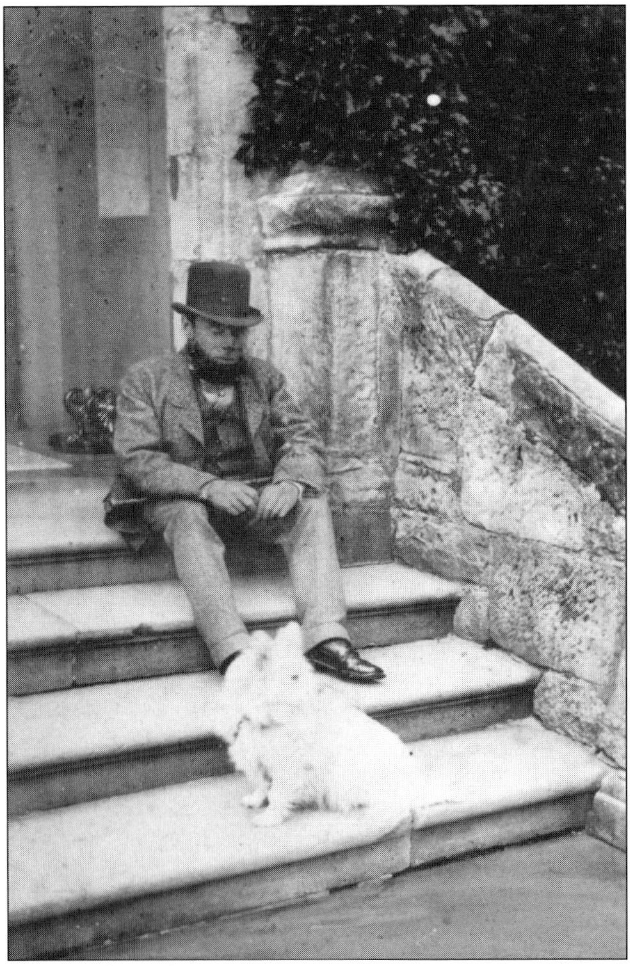

Ayscough Fawkes.

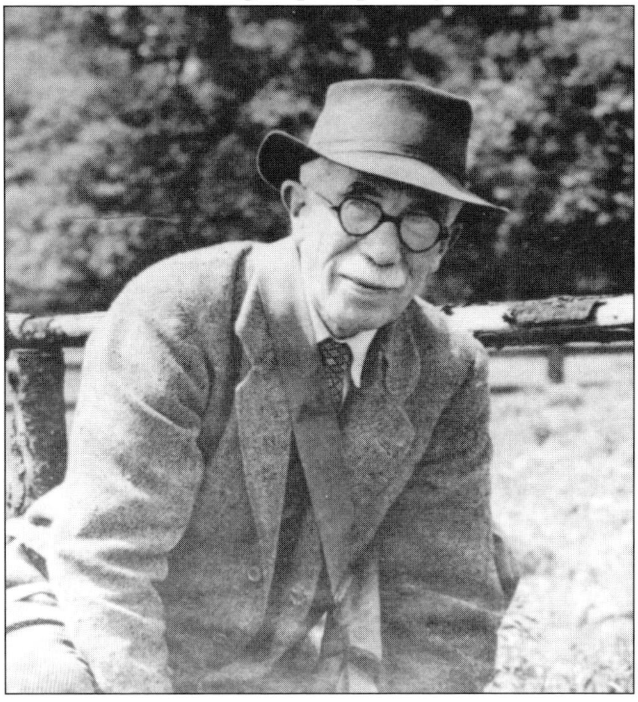

Major Le G. G. W. Horton Fawkes 1892-1982 – Squire of Farnley.

Charles himself, would have met anywhere in Menston other than at Menston (Fairfax) Old Hall, and in apparent confirmation the inscription on the table reads as follows;

> *'At this table which formerly stood in the orchard of Menston Hall the seat of Colonel Charles Fairfax, Oliver Cromwell (according to a tradition carefully handed down) dined June 30th 1644 two days preceding the battle of Marston Moor.'*

Windows at Farnley were acquired from Lindley, and a porch and dairy from Newall Old Hall at Otley. From Hawksworth Hall at Guiseley came panelling for the hall and a heraldic east window for the church at Farnley.

ALL SAINTS CHURCH, FARNLEY

A chapel is said to have been in Farnley since 1250 and archaeology has revealed Roman tooling on some exterior stone, a stone of the medieval period in the inner wall of the gallery and evidence of a Norman arch at the west end. References to a chaplain at Farnley occur as early as 1379, and in 1529 Brian Palmes of Farnley left three shillings and four pence to the 'Chappel at Farnley'. In 1548 the priest there was said to be 'sixty years of age and full of sickness.' In 1825 an inventory records that 'The chapel is kept in good repair by the inhabitants ... and the furniture thereof is one Surplice, a Bible and two Prayer books, a Pulpit-Cushion and one small bell.' The present building, restored by the Fawkes family in 1851 and intended as a chapel of ease for Otley, was served once a month by the vicar of Otley for which he received the sum of £5. In 1926 Farnley became a separate parish before being united with the parish of Leathley as one benefice.

The glass in the church belongs to the seventeenth, eighteenth and early nineteenth centuries. The east window which shows the armorial panels of the Hawksworth and Fawkes families was previously installed in the conservatory at Farnley Hall, and prior to that at Hawksworth Hall, the former residence of Walter Hawksworth Fawkes which explains the depiction of hawks. The artist Henry Gyles (1645-1709) was also responsible for another beautiful window, that of St Cecilia, King David and an angel choir in St. Helen's church, Denton 3miles west of Farnley. An accomplished and well-connected artist of the York school, Gyles was a member of the York 'virtuosi', a group of distinguished artists, antiquarians and academics.

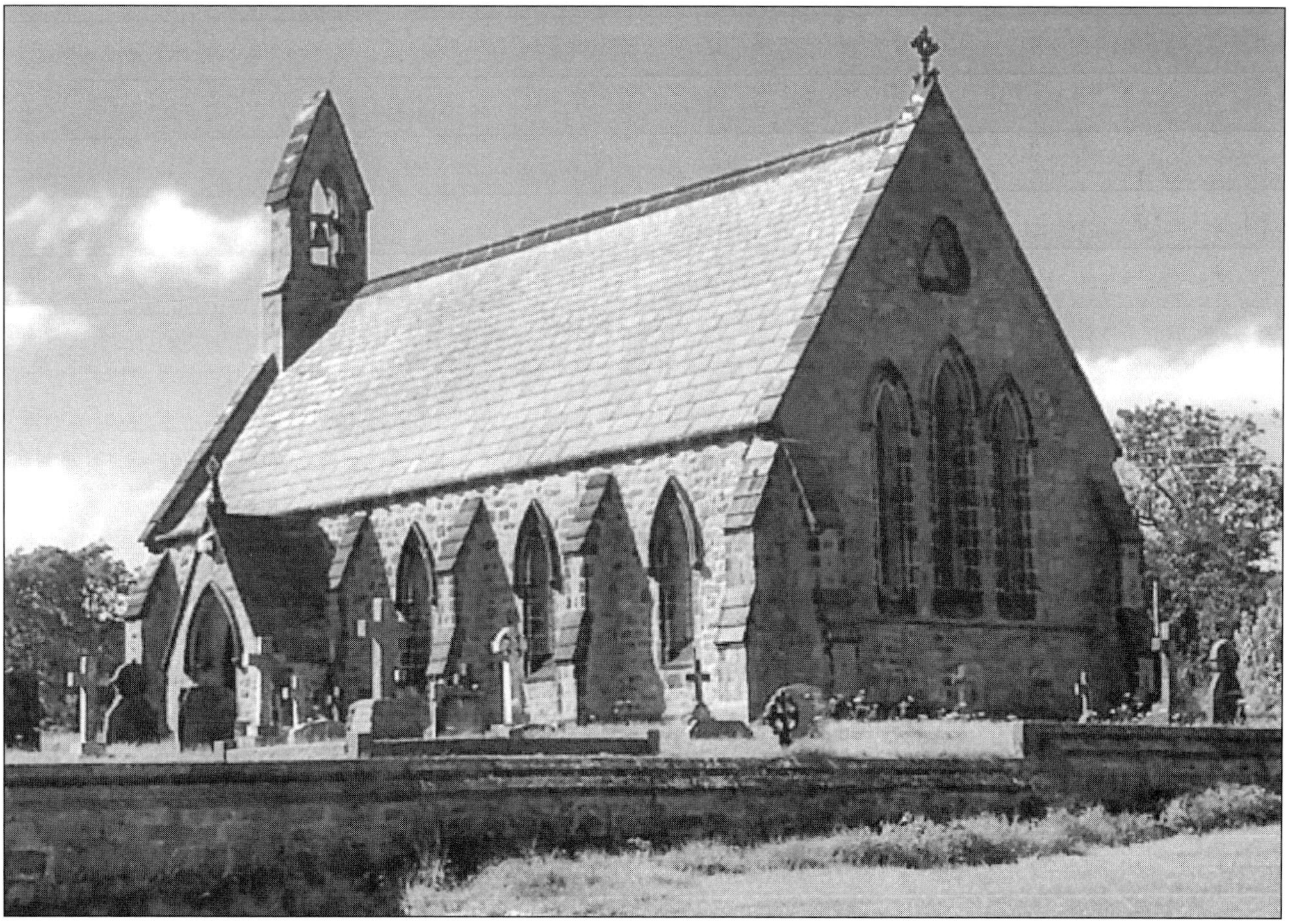

All Saints church, Farnley.

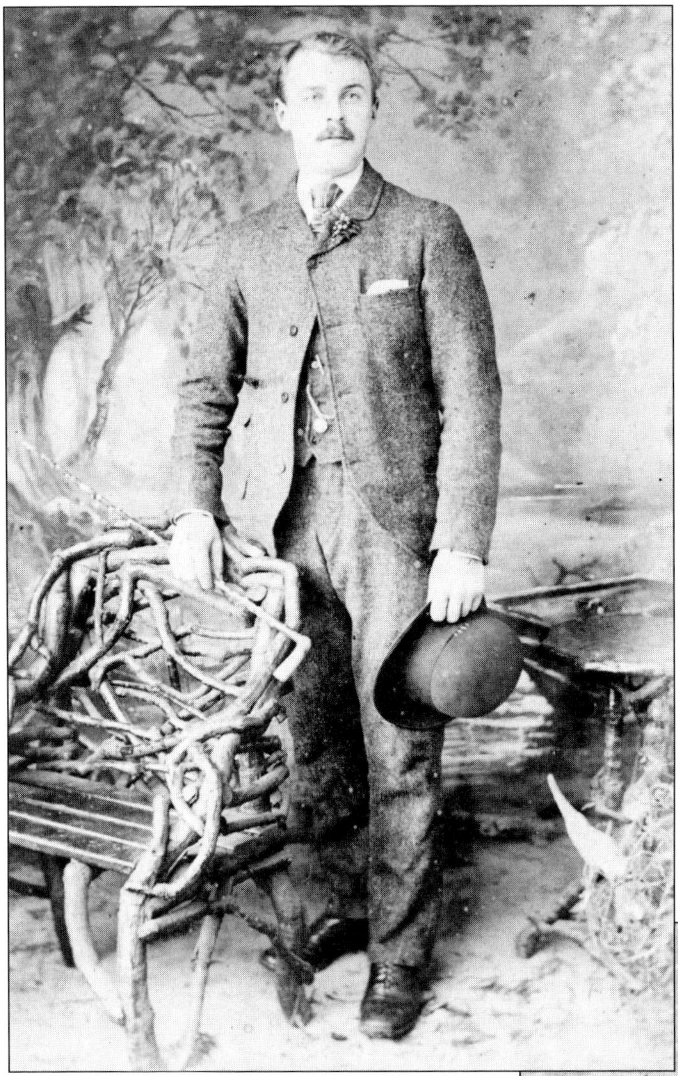

Humphrey Rodgers – Farnley blacksmith.

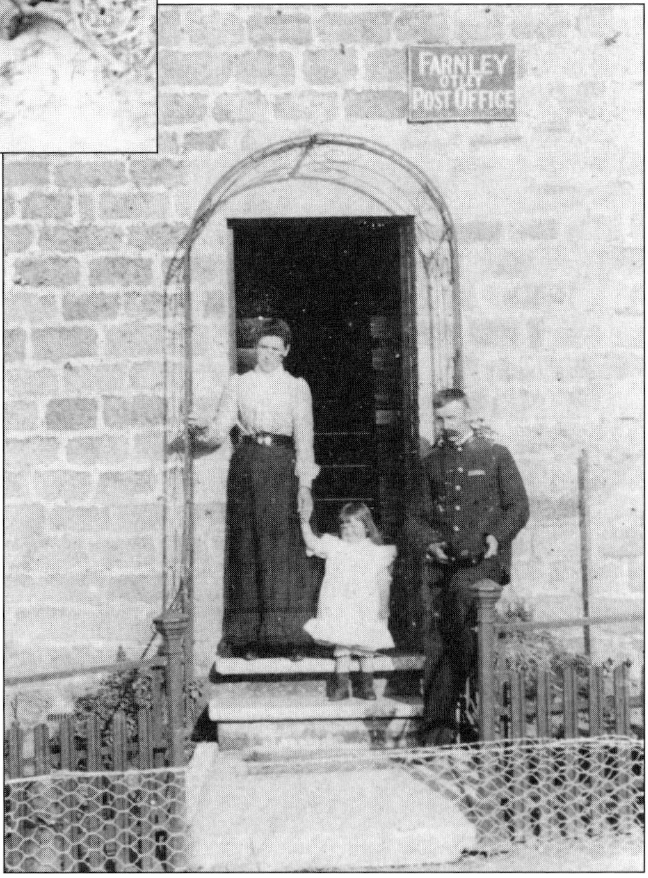

The Cryer family at Farnley Post Office. Alice Ann Cryer with her parents, Fred and Mary Alice. Fred, born c.1865 was both a farmer and postmaster in the village.

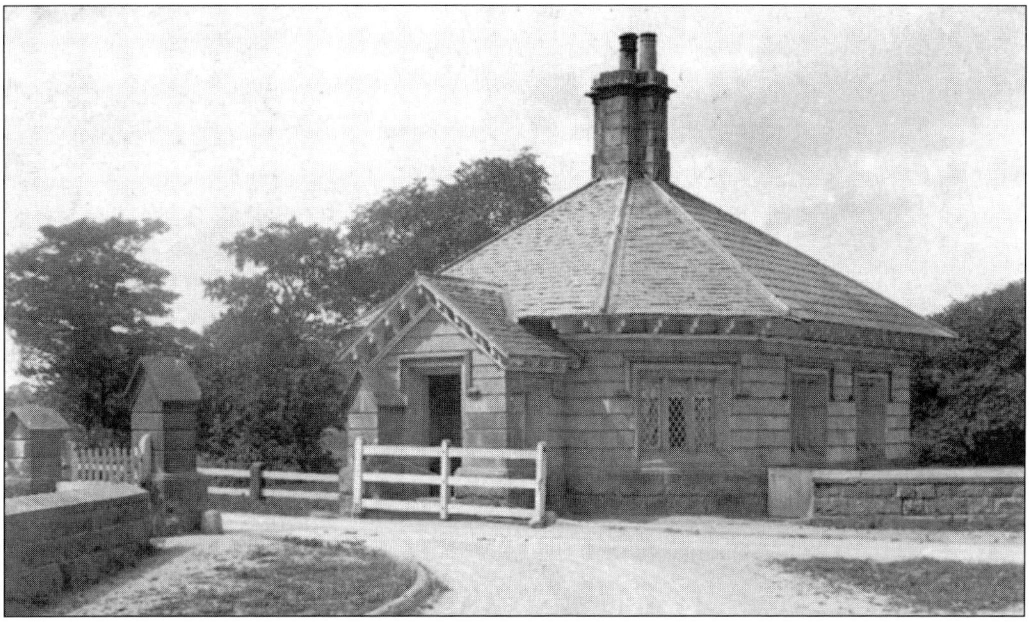

Farnley Toll Bar House. In 1861 the toll collector was Thomas Adamson born at Outwood, Wakefield who lived in the house with his wife Sarah and daughters Sarah and Mary, both dressmakers.

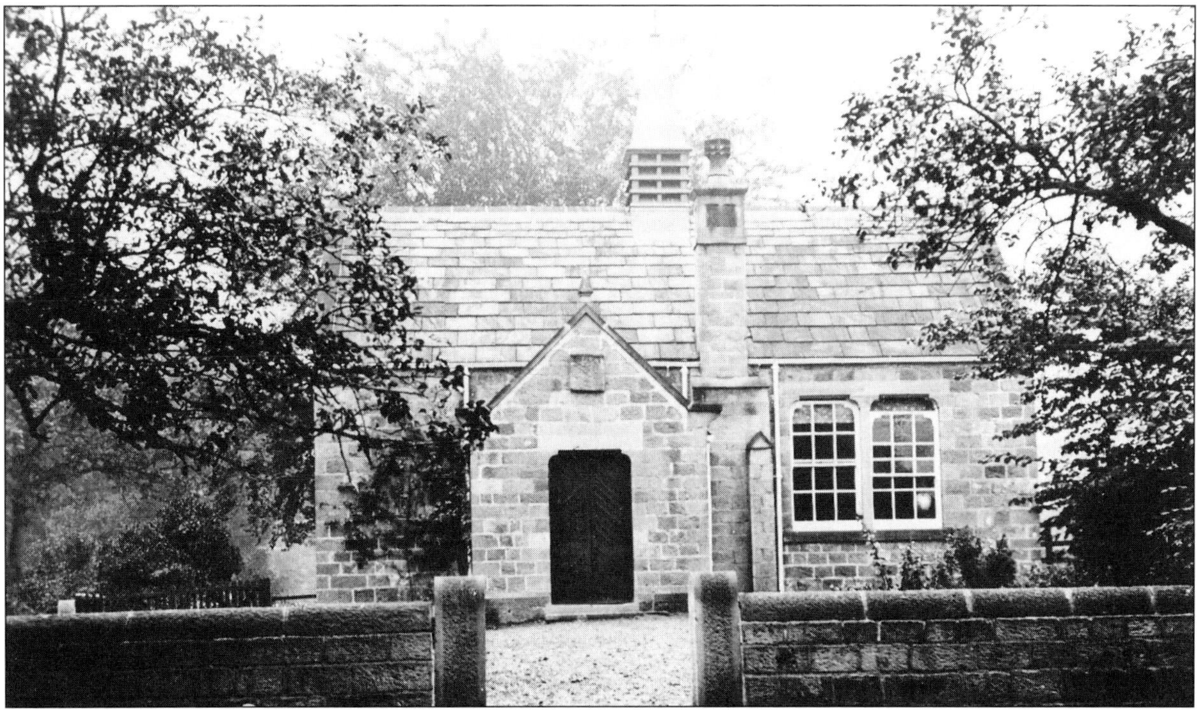

Farnley Schoolhouse. On the 31 August 1898 John Dickinson reported 'we are building a new school at Farnley. My nephews John & George Archer are in charge of the mason's work.'

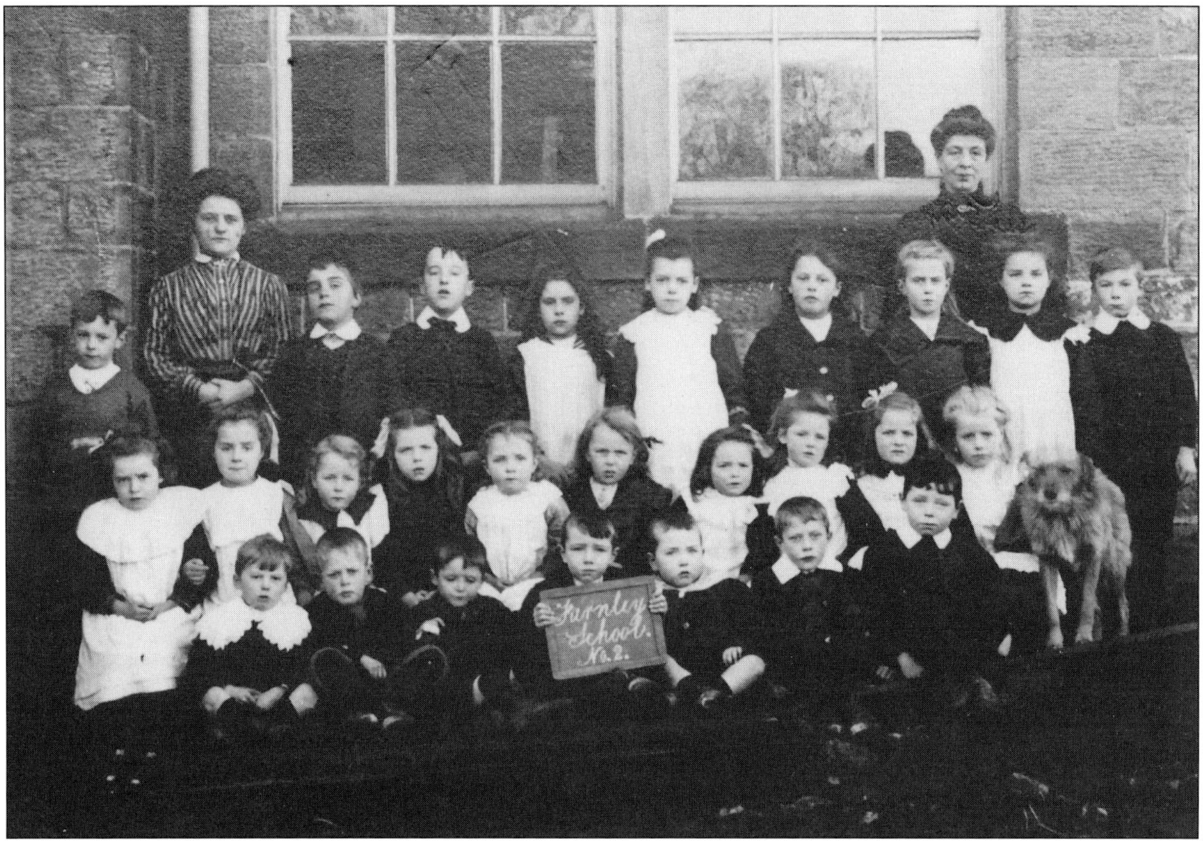

Farnley school pupils.

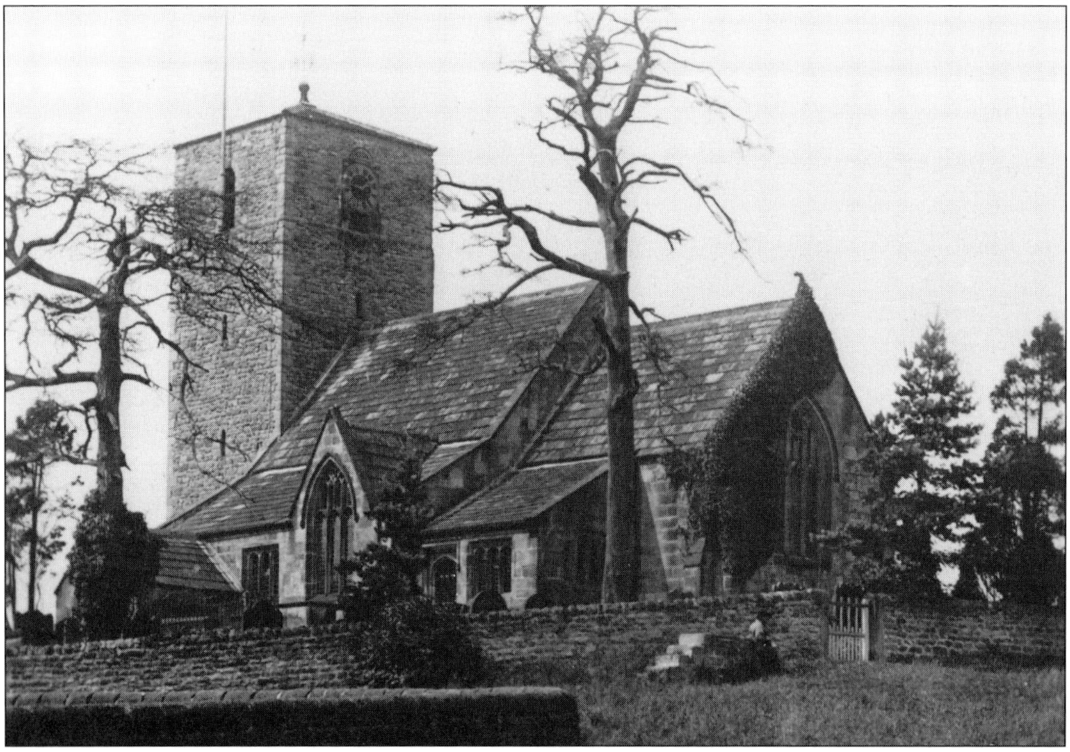

The church of St Oswald, Leathley.

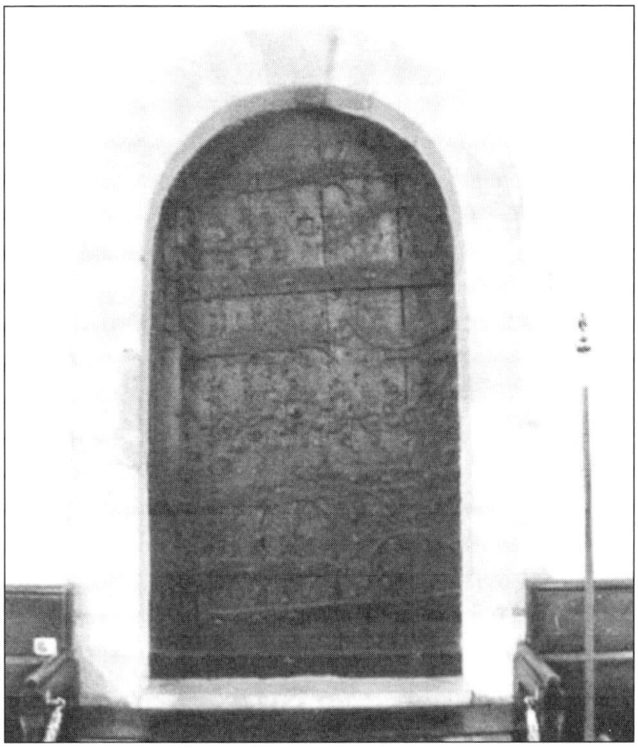

Leathley church – door in west wall.

The dedication of the church to St. Oswald suggests an early foundation, perhaps on a pre-Christian burial site. However, the tower, east and west walls of the nave and chancel arch are of the early Norman period. The first rector dates from 1251. The north and south aisles are of the late fifteenth century, and the capitals bear a number of symbols including the Tudor rose, the crescent and fetterlock of the Percy family and a Tau cross, once considered beneficial in warding off illness. A door into the tower is heavy with highly decorative ironwork, probably of an early date.

The panelling in the chancel is said to have come from nearby Castley Hall. In 1869 the church was restored by Francis Horton Fawkes at a cost of £2000. At that time the roof was renewed, the seventeenth century pews replaced, and an organ installed. The east window is in memory of the Revd Ayscough Fawkes. Wall tablets in the chancel commemorate members of the Hitch family including Robert Hitch of Leathley Hall, and Martin Flathers, a former rector, who died in 1633 aged eighty-three. He may have been related to Matthew Flathers, a Catholic priest born at nearby Weston in 1560 who was hanged, drawn and quartered for his faith at York in 1608.

The annual Rogationtide service held in April was introduced into England in the eighth century in order to pray for a good harvest. During the perambulation members of the congregation, carrying crosses and boughs of greenery, stopped at various places to sing a hymn, say a prayer and bless various aspects of agricultural life, for example the stock, crops, water, implements, and also the farmer and his family. An undated newspaper extract describes the service:

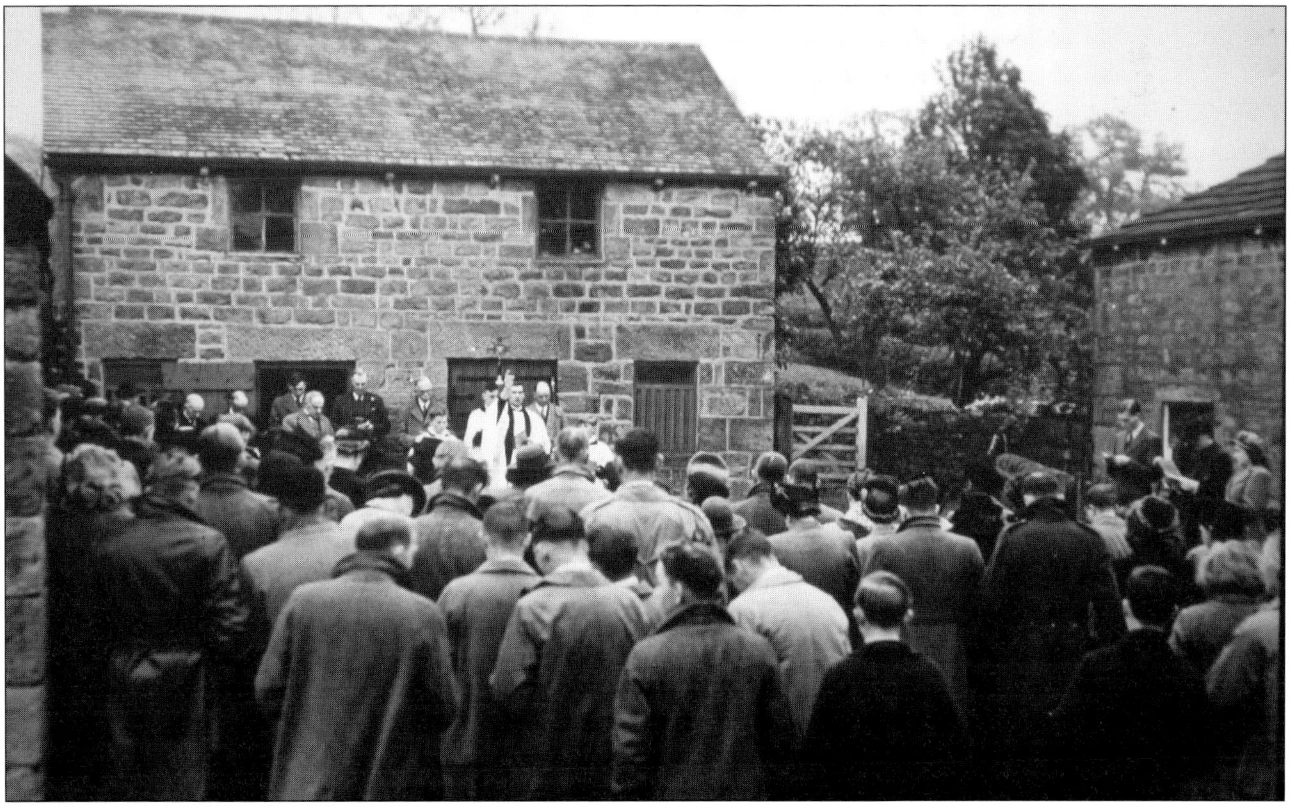

Rogationtide at Leathley.

'Squire and Rector, farmer and farmworker, stood bare headed together on Leathley village green on Sunday, and asked a blessing on their community ... It was a glimpse of the real England that still lives in the countryside. Through the lanes, between hedgerows heavy with blossom wound the Rogation day procession; and village life waited for it. In the farmyard where a blessing was sought for home life, a sheepdog lay beside his kennel, head on paws. At the field gate where crops and livestock were remembered, two horses waited patiently to play their part in a symbolism that captured something of the peace and serenity and simple faith of those who live very close to nature.'

LEATHLEY WESLEYAN METHODIST CHAPEL

A Grade II building, the plaque over the door bears the date MDCCCXXVI (1826) with the quotation:

'And this gospel of the kingdom shall be preached in all the world for a witness unto all nations; and then shall the end come.'

Matthew ch.24 v.14.

THE HITCH ALMSHOUSES

The almshouses on the green at Leathley were founded in 1769 by Ann Hitch for 'people of the parish with a need.' A stone on the central portion bears the inscription 'Through the benevolent intentions of Henry Hitch, Esq., this school and hospital were erected and endowed by Ann Hitch, his only surviving sister and executrix 1769.' Ann was the daughter of Robert Hitch of Leathley, and the great grand-daughter of the Dean of York. In her will of 1769 she left £4 each for four alms people and £14 to the poor of Castley.'

A notable resident of the almshouses Mrs Elizabeth Watson's local fame rests on the fact that she claimed to have lived to the age of a hundred and three. It is said that she was born at Hampole, near Doncaster, on 1 September 1795, and baptised at Hooton Pagnell church at the age of ten. However, this is not borne out by the registers of Hooton Pagnell which in 1805 state that she was born to George Cutt and Ruth (née Brown) on the 26 May 1805 and baptised on the 7 July in the same year. This means that at the time of her death in 1898 she was in fact only ninety-three.

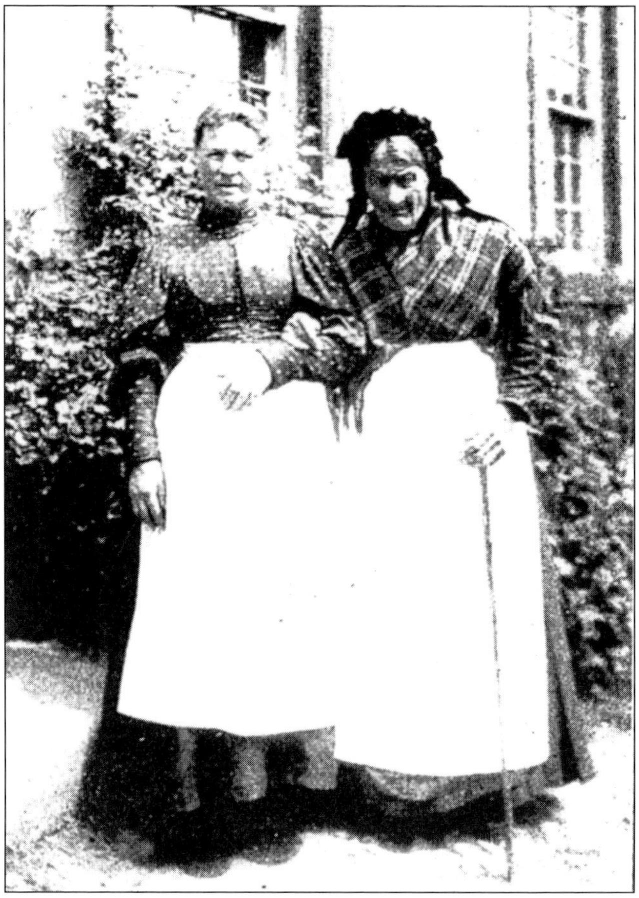

Mrs Watson and her daughter.

Her parents married on the 2 April 1804 when George would have been in his sixteenth year which accounts for Elizabeth's statement that she was her parents' first child. For forty years George Cutt was employed as a coachman by the rector of the neighbouring church of South Kirkby, the Rev. George Allott.

There is however no doubt that Elizabeth was a remarkable lady. The widow of Henry Watson, a

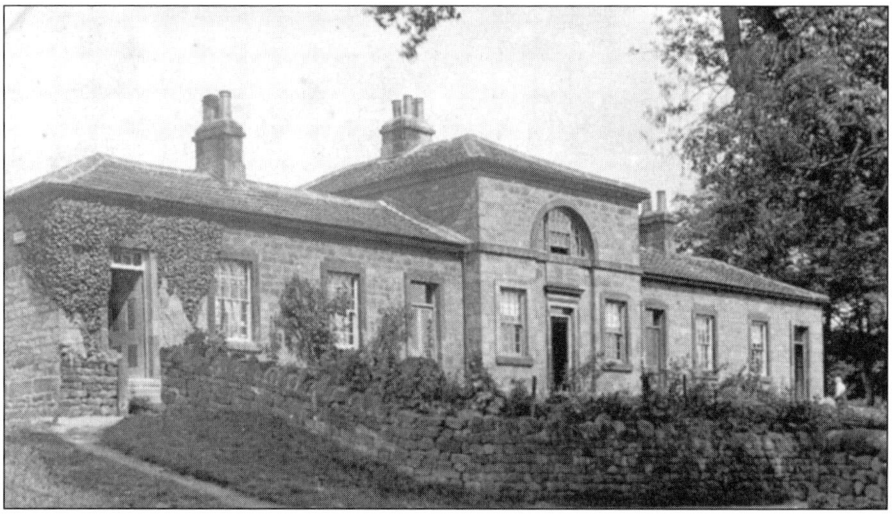

The Hitch Almshouses.

hind, or farm servant, once employed by the Earl of Mexborough, the couple produced thirteen children. After the death of her husband she lived with a daughter, remaining active almost to the end of her life. Her sight and hearing were said to be unimpaired and the year before her death she walked to Otley and back, all of which she attributed to having been a lifelong teetotaller.

LEATHLEY SCHOOL

Among the bequests of Ann Hitch was the sum of £12 a year for the schoolmaster. Initially the children were taught in his sitting room in the central portion of the almshouses before moving to an old tithe barn belonging to the rectory. Among the teachers at Leathley between 1857 and 1861 were John Bell and John Mitchell born in Blubberhouses, and his wife, Isabel, described as 'Master and Mistress of the Free School at Leathley'. In an account of their family history their daughter, Eliza, recalled that a bible belonging to her great-grandfather, Alexander Hay (1751-1817), and given to him by his mother, 'was stolen from our school room at Leathley'. In 1861 the school, then the National School, had an average attendance of twelve boys and girls between the ages of four and fourteen. Hours were from 9 to 12 and 1 to 4, the half hour between 11.30 and 12.00 being reserved for religious instruction 'of a general description'. The subjects taught were those of the original deed with the addition of drawing. According to a School Inspection Report the school's net grant for 1892-3 was £34.1s.8d. In 1901 Frances Seaman became the first head teacher having formerly held the same position at Stainburn.

THE FORREST FAMILY

On the village green opposite the church the Forrest family, blacksmiths for many generations, occupied a forge. In his will of 1701 Thomas Forrest left his son, William, one shilling, and William's two children five pence each 'as a token of my love,' to his daughter, Anne, wife of John Newsome 'one heifer ... and one desk that was her mother's', and to their five children 'two ewe sheep equally amongst them. All the rest ... I bequeath unto my loving son, Thomas.' The inventory of Thomas's goods shows that he also left clothing, furnishings, kitchen and farming equipment, bellows and the other tools of his trade, two cows, a heifer and four sheep with some corn, all amounting to £31.7.10.

LEATHLEY MILL

The mill, which is believed to date from the early seventeenth century, still stands although it is now a private house. The wheel, 14 feet in diameter and 5 feet wide generated about 25 horsepower. In 1861 Reuben Oliver was the miller; later millers included James Mason, John Dibb, John Clapham and Edwin Blakeborough.

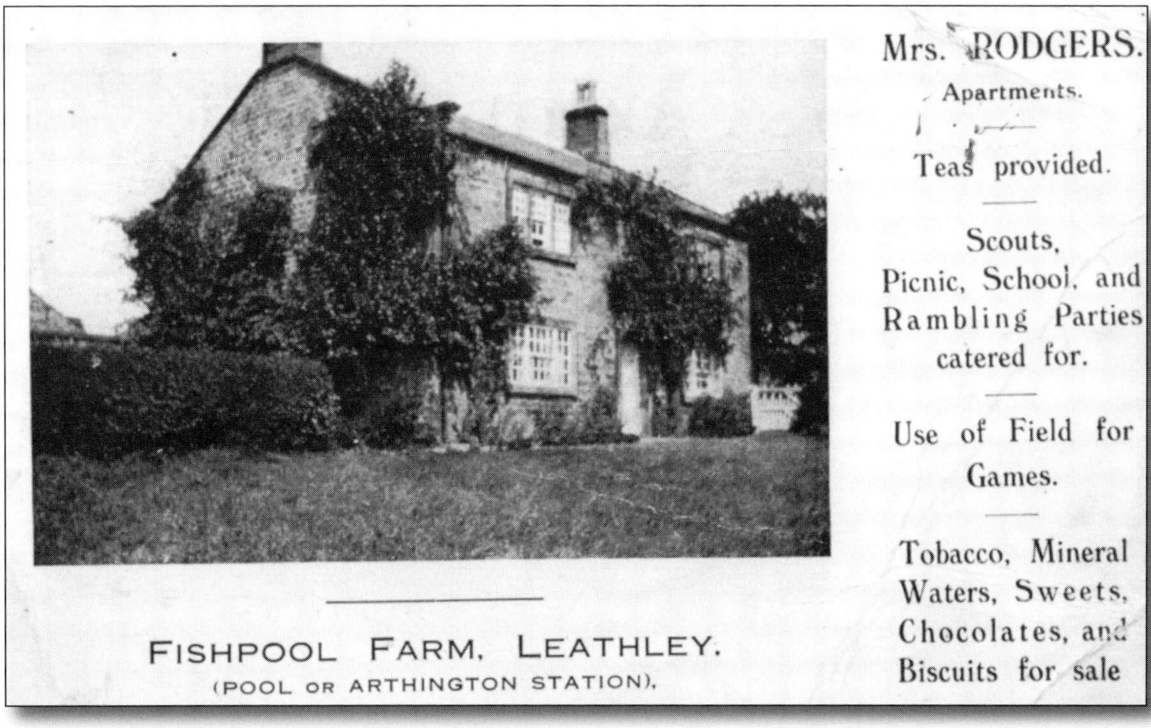

Mrs Rodger's advertisement – Fishpool Farm.

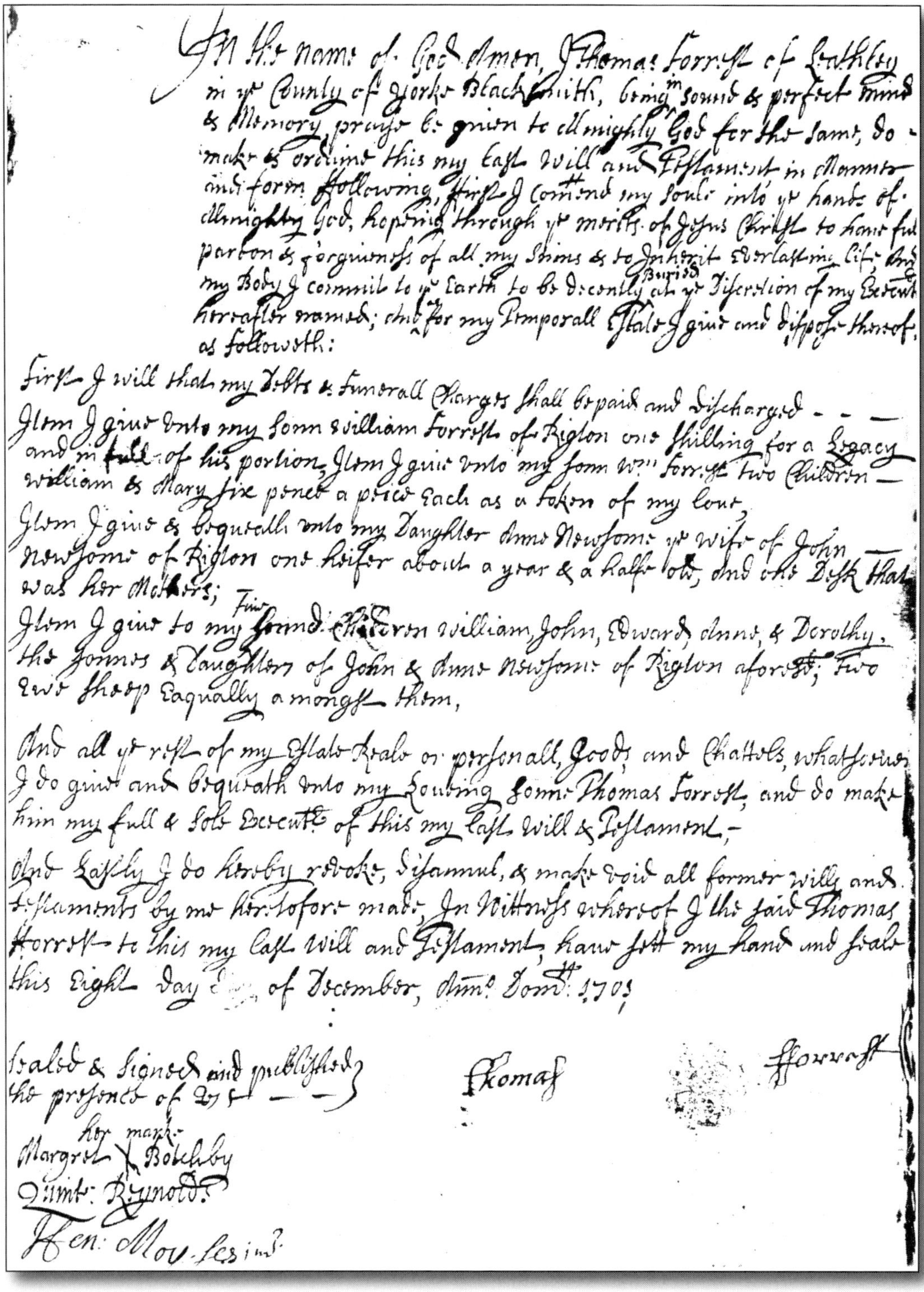
In the name of God Amen, I Thomas Forrest of Leathley in ye County of Yorke Blacksmith, being in sound & perfect mind & Memory praise be given to Almighty God for the same, do make & ordaine this my Last Will and Testament in Manner and form following, First I commend my Soule into ye hands of Almighty God, hoping through ye merits of Jesus Christ to have full pardon & forgiveness of all my Sins & to Inherit Everlasting Life; And my Body I commit to ye Earth to be decently Buried at ye Discretion of my Executr hereafter named; and for my Temporall Estate I give and dispose thereof as followeth:

First I will that my Debts & Funerall Charges shall be paid and Discharged - - -

Item I give unto my Sonn William Forrest of Rigton one Shilling for a Legacy and in full of his portion, Item I give unto my Sonn Wm Forrest two Children William & Mary six pence a peice Each as a token of my love,

Item I give & bequeath unto my Daughter Anne Newsome ye wife of John Newsome of Rigton one heifer about a year & a halfe old, and the Desk that was her Mothers;

Item I give to my Grand Children William, John, Edward, Anne, & Dorothy, the Sonnes & daughters of John & Anne Newsome of Rigton aforesd; Two Ewe Sheep Equally amongst them,

And all ye rest of my Estate reale or personall, Goods and Chattels, whatsoever I do give and bequeath unto my Loving Sonne Thomas Forrest, and do make him my full & sole Executr of this my Last Will & Testament, -

And Lastly I do hereby revoke, disannul, & make void all former wills and Testaments by me heretofore made, In Witness whereof I the said Thomas Forrest to this my Last Will and Testament, have sett my hand and seale this Eight day of December, Anno Domi 1703

Sealed & Signed and published the presence of us - -

her mark
Margret X Botchby
Quint: Reynolds
Hen: Moulesin

Thomas Fforrest

Will of Thomas Forrest, blacksmith.

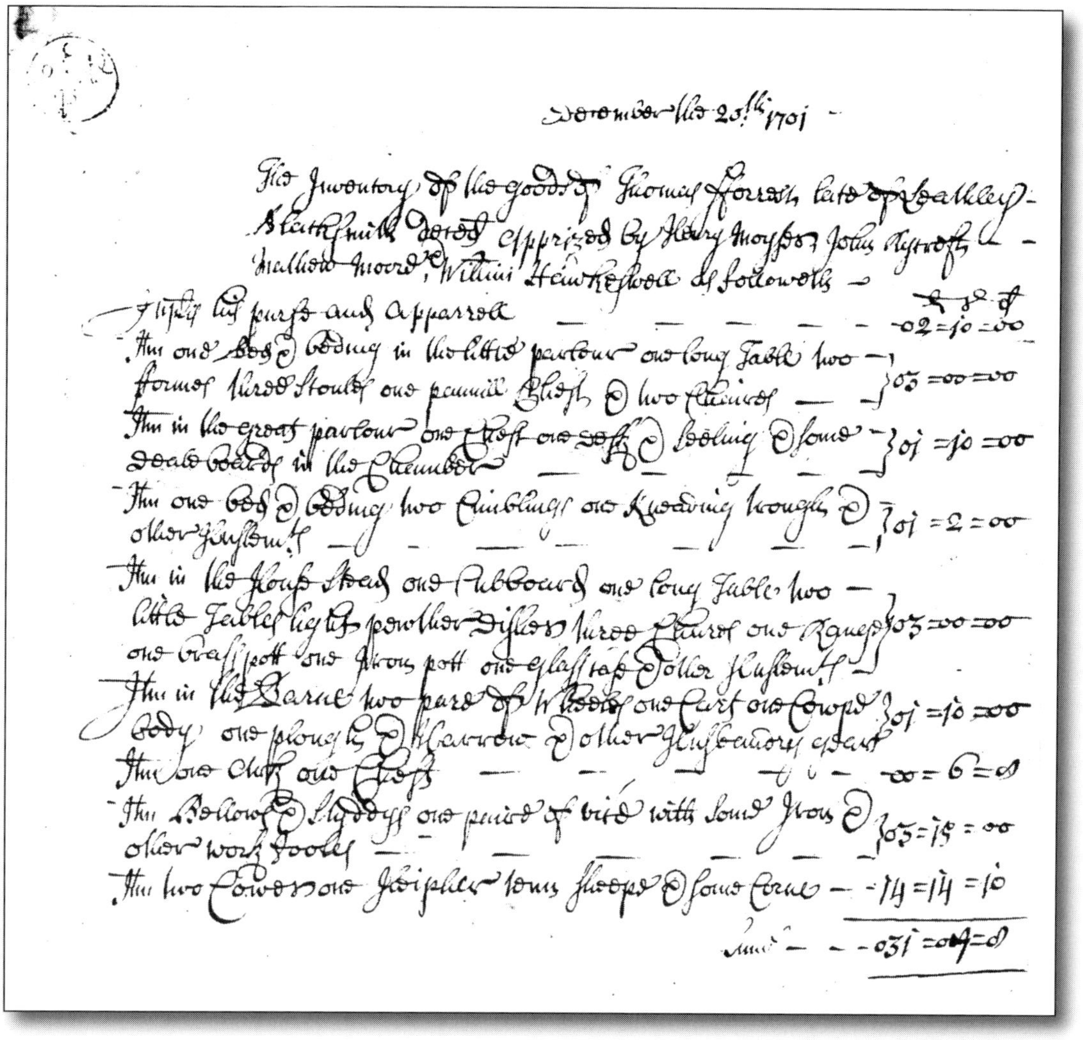

November the 20th 1701

The Inventory of the goods of Thomas fforrest late of Balley Blacksmith deced apprized by Henry Moyser John Ayrcroft Matthew Moore & William Hawkeshead as followeth

Imprimis his purse and apparrell	£ s d 02=10=00
Item one bed & bedding in the little parlour one long table two formes three stooles one pennill chest & two chaires	03=00=00
Item in the great parlour one chest one bed & bedding & some deale boards in the chamber	01=10=00
Item one bed & bedding two tubbs one kneading trough & other husslements	01=2=00
Item in the house stead one cubbord one long table two little tables eight pewther dishes three chaires one range one brass pott one iron pott one glass case & other husslements	03=00=00
Item in the barne two pare of wheeles one cart one cowpe body one plough & harrow & other husbandry geare	01=10=00
Item one chest one ...	00=6=8
Item bellows & stythyes one pare of vice with some iron & other work tooles	03=15=00
Item two cowes one heifer some sheepe & some corne	14=14=10
Sume	031=07=8

Inventory of Thomas Forrest.

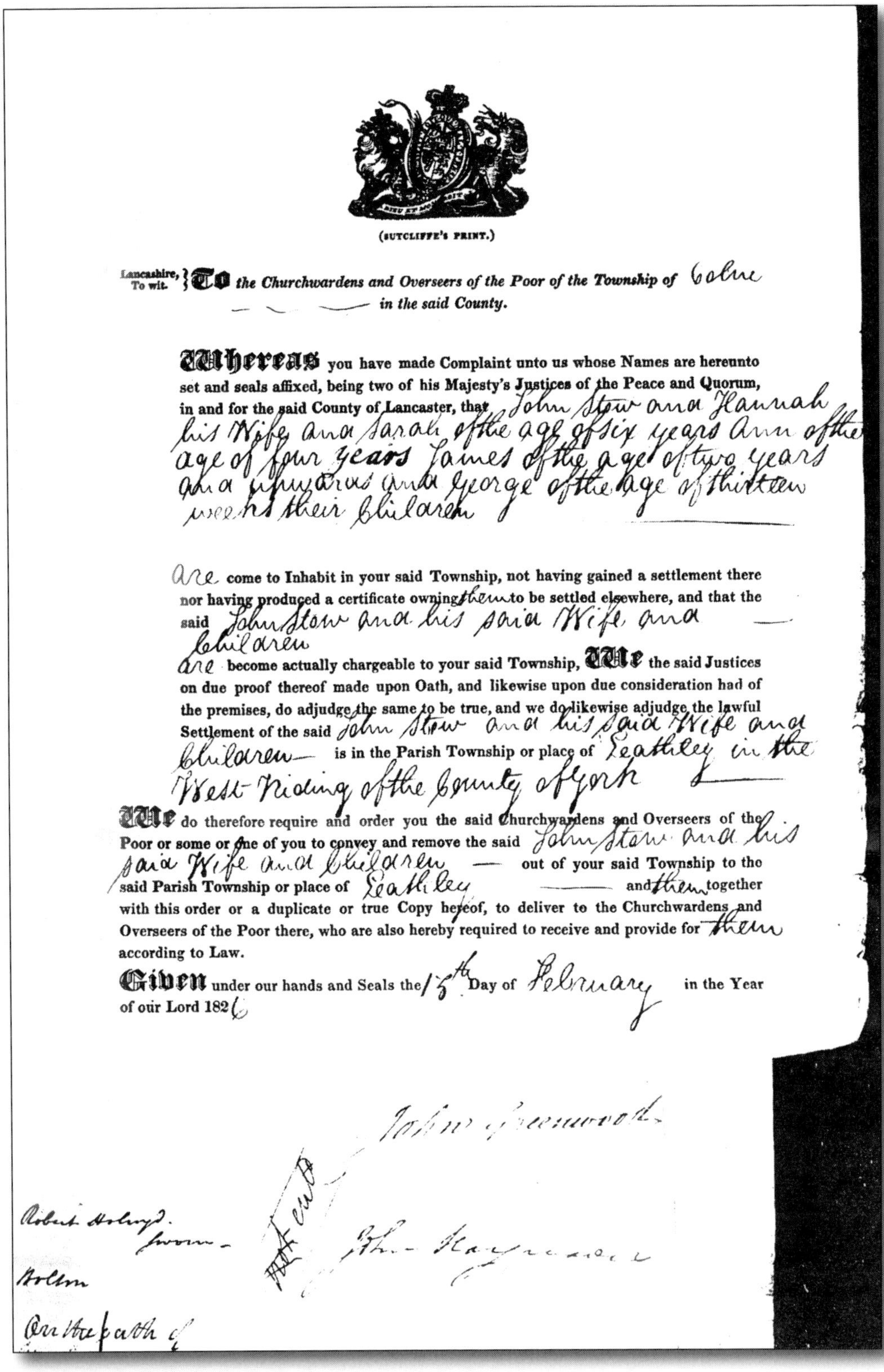

(SUTCLIFFE'S PRINT.)

Lancashire, To wit. } TO the Churchwardens and Overseers of the Poor of the Township of Colne in the said County.

WHEREAS you have made Complaint unto us whose Names are hereunto set and seals affixed, being two of his Majesty's Justices of the Peace and Quorum, in and for the said County of Lancaster, that John Stow and Hannah his Wife and Sarah of the age of six years Ann of the age of four years James of the age of two years and upwards and George of the age of thirteen weeks their Children

are come to Inhabit in your said Township, not having gained a settlement there nor having produced a certificate owning them to be settled elsewhere, and that the said John Stow and his said Wife and Children are become actually chargeable to your said Township, WE the said Justices on due proof thereof made upon Oath, and likewise upon due consideration had of the premises, do adjudge the same to be true, and we do likewise adjudge the lawful Settlement of the said John Stow and his said Wife and Children is in the Parish Township or place of Leathley in the West Riding of the County of York

WE do therefore require and order you the said Churchwardens and Overseers of the Poor or some or one of you to convey and remove the said John Stow and his said Wife and Children out of your said Township to the said Parish Township or place of Leathley and them together with this order or a duplicate or true Copy hereof, to deliver to the Churchwardens and Overseers of the Poor there, who are also hereby required to receive and provide for them according to Law.

GIVEN under our hands and Seals the 15th Day of February in the Year of our Lord 1826

John Greenwood

John Hargreaves

Robert Holroyd sworn Bolton

On the oath of

A settlement order of 1826 concerning John and Hannah Stow and their four children aged six, two, four and thirteen weeks who had become chargeable to the township of Colne and were therefore to be returned to their 'lawful settlement of Leathley'. John, born and baptised at Bolton Priory in 1792, was the son of David Stow and Elizabeth (Myers) who had married in the Priory church in 1792.

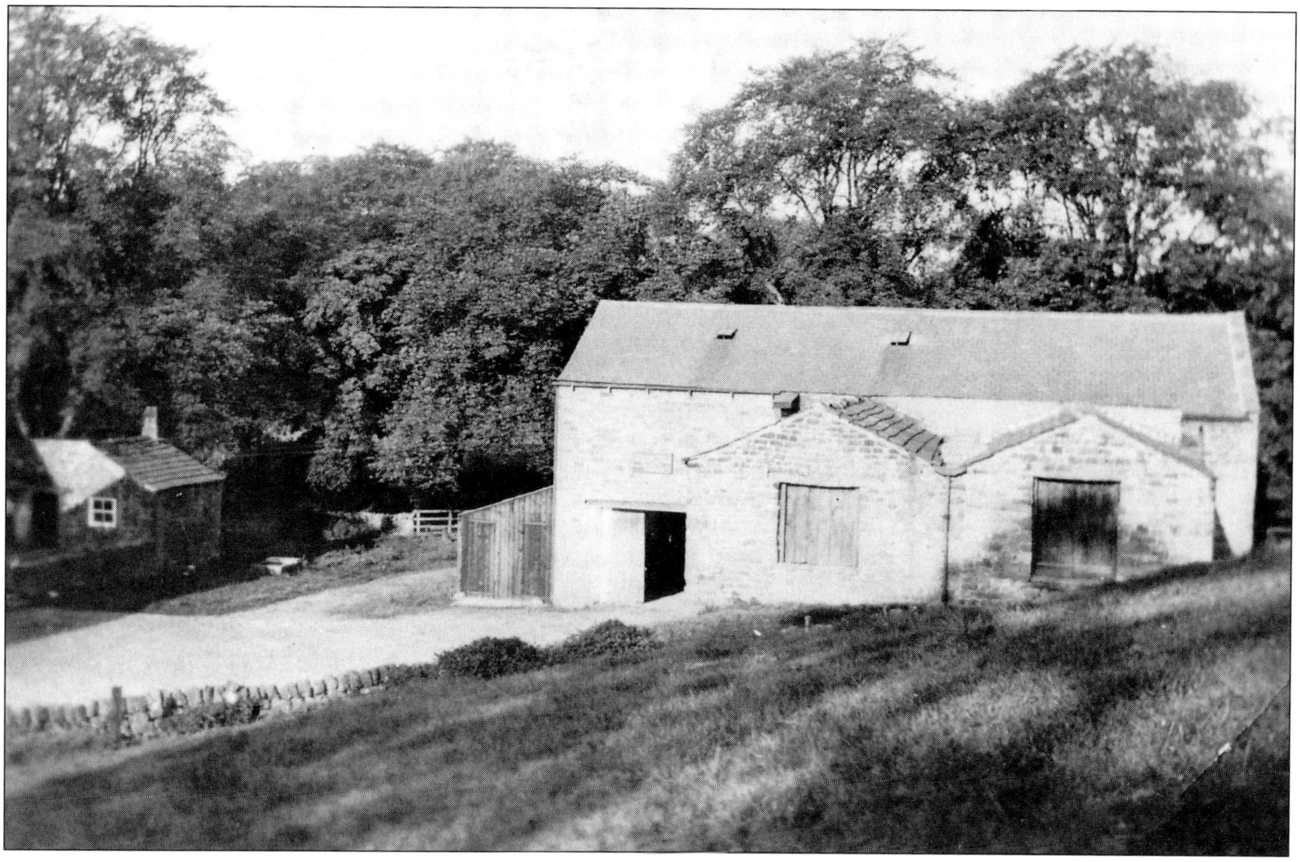

Leathley Mill.

LEATHLEY HALL

The present house, formerly known as East Hall to distinguish it from West Hall which probably stood at the other side of the village, dates from around 1715. In 1718 a guest described the house as a 'large and convenient edifice, improved by the worthy owner, who hath been at great expense in adorning and beautifying it with a new south front [and] a wing to the east.'

THE CHURCH OF ST MARY, STAINBURN

The Grade I church of St Mary belongs to the Norman period. Originally built as a chapel of ease, it was temporarily licensed for burials in 1362 when muddy

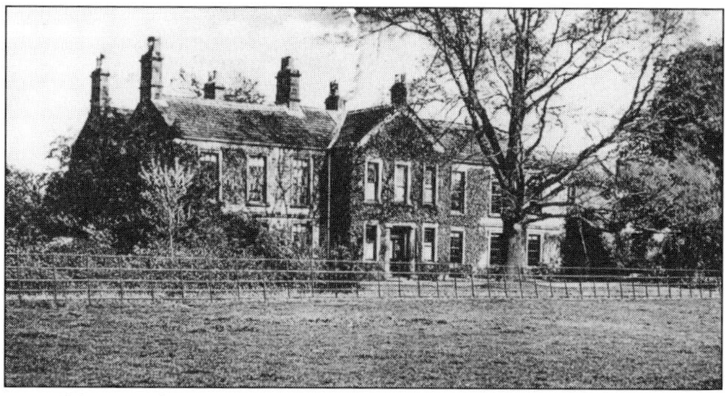

Leathley Hall.

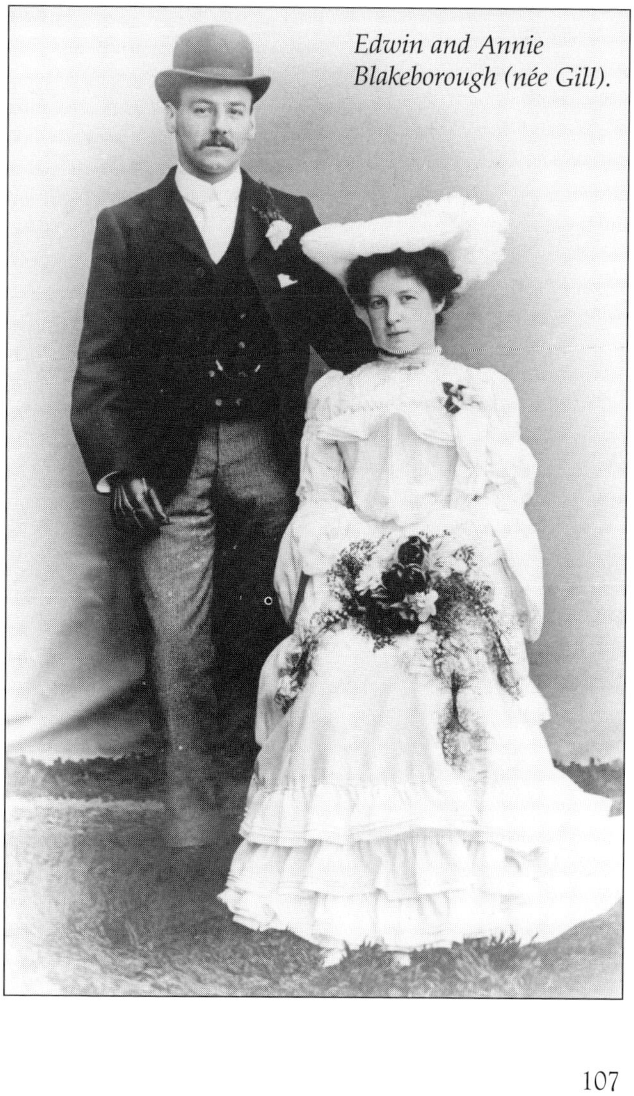

Edwin and Annie Blakeborough (née Gill).

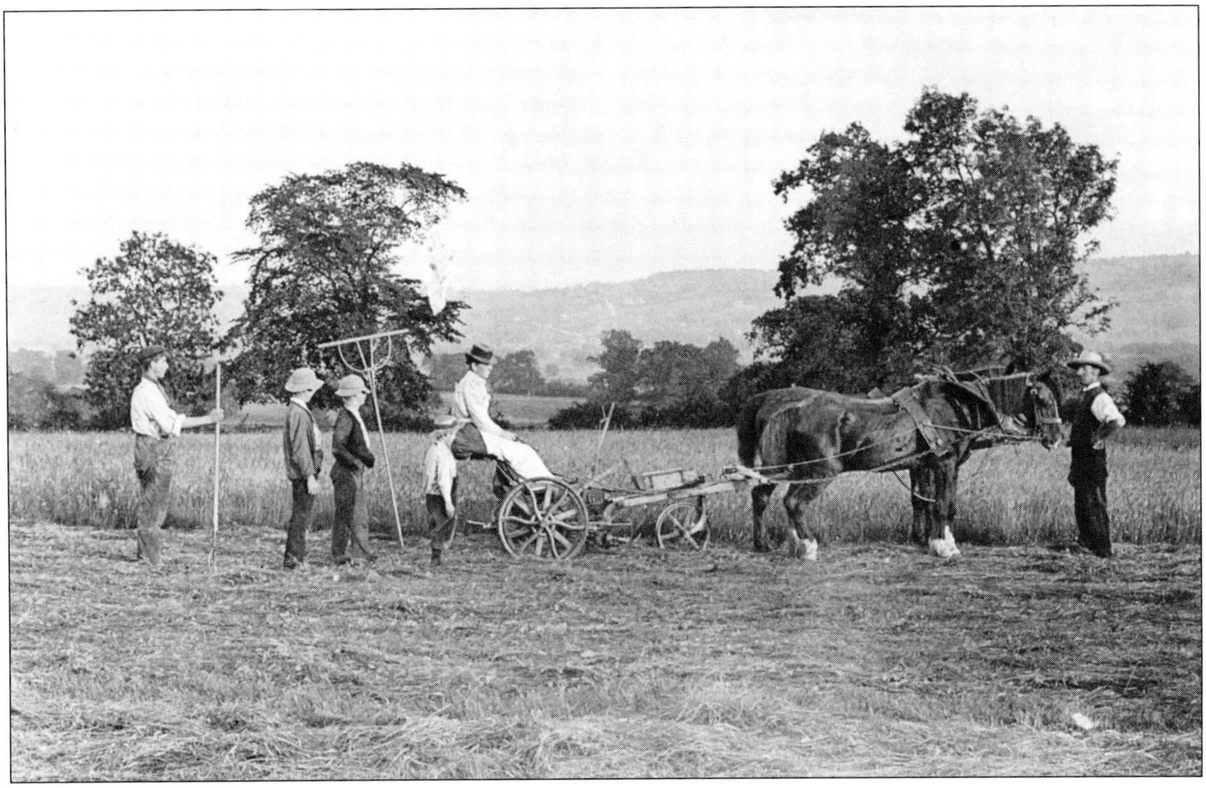

Posed photograph of the Todd family, Glebe Farm, Leathley, c.1900.

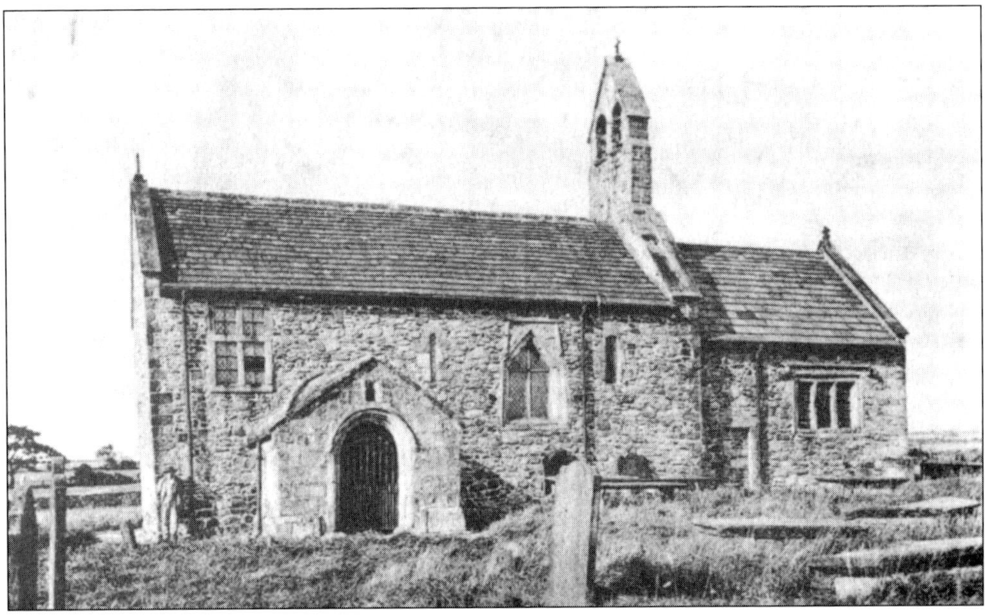

The church of S. Mary, Stainburn.

lanes prevented the transportation of plague victims to the mother church at Kirkby Overblow. The church consists only of a nave and lower chancel with a south porch and a seventeenth century bell-cote between the two. Some of the windows, the doorway, the font and chancel arch belong to the Norman period. The south porch is probably fifteenth century, and the bell cote seventeenth century. Formerly with a west gallery, the church has bench ends possibly of the sixteenth or seventeenth centuries, three with turned finials. Declared redundant in 1975 it is now in the care of the Historic Churches Trust.

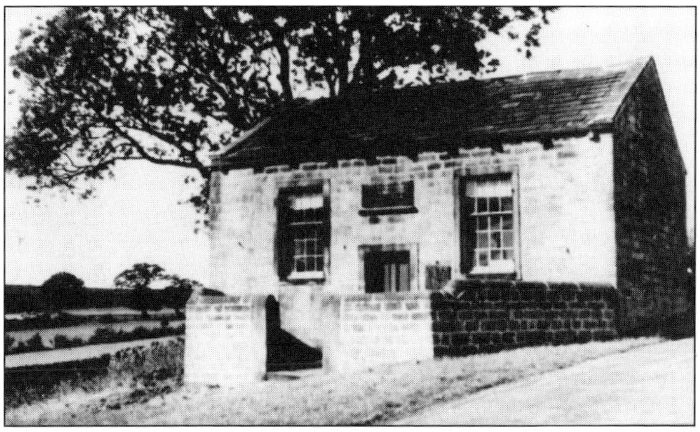

Stainburn Wesleyan Methodist chapel.

STAINBURN WESLEYAN METHODIST CHAPEL

The chapel was built in 1836. A visitation by the Archbishop to the parish in 1764 records that 'Thomas Bradley keeps an unlicensed meeting house for Methodists to be taught by Joseph Bradley of Otley, mole catcher.' It was also recorded that Thomas Bradley was presented for 'keeping a disorderly Meeting House in the town of Stainburn.'

STAINBURN SCHOOL

With an attached teacher's house, the school was established in 1862 by the Fawkes family. Other teachers at Stainburn between 1871 and 1901 were Elizabeth Charlesworth, Annie Lumby and Annie Clough.

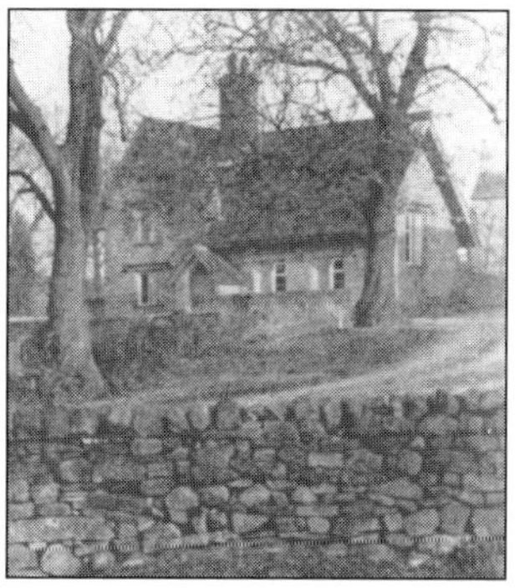

Right: *Stainburn School.*

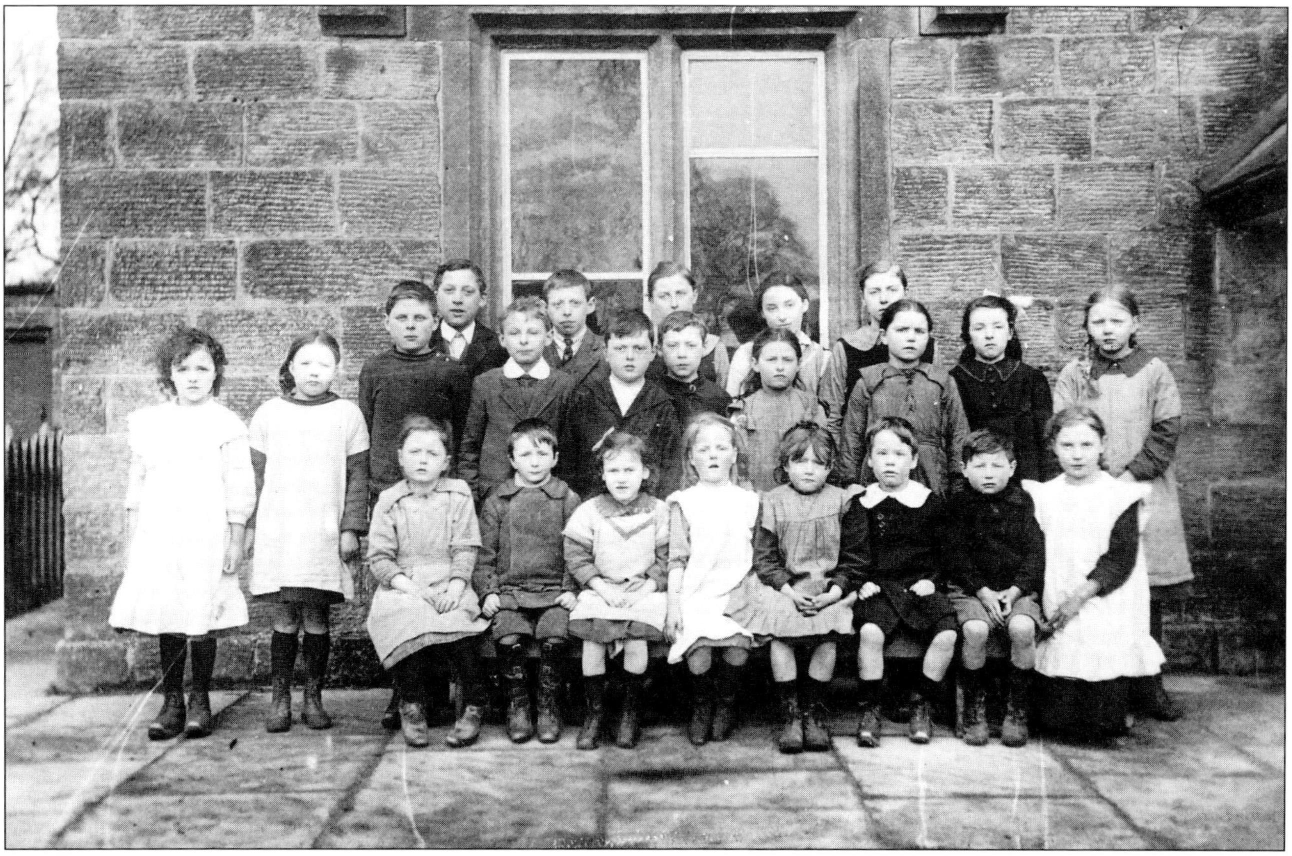

Stainburn School pupils.

Chapter 5

'The Beautiful Pellucid Waters'

Up to the middle of the nineteenth century the communities of the Washburn Valley were still largely isolated from the outside world, their inhabitants secure in a way of life they had always known and with which, knowing of little else, they were apparently largely content. In the latter part of the century all this was to be destroyed when their way of life was changed for ever by a development destined to rip out the heart of the valley. Buildings, including a church which had stood for centuries, disappeared, land was torn up, old roads and tracks were obliterated and the village of Fewston was almost completely destroyed. Later most of the top of the valley would also vanish. All of this was designed to produce what is now the most prominent feature of the area – the four reservoirs of Thruscross, Fewston, Swinsty and Lindley Wood – destined to serve the population of the city of Leeds 10 miles to the south.

There is no doubt that such facilities were desperately needed. From the early-nineteenth century the city had experienced a continuous expansion of its population which rose from 53,000 in 1801 to 123,000 by 1831. To accommodate this increase scores of jerry-built houses had been crammed into the courts and yards of the city, few of which were either paved or drained. For drinking water most of the homes in Leeds relied on wells, boreholes, or the River Aire which was heavily polluted. It was therefore not surprising that the average life expectancy in the city was under thirty years of age; in 1832 an outbreak of cholera claimed 700 lives within six months. Despite the efforts of Robert Baker, the city's poor-law surgeon and factory inspector who was himself a victim, and who demonstrated a link between cholera and the state of the drains, no immediate action was taken. Not until 1841 did the Leeds Waterworks Committee stop using the River Aire for drinking water.

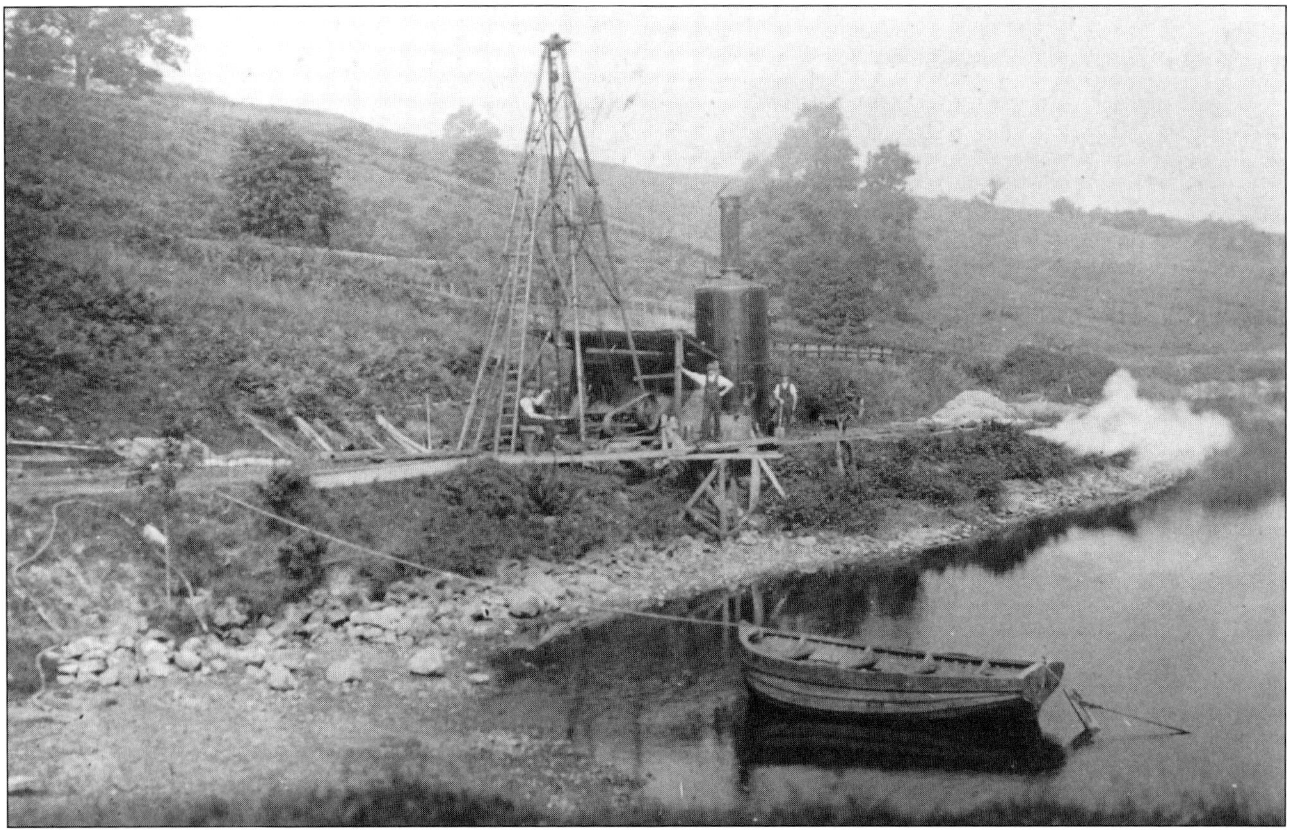

Steam driven pile driver in construction of Lindley Wood Reservoir.

In 1846 John Wignall Leather, the Leeds Borough Engineer, submitted plans to take pure water to the city, but twenty years were to elapse, and two more significant outbreaks of cholera to occur, before the Leeds Corporation Water Board commissioned a report from a civil engineer, Edward Filliter, whose recommendation was that a chain of nine reservoirs should be constructed in the valley; in fact, under the 1867 Waterworks Act, only four were eventually authorized – at Lindley Wood in the lower valley, Swinsty and Fewston, in the middle, and Thruscross in the north where construction did not take place until the 1960s.

The first reservoir to be constructed was at Lindley Wood, where the Corporation requistioned 150 acres of land belonging to the Fawkes family at Farnley. Although Francis Hawksworth Fawkes vigorously opposed the scheme, describing its perpetrators as 'water pirates', his protest was in vain. In compensation the family eventually received just over £48,000 for both land and timber and the first sod was cut at a ceremony in 1869, the snapping of the silver spade in the process not apparently perceived as an ill omen.

Not surprisingly progress was slow. Some of the stone used was acquired from abandoned buildings including Dob Park Mill, but most of the other materials had to be transported by train to Starbeck at Harrogate and then taken several miles by steam engine along the old turnpike, now the A59, in the process causing much damage to the road surface. They were then moved around the site by a narrow gauge railway equipped with two locomotives. Meanwhile four hundred and fifty men were employed to dig by hand to a depth of 60 feet, and create an embankment 360 yards long and 500 feet thick at the base, with a 1000 foot long bywash. The capacity was to be 750 million gallons.

In 1871 the construction of the second reservoir, Swinsty, began. Here some of the stone was taken from the hillside below Fewston village. Many cottages and farms including Newhall, the old home of the Pullens and Fairfaxes, bridges, a corn mill and a tanyard, vanished completely while much of what was left, including Fewston church and its vicarage, was so destabilized that it, and the area around, never completely recovered. In terms of capacity Swinsty was the largest of the three reservoirs, holding 866 million gallons. The embankment is 500 yards long and 75 feet wide at the base; the bywash 880 feet in length.

The construction of the nearby Fewston Reservoir began in 1874 and was completed in 1879. This time some of the stone from the redundant Westhouse Mill at Blubberhouses and the old corn mill at Fewston was used, to provide an estimated capacity of 770 million gallons. Although the initial estimate for the whole scheme had been £500,000, an appeal had to be made in Parliament for a further £300,000. In fact the cost of the work on all three of the reservoirs was finally estimated to have been in the region of one and a half million pounds.

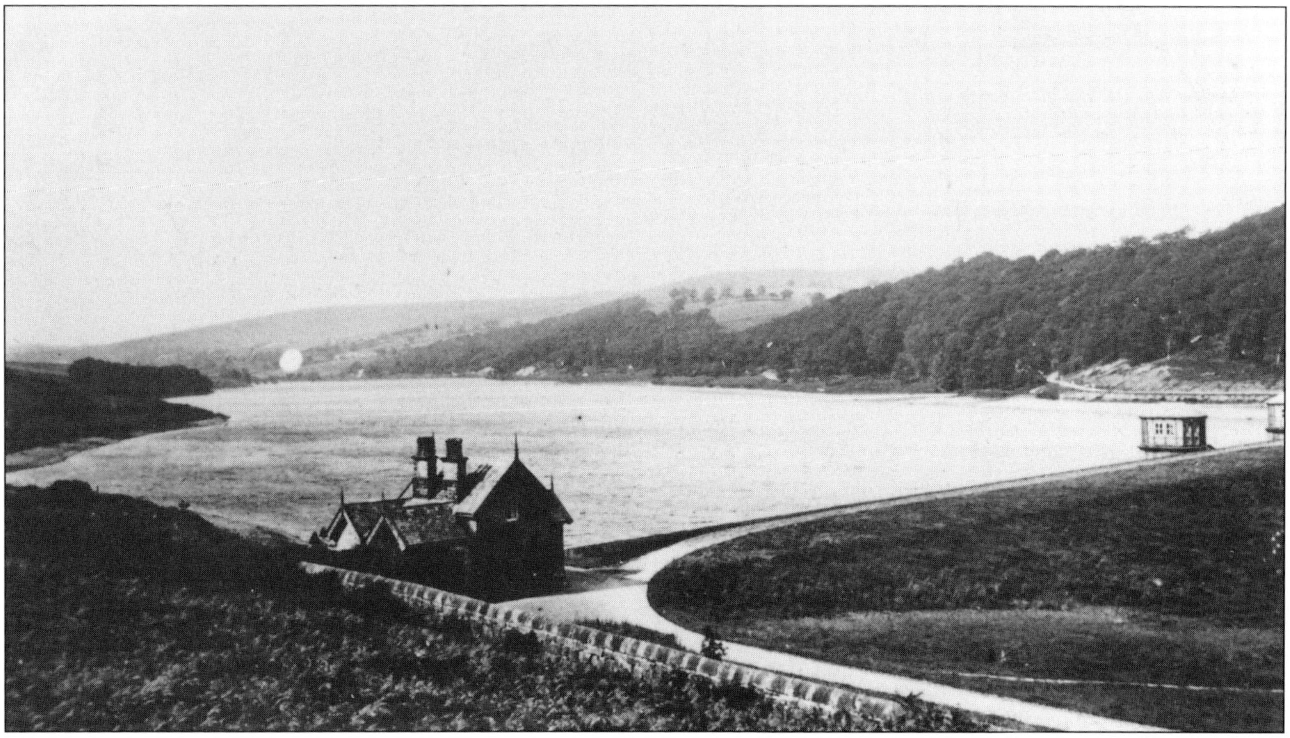

Lindley Wood Reservoir looking north west from lodge and embankment.

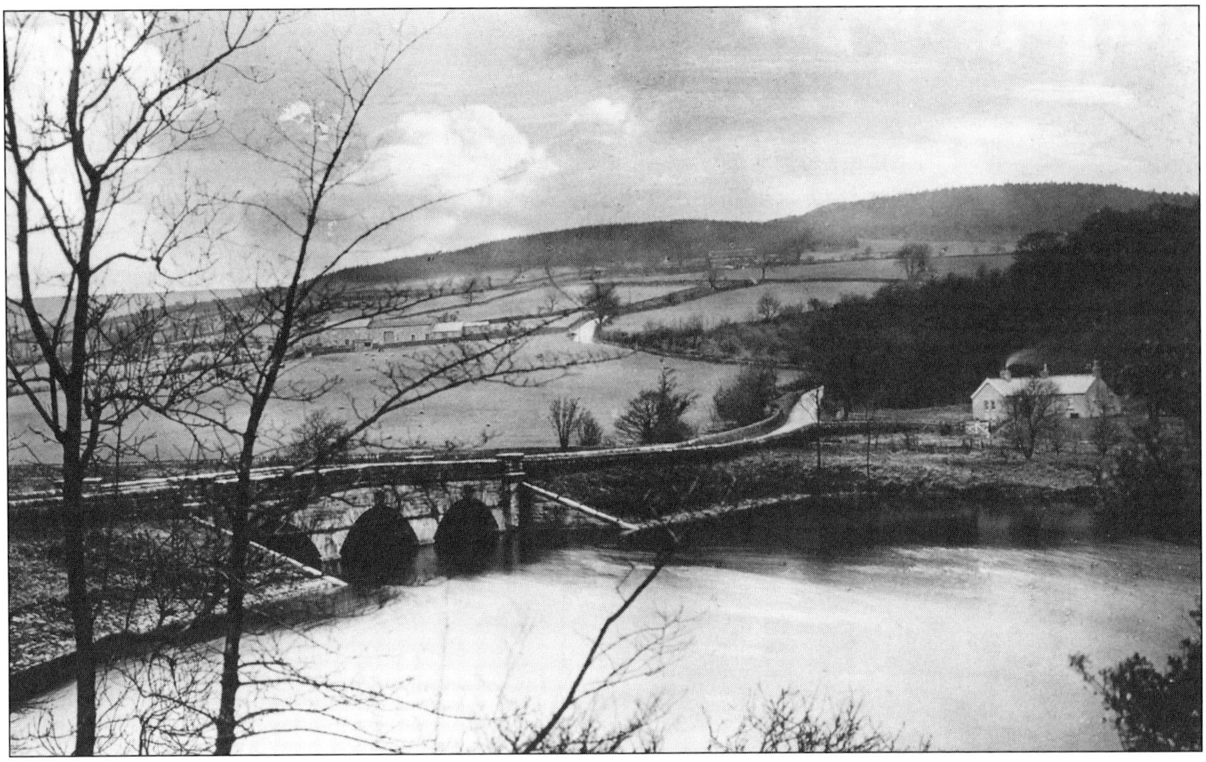

Road Bridge at head of Lindley Wood Reservoir. The hill known as Norwood Edge climbs past Sunny Bank Farm and Norwood Chapel, on left and Norwood Hall, on right.

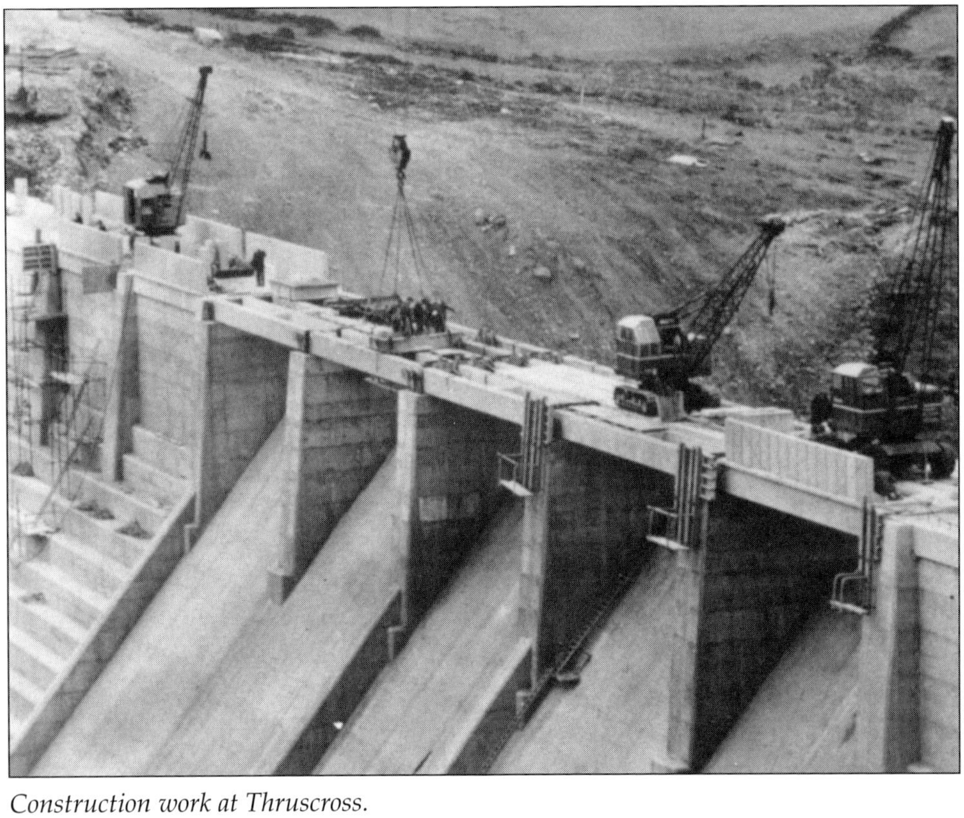

Construction work at Thruscross.

Throughout the construction of the first three reservoirs many people, including the men of Leeds Corporation and their wives, made regular trips to the valley to view the progress which became something of a social attraction. Parties travelled by horse-drawn bus from Leeds to Lindley where their horses were changed for four 'splendid' horses owned by the Corporation and, after a conducted tour of the valley, the party enjoyed a lavish tea before returning home.

Ten years after their commencement three of the reservoirs were complete. Via a pumping station at Arthington 3 miles east of Otley, and Eccup reservoir to the north of Leeds, 17 miles of piping now carried clean water to the people of the city. At last they were able to enjoy what the Leeds City Engineer described as 'the beautiful pellucid waters of the Washburn Valley'. On 13 September 1879 John Dickinson wrote 'The navvies are nearly done so we shall be ourselves again.' The reality was that the communities of the Washburn Valley would never again be themselves.

The delay in constructing the fourth and highest reservoir, Thruscross, probably owed much to the intervention of two World Wars but not surprisingly there was considerable bitterness over the way in which the area had been prematurely depopulated some fifty years previously when many of the inhabitants could have lived out their lives in the valley. In fact the delay meant that some buildings had been vacated for so long that it proved impossible to trace the owners who therefore received no financial recompense. This must have been very convenient for the Corporation which had never been inclined to generosity in such matters, and was the target of several unsuccessful court claims in the nineteenth century. Begun in 1961 the reservoir was finally completed in 1966. Covering an area of 142 acres and 120 feet deep it has an estimated capacity of 1.7 million gallons. The 120 foot high dam has a span of 600 feet and cost one and a half million pounds to build.

THE NAVVY VILLAGE

The effect of the reservoir construction on the valley was in itself dramatic. The population of the valley increased five fold as a huge and alien force of navvies, carpenters, blacksmiths, quarrymen, masons, mechanics and engine drivers arrived from all over the country as well as from Wales and Ireland. Mostly itinerant, such men also worked on the construction of railways and canals.

Some of the men sought lodgings in surrounding farms or inns. Henry Faux and his mother lived in Fewston with his two children, while James Marston, landlord of the Seven Stars Inn at Norwood, accommodated several navvies. Many more were housed in a 'navvy village', rows of specially constructed brick built cottages, or huts as they were called, set in woodland by the side of Lindley Wood Reservoir. Conditions were primitive, most of the huts housing a husband and wife with their children together with a number of navvy lodgers. Edward Horne, his wife Anne and their four children shared Hut 21 with nine lodgers. The upper storey of all the huts consisted of a half-floor providing a loft where one or other group of the inhabitants slept.

The village also had a 'shant' or canteen and a 'drinking shop,' although opening hours of the latter were confined to four hours a day. Men were only allowed six pints of ale a day – no doubt considerably weaker than now. Rules were strict. Women 'followers' were not allowed, and any form of gambling including even shove ha'penny and marbles was forbidden. The site was almost completely self-supporting with its own manager Henry Bower, a policeman William Balderston, and a nurse, Jane

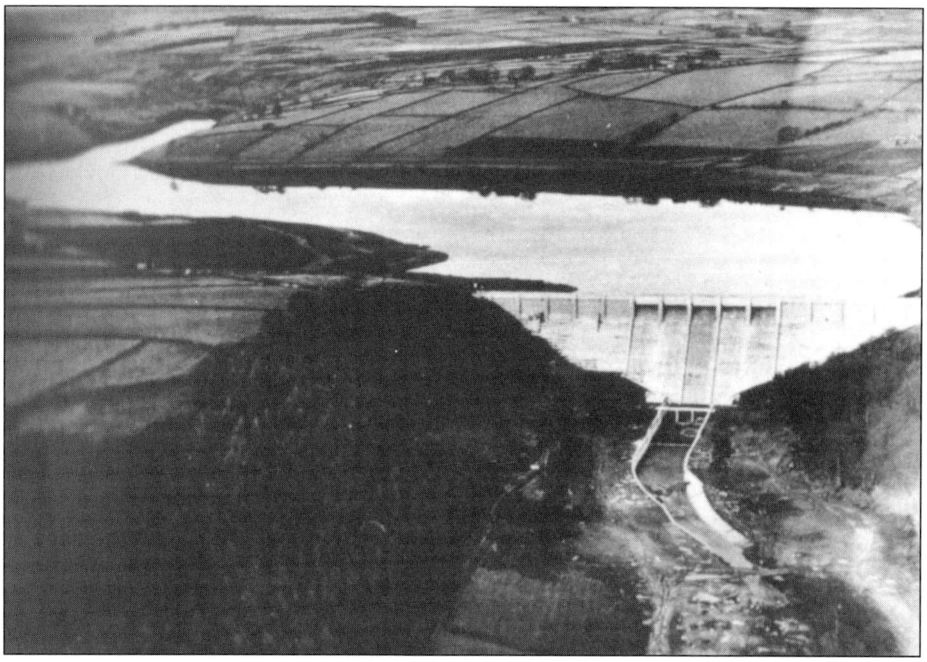

Thruscross Reservoir on completion.

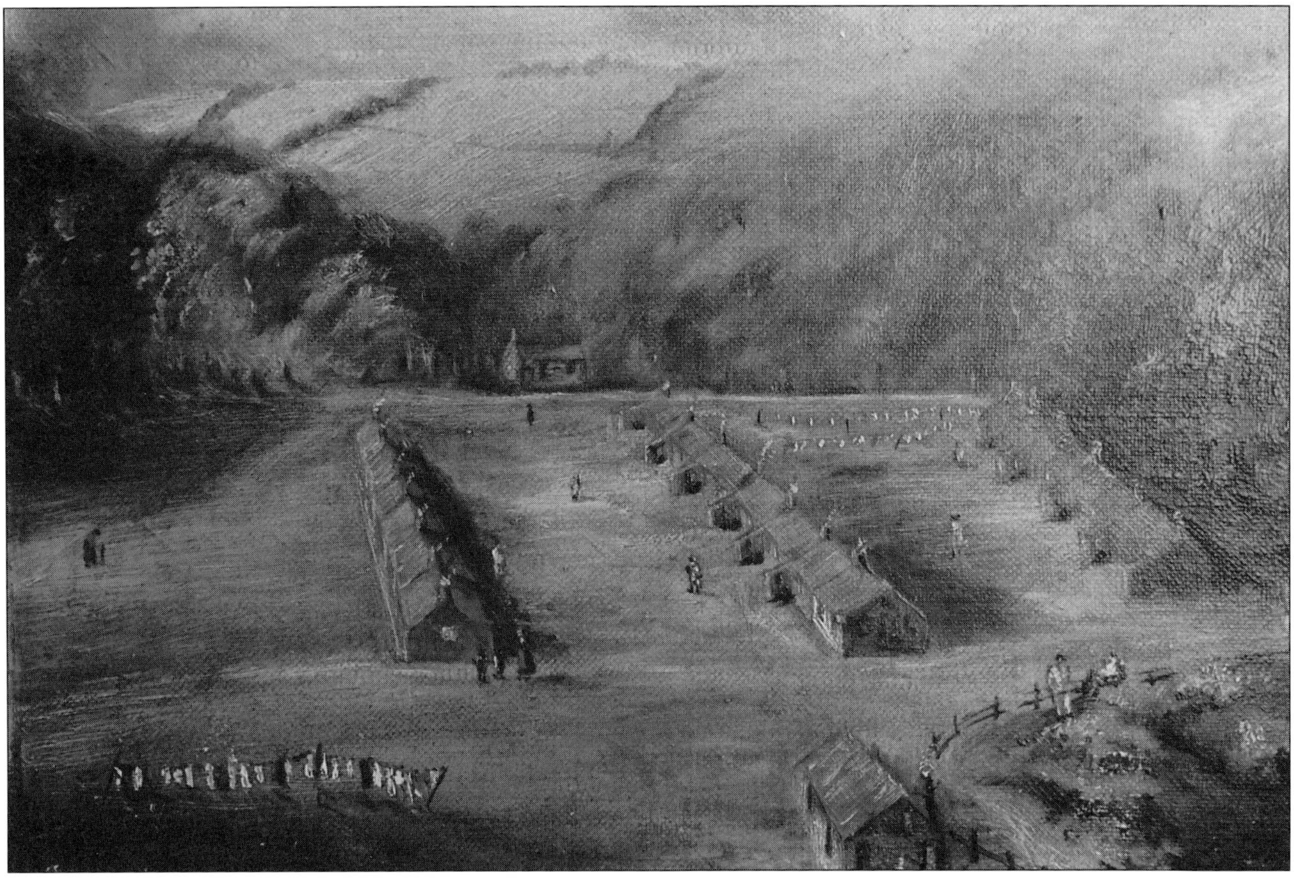

Navvy camp. A painting believed to be the work of an Irish navvy.

Denson. The site hospital, which catered for illnesses such as smallpox, typhoid and tuberculosis as well as the many injuries incurred on site, astonishingly also doubled as a school. There was also a church, a small wooden building with an open belfry, white-washed interior and stove heating. The men were not always welcome in the valley churches. One vicar described the navvies as 'vile and immoderate' and said that there was 'not an atom's worth of honesty amongst them'. However despite their unsavoury reputations – in 1878 one navvy was murdered by another – some good words were expressed by Lord Walsingham's gamekeeper, who reported no trouble with either trespassing or poaching by the navvies. Indeed one of them is believed to have been instrumental in starting a Sunday School at Blubberhouses.

Eventually the village at Lindley moved on to Fewston, and a second village, this time built of stone, was created on Swinsty Moor. Here there was also a butcher's shop and a meeting room where a variety of social events including magic lantern shows were held, and in summer there were sports days with races and a tug of war. The navvies also joined in village affairs such as the Timble Feast, while on Christmas Day the navvy band played for the villagers.

THE NAVVIES FRIEND

In the early 1870s Elizabeth Garnett of Otley visited the valley. Born in 1839, Elizabeth was the daughter of the vicar of Otley, Joshua Hart, who had consecrated the elaborate memorial in Otley churchyard to those navvies who died during the construction of

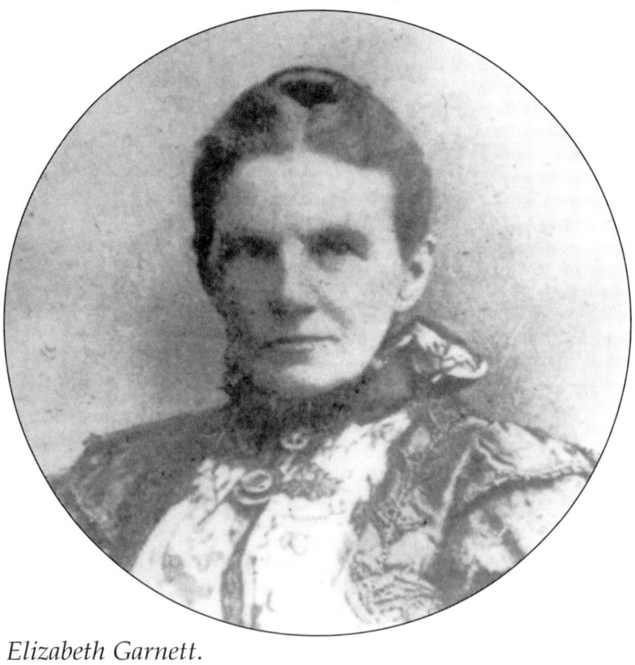

Elizabeth Garnett.

the Bramhope railway tunnel between Otley and Leeds. In 1861 she married Charles Garnett, an Anglican clergyman, the son of an Otley paper manufacturer, but was widowed almost immediately.

Elizabeth's interest in the navvies, kindled initially by her father, led to her visiting those at Lindley Wood with a friend. She found the valley dark and cold with a puddle trench being sunk, illuminated by pumping engine fires. The men hand-filled the trench, which was the core of the embankment, with blue clay or puddle, stamping on it to form an oily wall through which water could not escape. The huts where they lived were nearby beside the shingled church with its high pitched roof.

So disturbed was Elizabeth by the conditions in which the men and their families lived that she decided to begin missionary work in the navvy village starting with what she perceived as the most dire need, a Sunday School for the navvy boys. She also started a magazine *The Navvies Friend*, and eventually, despite considerable family opposition, moved onto the settlement herself to live among the families. She had 'found a new vista of interest in a lonely life'.

In 1874 she was joined in her work by the rector of Leathley, the Rev. Lewis Moule Evans, who shared her concerns after visiting a dying girl in one of the huts, 'the daughter of a navvy, the wife of a navvy ... born in a navvy's hut, wandering all her life with her parents ...' The joint efforts of Evans and Elizabeth eventually resulted in the founding of the 'Christian Excavator's Union', or 'Navvies Mission', and four hundred letters of appeal were sent to well-to-do Anglicans alerting the wider world to the navvy's plight. By 1917 the Union had acquired more than 700 members.

Elizabeth Garnett was a redoubtable woman. She has been described as 'a natural-born organiser, unasked, of other people's lives', and it has been said that if her husband had not died 'she would without doubt have terrorised some hapless parish into Christianity'. There is no doubt that she had been deeply affected by the plight of the navvies, who knew little of religion and probably did not wish to be told. One of them remarked that although 'the Navvy Mission is a bloody good thing, they were always preaching at you at dinner time and I didn't want no ... preaching at me while I was eating my bit of snap.' Some even regarded the parson as their foe. One vicar is reputed to have overheard a navvy say 'ere comes't parson, let's 'eave a truck at 'im.'

Elizabeth Garnett made no distinction between herself, the men and their families. She referred to herself as a navvy, they were 'her mates', and their welfare became her whole life. It is said that she mercilessly scolded, nagged and bullied the rough, drunken and usually illiterate men while never looking down on them, assuring them 'there are those in the world who love you still,' later adding 'Hitherto the navvies have not been duly cared for, that day is past.'

Lewis Moule Evans died of tuberculosis in 1878 and although no trace of his grave has been found, he is said to have been buried in the churchyard at Leathley 'within sight of Lindley Wood'. Despite being recorded as the sole founder of the Society, it was in fact, Elizabeth who, in writing a number of 'navvy' novels as well as papers for various societies and editing a quarterly letter to all navvies for thirty nine years, was able to provide most of the funds for the enterprise. In the course of her work, with and without Lewis, she had been instrumental in the formation of mission rooms, missions and missionaries, evening classes, sick clubs, savings banks and soup kitchens which surely at least entitles her to the honour of co-founder. She died at Croydon, Surrey on the 22 September, 1921 and is commemorated in Ripon Cathedral by a plaque which also bears the badge of the Navvy Mission Society.

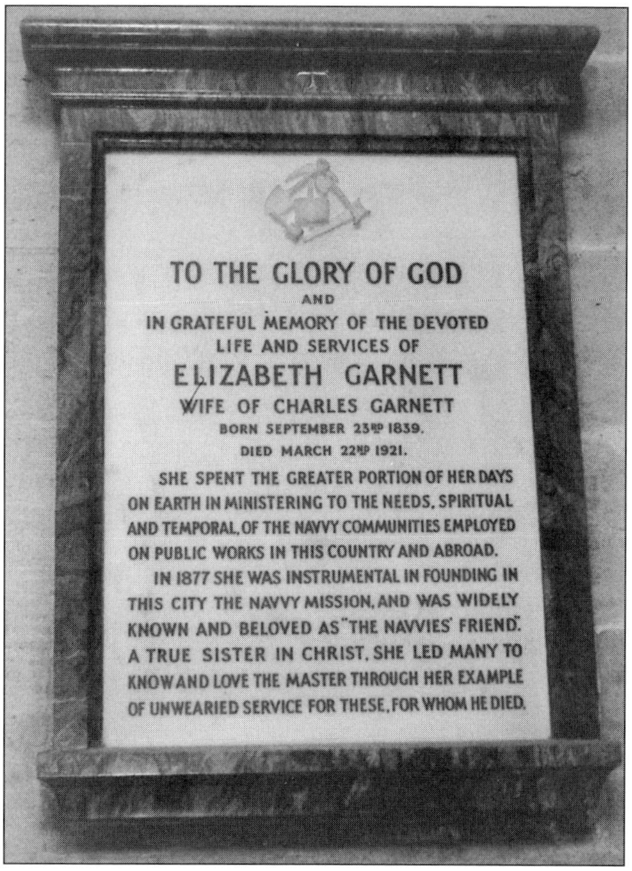

Plaque in Ripon Cathedral.

Chapter 6

Lest We Forget

The residents of this peaceful valley rarely travelled far even within their own district, and it is easy to forget that they have twice been called upon to serve in the forces throughout the world. The Roll of Honour in Fewston church records the names of ninety-four men from Fewston, Timble, Norwood and Blubberhouses who fought with the armed services in the First and Second World Wars, fifteen of whom never returned. A similar memorial at Leathley simply records the names of a further forty-five from Leathley, Lindley, Stainburn and Farnley who also served. Most if not all were from families with long associations with the valley who were previously employed in a variety of trades related to agriculture and forestry.

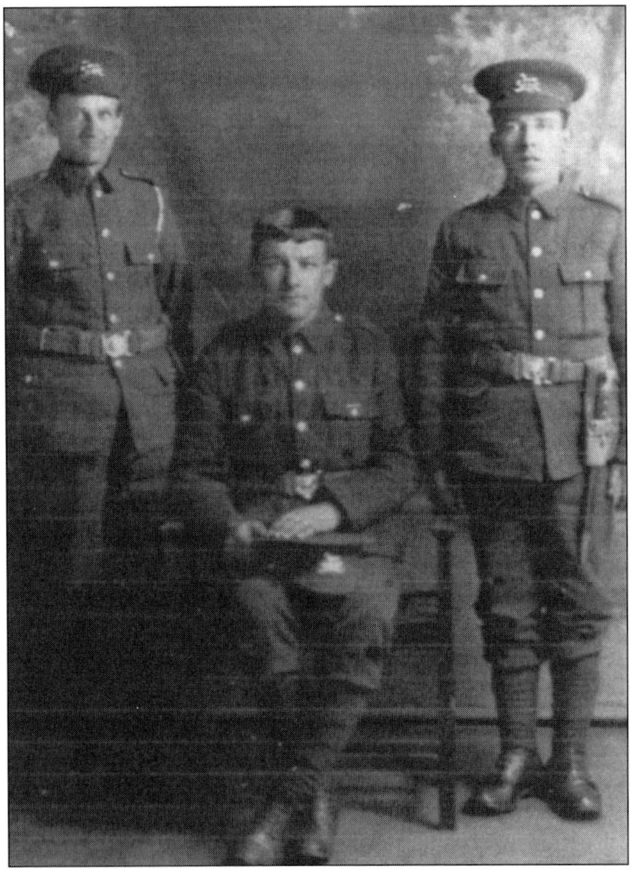

Sgt Frank Driver (centre).

SGT FRANK DRIVER

Frank was the son of a farmer, Joseph Driver, and his wife Mary of Norwood. He served with the West Yorkshire Regiment and was killed in action in France in May 1917, perhaps during the Battle of Arras. His commanding officer wrote to his family that he was last seen heading through heavy fire, 'firing his Lewis gun from his shoulder supported on his arm, calmly and steadily' before being shot dead. Aged twenty-two, his memorial is in the Arras Military Cemetery. His older brother, Tom, who served with the Coldstream Guards, received a Gallant Conduct Certificate and despite being badly gassed survived the war. He never married.

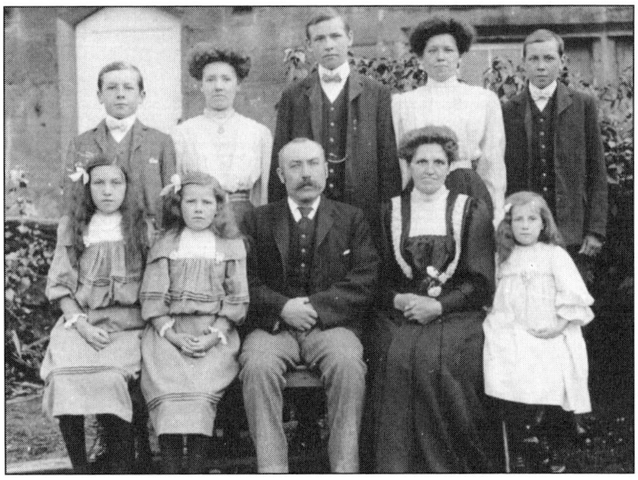

Driver family. From left standing: *Frank, Mary Ann Isabel (Annie), Tom, Florence and Joe* – front *Alice, Joseph and Mary, Dora and Elsie.*

WILLIAM HENRY CLAPHAM

A private in the 1st battn East Lancashire Regiment, William was born at Castley near Otley. He arrived in France in 1916 and his battalion was ordered to prepare trenches in torrential rain under the command of 2nd. Lieut Conan Doyle, the son of the creator of Sherlock Holmes.

At the end of July the battalion marched on Elverdinghe when William is believed to have been killed on the 4 August 1916. He was aged twenty-nine. His widow moved to Wales and later remarried.

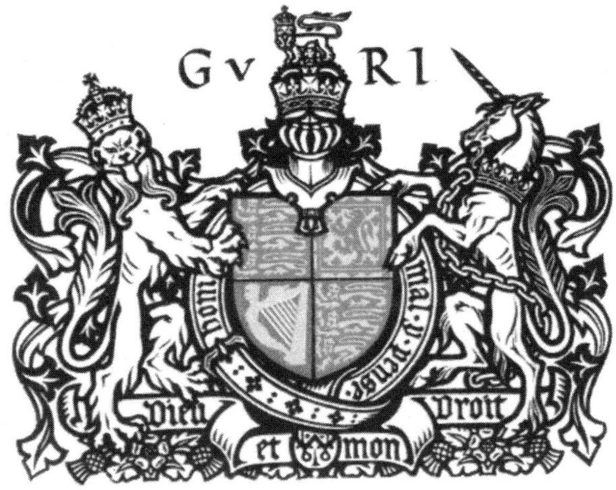

HE whom this scroll commemorates was numbered among those who, at the call of King and Country, left all that was dear to them, endured hardness, faced danger, and finally passed out of the sight of men by the path of duty and self-sacrifice, giving up their own lives that others might live in freedom.

Let those who come after see to it that his name be not forgotten.

26481, PRIVATE, William Henry CLAPHAM

1st Battalion.
East Lancashire Regiment
Killed in action, France & Flanders, 04/08/16
Born: Otley, Yorks, Enlisted: Durham, Residence: Rhosymedre, Denbigh

A scroll given to all who served in the First World War.

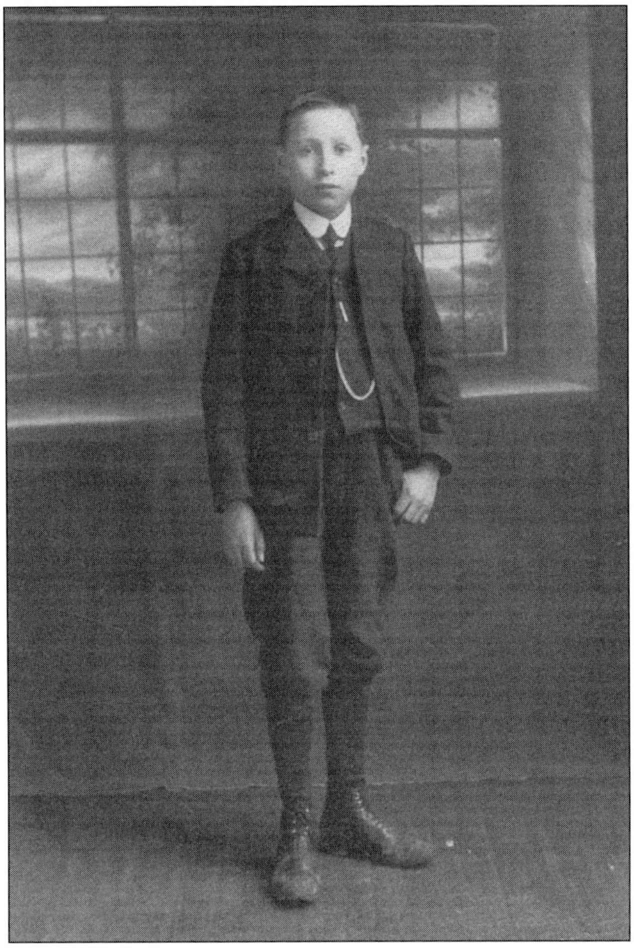

Samuel Henry Pennington as a boy.

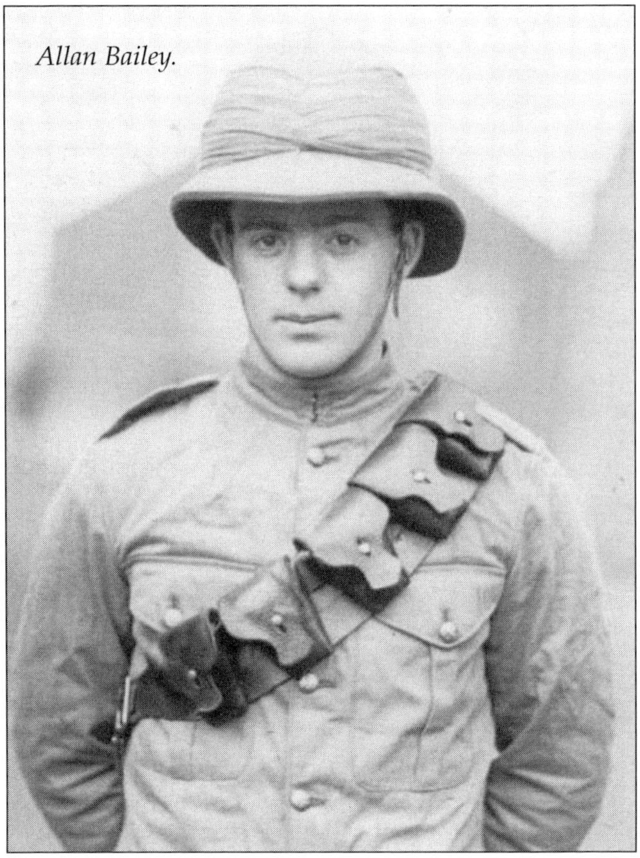

Allan Bailey.

SAMUEL HENRY PENNINGTON

Some men had a lucky escape. Samuel Henry (or Harry) from Bents Farm, Fewston, joined the East Yorkshire Regiment at the age of eighteen in 1917 but was captured in the retreat at Ypres. Put on a train, he cut a hole in the floor of the carriage and escaped while it was stationary on a bridge. His less fortunate companion was shot dead after standing up too soon. After his return Harry married Dora Driver, sister of Frank, and farmed at High House, Blubberhouses.

JACK LUPTON

Gunner Jack Lupton, who served with the Royal Artillery was wounded in the leg by a shell, repatriated and hospitalised at Easton Park, Wickham Market in Suffolk, the home of the Duke of Hamilton, where the Duke's wife and daughters were nurses.

ALLAN BAILEY

Allan served with the Royal Artillery in Mesopotamia – now part of Iraq. He was the eldest child of Benjamin C. Bailey, farmer, of Brame Lane Farm, Norwood, and Alice (née Hobson) the daughter of John and Hannah Hobson, licensees of the Sun Inn. After the war he married, lived at Whistle House Farm, had four children, and was very active in public life. He died in 1984 aged ninety.

WILLIAM STOBBS

Born c.1893, the son of Wilkinson Stobbs, blacksmith and farmer, and his wife Alice of Bland Hill, Norwood, William served as a private with the Royal Field Artillery.

WILLIAM DOLPHIN

A rifleman in the King's Royal Rifles he married Emma Dickinson in 1919.

WILLIAM FIRTH

A corporal in the West Yorkshire Regiment he was born at Birstwith in c.1879, the second of four children of Joseph, a farmer, and Emma Firth, who farmed at Jack Hill, Norwood. He also survivied the war.

SAMUEL MORRELL

A sergeant in the West Yorkshire Regiment, Samuel was the son of Thomas Morrell, a stonemason. After the war he returned to the valley, married Sarah Ellen Spence, and farmed at Wydra.

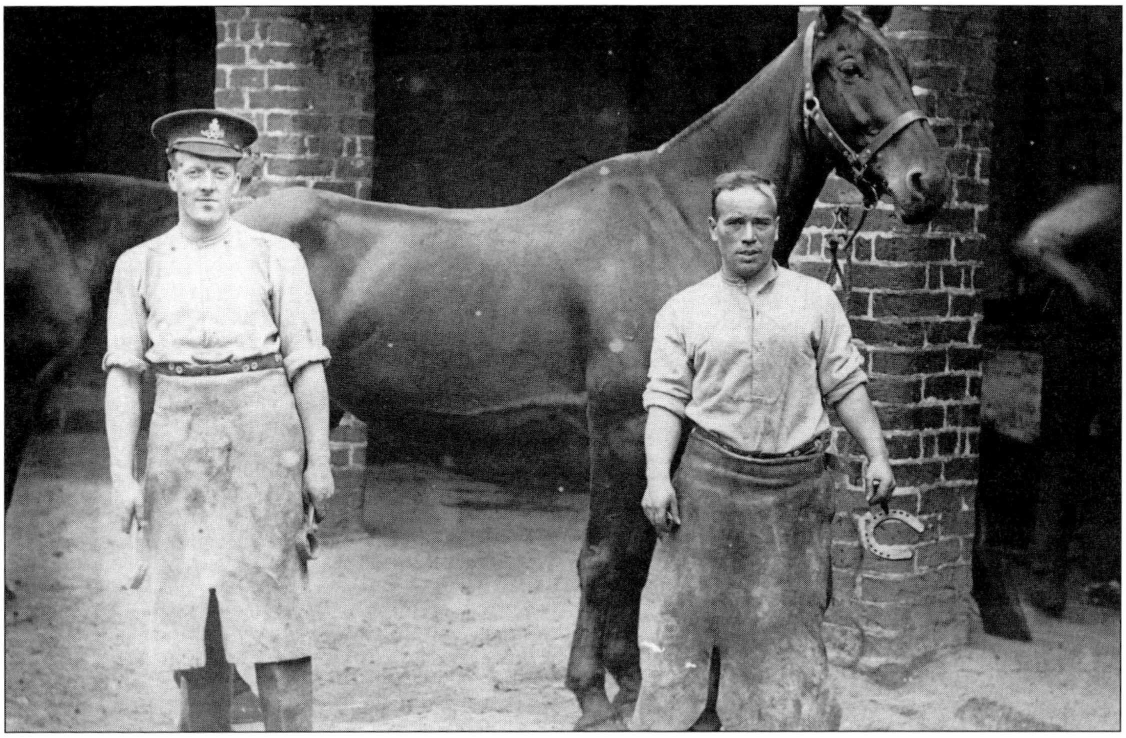

William Stobbs.

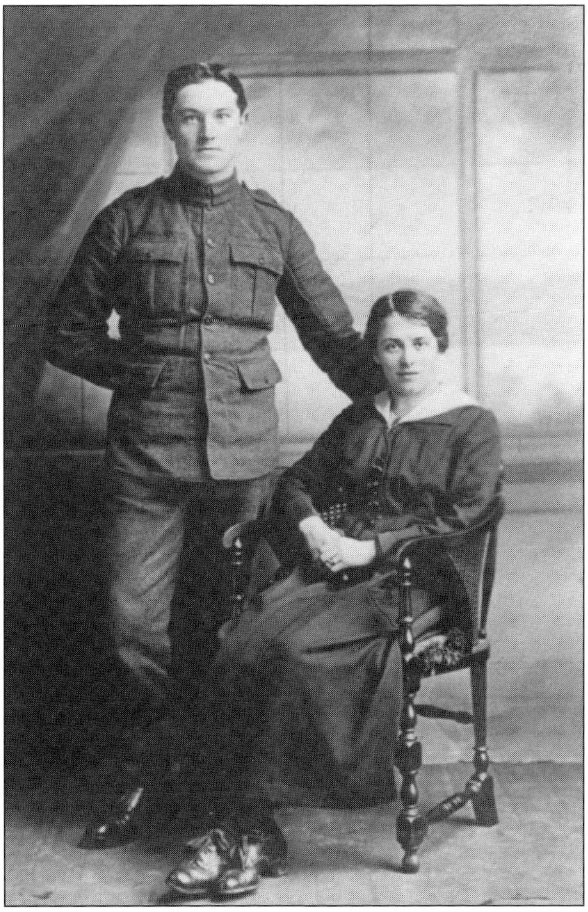

William and Emma Dolphin.

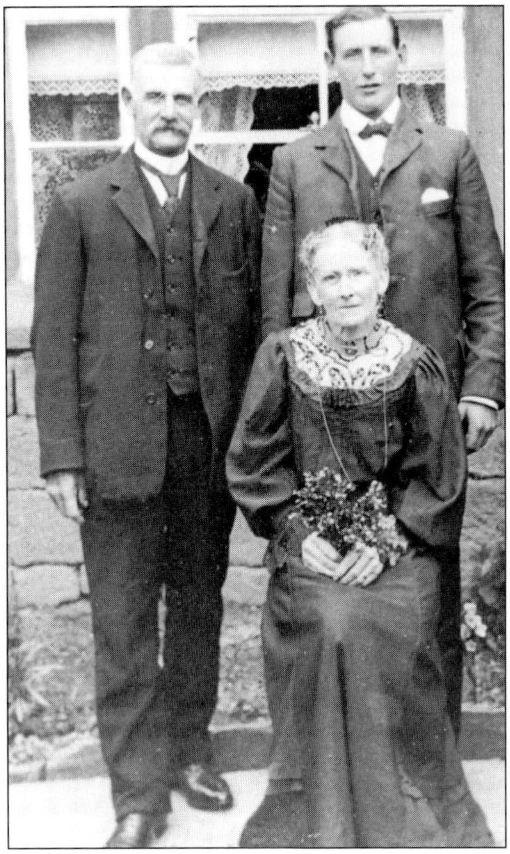

William Firth with his parents.

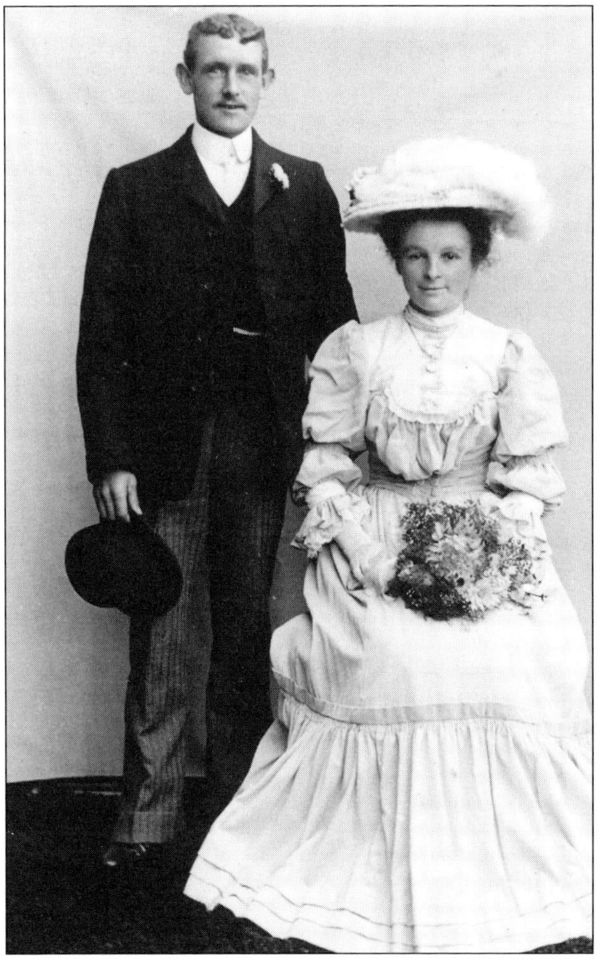

Samuel and Sarah Morrell.

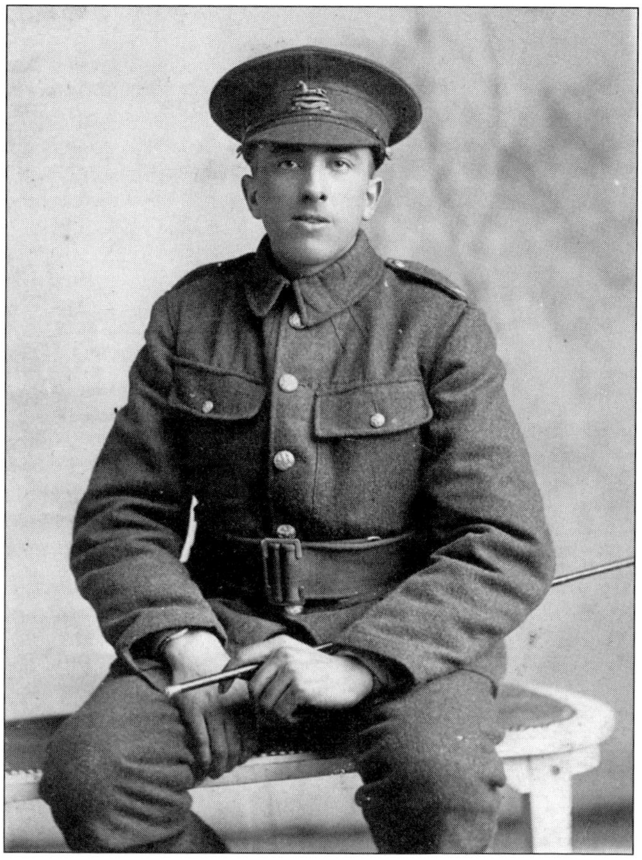

Stanley Robinson.

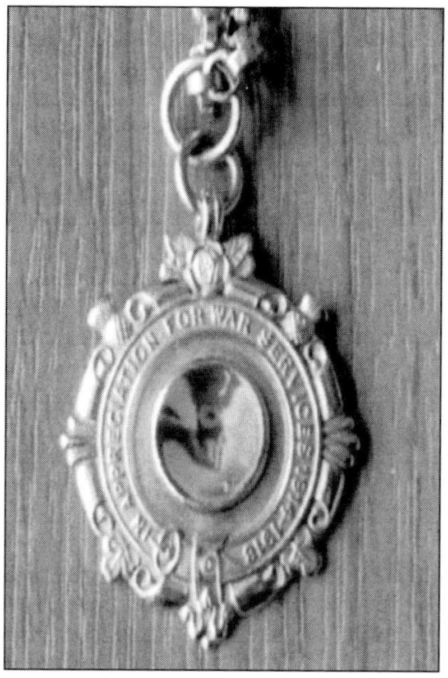

WASHBURN MEDAL

Awarded to Pte Stanley Robinson of the West Yorkshire Regiment, son of Freeman and Sarah of Catchem Corner Farm, Fewston where he was born in 1898. A prisoner of war in Germany for a year, on his return he married Annie Skaife of Darley and lived at Nesfield Farm. He died in 1979 and was awarded the Washburn Medal to commemorate his service as did all the men of the valley who returned.

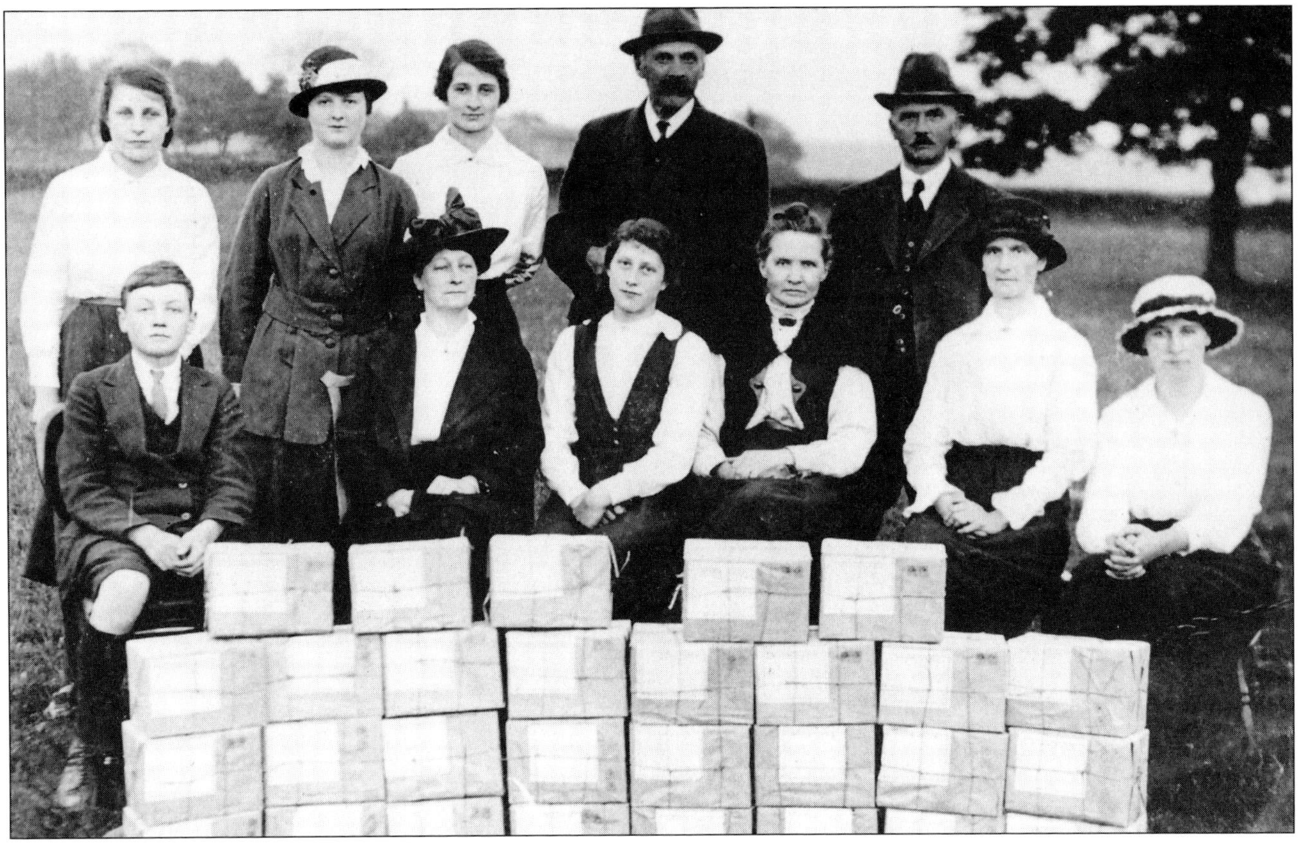

Comforts Fund Committee.

COMFORTS FUND COMMITTEE

In both World Wars the servicemen of the valley were supported via a number of fund raising efforts. During the first war a collection in Thruscross church for the Prince of Wales Regiment fund raised £2.11s., while Mrs Hiley, the Rocking School head teacher, visited every house in the valley to collect £13 divided equally between the regiment and the West Riding Distress Committee. The Washburn Valley Soldiers and Sailors Fund held concerts in Norwood School, and numerous whist drives and dances provided a parcel of 'comforts', or five shillings, every two weeks. Families most involved in the Comforts Fund were the Patricks, Powells, Hardwicks, Pounders, Penningtons, Crosses, and also the Rev Donald Milligan, vicar of Fewston. Mrs Galloway of Skaife Hall provided £1 to be spent on wool knitted up by the ladies into thirty six pairs of socks sent to Queen Mary's Needlework Guild founded in 1914 specifically to 'provide comforts for serving soldiers and their families.' Gunner Robert Bidewell wrote from the front to thank them adding that 'the bit of news from England brightens the men up.'

RONALD HOUSEMAN

Sergeant Ronald Houseman was a casualty of the Second World War. Born at Watson Lane Farm, Norwood, in 1924, the son of Robert and Emma, he attended Norwood School before working on the farm. Shortly after the death of his mother he joined the Royal Air Force. He was killed in action on the day before his twentieth birthday, having replaced a sick member of the regular crew who was left to wonder if his greater experience would have changed the outcome of the mission.

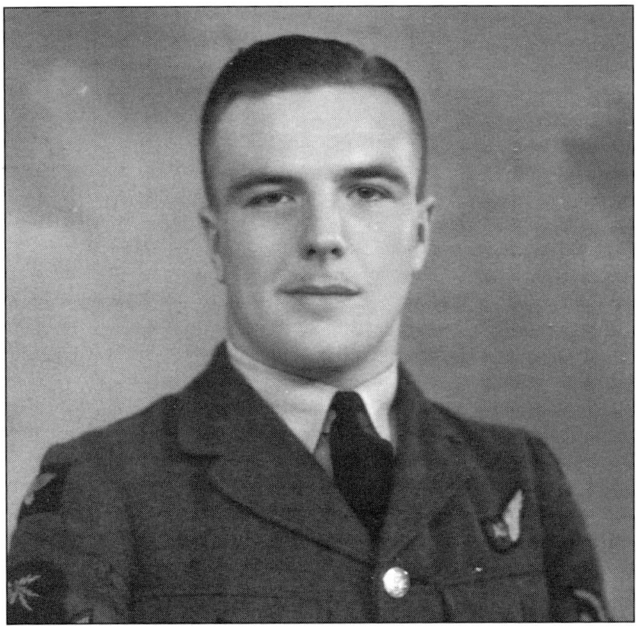

Ronald Houseman.

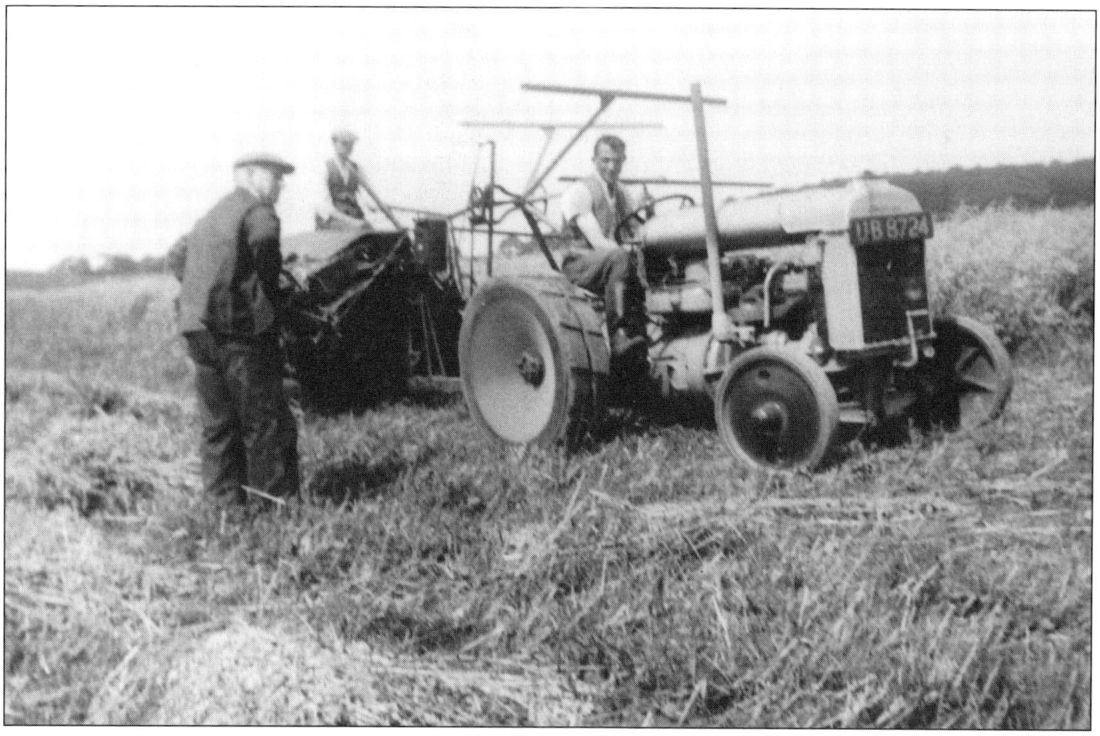

Combining oats for the Second World War effort.

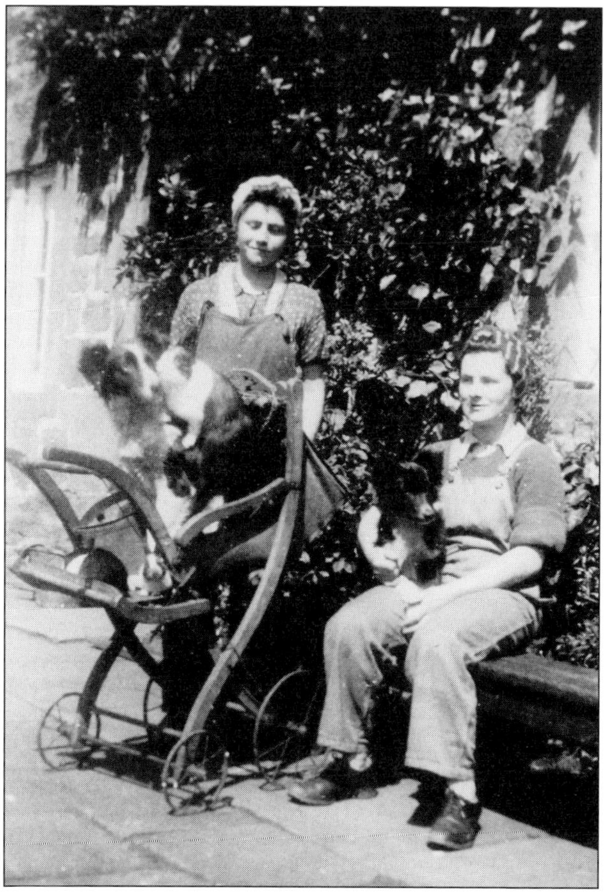

Land Girls Annie and Ellen Stone at Bray House Farm.

In 1957 there was an unfortunate sequel to the Second World War when a party of beaters lunching on Pock Stones Moor found an unexploded device which killed four members of the party, and seriously injured several others. Two of those killed were Dennis and Arthur Peel, sons of Arthur and Olive Peel of Bank Farm, Thruscross Green. Dennis had only recently gained the tenancy of High Flatts Farm and was due to be married. Among the injured were Gerald Harrison who lost both legs and Leslie Pullan who lost an arm.

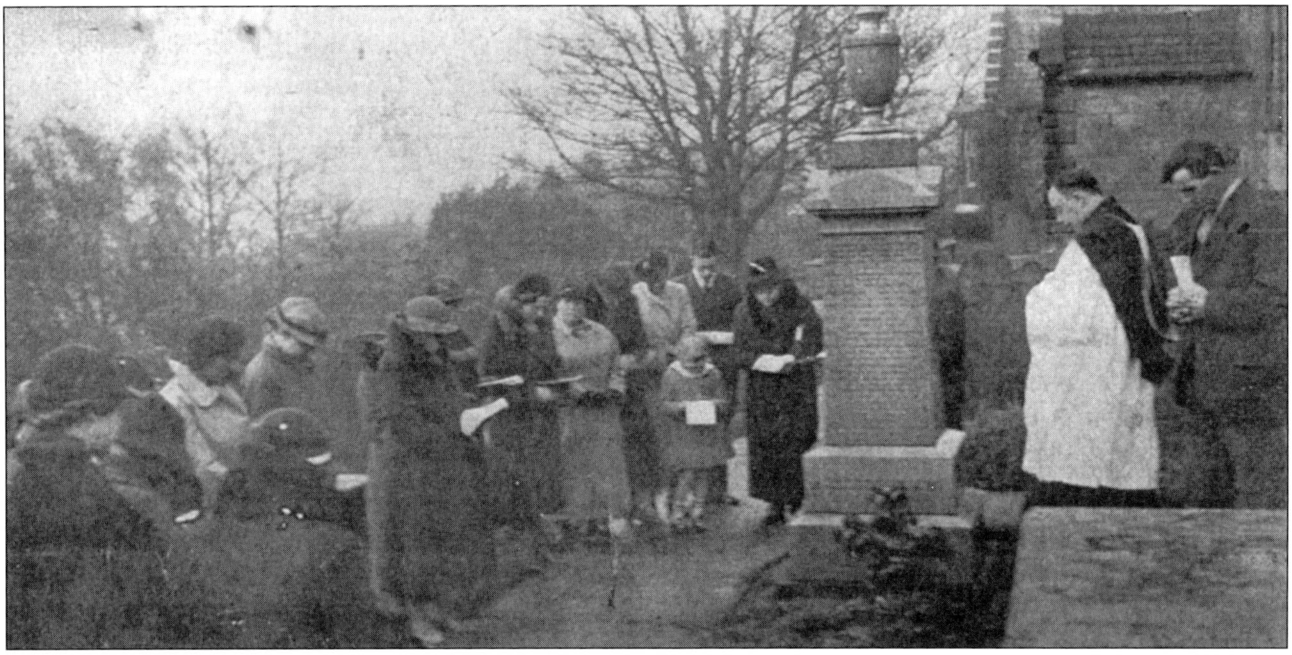

On the 7 November 1948 a Remembrance Service was held in Fewston church and the names of those killed in the Second World War were added to those of the First.

Principal Printed Sources

Brown, A. J., *Broad Acres,* Country Life, London 1948.
Brunfitt, E., *Otley and Menston*
Burt, Stephen, *Roundhay park: an illustrated history,* 2000.
Curnock, Nehemiah (ed.), *Journal of the Rev. John Wesley, vol. 5, 1909,*
Curtis, S. J., *The History of Education in Great Britain (6th. Edit.,)* University Tutorial Press, London, 1965.
Creaser, Mary, *William Vavasour: the Squire of Weston 1798-1933,* Thoresby Society, Leeds LVI.
Cross, C. & Vickers, N., *Monks, Friars & Nuns in 16th century Yorkshire,* YASRS, 1991/2.
Fletcher, J. S., *A Picturesque history of Yorkshire,* J. M. Dent, London, 1900.
Giles, C. & Goodall, I. H., *Yorkshire Textile Mills: the buildings of the Yorkshire Textile Industry 1770-1930,* London HMSO, 1992.
Grainge, William, *History of the Timbles & Sowden,* William Walker, Otley, 1895.
Ibid., *The History and Topography of Harrogate and the Forest of Knaresborough,*
Rigg Publications (Guiseley fac. Edit., 1988), first pub. 1871.
Grant, R. K. J., *The Royal Forests of England, Sutton, 1991.*
Harker, Ronald, *Timble Man: selected diaries of a dalesman 1878-1912,* Hendon Publishing, Nelson, Lancs.
Hartley, M. and J. Ingilby, *A Dales Heritage, 1982; Dales memories,* 1986; *Yorkshire Album,* 1988; *A Dales Album,* 1991, Dalesman Publishing Co. Ltd., Clapham, Yorkshire.
Ibid *Fifity Years in the Yorkshire Dales,* Smith Settle, Otley, 1992.
Hey David, *A History of Yorkshire: county of broad acres,* Carnegie Publishing, Ltd., Lancaster, 2005.
Hill, David, *Turner's Birds,* Phaidon, Oxford, 1988.
Higginbotham, Peter, www.work houses.org.uk/wharfedale/
Honeyman, Katrina, *Child Workers in England 1780-1820: parish apprentices and the making of the early industrial labour force,* Aldershot, Ashgate, 2007.
Horn, Pamela, *Education in Rural England 1800-1914,* Gill & Macmillan, 1978.
Hurworth, N. R., *A short history of Roundhay to the Twentieth century,* priv. pub.2000.
Ingle, George, *Yorkshire Dales Textile Mills,* Royd Press, Hebden Bridge, 2009.
Jennings, Bernard (ed), *A history of Nidderdale* (2nd Edit.), Nidderdale History Group Advertiser Press, Ltd., Huddersfield, 1967.
Laurence, Alastair, *West End,* Smith, Settle, Otley, 1992.
Marjerrison, Allan, *Strike at Timble School,* priv. pub., 1995.
Maxwell, Sir Herbert, Translat. *Chronicle of Lanercost 1272-1346,* Maclehose, Glasgow 1913.
Mitchell, W. R., *J. B. Priestley's Yorkshire,* Dalesman, 1987.
Muir, Richard, *'Old Yorkshire',* Michael Joseph, London, 1987.
Neesam, Malcolm G., *Harrogate Great Chronicle, 1332-1841,* Carnegie Publishing, Lancaster 2005.
Parkinson, Thomas, *Lays and Leaves of the Forest,* Kent & Co., London 1882.
Power, Eileen, *Medieval English Nunneries,* Cambridge University Press 1922.
Pullein, Catherine, *The Pulleyns of Yorkshire,* J. Whitehead, Leeds, 1915.
Parish Comunications Group, Otley, *Our Lady of All Saints Catholic Church, Otley: the story of the Parish, 2001.*
Laurence, Alastair, *West End: a sunken village,* Smith, Settle, Otley, 1992.
Ibid., *A history of Menston & Hawksworth,* Smith, Settle, Otley, 1991.
Sharples, Marion, *The Fawkes family and their estates in Wharfedale 1819-1936,* The Thoresby Society of the Leeds Historical Society, 2nd series, vol. 6, 1997.
Skempton, A. W., *A biographical dictionary of civil engineers in Great Britain and Ireland, 1500-1830,* London, 2002.
Smith, A. H., *The Place names of the West Riding of Yorkshire, pt. V Upper & Lower Claro,* Cambridge University Press, 1961.
Speight, H., *Upper Wharfedale,* Elliott Stock, London, 1900.
Sullivan, Dick, *Navvyman,* Coracle Press, 1983.
Turner, Maurice, *Kith and Kin: Nidderdale families 1500-1750,* Summerbridge Tutorial Group.
Wheater, William, *Knaresborough and its rulers,* R. Jackson, Leeds, 1907.
Wood, Donald, *Bolton Abbey: the time of my life.*
Wood, Paul, *A Guide to the Landscape of Otley,* 1999; *Otley and District,* Sutton, Stroud, 1995.
Wright, G. N., *Roads and Trackways of the Yorkshire Dales,* Moorland Publishing, Ashbourne, Derbyshire, 1985.

Acknowledgements

My thanks must first of all go to the Washburn Heritage Centre based at Fewston church who now hold the photographic history of the valley and who granted me access to the collection without which this book could not have been written. Secondly, I must also thank David Alred, who during the 1980s and '90s had the foresight to collect and preserve the valuable photographic archive of the valley, and also the people of the valley and beyond who generously shared their family history. In this context I would also like to thank Denise Rawson of East End Manor and Ray Wilson and Gisela Moritz of Padside Hall for allowing me to view the interior of their homes. During the writing of this book I also benefited from the help of many people sadly no longer with us, and in this context I would particularly like to mention the late Pauline Barnes, Joanna Dawson, Raymond Gill, Edna Peel and Ernest Wood.

Others to whom I would like to record my thanks are Lucy Atkinson, Mary Barley, Maureen Beanland, Cherida Beaumont, Ruth Brown, Dawn Bussey, John Charman, Rowland Coates, Olive Cooper, Mary Creaser, Kenneth Dickinson, John Duncalf, Michael Ellison, Mikki French, Tom Grange, Michael Grunwell, Peter Hannam, Shelagh Harrison, Stuart Horsman, George Ingle, Cynthia Jewitt, Gerry McIlwraith, Douglas, Olwen & Marjorie Middleton, Sally Moxon, Roger Nelson, Bernard & Rosa Peel, Mary and Selwyn Pennington, Terry Porter, Adrian Ramshaw, Ann Skelton, Kay Ewen-Smith, Marcia Smith, Graham Steel, Martin Stray, Phyllis Stevenson, Walter Thackwray, Mary Wilson, Canon Peter Winstone and Barbara Wright. For anyone I have inadvertently omitted I can only apologise.

My thanks are also due to the Local Studies Section of the Leeds Reference Library, the North Yorkshire County Record Office, Northallerton, the West Yorkshire Archive Service Bradford for access to the notebook of Stephen Hudson, the West Yorkshire Archive Service Leeds for permission to publish the plan of Craggs Mill, the Lancashire Record Office Preston for the Stow family Removal Order, the museums of Nidderdale (at Pateley Bridge) and Otley, and Professor Michael Dixon for the picture of Robert Collyer's anvil.